MAHOMET THE PROPHET

or

FANATICISM

Voltaire

MAHOMET
THE PROPHET

or

FANATICISM

A tragedy in five acts

Translated, with an introduction, by
ROBERT L. MYERS
University of Waterloo

FREDERICK UNGAR PUBLISHING CO.
NEW YORK

MILESTONES
OF THOUGHT
in the History of Ideas

General Editors

HANS KOHN
The City College of New York

SIDNEY HOOK
New York University

INTRODUCTION

In 1685, only nine years before the birth of Voltaire, Louis XIV of France revoked the Edict of Nantes, thus ending the hope of religious freedom in France for many generations to come. Voltaire's youth and early manhood were therefore spent in an atmosphere of increasing religious intolerance, a fact that had a lasting influence upon his character. As early as 1718, in his dramatic adaptation of the Greek legend of Oedipus, Voltaire expressed the conviction that the power of the church rests primarily upon the credulous attitude of the unenlightened people. Throughout his career, therefore, he strove with unfailing energy to put an end to ignorance, bigotry, and prejudice, to enlighten his fellow countrymen in every area of thought.

Voltaire's investigations into man's cultural and political history led him to the unhappy conclusion that of all the causes of man's sufferings none perhaps could equal religious fanaticism. His now dusty epic poem, *La Henriade* (1723), is a description in verse form of the horrors of the religious wars of sixteenth-century France. His tragedy *Zaïre* (1732) presents the picture of the tragic results when two religions clash. In his *Lettres philosophiques* (1734), he extols the moderation and tolerance of the English Quakers. In his *Candide* (1759) he ridicules the excesses of the inquisitorial spirit. His pamphlet war against intolerance in all domains was summed up in the famous motto *écrasez l'infâme*, "crush the infamous." By *l'infâme* was meant not religion itself, but rather the blind, unenlightened use which fanatics have ever made of the religious sentiment in man.

Although not an atheist like so many of his fellow thinkers of the eighteenth century (Diderot, for example), Voltaire, precisely because he had found so many examples in history of the destructive force of religious fanaticism, was attracted to deism. He recognized the need of God as the creator, but felt that man, by the wise use of his rational gifts, would henceforth be capable of solving his own problems. This attitude, typical of other thinkers of that materialistic age (Montesquieu, for example), had the unfortunate consequence of blinding Voltaire to the beauties and, indeed, the importance of the religious and emotional drives. Thus his complete misunderstanding of the Middle Ages (in his *Essai sur les mœurs*, (1756), and his biting satirical references to biblical tradition (as in his *Le Mondain*, 1736).

Voltaire's iconoclastic nature resulted, as might be expected, in his experiencing the powerful hand of authority in a very personal way. On several occasions he was imprisoned or threatened with imprisonment for speaking out against tradition. In 1726, he had to leave Paris. He chose to go into voluntary exile in England where he spent three extremely fruitful years. There, he came to know more intimately the works of the new revolutionary thinkers whose influence upon later French philosophers was incalculable. The writings of Locke, Shaftesbury, and Newton, largely through the propagandizing genius of Voltaire, became better known in France upon his return in

1729. Again in 1734, after the publication of his critical *Lettres philosophiques,* Voltaire was forced to flee Paris and seek asylum in the far reaches of the provinces. Indeed, after this date, Voltaire lived for only short periods in the cultural center of Europe, Paris. After his unhappy sojourn with Frederick II of Prussia (1750-1753), he lived for a time in Switzerland and then permanently on his property in Ferney on the French-Swiss border. The "patriarch of Ferney" did not, by any means, lose contact with the seething intellectual life of Paris, and indeed, through his countless pamphlets and the endless stream of his correspondence, was the veritable leader of cultural activity in the capital. His triumphant return to Paris early in 1778 attests to his never failing popularity there. Perhaps it was fitting that his life should have ended only weeks later in the city he loved so well.

The tragedy *Mahomet* (1741) is the most violent and successful attempt by Voltaire to dramatize his belief that fanaticism, whether it be religious, political, or intellectual, can wreck havoc on the lives of innocent bystanders. Ostensibly drawing a portrait of the historical Mahomet (he even dared to dedicate the play to Pope Benedict XIV, who accepted the honor), Voltaire's satire is not limited to the Moslem religion but reaches out to touch Christianity itself. It has even been suggested that the character of Mahomet represents to a certain degree that of Christ. The ironic conclusion to the action of the tragedy expresses clearly Voltaire's despairing belief that deceit and intolerance are forces difficult to overcome and perhaps invincible. Here we do not have the reassuring optimism of the conclusion of *Candide* but we are left with the picture of a tyrant, although torn with personal grief, still insisting that deceit is his only means of maintaining control of men's minds.

As an example of neo-classical French tragedy, *Mahomet* reveals all the weaknesses of the genre. Its essentially superficial characterizations, its melodramatic action, its servile adherence to classical formulas, consign it to the domain of the scholar, not that of the actor. Yet despite its weaknesses as a piece of theatrical literature, it is still interesting as the ardent cry of a man whose vision of universal tolerance and peace is still pertinent in the troubled "enlightened" world of the twentieth century.

SELECTED BIBLIOGRAPHY

In English

The Works of Voltaire, translated by the Reverend Mr. Franklin. 40 volumes. London, 1763.

The Works of Voltaire, translated by William F. Fleming. New York, Craftsmen of the Hubert Guild, 1901. (*Mahomet* not included.)

Bottiglia, William F., *Voltaire's Candide.* Geneva, Institut et Musée Voltaire, 1959.

Maurois, André, *Voltaire.* Translated by Hamish Miles. Peter Davies Ltd., 1932.

Tallentyre, S. G., *The Life of Voltaire,* London, Smith, Elder & Co., 1910.
Thaddeus, Victor, *Voltaire: Genius of Mockery,* New York, Brentano's, 1928.

In French

Œuvres complètes, éd. Moland. Paris, Garnier, 1877.

Lanson, Gustave, *Voltaire,* Paris, Hachette, 1910.
Pomeau, R., *La religion de Voltaire,* Paris, Nizet, 1956.

MAHOMET THE PROPHET

or

FANATICISM

DRAMATIS PERSONÆ

MAHOMET

ZOPIR, sheik of Mecca

OMAR, Mahomet's second in command

SEID,
PALMIRA, } slaves of Mahomet

PHANOR, senator of Mecca

Company of Meccans

Company of Musulmen

The scene is in Mecca.

ACT I

SCENE 1

ZOPIR, PHANOR

ZOPIR: What did you say? *I* should bow humbly before his false miracles! *I* should pay homage to the miracles of that fanatic! *I* should greet him with open arms in Mecca after having banished him! No. May I be punished by the righteous gods if ever you see this hand of mine, 'til now free and pure, encourage revolt and flatter imposture.

PHANOR: Your subjects, my lord, cherish this paternal zeal of the august and saintly head of Ismael's senate. But this zeal is highly dangerous. Such great resistance, far from wearying Mahomet, merely spurs on his desire for vengeance. In other days you could with impunity invoke the holy force of the laws in opposition to his bold desires, and snuff out the first spark of deadly war. The citizen Mahomet at that time seemed but a mere obscure insurrectionist, the instigator of vile rebellion. But today he is a prince; he triumphs everywhere, everywhere he is in command. An impostor in Mecca, but a prophet in Medina. He has succeeded in winning the adoring adulation of some thirty nations for the very crimes which here in Mecca we abhor. But what am I saying? Within these very walls a misguided troupe of fanatics, intoxicated by his in-

3

sidious poison, proclaim the veracity of his false miracles and spread fanaticism and sedition. They summon his army, believe that a terrible god inspires him, leads him and renders him invincible. But all true citizens are united behind you; yet, is the best counsel always followed? The love of change, false zeal, fear, alarm our citizens who, always the recipients of your kind deeds, now cry out to their father and ask for peace.

ZOPIR: Peace with that traitor! Ah, cowardly people, you can expect only hideous slavery under him! Go then, carry aloft in pompous triumph that idol whose very weight will crush you all. Fall on your knees before it if you will! As for me, I shall always feel an invincible hatred for this scoundrel; the wound in my bleeding heart will never heal. Besides, he too has too many bitter feelings towards me. The savage killed my wife and my children and in revenge I have carried the banners of our army to his very camp. The fires of hatred are lit and never will they be extinguished.

PHANOR: Don't extinguish them—but hide their burning flame. Sacrifice the pain in your heart for your people's good. Will your unfortunate children be avenged when our lands have been plundered? Yes, you have lost all: son, brother, wife, daughter. But do not lose the state for it now is your only family.

ZOPIR: Only through cowardice does one lose one's state!

PHANOR: Too often one perishes by being too obstinate.

ZOPIR: Let us perish then!

PHANOR: What misguided spirit exposes you to shipwreck at the very moment when you are safely reaching harbor? Heaven, don't you see, has placed in your hands the means of overcoming this tyrant of mankind. The youthful Palmira, raised in his camp, was captured by you in your last battle. Is she not an angel of peace descended amongst us, who can calm the fury of Mahomet? Already his heralds have asked for her return.

ZOPIR: It is your desire that she be turned over to this savage? You wish that his bloody hands receive so dear and noble a treasure? The most tender and sweet charms are to court his favor at the very moment when his army enslaves and ravages our lands? Beauty should be the prize of madness! It is not that I, old as I am, feel any shameful envy of Mahomet's fortune; this saddened and withered heart, whose ardor the years have cooled, is incapable of feeling the senseless pangs of love. However, whether because a person born to please always wins our involuntary homage, or whether because I, having lost my children, strive to dissipate the gloom which envelops me, an inexplicable fondness for this unfortunate girl fills my empty heart. Whether it be weakness or reason, I can view only with horror this girl in that monster's grips, that propagator of falsehood! How I would wish that she might secretly come to love the haven we offer and that, responding to my kindness, she might come to detest Mahomet as I detest him. She wishes to speak to me beneath these sacred portals, close to this altar of our domestic gods. She comes, and her candid brow proclaims with its blush the virtue of her heart.

SCENE 2

ZOPIR, PALMIRA

ZOPIR: Young and sweet Palmira, who by the pro-
pitious fate of war bring honor to our land, be assured that you have not fallen into the hands of
barbarians. We all respect your unhappy lot, your
age, your beauty, your sweet innocence. Speak, and
if I have any power left, if I can fulfill your just
requests, these last days of mine will indeed be
happy ones.

PALMIRA: My lord, for two months I have been your
prisoner. I have been obliged to forgive the fates
for my misfortunes. Your kind hands now hasten
to dry the tears that heaven condemns me to shed.
Emboldened by you and your kindness to speak, I
await my life's happiness from you alone. I dare to
add my prayers to those of Mahomet; he has asked
you to free me. May you heed his words! And may
I be able to say that after heaven and him, I owe
all to you!

ZOPIR: So you pine for Mahomet's chains, for the tu-
mult of the army, for the horrors of the wilderness,
for that wandering home abandoned to discord?

PALMIRA: Home is where the heart is. Mahomet shaped
my earliest feelings and his women guided peace-
fully my early years. Their home is a temple in
which those holy women raise to heaven hands

6

adored by their master. The day of my misfortune was, alas, the only day on which their tranquil haven had been disturbed by the fury of war. My lord, have pity on me, for my heart is ever present in those lands from which I have been snatched.

ZOPIR: I understand. Your hope is that one day you should share this proud villain's hand and love.

PALMIRA: My lord, I revere him and my trembling heart sees in Mahomet a terrifying god. No, my heart does not cherish the hope of such a union. Such splendor would ill become one as obscure as I.

ZOPIR: Ah! Whoever you may be, he was perhaps not born to be your spouse, still less your master. You seem to possess blood formed to administer laws to that Arab who walks insolently with kings.

PALMIRA: We women do not possess the pride of birth; deprived of our parents, without a homeland, slaves since earliest youth, we have come to love our bonds because we are all equal. All is foreign to us except the god I serve.

ZOPIR: All is foreign? Can such a state satisfy you? You serve a master and yet have no father? Alone in my empty palace, deprived of my children, I might have found in you the support of my advancing years. The care of forming a happier destiny for you would surely have sweetened the long injustices I have suffered. But that is not to be! You abhor my land and my laws.

PALMIRA: How can I be yours? I am not my own mistress. You would but see me full of regrets, although your kindness is dear to me—for Mahomet has always been a father to me.

ZOPIR: What a father! Ye Gods! Mahomet? That monster of hypocrisy!

PALMIRA: Ah! what foul names you call him, my lord!
He who for so many lands is the true prophet, he,
the envoy of heaven, and its sole interpreter!

ZOPIR: Strange blindness of misguided men! Everyone abandons me to build altars to this lucky criminal whom I, in my justice, once spared, and who
now, having escaped punishment, sets his eyes on
the throne.

PALMIRA: You make me shudder, my lord. Never in
my life have I heard such language. I confess that
my fondness for you and my gratitude were winning you over to my heart, but your frightful blas-
phemies against Mahomet, my protector, have made
this fondness change into horror!

ZOPIR: Superstition! How its harsh power deprives
mankind of its most tender hearts! How I do pity
you, Palmira! And what tears my pity for your misguided thoughts makes me shed!

PALMIRA: Do you refuse then . . .

ZOPIR: Yes! I cannot surrender you to that tyrant
who deceived your sweet and impressionable heart.
Yes! You are too precious to me and you make Mahomet even more odious to me.

SCENE 3

ZOPIR, PALMIRA, PHANOR

ZOPIR: What do you wish, Phanor?

PHANOR: Omar has arrived at the gates of the city
from which the fertile fields of Moad are visible.

ZOPIR: Who? That fierce Omar who today blindly follows the chariot of Error, who long fought the tyrant whom he now worships, who once avenged his homeland?

PHANOR: Perhaps he loves his home still. Less ferocious in appearance, this insolent soldier, bearing in his hands the sword and olive branch, has turned over to our chiefs the pledge of peace. A conference has taken place. He requests and has been granted a hostage. Seid is with him.

PALMIRA: Great god! Sweetest destiny! Seid?

PHANOR: Omar comes towards us.

ZOPIR: We must hear him. Leave us, Palmira. (*Exit Palmira.*) Omar dares to appear before me! What will he say? O gods of my country, who for three thousand years have protected the righteous children of Ismael, O Sun, sacred brand, image of our gods, who in your circular course lend us your light, watch over me and sustain my righteous steadfastness in the face of iniquity!

SCENE 4

ZOPIR, OMAR, PHANOR, attendants

ZOPIR: Well! After six years you gaze again upon your native land, which once you stoutly defended, but which now your heart has betrayed. These walls still ring with your first great deeds. Deserter of our gods, deserter of our laws, persecutor of this sacred city, whence comes this audacity of yours to pro-

fane these hallowed halls? The minister of an out-
law who should long ago have been exterminated,
speak! What do you want of me?

OMAR: To pardon you. God's one prophet, through
pity for your great age, for your former griefs, and
especially for your courage, offers you a hand which
could easily destroy you. I bring you the peace which
he deigns to offer you.

ZOPIR: A vile rebel has the audacity to grant us peace
and not ask our pardon? Will you allow, great gods,
that Mahomet, according to his whim, deprives us
of peace or grants it to us? And you, the messenger
of this traitor, do you not blush in shame to serve
him? Did you not once see him, honorless and pen-
niless, grovelling among the meanest of our citizens? How far he then was from such renown!

OMAR: Accustomed as you are to vile magnificence,
who are you to judge a man's merit, to weigh human worth according to the scales that fate has
granted you? Do you still not know, you paragon
of weakness and pride, that the senseless insect
buried beneath the earth, and the imperious eagle
which soars aloft in the heavens, are of equal worth-
lessness in the eyes of God? Mortal men are all equal;
birth does not count—virtue alone determines the
difference between them. There are men, favored
by heaven, who accomplish everything by their own
efforts and gain nothing from their ancestors. Such
a man, indeed, is he whom I have chosen as my
master. He alone among all men deserves my allegiance. Every man must one day obey him and I
have shown the way for future generations.

ZOPIR: I know you well, Omar. In vain do you strive
to deceive me with this fanatic's portrait; in vain

elsewhere do you dazzle the eyes of the multitude. What your people adore excites merely my scorn. Dispel all deceitful delusion and look wisely upon this prophet to whom you do homage. See the man in Mahomet. Realize clearly how, by your help, this worshipped phantom rises to divinity. Whether you act in all sincerity or for personal gain, you must cease this behavior. Use your reason, judge your master impartially. You will see a gross, uncouth camel driver, an insolent deceiver of his first wife, who, enticed by the vain dream of glory, seeks to deceive the credulous faith of the humblest of men. Brought before me, this rebel was condemned to exile by forty city fathers: too light a punishment which emboldened him to greater crime. From cave to cave he fled with Fatima. His disciples, wandering from city to desert, outlawed, persecuted, banished, enchained, paraded their madness which they said was divinely inspired. Soon they infected Medina with their poison. Then, you, you, Omar, hearing their madness, you tried to stop up the poison at its very source. Happier, wiser, braver were you then when you opposed the tyrant whose slave you now are. If he is really a divine prophet, how did you then dare to attack him? If he is really an impostor, how do you now dare to serve him?

OMAR: I wished to punish him only because in my blindness I did not recognize the early steps of this great man. But when, at last, I saw that Mahomet was born to change the astonished world, when my eyes, illumined by the fire of his genius, saw him begin to rise in his infinite flight, eloquent, intrepid, admired by all; when I saw him act, speak, punish or pardon as a god, I gave my life to his holy work. Thrones and altars have been the rewards. As you, I too was once blind. Open your eyes, Zopir, and change as I have changed. And without further flaunting your zeal, your vain and cruel persecution of Mahomet, our suffering brothers or our blasphemed God, fall at the feet of a hero whom you yourself have oppressed. Come and kiss the hand that bears the thunder of heaven. You see in me, after Mahomet, the most powerful man on earth. The position awaiting you is sufficiently noble if you will but yield and recognize your new master. Consider what we were and what we now are. The multitude, blind and weak, is born to serve great men, to admire, to believe, to obey us. Come and reign with us if you are afraid to serve. Share our power rather than hold yourself aloof from it. Instead of imitating the vile mob, henceforth make them tremble.

ZOPIR: My sole desire, Omar, is to inspire fear in Mahomet, in men like him and you! Do you really expect me, the chief of our senate, to be unfaithful, to worship an impostor, to crown a rebel? I will not deny that this proud seducer has great wisdom and much valor; I know as well as you your master's talents. If he were virtuous, he would perhaps be a great hero. But this hero, Omar, is a traitor, a cruel man, and the most criminal of all tyrants. Stop proclaiming his deceitful clemency. The only skill he possesses is the art of vengeance. In the course of our battles, fate decreed that my hand should deprive him of his son. My arm destroyed the son, my voice banished the father. My hatred for him is inflexible, as is his anger with me. If he wishes to reenter Mecca, he must kill me, for the just can never pardon the wicked.

OMAR: To prove to you that Mahomet really pardons you, and to persuade you to follow his example, share with him and distribute among your tribes the royal bounty that we have won. Put a price on peace, put a price on Palmira. Our treasures are yours.

ZOPIR: You think you can seduce me. What! Sell my honor, bargain for peace with vile bounty, bounty won by his infamous crimes? You expect me to allow Palmira to surrender herself to Mahomet? She is too virtuous to be his subject. My sole desire is to protect her from tyrannical impostors who overthrow laws and corrupt morals.

OMAR: You always address me as would an implacable judge intimidating a criminal from his bench. Think and speak as a minister. I warn you, treat me as the envoy of a great man and a king.

ZOPIR: Who made him king? Who crowned him?

OMAR: Victory! Humor his power, respect his fame. He wishes to add the name of peacemaker to that of conqueror. His army is still on the banks of the Saibare. We are preparing to besiege the walls within which I was born. Let us spare the blood that is about to flow. Mahomet wishes to see you and to speak to you here.

ZOPIR: Mahomet!

OMAR: Yes. He begs you.

ZOPIR: Traitor! If I were the sole master of these holy grounds, I would have answered by punishing you.

OMAR: Zopir, I pity your false virtue. But since an abject senate insolently shares with you the reins of your fragile government, I hasten to betake myself to it.

ZOPIR: I shall follow you. We shall see to whom they will listen. I shall defend my laws, my gods, my country. Against my words lend your impious voice to your persecuting god, the terror of the human race, a god whom an armed impostor claims to represent. (*To Phanor:*) Aid me, Phanor, to repulse a traitor. To suffer him amongst us, to spare him, is to be a traitor like him. Let us destroy his plans, let us crush his pride, let us prepare his punishment and dig his grave. With the senate's approval, I shall deliver my native land and the world from a tyrant.

End of Act I

ACT II

SCENE 1

SEID, PALMIRA

PALMIRA: Has a god guided you to my cruel prison?
Are my sufferings over, Seid? Do I really see you?

SEID: Oh sweet charm of my life and of all my misfortunes! Palmira, for you alone I have shed many
tears. Since that bloody day when a barbarous enemy, near our master's camp on the banks of the
Saibare snatched you as his prey from my bleeding
arms, since that day when, as I lay collapsed upon
a heap of dying soldiers, my cries, unheard upon
that foul bank, summoned cruel death in vain; oh
my beloved Palmira, how your peril and the loss of
you have plunged my heart into an abyss of terror!
My love for you, my fears and my impatience cursed
the slow arrival of my chance for vengeance! I
urged on the assault so long delayed, that hour of
carnage in which, intoxicated with blood, I with
my own hands was to burn down this impious city
in which my Palmira wept for her ravished freedom! Finally Mahomet, in his infinite wisdom
which we humble beings dare not try to understand,
sent Omar into this den of slavery. I learned of this
action and hastened here. A hostage was demanded.
I entered and offered myself. They accepted me on

15

my word. Either I become a prisoner or I die with
you.

PALMIRA: My Seid, at that very moment, before your
presence here could soothe my despair, I was kneeling before my proud captor: "I reveal to you my
innermost secrets," I said. "My heart is in the camp
where you found me. Give me back my freedom!"
My tears, as I spoke, wet his feet. His immediate refusal terrified me. My eyes became clouded, my
heart, without beating, without warmth or life, felt
no shadow of hope to sustain it. All was coming to
an end for me when suddenly you appeared.

SEID: Tell me the name of this insensitive man!

PALMIRA: It was Zopir. He seemed moved by my an-
guish, but cruelly he told me that nothing could
free me from my prison here.

SEID: The wretch is mistaken! Mahomet, my master,
along with the invincible Omar and myself (if I
dare to include myself along with these two famous
names, pardon your lover's proud hope), we will
break your bonds and dry up your tears. The god
of Mahomet, the protector of our army, the god
whose holy standards I have carried, the god who
has destroyed the ramparts of Medina, will destroy
Mecca before our eyes! Omar is here, and the people have not shown the fear and terror that the
sight of an enemy conqueror usually inspires. A
great purpose brings him here in the name of Mahomet.

PALMIRA: Mahomet loves us. He will free us. He will
unite our hearts which we offer to him alone. But
he is so far away! And we are in chains!

SCENE 2

SEID, PALMIRA, OMAR

OMAR: Your chains will be broken; don't lose hope. Heaven looks upon you with favor, for Mahomet comes.

SEID: Mahomet!

PALMIRA: Our august father!

OMAR: Through my mouth Mahomet's spirit has spoken to the assembled senate: "This man, favored by the god who presides over the battlefield, this great man, I said, was born within the walls of this city. He has become both the master and defender of kings, and you refuse him the rank of citizen! Does he come to enchain you, to destroy you, to annihilate you? No! He comes to protect you, and above all, to enlighten you. He comes to establish his power within your very hearts." More than one judge seemed moved by my words. An argument ensued. Obstinate Zopir, who fears the inevitable dominion of reason, wanted to assemble the people and seek support from them. The people were called together. I hastened to the meeing place with him. I spoke to the citizens, I threatened them, I exhorted them. Finally I won their permission to let Mahomet enter. After fifteen years of exile he sees his homeland again. He entered, accompanied by his bravest warriors, Hali, Ammon, Hercides, and the members of his personal guard. The people swarm after him; each one looks at him differently. Some see in him a hero, others a tyrant. One blasphemes him and threatens him, another falls at his feet, kisses them and worships him. We shout out to this agitated crowd the blessed names of God, of Peace, and of Liberty. Meanwhile Zopir and his powerless group vainly spew forth their fruitless rage. In the midst of their cries for revenge, Mahomet, his brow calm and serene, walks like a lord, and carries the olive branch in his hand. Truce is proclaimed. But here is Mahomet now.

SCENE 3

MAHOMET, OMAR, HALI, HERCIDES, SEID,
PALMIRA, attendants

MAHOMET: Invincible supports of my supreme power, noble and sublime Hali, Morad, Hercides, and Ammon, return to the people, instruct them in my name. Promise, threaten, let truth be known, make them adore my God, but see especially that they fear him. Seid! What are you doing here?

SEID: My father! My king! The god who inspires you guided my steps. Ready to die for you, ready to undertake anything, I anticipated your order.

MAHOMET: You should have waited for it! He who does more than he should does not obey me. I obey my God; you, learn to obey me.

PALMIRA: My lord, excuse his impatience. Brought up

together since our earliest childhood, we both have the same feelings. Alas, my life is sad enough! Far from you, far from him, I have languished here in my prison. Seid brought new light to my tear-drenched eyes. Would you have deprived me of this happiness?

MAHOMET: Enough, Palmira. I can read your heart. Do not be alarmed, do not be dismayed. Despite my religious and kingly duties, I shall never lose sight of you. I shall watch over you as I do over the rest of the world. (*To Seid:*) You, follow my soldiers, and you, youthful Palmira, you will serve your god best by fearing only Zopir. (*Exeunt all but Mahomet and Omar.*)

SCENE 4

MAHOMET, OMAR

MAHOMET: You, Omar, remain. It is time that I reveal to you the innermost secrets of my heart. The usual length of a siege which is already doubtful can delay my progress and limit my career. Let us not waste time reassuring the mob which is so easily bedazzled by pomp and ceremony. Prejudice, my friend, is the common man's king. You know well which oracle and which rumor promised the world to God's envoy, who, received in Mecca, and everywhere the victor, would enter this city bearing the branch of peace. I intend to take advantage of the people's credulity. But while I renew my efforts to win over this fickle mob, tell me, Omar, what is your opinion of Seid and Palmira?

OMAR: Among all the children raised by Hercides, who, brought up under your stern hand, and nourished by your law, who know no god but yours, no father but you, none serves you with less scruple, none has a more docile heart, none a mind more credulous. Of all your subjects, they are the most submissive.

MAHOMET: My dear Omar, they are my greatest enemies, for they love each other.

OMAR: Do you criticize their love?

MAHOMET: Ah, must I reveal to you my madness and my weakness?

OMAR: What do you mean?

MAHOMET: You know well enough the reigning passion of my soul. Burdened with the world's cares, besieged by peril, I carry not only the censer, but the scepter and arms. My life is one long battle and I have conquered my nature only by austerity and self-denial. I have forsworn the use of that treacherous liquor which nourishes brutish feebleness in mankind. On burning sands, on desert rocks, I share with you the inclemencies of the weather. Love alone is my consolation, my reward, the object of my pains, the idol I worship, my very god! And this passion is no less strong than my ambition. I'll tell you my secret. I prefer Palmira to all my wives. Can you imagine my jealousy when Palmira, at my very feet, by her own confession, insulted me by telling me she loves another!

OMAR: And you did not avenge yourself?

MAHOMET: Judge for yourself what I should do. If you knew who he really is, you would detest him

even more. Learn the extent of their crime. My two
enemies are the children of the tyrant of Mecca!

OMAR: What! Zopir is . . .

MAHOMET: Their father! Hercides, fifteen years ago,
turned them over to my care. I have nourished these
two serpents in my very bosom and already, without knowing their identity, they are insulting me.
It was I who kindled their illegitimate passion.
Heaven wished to center in them every crime. My
wish is . . . But Zopir comes. His hatred and anger
dart in flame from his eyes. Watch everything carefully, Omar, and tell vigilant Hercides to beleaguer
this gate with his men. Return and give me the
full account. Tell me then if I must hasten or delay my attack against him.

SCENE 5

ZOPIR, MAHOMET

ZOPIR: What a cruel burden for my grief-stricken
heart! Must I, Zopir, receive here the enemy of the
world?

MAHOMET: Approach, Zopir, and since heaven decrees
that we should meet again, look at me without fear
and speak to me without shame.

ZOPIR: I blush for you alone, for you whose deceit has
brought your native land to the brink of destruction, for you whose hand sows the seed of crime
and brings forth war in the midst of peace. Your
name alone divides our families, husbands, parents,

mothers, daughters, and the truce is but a new device by which you can pierce our hearts with your blade. Civil discord follows your every step. Unparalleled assemblage of hypocrisy and insolence, your own land's tyrant, is this the way that you bring us peace and announce your god?

MAHOMET: If I had to answer anyone but you, Zopir, I would use the voice of the god who inspires me. The sword and the Koran in my blood-soaked hands would impose silence upon anyone else. My voice would be as thunder to their ears, and they would grovel on the ground before me. But I address you, not as a god, but as a man, without any disguise. I consider myself great enough not to have to deceive you. Learn what I am really like, Zopir. We are alone. Listen. I am ambitious; all men doubtless are. But never did king, pontif, chief or citizen conceive a project as great as mine. Each land in turn has had its moment of glory—either by laws, by the arts, or especially by war. Arabia's turn has now come. This noble people, too long unknown, allowed its glorious qualities to be buried in its sands. But the day of its victory has now arrived. Look, the whole world lies conquered from north to south: Persia is still licking its wounds, its throne toppled; India is but a timid slave; Egypt is overwhelmed, and the splendor of Constantine's walls is eclipsed. Look, the Roman empire is crumbling, its great body in fragments, the parts of which languish honorless and lifeless everywhere. Upon the debris of the world let us raise Arabia. We need a new cult, we need new power, we need a new god for the blind world.

In Egypt Osiris, Zoroaster in Asia, Minos in Crete,

Numa in Italy, all gave with ease insufficient laws
to people without morals, cult or kings. I come
after one thousand years to change these crude laws.
I bring a more noble yoke for all nations. I shall
abolish false gods, and my purified cult is the first
step toward my ultimate greatness. Do not reproach
me for betraying my country. I merely destroy its
weakness and idolatry. Beneath one king, beneath
one god, I come to unite it, for, to make it illustrious, we first must enslave it.

ZOPIR: So that is your goal! You dare to assume that
you can change the face of the world at will? By
means of bloodshed and terror you intend to order
mankind to think as you do! You ravage the earth
and you believe you are enlightening it! Even
though we may be misled by our erroneous beliefs,
even though we stumble in the darkness of false
convictions, by what frightful torch do you intend
to illuminate our path? By what right do you teach,
predict, bear the censer, and affect imperious power?

MAHOMET: By the right that a vast intelligence, one
firm in its purpose, has over the gross minds of the
vulgar mob!

ZOPIR: So, every bold seditionist may enslave mankind in his own way! He may deceive with impurity
provided he deceives with a flair!

MAHOMET: Yes! Well do I know your people. They
need deceit. My cult, be it true or false, is needed
by them. What have your gods produced? What
good have they brought you? What laurels are to
be seen sprouting at the base of their altars? Your
obscure and vile sect debases man, saps his courage and renders him brutish. Mine elevates the soul,
makes it intrepid. My faith creates heroes.

ZOPIR: Say, rather, thieves. Take your lessons elsewhere. They but produce tyrants. Go, vaunt your
imposture in Medina where you reign, where your
deceived followers march beneath your banners,
where your peers grovel at your feet.

MAHOMET: My peers! I have not had any for a long,
long time! I terrify Mecca, and reign in Medina.
Believe me, Zopir, either you receive peace on my
terms or you risk destruction.

ZOPIR: Peace is easy to talk about, but your heart is
not sincere. Do you think you can trick me?

MAHOMET: I don't have to try. The weak man deceives, the strong man commands. Tomorrow I
shall order what I now request. Tomorrow I shall
see you bent beneath my yoke. Today, Zopir, I wish
to be your friend.

ZOPIR: We, friends! What god could produce such a
miracle?

MAHOMET: I know one who is powerful, always heed-
ed, and who speaks to you as I do.

ZOPIR: Which god?

MAHOMET: Necessity, that which is good for you.

ZOPIR: Before we are united by such a bond, heaven
and hell will be joined together! Self preservation
may be your god, mine is equity. There is no treaty
to be formed between these two. What, pray tell
me, would serve to bind together such a frightful
friendship? Answer me. Your son whom I killed, or
the blood of my children spilt by your hand?

MAHOMET: Yes, your own children. Let me tell you
something that I alone in the world know. You
weep for your children, but they are both alive!

ZOPIR: Alive! What did you say? Oh happy day, they
are alive! And such news I must hear from you!

MAHOMET: Brought up in my camp, I hold them both prisoners.

ZOPIR: My children are your prisoners! They are your slaves?

MAHOMET: My kind hands have deigned to nourish them.

ZOPIR: What? Your anger has not been felt by them?

MAHOMET: I do not hold them responsible for their father's crimes.

ZOPIR: Speak, enlighten me. What is their fate?

MAHOMET: In my hands I have the power of life and death over them. You have only to say the word— I make you their judge.

ZOPIR: You mean I can save them? At what price? Must I offer my own blood? Must I become your slave?

MAHOMET: No. But you must help me deceive the world. You must turn over Mecca to me, abandon your temple, be an example of trustfulness for all men; announce the validity of the Koran, serve as my prophet, and prostrate yourself at my feet. I shall return your son to you and become your son-in-law.

ZOPIR: Mahomet, I am a father and have a tender heart. After fifteen years of despair, to find my children again, to see them again, to die in their arms, is all that I ask. But if I must turn over my people to you, or kill my two children with my own hands, believe me, Mahomet, the choice is not difficult. Farewell. (*Exit Zopir.*)

MAHOMET (*alone*): Proud citizen, stubborn old man, I can be more cruel, more pitiless than you!

SCENE 6

MAHOMET, OMAR

OMAR: Mahomet, you must be pitiless or our cause is lost. The secret plan of these tyrants has been revealed to me—at a price. Tomorrow the truce expires and you will be arrested. Tomorrow Zopir assumes power again and will have your head. Half the senate has just condemned you, for, not daring to defy you, they will assassinate you. This murder of a hero is called "just punishment" by them. This shady plot they call "justice."

MAHOMET: They will feel my justice and my fury. Persecution has always brought me power. Zopir must die.

OMAR: Once his head has fallen at your feet, the others will be convinced of your power. But hasten. There is no time to lose.

MAHOMET: Yet, despite my anger, I must be careful to disguise the hand that will slay him and turn away from me the suspicions of the mob.

OMAR: Forget what the mob thinks.

MAHOMET: No, Omar, we must please the mob. I need a strong arm which will obey my command, and having committed the murder will let me enjoy the fruits of the crime.

OMAR: For such a deed, may I suggest Seid?

MAHOMET: Seid?

OMAR: He is the perfect instrument for such a murder. Zopir's hostage, he alone today can approach him and seek vengeance for you. Your other favorites, prudently zealous, are too experienced to risk everything for you. They are all too mature and have lost their early trust. We need a simpler man, blind yet courageous, a man who loves his own slavery. Youth is the time for such illusions. Seid alone is the prey to superstition, a lion docile to the voice which guides him.

MAHOMET: Palmira's brother?

OMAR: Yes, yes. Seid it must be. The son of your proud enemy, the incestuous rival of his own master.

MAHOMET: I detest Seid. His very name offends me. My own son's ashes cry out for vengeance. But you know the object of my fatal passion; you know what blood flows in her veins. You know that in this pit of iniquity I seek a throne, an altar and victims. You know I must dazzle the minds of these proud citizens, that I must destroy Zopir and his son. Let us go. We must deliberate what best will serve my interests, my hatred, my love, my unworthy love which, despite my efforts, drags me along in its chains; and religion to which all must submit, and necessity, the mother of all evil.

End of Act II

ACT III

SCENE 1

SEID, PALMIRA

PALMIRA: One moment, Seid. What is this secret sacrifice? Whose blood is demanded by eternal justice? Do not leave me.

SEID: God deigns to call on me. My arm must serve him, my heart speak to him. Omar, at this very moment, insists that I bind myself even closer to our invincible master by a new oath. I am about to swear to God to die for his law—my other oath shall be to love you always.

PALMIRA: Why am I not to be present at this oath? I would be less afraid if I were with you. Omar, far from consoling me, speaks only of betrayal, of blood about to flow, of the madness of the senate, of Zopir's plots. The sacred fires have been lit, the truce is soon to expire. The soldiers are armed and are about to strike. So says Mahomet, and he wouldn't deceive us. Zopir terrifies me and I fear for your safety.

SEID: I can scarcely believe that Zopir's heart is so base! This very morning, presented as a hostage to him, I admired his nobility and humanity. Secretly I felt a strange force attract my willing heart to him. Either it was respect for his name, or his prepossessing manner hid from me the dangerous

29

depths of his heart. Perhaps it was because at the
moment I saw you again, my overjoyed heart for-
got its grief and terror and did not hear or see anyone but you. I was indeed happy to be near Zopir.
I now hate him the more since he so deceived me.
Yet, Palmira, despite the anger I should feel, how
difficult it is to hate those one would wish to love!

PALMIRA: How strange it is to what degree heaven
has joined our destinies. What care it has taken to
unite our enchained hearts. Alas, Seid, were it not
for my love for you, this tender bond, were it not for
this sweet instinct which joins my heart to yours,
were it not for the religion inspired in me by Mahomet, I would have accused Zopir with great misgiving.

SEID: Forget this misgiving and let us heed the divine
voice we strive to serve. I must leave. I must take
this frightening oath. The god who will hear it
will be favorable to us and the pontif-king, who
watches over our lives, will bless our chaste love.
Farewell. To be yours, I am ready to try all.

SCENE 2

PALMIRA

A black foreboding torments me. This love which has
brought me such happiness and this long awaited
day bring only terror. I wonder what oath they will
exact from him. I suspect everything. Zopir fright-
ens me. I invoke Mahomet, yet his name fills my

heart with secret terror. Despite the profound respect I feel for him, I fear him almost as much as
Zopir. Free me, great God! Free me from my uneasiness. In fear I do serve thee, in blindness I do follow
thee. Alas, dear God, dry my tear-drenched eyes.

SCENE 3

MAHOMET, PALMIRA

PALMIRA: A kindly god has heard my prayers and
sent you, my lord. Has Seid . . .
MAHOMET: Why are you afraid, Palmira? Why do
you fear for him when you are by my side?
PALMIRA: Oh heaven! My uneasiness is increased
when for the first time I see Mahomet himself upset. What miracle is this? Why do you remain silent?
MAHOMET: It is your grief that upsets me. Is it thus
that your sweet innocence confesses a passion which
perhaps offends me? Can your heart feel without
fear an emotion not dictated by me? Is this heart
formed by me now only a rebel, ungrateful for all
my kindness, unfaithful to my laws?
PALMIRA: What are you saying? Trembling and
shocked I kneel before you with my terrified eyes
cast down in fear. My lord, did you not in this very
place smile upon our love and permit Seid to love
me? This passion, this pure love which God has
formed in our hearts is a tie which binds us even
closer to you.
MAHOMET: The ties formed by imprudence are to be

feared. Crime often accompanies innocence. The heart may be mistaken; love and its sweetness can be the cause of death and unhappiness, Palmira.

PALMIRA: Do not doubt, my lord, that I am ready to die for Seid.

MAHOMET: You love him so much?

PALMIRA: Since the day when Hercides brought us both beneath your holy care, this all-powerful instinct, as yet unrecognized by us, preceding the age of reason, growing with age, was the secret work of heaven which guides us all. Our feelings, you say, come only from heaven. God cannot change; could he today criticize a love that he himself inspired? What was once innocent, can it now become a crime? Can I really be guilty?

MAHOMET: Yes! You should shake with fear. Listen to what I have to tell you. Let my voice inform you about what you can and cannot do. Believe only in me.

PALMIRA: Whom else could I believe? Accustomed to your laws, my heart, your submissive servant, does not forget its respect for your holy person.

MAHOMET: Too much respect often leads to ingratitude.

PALMIRA: No. If ever I forget your kindness, may Seid punish me immediately.

MAHOMET: Seid!

PALMIRA: Why do you look at me with such anger?

MAHOMET: Be reassured, my Palmira; I am not angry. I wished only to test your innermost thoughts. Rely on me. I am worthy at least of your confidence. Your destiny depends upon your obedience to me. If you belong to me, be worthy of the kindness I can show you. Whatever the voice of heaven orders

Seid to do, strengthen his resolve and sense of duty.
He must abide by his oath. He must be worthy of
you.

PALMIRA: Have no fear, my father, he will do his duty.
I will answer for him as well as for myself. Seid
worships you even more than he loves me. In you
he sees his king, his father, his support. I swear at
your feet that I love him dearly. I hasten now to
urge him on to serve you.

SCENE 4

MAHOMET

Well, despite myself I must be the confident of her
love! In her innocence, which overwhelms my
anger, she naïvely plunges the dagger into my heart!
Zopir, Seid, Palmira, destined all to bring me grief,
baleful and inimicable race, today you will see what
hatred and love are capable of.

SCENE 5

MAHOMET, OMAR

OMAR: The time has at last come to seize Palmira. in-
vade Mecca, and punish Zopir. By his death alone
will these citizens be brought under your power.
Our cause is lost if you do not accomplish this.

Doubtless Seid alone can help you. He sees Zopir
often, speaks to him and hears his words. Do you
see this gloomy passage which leads from your palace to his? There, this very night, Zopir will offer
useless incense and vows to his fancied gods. There,
Seid, intoxicated with his zeal, will sacrifice Zopir
to the god who speaks through you.

MAHOMET: Yes. It is he who must sacrifice Zopir, for
he was born a criminal. Let him be the instrument
and the victim. My desire for vengeance, my love
for Palmira, my laws, my very safety, the irrevo-
cable decree of fate, all order it so. But are you certain that this youth, despite his fanaticism, is sufficiently enraged for this deed?

OMAR: He alone was divinely ordained to fulfill your
grand design. Furthermore, Palmira urges him to
serve you. Love and fanaticism blind this youth who
through his excessive weakness will serve you well.

MAHOMET: Has he sworn an oath to do the deed?

OMAR: The dark and frightening atmosphere of the
holy rite, the altar, the oath, all enchain Seid. I myself placed a holy sword in his murderous hand, and
religious enthusiasm filled his soul. He comes.

SCENE 6

MAHOMET, OMAR, SEID

MAHOMET: Child of God who has spoken to your
heart, hear by my voice his supreme wish. You must
avenge his cult, you must avenge God himself.

SEID: King, pontiff, and prophet, to whom I pledge

my allegiance, master of nations, recognized by heaven, you hold complete sway over my being. Deign only to enlighten me as to my task. A mortal man must avenge God?

MAHOMET: By your weak hands he desires to terrify impious mortals.

SEID: Doubtless this god, whose image you are, will honor my courage with a great battle.

MAHOMET: Do as he commands, there is no other form of honor. Blind executor of his divine decrees, adore him and strike! Your hands will be armed by the angel of death and the god of armies.

SEID: Speak. Tell me which enemies I must kill. What tyrant must I destroy? Whose blood must flow?

MAHOMET: The blood of that murderer whom I abhor, who has persecuted us, who still pursues us, who combats my god, who massacred my son! The cruelest blood of all our enemies . . . Zopir's!

SEID: Zopir's! My arm must . . .

MAHOMET: Presumptuous youth! Hesitation is sacrilege. I will have nothing to do with men who are bold enough to think for themselves or to look with their own eyes! He who dares think was not born to believe me! To obey in silence is your only hope of glory. Do you not know who I am? Do you not know in what holy grounds my voice instructed you in the will of heaven? If, despite its errors and idolatry, Mecca is the home for the people of the Orient, if this temple is promised to me and my command, if God has created me its pontiff and king, if Mecca is holy, do you know why? Abraham was born here and his ashes repose here; Abraham, who at God's command dragged his only begotten son to this altar, snuffing out the cries of nature in his obedience to God's will. And when this God wishes to be avenged through you, when I too demand Zopir's blood, when God chose you, do you dare to hesitate? Begone, vile idolater, forever destined merely to be so, unworthy Moslem, seek another master. The reward was all prepared—Palmira was to be yours. But you dare to defy Palmira and incensed heaven! You weak and cowardly instrument of divine vengeance, your blows will kill none but yourself. Begone, and grovel at the feet of my proud enemies, your new masters.

SEID: I seem to hear the voice of God. You speak and I obey.

MAHOMET: Obey, strike him! Stained with his impious blood you will merit eternal life if he dies. (*To Omar*:) Do not leave him, and keeping close by, watch carefully over all that he does. (*Exeunt Mahomet and Omar.*)

SCENE 7

SEID

I must sacrifice an old man whose hostage I am, defenseless and weighed down with age though he is! What difference does it make? A victim brought to the altar falls there defenseless and his blood is pleasing to heaven. God has chosen me for this great sacrifice. I have sworn to do it, so I must act. Ye gods, come to my aid. You who have given death to so many tyrants on this earth, add your fury to my intrepid zeal; strengthen my saintly murderous hand. Angel of Mahomet, angel of death, place your fierceness in the depths of my heart. But whom do I see?

SCENE 8

SEID, ZOPIR

ZOPIR: Why does the sight of me disturb you, Seid? I will tell you why I come. Unfortunate hostage granted me by fate, it is with much regret that I see you ranked among my enemies. The truce has stopped up the flow of blood; but this dammed torrent may find a weak spot and burst forth again. I say no more. Yet my heart, despite my efforts, trembles at the sight of the dangers which surround you. Dear Seid, during this time of upheaval, let my home be your safe haven. I will guarantee your life—it is dear to me. Do not refuse me.

SEID: Oh heaven! Have you no other desire, Zopir, but to protect me, to watch over my safety? *(aside)* On the point of spilling his blood, what words do I hear! How pitiful he looks! Pardon me, Mahomet, if my heart hesitates.

ZOPIR: Perhaps you are startled by my pity for you. I am but a man. This is sufficient reason for wanting to take solicitous care of unhappy innocent souls. Ye gods, exterminate from this world of ours all those who spill men's blood with glee!

SEID: How sweet such words sound to my ear! Is my god's sworn enemy really a man of virtue?

ZOPIR: If you are so easily surprised, you know little of virtue, my son. How mistaken you are! Your mind, fascinated by a tyrant's laws, believes that one can be virtuous only if one is a Moslem. Cruelly submissive to your master's preachments, you had condemned me before knowing me. A frightful prejudice holds your innocent heart in its claws of iron. But I forgive you the errors into which Mahomet has led you. But how can you believe in a god that orders only hatred?

SEID: Ah! I feel that I am about to disobey that god. No, my lord, no. My heart cannot hate you.

ZOPIR (*aside*): Alas, the more I speak to him, the more he interests me. His youth, his candor, excite my love. Can it be that a soldier of this monstrous impostor has found the way to my heart? (*To Seid*). Who are you? Whose blood flows in your veins?

SEID: I have no parents, my lord. I have only a master, whom until just now I have always faithfully served but whom I now have betrayed in my weakness after hearing your words.

ZOPIR: You do not know who your father was?

SEID: Mahomet's camp was my cradle, his temple my home. I know no other. Among those children who are offered to him each year as tribute, none more than I has felt his kindness.

ZOPIR: I cannot blame this boy's gratitude. Yes, kind deeds, Seid, speak to the heart. Heavens! Why was Mahomet his benefactor? He has been your father as well as Palmira's. But why do you tremble, why do you sigh? You turn your eyes away from me. You seem torn by some feeling of remorse.

SEID: Who would not feel remorse on such a frightful day as this!

ZOPIR: If your remorse is well founded, it is not the
fault of your heart. Come. Blood will soon be flow-
ing, and I wish to spare yours.

SEID (*aside*): Gracious heaven! And it is I who would
spill his! What vows have I taken! Oh Palmira!
Oh god of vengeance!

ZOPIR: Trust yourself to my care, but do not hesitate.
For the last time, come. Your life depends upon it.

SCENE 9

ZOPIR, SEID, OMAR, attendants

OMAR (*rushing in*): Traitor, what are you doing? Mahomet awaits you.

SEID: Where am I, oh heaven! Where am I? What
must I do? The thunderbolts strike from all sides.
Where can I run? Where can I hide my fright?
Where can I flee?

OMAR: To the feet of the king chosen by eternal God.

SEID: Yes! I will run to him and abjure an oath that
I abhor. (*Exeunt Seid and Omar.*)

SCENE 10

ZOPIR

Seid! Where are you going? He still flees from me.
He leaves in despair, overwhelmed with gloomy

fear. My heart goes out to him. His feeling of guilt, my pity, his appearance, his absence are too much for me to bear. I must follow him.

SCENE 11

ZOPIR, PHANOR

PHANOR: My lord, read this important note which an Arab secretly gave me a moment ago.

ZOPIR: Hercides! What have I read? Ye gods! Does your clemency put an end finally to sixty years of suffering? Hercides wishes to see me. He, who cruelly snatched my children from this bosom of mine! They are alive! Mahomet has them in his power, and Seid and Palmira are ignorant of their lineage. Are *they* my children? Sweet hope. Dare I listen to my heart? I am too unlucky, and I fear that I am misleading myself. Confused presentiment. Should I believe in you? Oh my family! Where can I go to weep and rejoice? My heart cannot bear such emotion. I will go to them and embrace them, my children. But I hesitate. I don't move. My fear gives careful heed to the voice of my blood. I must go. I must see Hercides tonight. Phanor, see that he is secretly led beneath that vault, to the foot of the altar, where your master's tears have importuned the gods who now perhaps are appeased. Ye gods, give me back my children! Ye gods, give back to virtue two nobly born hearts which a traitor has corrupted! If they are not mine, if such is to be my grief, at least I wish to adopt them and be a father to them.

End of Act III

ACT IV

SCENE 1

MAHOMET, OMAR

OMAR: Our secret is out, my lord. Your glory is in danger, your very tomb is opened. Seid will obey, but before his heart was rekindled by your words, he revealed this plot to Hercides.

MAHOMET: To Hercides!

OMAR: Yes. Hercides loves him as a father.

MAHOMET: Well, what was Hercides' reaction?

OMAR: He seems terrified, for he appears to pity Zopir somewhat.

MAHOMET: Hercides is weak. My friend, the weakling soon turns into a traitor. Frighten him! He now knows my secret and I know well enough how to deal with a dangerous witness. Have my orders been obeyed?

OMAR: I have done what you wish.

MAHOMET: Let us get on with it then. Within the hour either Zopir or I must die. If he dies, we win, for all the people will then adore my god who will have protected me. That is the first step. But, as soon as Seid's hands are bloodied by his father's death, do you guarantee that he too will die? Do you vouch for the poison we have had prepared for him?

OMAR: Have no worries on that score.

MAHOMET: Our shady plot must be hidden by their deaths and covered by death's shadows. Yet take care, Omar, to continue to incite the fanaticism of Seid even though he says he is quite ready to strike, to pierce the very source of Palmira's life-blood. Let us take extra care to hide the truth of her birth, for her own sake, for mine, and for my future happiness. My ultimate triumph is solely based on deceit. In vain was she born of this abhorred blood, one has no parents if one does not know who they are. The cry of the blood, its strength, its impressions are the illusions of deceived hearts. Nature, as I see it, is a matter of custom. Her only lesson in life has been to obey me. I am everything to her. Let's see that she comes into my arms over her own father's ashes, a father she doesn't even know. Doubtless her heart will secretly exult in capturing her master. But already the hour approaches in which Seid must sacrifice his father here before the eyes of the gods. Let us retire.

OMAR: Here he comes. See how he stumbles—his soul is devoured by his desire to obey.

SCENE 2

MAHOMET, OMAR (*in the foreground and to one side*); SEID (*in background*)

SEID: Must I then fulfill this terrible duty!

MAHOMET: Come, Omar, let's strengthen my power by striking elsewhere.

SEID (*alone*): I was incapable of answering them! A single word from Mahomet was enough to silence me! Yet even though he filled me with holy terror, I was not entirely persuaded. If it is heaven's wish, I shall obey. But the cruel obedience! Oh heaven! At what a price!

SCENE 3

SEID, PALMIRA

SEID: Palmira! What are you doing here? What brings you to this baleful spot consecrated to death?

PALMIRA: Fright and love are my guides, Seid. My tears anoint your justly murderous hands. What a horrible sacrifice! Alas, must you offer it? Must you obey Mahomet and god?

SEID: Oh my beloved, speak, strengthen my will, enlighten me and guide my arm. Be as a god for me for I do not understand. Why have I been chosen? Is terrible Mahomet really God's sole interpreter?

PALMIRA: We must not question. Mahomet reads our very hearts, hears our sighs, and observes our tears. Everyone fears in him God himself. That is all I know. Doubt is a blasphemy and the god he proclaims so proudly, Seid, is the real god since Mahomet is victorious everywhere.

SEID: Since you believe in him and adore him, he must be the real god. But my confused mind cannot yet understand why this good god, this father of mankind, chose me to commit so frightful a murder. I know only too well that my doubt is a crime, that a priest remorselessly slaughters the sacrificial victim, that Zopir has been condemned by heaven's decree, and that I was predestined to support the divine will. Mahomet explained it all to me and I had to be silent. Proud to serve divine anger, I was about to bring death to God's enemy. Another god, perhaps, stayed my arm. At least, when I saw that unfortunate Zopir I felt the strength of my zeal weaken. In vain did my sense of duty urge me on, humanity spoke to my stricken heart. With what anger, what tenderness does Mahomet reproach my weakness! With what grandeur, what authority has his voice strengthened my resolve. How terrible and powerful is religion! I felt fury reborn in my breast. Palmira, I am weak, and afraid of this murder. I feel to much pity for Zopir. I am besieged by confused feelings. I fear being cruel or being sacrilegious. I do not consider myself born to be a murderer. Yet God orders me and I have promised my hand. I still weep tears of grief and rage. You see me, Palmira, the prey to this storm of passions swimming in the tide of contrary feelings which buffets back and forth my feeble will. You must secure my wavering heart, for our hearts are joined by the strongest of bonds. Yet, if I do not go through with this sacrifice, our union is forever doomed, for only at this price will I win your hand.

PALMIRA: *I* am the reward for spilling poor Zopir's blood?

SEID: Heaven and Mahomet have so decreed.

PALMIRA: Can love withstand such cruel blows?

SEID: Mahomet will give you only to Zopir's murderer.

PALMIRA: What a frightful dowry.

SEID: But if it is heaven's command? If I am really serving love and religion?

PALMIRA: Alas!

SEID: You know the curse that forever damns those who disobey.

PALMIRA: If God himself has entrusted his vengeance to you, if he demands the blood which you said would . . .

SEID: Tell me, Palmira, what must I do to be yours?

PALMIRA: I tremble.

SEID: I understand. His condemnation has issued from your mouth.

PALMIRA: Who? I?

SEID: You have willed it.

PALMIRA: Ye gods, what a frightful decree! What have I said?

SEID: Heaven has used your voice. It is its last pronouncement and I shall obey. Here is the moment when Zopir is to offer prayers at this altar to the gods I detest. Palmira, go away from here.

PALMIRA: I cannot leave you.

SEID: Do not witness this murder, Palmira. Such moments are terrifying. Go! Flee! This retreat is close to Mahomet's house. Go, I say!

PALMIRA: So this kindly old man is to die!

SEID: So it has been decreed. I must drag him in the dust with my own hand, strike him three times in the chest until he is dead, and splash his spilled blood on this overturned altar.

PALMIRA: He must die by your hands! My blood has turned to ice. Here he is, righteous heaven! . . .

(*The back of the stage opens. An altar is seen.*)

SCENE 4

ZOPIR, SEID, PALMIRA (*in foreground*)

ZOPIR (*near the altar*): Oh gods of my country! Gods ready to die beneath an impious sect, it is for you alone that my weak voice implores you here for the last time. War is about to begin again and its murderous hands will soon break down the walls of this weak peace. Gods, if you support the cause of a scoundrel . . .

SEID (*to Palmira*): Do you hear him blaspheme?

ZOPIR: . . . grant me death. But grant me my children before I die. Let me expire in their arms; let them close my lids. Alas, if I were to believe my secret feelings, if your divine hands have guided them here. . . .

PALMIRA (*to Seid*): What does he say? His children?

ZOPIR: Oh my gods whom I adore, I would die from the pleasure of seeing them again. Arbiters of destiny, deign to watch over them. May they think as I, but may they be happier!

SEID: He speaks to his false gods! I must strike! (*He draws his dagger.*)

PALMIRA: What are you going to do? Alas!

SEID: Serve heaven, deserve you, please you! This blade has just been sacrificed to our god. May our god's enemy be massacred by it! Let's hurry. Can't you see those bloody traits, that ghost, those wandering shades in this gloomy abode?

PALMIRA: What are you saying, Seid?

SEID: I follow you, ministers of death! Show me the altar, guide my arm. Let us go!

PALMIRA: No! This place is too filled with horror. Wait a moment.

SEID: There is no time. We must go forward—the altar trembles.

PALMIRA: Heaven reveals itself, we must doubt no more.

SEID: Does heaven urge me on to kill or does it hold me back? I hear the voice of God's prophet—he admonishes my weak and tender heart. Palmira!

PALMIRA: Well?

SEID: Pray to heaven. I am going to strike (*He steps behind the altar where Zopir is praying.*)

PALMIRA: I am dying. Oh dreadful moment. What frightful voice do I hear ringing in my heart? Why does my blood run cold? If heaven wants a murder, who am I to judge? Who am I to complain, to question? I obey. Why then am I overwhelmed with remorse? Ah! Who in the world ever knows for sure whether he is right or wrong? I am mistaken, or else the blows have been struck. I hear the plaintive cries of a dying voice. Seid! . . . Alas!

SEID (*comes back distracted*): Where am I? Who calls me? I do not see Palmira. A god has snatched her away!

PALMIRA: What! Do you not recognize the one who lives for you alone?

SEID: Where are we, Palmira?

PALMIRA: Tell me, Seid, has this frightful law, this promise been fulfilled?

SEID: What do you say?

PALMIRA: Is Zopir dead?

SEID: Who is Zopir?

PALMIRA: Ye gods, bloodthirsty gods, do not persecute Seid any more! Let us flee from here!

SEID: My knees feel weak. (*He sits down.*) Ah, I see light again; my strength is coming back. Is it you, Palmira?

PALMIRA: What have you done?

SEID (*standing up*): I have just obeyed . . . I seized him with my desperate hands, I dragged my victim by his white hair. Oh heaven! you wished it so! How can you desire a crime? Trembling, seized with fright, I plunged this consecrated blade into his side. I wanted to strike again. But that venerable old man uttered such a lamentable scream in my arms, nature revealed such great character in his dying glance, such moving traits on his face! . . . My heart was filled with pity and terror, and more dead than my victim, I hate life.

PALMIRA: Let's flee to Mahomet who will protect us. Near this bloody corpse you are in danger. Follow me.

SEID: I cannot. I am dying. Ah! Palmira . . .

PALMIRA: What terrifying disorder rends him before my eyes?

SEID (*weeping*): Ah! If you had seen him, the dagger in his side, show affection for his cowardly assassin! I was about to flee. Would you believe that he summoned enough strength to call me back. He pulled the dagger from his side. "Alas!" he said with a sad glance, "dear unfortunate Seid." This voice, that glance, that murderous dagger, that kindly old man washed in blood at my feet—I can still see him as I stand here before you. What have we done?

PALMIRA: Someone is coming. I am afraid for you, Seid.

Flee in the name of our love and the bond that binds us.

SEID: Go, leave me alone. How could our love have ordered such a frightful sacrifice? No, cruel Palmira. Without you, without your order, I could never have obeyed heaven.

PALMIRA: Do you dare blame me! Alas! More than you, I feel my heart ache. Dearly beloved, have pity on your distraught Palmira.

SEID: Palmira! What frightful object do my eyes see? (*Zopir appears, leaning on the altar, after having stood up behind it where he had received the blow.*)

PALMIRA: It is that hapless man struggling against death. He drags himself all covered with blood towards us.

SEID: Wait! Are you going to him?

PALMIRA: Devoured by remorse, I must yield to the pity I feel for him. I cannot help myself—it drags me to him.

ZOPIR (*advancing and leaning upon her*): Alas! be a guide for my faltering steps. (*He sits down.*) Seid, you ingrate! You have killed me. You weep! Does pity now replace madness in your heart?

SCENE 5

ZOPIR, SEID, PALMIRA, PHANOR

PHANOR: Heavens! What ghastly sight do I see?

ZOPIR: If only I could see Hercides! . . . Ah, Phanor, is it you? There is my assassin.

PHANOR: Oh crime! Fearful mystery. Wretched murderer, this is your father.

SEID: My father!

PALMIRA: Zopir!

ZOPIR: Ye gods!

PHANOR: Hercides is dying. He saw me, called to me and cried out: "If there is still time, stop a patricide. Run and snatch the dagger from Seid's hands. The unhappy confident of a horrible secret, I have been punished and put to death by Mahomet. Run, hasten to inform the unfortunate Zopir that Seid is his son and the brother of Palmira.

SEID: Palmira!

PALMIRA: My brother!

ZOPIR: Oh my children! Oh nature! Oh ye gods! You did not deceive me when you spoke to me on their behalf. Doubtless you were trying to enlighten me. Ah, wretched Seid! Who ever commanded you to do such a deed?

SEID (*falling on his knees*): It was love of my duty and of my country, my gratitude and my religion. All that man most reveres inspired me to commit the most heinous of crimes. Return, please return that dagger to me.

PALMIRA (*on her knees and grasping Seid's arm*): My father, ah, my lord! Plunge it into my bosom. I alone it was who urged Seid on to this crime. Incest was for us the reward of murder.

SEID: Heaven has not sufficient punishment for us. Strike your killers.

ZOPIR (*embracing them*): I embrace my children. In the suffering it sends me, heaven desired to mingle the greatest horrors and the greatest joys. I bless my destiny for I die while you live. You, whom I found

at last at my dying hour, Seid, and you, Palmira, in
the name of nature, by this last drop of blood that
flows from my wound, by your father's blood, by my
very death, avenge yourselves, avenge me! But be
careful, my children. The hour approaches when
the truce was to come to an end. I was to have been
able to fulfill my plans. The gods have had pity on
my great sufferings. Your hands' crime is but half
committed. Soon, with daylight, the people will
show themselves here. You, my son, will lead them.
They will punish a traitor. Wait for them.

SEID: My father, I go now to slay that monster, and
hasten my own death. I will punish myself and
avenge you.

SCENE 6

ZOPIR, SEID, PALMIRA, PHANOR, OMAR, attendants

OMAR: Arrest Seid! Help Zopir! Enchain the murderer. Mahomet has come only to avenge the laws.

ZOPIR: Heavens! What crime is this? What are you
doing to Seid?

SEID: Mahomet is punishing me?

PALMIRA: What! Mad tyrants, after this horrible murder which you yourself ordered!

OMAR: We ordered nothing.

SEID: I have well deserved this reward for my credulity!

OMAR: Soldiers, obey!

PALMIRA: No! Stop! Treacherous Omar!

OMAR: Palmira, obey me if you love Seid. Mahomet will protect you and his righteous anger, ready to strike everyone else, will stop short of you. You must come with me now to see him.

PALMIRA: Great god! May death deliver me from such horror. (*Palmira and Seid are led out.*)

ZOPIR (*to Phanor*): They have taken them. Oh heaven, oh wretched father! The blow that has killed me is one hundred times less painful.

PHANOR: Already dawn comes. The people are moving forward. They are arming and are coming to defend you.

ZOPIR: What! Seid is my son!

PHANOR: Do not doubt it.

ZOPIR: Alas! Oh crimes, oh nature! ... Let us go. Help me, Phanor, for I am dying. Ye gods, save from Mahomet's barbarous hands my two children whom I love and who have taken my life from me!

End of Act IV

ACT V

SCENE 1

MAHOMET, OMAR, attendants (*in background*)

OMAR: Zopir is dying. The desperate populace is raising its dust-covered face in alarm. Your prophets
and I, inspired by your spirit, all disavow the murder of Zopir. In one place we claim to this furious
mob that it is the manifestation of God's support of
you. In another place we weep and moan; we promise vengeance; we vaunt your justice as well as your
forgiveness. Everywhere they listen, they wince at
the sound of your name. Their desire for rebellion
is now but the quiet tossing of the waves after the
storm, waves whose dying roar still strikes the shore
while serenity reigns in the lofty heaven.

MAHOMET: Let us impose eternal silence upon these
waves! Have you brought our army up close to the
ramparts?

OMAR: It has marched all night towards the alarmed
city. Osman was guiding it by secret routes.

MAHOMET: Must men forever be won by force of arms
or deception? Does Seid know that in his blind fury
he stabbed the author of his life?

OMAR: Who could have told him? Eternal oblivion
seals the lips of Hercides who alone knew the secret.
Seid is soon to follow him, and his death has al-

55

ready begun. I have destroyed the instrument of your vengeance. You are aware that he has drunk from the cup into which poison was skillfully placed. His punishment had begun before his crime was committed. At the very moment he was dragging his victim to the altar, while he was plunging his dagger into his father's bosom, he was carrying his own death in his veins. He is in prison now and soon will die. Meanwhile, I have had Palmira kept under guard here. She can still be of help in your plans. Thinking she can save Seid, she will obey you. I have led her to believe that he can be pardoned. She still refuses to speak. Her ever docile heart, born to adore you, will still not openly complain. Lawgiver, prophet, king in your native land, your life's happiness, Mahomet, will be attained through her. Look, the guards are leading her here. She trembles and is pale.

MAHOMET: Assemble my chiefs and then hasten back here.

SCENE 2

MAHOMET, PALMIRA, their attendants

PALMIRA: Heaven! Where am I? Ah, great God!

MAHOMET: Be not alarmed, Palmira. I have decided on your destiny and that of this people. The great event which so fills you with terror, Palmira, is a sacred mystery between heaven and me. Forever freed from your unworthy chains, you are free here

now, happy, and avenged. Do not weep for Seid, and
leave to me the task of deciding men's destinies.
Think only of your own future. And if you are dear
to me, if ever I have seemed like a father to you,
know that a nobler fate, a grander title, if you so
deserve, perhaps await you. Cast your bold glance
on the heights of glory—snuff out the memory of
Seid and all that has happened. All your first emo-
tions must now be forgotten in view of the gran-
deurs which once you dared not contemplate. Your
heart must respond to my kindness and obey my
laws, just as the world obeys them.

PALMIRA: What is this I hear? What laws? Oh heaven!
And what kindness! You blood-smeared impostor, I
abjure you forever! Executioner of all my loved
ones, this final outrage was wanting to complete my
misery and your madness. So there you are! Ye gods!
The holy prophet, the king I served, the god I worshipped! Monster! whose madness and treacherous
plots have made two murderers out of two innocent
hearts! Infamous seducer of my weak youth, be-
smeared with blood, you think I will marry you!
Your conquest is not yet assured, Mahomet. The veil
is torn away, vengeance is being prepared. Do you
hear that noise? Do you hear those shouts? My father pursues you from the shadows of death; the people rise up and arm in my defense. They will snatch
youthful innocence from your greedy arms. Would
that I had the strength to plunge a dagger in your
side, to see you and your crowd die and drown in
your own blood! May Mecca, Medina, and Asia together punish such madness and hypocrisy. Let the
world, deceived and ravaged by you, blush at its
chains, break them, and be avenged! May religion,

the source of deceit, be henceforth held in scorn by
the human race! May hell, whose horrors you so
often threatened to inflict upon those who doubted
your worthless laws, may hell, I say, that realm of
pain and madness, be prepared for you alone, be
your just reward! Those are the sentiments I feel for
your kindness! That is the homage, the oath, the
prayer I make for Mahomet!

MAHOMET: I see I have been betrayed. But so be it!
Whoever you are, obey me and know that this
heart of mine . . .

SCENE 3

MAHOMET, PALMIRA, OMAR, ALI, attendants

OMAR: The secret is out, Mahomet. Hercides, before
he died, revealed everything. The people know all;
the prison has been besieged. Everyone is in arms
and rebelling. A maddened crowd, raising its fearful
cry against you, is bearing here the bloody corpse of
Zopir. Seid is at their head and in baleful tone of
voice is exhorting them to seek vengeance for his
father. The blood-smeared body is the signal for re-
newed effort by the people. With sobbing voice,
Seid shouts: "I murdered my father!" Grief restores
his strength, rage guides him. He seems to breathe
only the desire to avenge himself on you. They all
detest your god, your prophets and you yourself.
Those traitors who this very night were to have
opened Mecca's gates to admit your army, intoxi-

cated too by the zealous common madness, come towards you with raised sword. I heard only shouts of
death and vengeance.

PALMIRA: Righteous heaven, finish the task! Sustain
innocence. Strike him!

MAHOMET (*to Omar*): Well, why are you so afraid?

OMAR: You still have a few friends who hardened to
danger as I am are armed (vainly I fear) and will
face such a storm. We are all ready to die courageously at your feet.

MAHOMET: I alone shall defend them. Stand near me
and realize at last what kind of man your king is!

SCENE 4

MAHOMET, OMAR, their attendants, *on one side;*
SEID and the people *on the other;*
PALMIRA *in the middle.*

SEID (*a dagger in his hand, already weakened by the
poison*) : My people, avenge my father! Kill this
traitor!

MAHOMET: Citizens, you were born to follow me!
Hear your master!

SEID: Do not listen to this monster; follow me . . .
Great gods, what dark shadow passes before my
eyes? (*He moves forward, staggers.*) Let us strike!
. . . I am dying!

MAHOMET: And I triumph!

PALMIRA (*rushing to Seid*): My brother! Will you
have shed only your father's blood?

SEID: Let us advance! . . . I cannot . . . What god
overwhelms me? (*He falls into the arms of his men.*)

MAHOMET: Thus must every fanatic tremble before
me! Unbelieving people, inspired by blind zeal,
you who dare to curse me, and who wish to avenge
Zopir, my arm alone which is universally feared,
my arm alone can punish you for daring to doubt.
God, who granted me his voice and power, if I desire vengeance, will reduce you to ashes! Wretches!
Know his prophet and his law! Let God judge between Seid and me. Let the guilty one die this very
moment!

PALMIRA: Seid! What! does this monster wield such
power over the people? They stand transfixed, they
tremble when he speaks! Mahomet, like a god, still
dictates his laws. And you, Seid, you too!

SEID (*in the arms of his men*): Heaven punishes your
brother, Palmira. My crime was as horrible as it was
involuntary. In vain did virtue dwell in my heart.
You, Mahomet, you villain, if God punished our errors, beware the thunderbolt that awaits you and
your mob. Tremble, Mahomet! God's right arm is
about to strike its victims! Spare her, my god, the
death that I deserve.

PALMIRA: No! Citizens, no god punishes Seid. Poison
doubtless . . .

MAHOMET (*interrupting her and addressing the people*): Learn from this, you infidels, the punishment
that awaits those who plot criminally against me.
From celestial vengeance learn the power I wield.
Both nature and death heed my voice. Death, which
obeys me, which, in my defense, has traced its vengeance on Seid's paling brow, death is ready to strike
you! Thus will my enemies ever feel my anger.

Thus shall I punish senseless error, vile rebels, and impious doubters. If now you see the light of day and still live, thank me, the pontiff to whom you owe all. Flee, run to the temple to appease my anger! (*The people withdraw.*)

PALMIRA (*regaining her composure*) : Citizens! Stop! This barbarian poisoned my brother! Monster, his death will have justified your cause! By means of crime you have deified yourself. Wretched assassin of my entire family, take from me my few remaining years! Oh Seid! Oh my sweet Seid! At least may I follow you! (*Snatching her brother's dagger, she stabs herself.*)

MAHOMET: Stop her!

PALMIRA: I am dying. I no longer see you, villainous impostor. As I die, I trust that some more equitable god reserves a future life for innocent souls. Yes, you will reign on earth, for the earth is made for tyrants.

MAHOMET: I have lost her! . . . Ah, my sweet Palmira. I have lost the only reward of my crime. I, the hated enemy of her appealing charms, the victor and all-powerful conqueror, I it is who am punished! So remorse does exist! Oh madness, oh justice. My crimes have thus brought my heart great suffering! God, whom I have used for the wretchedness of mankind, adored instrument of my frightful designs, thou whom I have blasphemed, but whom I fear still, I feel myself condemned, even though I am universally adored. In vain do I defy thy power which now I feel. I have deceived men, but not my-self. My father, my sweet and innocent children, sacrificed to my madness, avenge the world and yourselves, and heaven too which I have outraged. Come, kill me, tear out my perfidious heart, this heart born to hate which burns with madness. (*To Omar:*) You, blot out the memory of such shame. Conceal my weakness, but save my glory. I must rule this deluded world like a god. My dominion is finished if my character be known.

End of the tragedy

WHAT A WOMAN OUGHT TO BE AND TO DO

WOMEN IN CULTURE AND SOCIETY

A series edited by Catharine R. Stimpson

WHAT A WOMAN
Ought TO BE AND TO DO

BLACK PROFESSIONAL WOMEN WORKERS
DURING THE JIM CROW ERA

STEPHANIE J. SHAW

THE UNIVERSITY OF CHICAGO PRESS
CHICAGO & LONDON

Stephanie J. Shaw is associate professor of history and women's studies at Ohio State University.

The University of Chicago Press, Chicago 60637
The University of Chicago Press, Ltd., London
©1996 by The University of Chicago
All rights reserved. Published 1996
Printed in the United States of America
04 03 02 01 00 99 98 97 96   1 2 3 4 5

ISBN: 0-226-75119-8 (cloth)
        0-226-75120-1 (paper)

Library of Congress Cataloging-in-Publication Data

Shaw, Stephanie J. (Stephanie Jo), 1955–
    What a woman ought to be and to do : Black professional women
  workers during the Jim Crow era / Stephanie J. Shaw.
        p.   cm.
    Includes bibliographical references and index.
    1. Afro-American women in the professions—History.   I. Title.
HD6054.2.U6S53   1996
331.4'089'96073—dc20   95-33063
                                                        CIP

This book is dedicated to the blessed memory of
Aaron Vernard Shaw, my father, and Vera A. Shaw Moreland, my sister;
to Jennie Lee Thompson Shaw, my mother;
and to my aunt Vera L. Thompson and uncle Richard Thompson.

CONTENTS

Foreword, by Catharine R. Stimpson   ix
Preface   xi
Acknowledgments   xiii
Introduction   1

PART 1   WHAT A WOMAN OUGHT TO BE

1   "Aim always to attain excellence in character and culture":
Child-rearing strategies   13
2   "The daughters of our community coming up": Developing
community consciousness   41
3   "We are not educating individuals but manufacturing levers":
Schooling reinforcements   68
Epilogue to Part 1   104

PART 2   WHAT A WOMAN OUGHT TO DO

Prologue to Part 2   109
4   "I am teaching school here . . . [but] I find it rather hard . . .
with my housekeeping": Private sphere work   111
5   "It was time . . . that we should be members": Personal
professional work   135
6   "Working for my race in one way or another ever since I was a
grown woman": Public sphere work   164

Conclusion   211
Appendix: Biographical sketches   221
Abbreviations and Sources   239
Notes   245
Index   333

The publication of *What a Woman Ought to Be and to Do,* a major history of African American professional women, is a signal event.

Stephanie Shaw has studied members of three generations of these women. Growing up after the Civil War but before World War II and the postwar Civil Rights movement, they were raised to be leaders. Although their parents and grandparents may have been slaves, they were not, a fact that empowered them.

With care, clarity, and respect, Shaw first explores the institutions that shaped these women: the family, with its realistic but hopeful child-rearing strategies; the African American community; and the education that prepared them to be social workers, librarians, nurses, and teachers. The young women were to work hard. They were to behave scrupulously, responsibly, exercising self-discipline and self-control. They were to believe in themselves and their aspirations. "Look up and not down Little girl," Archibald Grimké wrote his daughter Angelina, "and never say die" (p. 37). Because they had been brought up with comparative advantages, they were to both set an example for and "lift up" the African American community. This "race consciousness" transcended intraracial class divisions. For Shaw, such women exemplify an important ethos, "socially responsible individualism."

Shaw next shows how these women—socialized as they were— managed a triple burden of domesticity, professionalism, and community improvement. As they knew, they did not dwell in a democratic, color-blind America. Jim Crow was a violent and repressive period. If they had high status at home, they had low status away from it. In 1940, for example, only 42 out of the 1200 nursing schools in America admitted African Americans; 28 of the 42 were at historically black institutions. Courageously, with a subtlety and grace white people usually did not recognize, African American women began to work to "uplift the white race" as well (p. 210).

Poised and serious, *What a Woman Ought to Be and to Do* also extends a historical method that has interdisciplinary implications. Shaw is one of the notable scholars who stand at the intersection of the histories of African Americans and of women. This vantage point permits them to observe both a complex location and the landscape of American history at large. Shaw's account, for example, of African American community-building deepens our understanding of Progressive Era reforms. Moreover, she underscores the historical importance of people's perceptions. Thought by other African Americans to be capable of strong, active, moral, and productive behavior, African American professional women saw themselves in this way and acted accordingly.

A common complaint about America is that our leading figures have celebrity but no character. *What a Woman Ought to Be and to Do* tells of women of a heroic and inspirational character. They and their book are to be celebrated.

CATHARINE R. STIMPSON

When I was growing up in the South, family members often went to a local seafood restaurant to purchase takeout orders. Until I was well into my teens, we always went to the back of the restaurant, to the kitchen, to place and pick up our orders. Though nobody ever told me so, I always believed that we went to the back because Mr. Hunter, who attended the same church as my father, worked in the kitchen, and if he saw that the order was ours, he would put extra food in it. I grew up believing that we went to the back door because it gave us special privileges.

When I try to interpret earlier events of my life now, I have to acknowledge that *not* knowing why we *really* went to the kitchen shaped my life as much as knowing would have, though knowing the truth would undoubtedly have shaped my life differently. The example suggests not only that it is possible that you cannot understand another person's life without walking the proverbial mile in her shoes, but that indeed you can walk that mile in your own shoes and still not fully understand what you have been through. At the very least, our own understanding is peculiar and perhaps even unique.

I became more intensely aware of the peculiarity of historical experiences as I was working on this book, and so I shall comment on perceptions repeatedly. The professional women who are the subjects of this study fit several categories easily stereotyped from the different viewpoints of both liberals and conservatives. The challenge therefore became how to write about these women not only as I can see them now but also as they saw themselves. Notwithstanding the many ways black women's history intersects with the history of white women and the history of black men, the differences are dramatic and complex. They cannot be explained merely by degrees of oppression. Perception lies at the heart of the matter—as it does for the women about whom I write. For black women who reached the age of majority before 1920, the fact that they were not enslaved, as their mothers and grandmothers often had been, was at least as important to them—and in some ways more so—as the fact that they had no right to vote.

The point is not that each generation was satisfied with simply doing better than the previous one did, but that these women were keenly aware of their collective history. They knew that their forebears had endured slavery. As slaves, their parents and grandparents lived in a socially approved and legally enforced state of poverty, illiteracy, and bondage. Yet they produced and educated these daughters. Thus in one way the daughters could not perceive themselves as powerless, disadvantaged, or handicapped. They were the empowered, the advantaged. Nor did the rampant racism and sexism of society permeate their lives. They lived in a segregated society but mainly in one half of it. And while the impact of racism and sexism on and in African American communities was profound, in these communities black women were enabled as much as they were disabled. They saw endless possibilities for themselves rather than limited ones. And all together, the role model that black professional women represented was not pathological, it was ennobled. They were among the well-educated, self-confident "race" leaders. They had influence in their community and authority beyond their households. Their lives compel us to understand them in the context of the community in which they lived and worked as well as in the national context.

I have benefited from the support of many people, and, quite honestly, I fear that even my best effort to recall them all will fall short. Some people contributed in ways that were not always obvious. As important as their contributions were, they sometimes occurred in situations that were less than memorable, and, regrettably, those situations were forgotten. Thus a source was lost, even when the contribution was not.

One that was not lost is Linda Sledge, a secretary at the Virginia State Library, with whom I occasionally had lunch when I was conducting research during the summer of 1988. At the time, I was still waiting for that moment to occur when one finally comprehends the difference between the dissertation and "the book," and because that moment was slow in coming, I had started research on another project. At lunch one day, Linda began to talk about a black family in Richmond that she thought I knew. When I tried to convince her that I (a North Carolinian) did not know the family to whom she referred, she announced in exasperation that I *must* know them, they were "people who stood for something!" I had not heard the expression in many years, but the minute Linda said it, I knew that the ideas it embodied were very much related to what "the book" should be about. Linda's characterization of this family—they were people intensely involved in community work—helped me to understand the significance of suggestions that other people had made when they read my dissertation. In particular, Elsa Barkley Brown had suggested that I definitely write a chapter on education (instead of talking only about schools) and perhaps one on community too. Linda's and Elsa's comments came together for me, and I began to understand the difference between my dissertation and this book.

Numerous people generously read and commented on one or more versions of the entire manuscript, or some of the chapters in it, and offered me their best advice. Sometimes it was practical advice, designed to enable me to meet externally imposed time constraints. At other times it was more extensive, in case I decided to abide by my own rhythm. All of this advice was invaluable, and I hope I have appropriately used the best suggestions of both types. For this help, I wish to thank James D. Anderson, Kenneth Andrien, Ross Bagby, Mary Frances Berry, Richard J. M. Blackett, John B. Boles, John Bracey, Elsa Barkley Brown, John C. Burnham, Kimberlynne Darby, Mary Margaret Fonow, Elizabeth Fox-Genovese, James R. Grossman, Kenneth W. Goings, Kenneth M. Hamilton, Susan M. Hartmann, Jacqueline Jones, Robin D. G. Kelley, Earl Lewis, Charles E. Payne, Paulette Pierce, Gary W. Reichard, Leila J. Rupp, Tiwanna Simpson, and Joe William Trotter. Elsa Barkley Brown and John Boles provided comments on the very first draft of the book, and still continued to encourage me. After a major reconceptualization of the book, Kenneth Goings read each chapter in its first draft and insisted, in his comments, that I was getting somewhere. Charles Payne read and commented on one chapter over and over, beginning when it was only two pages long. John C. Burnham not only endured this entire process, beginning as my dissertation adviser, but convinced me with each draft of the manuscript that his reading it was not a burden.

Librarians and archivists around the country contributed greatly to my effort to complete this book. At a small conference on researching and writing black women's history at Oberlin College in 1982, I met Mary Mace Spradlin, then a librarian in Kalamazoo, Michigan, and Ann Allen Shockley, archivist at Fisk University. Their presentations inspired me to begin thinking about the work of black women librarians, and thus I had the beginning of a dissertation topic. Mrs. Spradlin's subsequent correspondence spurred me on. Indirectly, Ms. Shockley introduced me (through the mail) to E. J. Josey, a New York State librarian, then president of the American Library Association, and he generously agreed to meet and talk with me when the association met in Columbus, Ohio. Ms. Shockley's assistance is evident throughout this study, as is that of Ms. Minnie H. Clayton of Clark-Atlanta University, Mrs. Beth Howse and Mr. Sam Cameron of Fisk University, Dr. Daniel T. Williams of Tuskegee University, Dr. Fritz Malval of Hampton University, Mr. Ronald Shelton and Dr. Vonita Foster of Virginia Union University, Mr. Lucious Edwards of Virginia State University, Mrs. Barbara Simmons, formerly of the Louisville Free Public Library, Dr. Esme Bhan, formerly of the Moorland-Spingarn Research Center, Mrs. Wilda Logan Willis, now at the National Archives, Ms. Brenda Banks of Spelman College, Ms. Diana Lachatenere of the Schomburg Center for Research in Black Culture, Ms. Barbara Teague of the Kentucky Department for Libraries and Archives, and the late Dr. Annette Phinazee of North Carolina Central University School of Library and Information Sciences. I am indebted to all these people and to their staffs, and to the archivists and staffs of the Rockefeller Archives Center, Boston University's Mugar Library–Special Collections, Radcliffe College's Schlesinger Library, the Washington State Archives, the Robert Scott Small Library at the College of Charleston, Avery Research Center for African American History and Culture, the Stanford L. Warren Public Library, the Minnesota Historical Society, and the Richard B. Harrison Public Library.

I must also thank Dr. Patricia E. Sloan, of Hampton University's School of Nursing, who opened all her records to me when I began to incorporate nurses into this study. Dr. Evelyn Tomes of Meharry Medical College was equally generous and shared her oral histories of black nurses with me. Whenever I did research in New York City, Anthony G. Moore stayed near his telephone with train schedules and city maps—just in case I got lost. William Green, now a graduate of Coppin State University, and Pat Pannell Bullock, currently a graduate student at the University of Pittsburgh, were superb research assistants when they worked with me as Summer Research Opportunity Program students. They not only uncovered important materials in newspaper files here in Columbus but also made my work easier in libraries and archives in Tennessee and Kentucky.

Along with my parents, aunt, and uncle, my sisters and brother remain important links in my lifeline. Whenever I got stuck in the writing phase of this project, Aaronia Shaw McAdams told me to go on to something else. And, yes, in my compulsion (or overwhelming desire) to finish one part before going on to another, I occasionally needed someone to tell me to "move on." Vera Allethia Shaw Moreland, my oldest sister, played a significant role in my getting through undergraduate school, sticking with graduate school, and revising my dissertation for publication. She and Robert Moreland talked to me the entire day before my general examination began—and paid the telephone bill. Susithea Dianne Shaw Tyson and Kevin Vernard Shaw still regularly go out of their way to accommodate me and to promote my career. For these and many other reasons, I am blessed to have such a family of friends.

Cynthia Zachary Smith instructs me on community in ways that I will be contemplating for a long time and possibly will never fully understand. Connie and James Gillam (and Damon, Jessica, and Whitney), Robert Hall and Jacqueline Goggin, Robin J. Hailstorks, and Barbara and Alvin Hailstorks opened their homes to me whenever I did research in their neck of the woods—and even when I was not doing research. For general moral support and consistent enthusiasm about this project, thanks also to Michelle and Julius Gordon, Mrs. Ella Stephens, Thaddeus Smith, Jan Leone and Ken Schmitz, Lynette Helms Loury, Darlene Clark Hine, Carlton Wilson, Mildred Pratt, Annetta Jefferson, Lydia Lindsey, Julie Gowen, Beverly Moss, Freddie Parker, Mrs. Ann Scott, and Tullia and Irvin Hamilton.

Finally, I wish to acknowledge the financial and academic support I received as a postdoctoral fellow at the University of Virginia's Carter G. Woodson Institute for Afro-American and African Studies and as a Mellon Visiting Assistant Professor in the Humanities at Rice University. Dean Virginia Owen, through her office in the College of Arts and Sciences at Illinois State University, also provided critical financial support just as I began new research for the revision of my dissertation, and Ohio State University's College of Humanities provided financial assistance as I was completing the book.

And a special thanks to Mary Rose, of the Woodson Institute, who taught me how to use computers and assisted me often when my skills, patience, or time ran out.

INTRODUCTION

In her classic novel *Their Eyes Were Watching God,* Zora Neale Hurston created a conversation that poignantly illustrates a major theme of this book. In that conversation, Janie Crawford's grandmother, Nanny, says that because she was born a slave, she never had the opportunity "to fulfill [her] dreams of whut a woman oughta be and to do." She says, "Ah didn't want to be used for a work-ox and a brood-sow." But to some extent she was. And upon emancipation Nanny found herself with an infant daughter and with no way to achieve her dream of becoming a great pulpit preacher. She had to content herself with devising a plan that would allow her to "take a broom and a cook-pot and throw up a highway through de wilderness" for her daughter.[1]

A variety of people in African American communities worked to "throw up highways" for sons and daughters, brothers and sisters, cousins and others. Over and over, those highways paved the way past obstacles around which many scholars still cannot see. The lives of the black professional women examined here provide a case in point. These women were educated to the best abilities of their families and communities, not in spite of their being black women but *because* they were black and female and would otherwise have few economic alternatives to a lifetime of "work-oxen and hoes," "brooms and cook-pots." In the minds of many parents, their daughters would be far too vulnerable to economic and sexual exploitation as female domestics or agricultural laborers. Formal education, *and* the people who made it possible, were "highways" around those limitations.

The education process went beyond simple schooling—it imparted an orientation toward achievement. Family members supplemented formal schooling by encouraging these daughters to believe that regardless of the limitations others might impose on them because of their race, class, or sex, none of those conditions necessarily determined their abilities, and neither should race, class, or sex inhibit their aspirations. Parents knew that if they were not convincing, their children would have little chance of developing fully and achieving highly, for not only would the larger society fail to encourage their success, but the children themselves would have too much doubt about their abilities. Thus the women studied here came to possess an achievement orientation largely because their families devised child-rearing strategies that included much attention to providing the mental (attitudinal) as well as the material preparation necessary to undertake whatever task was at hand.

This powerful enabling process was in one way highly individualistic and destined to create or ensure class privileges. It did, after all, enable these women, psychologically and intellectually, to undertake tasks that others were less apt and less able to undertake. But at the same time that the process set these women apart from others of their community, it also made them *a part of* that community. The individualistic aspects of the process were accompanied by and reinforced a sense of mutual obligation among the women, their families, and the larger black community and had important collective consequences as well. The child-rearing strategies transformed individualistic notions of self-help and the so-called Protestant work ethic into an ethic of *socially responsible individualism.*[2] At a time when relatively few African Americans achieved much formal education, those few who did were looked to, encouraged to, and expected to "take up the crosses" of those who were less able than they. Community and educational mentors joined with the families to imbue such women with a determination to use their education in a socially responsible way. And consequently, these women became not simply schoolteachers, nurses, social workers, and librarians; they became some of the political and social leaders in the formal and informal movements of the larger group.

In spite of this self-affirming socialization, the debilitating aspects of the Jim Crow system cannot be ignored. The average annual income for black families never came close to that of white families between 1870 and 1950. Between the 1870s and the 1890s, African Americans were effectively disfranchised by force throughout the South, where more than 90 percent of them still lived.[3] And numbers alone cannot convey the intimidation, including violence, that accompanied disfranchisement. Lynchings increased steadily between 1870 and 1900, and the decline after 1900 was inconsistent for three more decades. All the while, Congress refused more than half a dozen times to pass an antilynching bill.[4] State and local governments regularly outlawed integrated schools while refusing to fund separate public education for black children. Where public funds were allocated for black schools, the amounts were often so meager that neither adequate facilities nor well-trained teachers could be supported.[5] Social Darwinist writers of the late nineteenth century sought to justify the continued subordination of African Americans, and pseudoscientific works on their alleged inferiority had become mainstream popular literature by the 1920s.[6] The odds against black women's ultimate success were clearly overwhelming, but the importance of child-rearing strategies and lifetime goals that defied the negative odds is equally manifest.

This book is based on records of the lives of approximately eighty African American women who worked throughout the country in the feminized professions—as social workers, librarians, nurses, and teachers—from the 1880s to the 1950s. Forty-five of these women, for whom extensive documentation of their lives is available, form the core.[7] Isolated details from the lives of thirty-two others, for whom such complete biographical sources are lacking, are also included in the narrative.

A word about the terms used throughout the study is necessary. I have elected not to use the sociological expressions "semiprofessional," "pseudoprofessional," and "quasi-professional" to refer to these women and their work. None of these traditional, and technically more correct, terms conveys the relatively high placement of these women in the public workforce. I have, however, occasionally used "lower-level professional" when my intent is to imply the position of the feminized occupations in a hierarchy of professions topped by physicians and attorneys, whose training, self-perception, earning potential, and community recognition (status) placed them more highly. My reason for otherwise referring to these women as professionals is threefold. First, the occupations represented here were generally the highest ones attainable by black women during the years I cover. Second, the people who worked in these areas considered themselves professionals. And finally, the women studied here meet the traditional definition of "professional" in their preparation, work, personal attitudes, and community images.[8]

● ● ●

Because of the historical visibility of African American women who worked in these professions, scholars have examined some aspects of their lives in great detail. In particular, these studies note the extensive public work that African American women have historically undertaken on behalf of "the race." Much of this scholarship, old and new, concentrates on the period 1880–1920 and appropriately characterizes their activism as reformist, like other Progressive Era activism. While exploring the impulses of a diverse group of African Americans, this fine literature has developed a narrative of the formerly enslaved people and their descendants and related it to the events of a larger American society.[9]

One of the tasks of this book is to refigure this history of the leadership of black women professionals so as to reveal both the roots of their community commitment and the process of their becoming the leaders they became. A second task is to determine how their leadership manifested itself during and beyond the Progressive Era. Readers will find that these women's lives were embedded in a familiar context—the usual industrialism, urbanization, progressivism, wars, depressions, and reforms, with parallel socializing institutions and histories—that has been well described by others. The socializing institutions and processes that help to explain black professional women's lives must be understood to have parallels in institutions of other middle-class American groups. But this book is about the special ways the usual socialization and social institutions functioned for people who were black and female.

African American women hold a unique place at the confluence of the histories of African Americans and of women. From one angle, black women faced a variety of constraints in their lives because of private sphere responsibilities bequeathed to them as women. From a second angle, they were consigned grave public responsibilities because of the needs of the race. Reconciling these seemingly opposing traditions (among others) is both necessary and difficult, as numerous scholars from a variety of disciplines have noted. And as those scholars eloquently demonstrate, the pitfall to avoid is one of forgetting or ignoring the circumstance that African American women are both black and female.[10] More concretely, and in the specific context of this narrative, if one makes race the all-important "category of analysis," black women can be excused from public sphere restrictions placed on other women (chiefly white and middle-class), and black women's seemingly aberrant public roles can be more easily explained. But African American women would thus not only be "excused" from traditional restrictions set up for women in general, but would also be bound to another stereotype, based on race. Ultimately, in the tug-of-war between the centrality of race and of sex that would logically ensue from such false dichotomizing, black women's lives would be fractured beyond recognition.

In the communities where these women were reared, there was no confusion about who they were. They were African American women whose individual futures ultimately depended on their abilities to work effectively in both the public and private spheres. To increase the likelihood of their success, interested persons generated a process that encouraged these women to take responsibility for their own futures and simultaneously to become agents of social change. The process produced some notable leaders among black women and had far-reaching consequences in and beyond African American communities.

Certainly, as scholars have repeatedly demonstrated, American women—and especially African American women—faced many barriers during their lives that prevented them from living as freely and as fully as they wanted. But scholars have not yet adequately looked at black women's lives in a manner that allows us to see beyond their victimization and apply the commonsense knowledge that their experiences often transcended their being oppressed. It is imperative to understand the objective reality of racism and sexism and at the same time to distinguish it from the subjective experiences of individuals who lived in a racist and sexist society.

Without denying the imperious nature of racism and sexism, then, this book looks past oppression to investigate what these women could and did do as much as what they could not do. It explores the ways they lived in time and place—their roles as African American women workers as they themselves and those with whom they lived and worked defined them. The women studied here were participants in family groups, class groups, gender groups, and others while simultaneously operating within larger social, political, and economic groups. In the course of history, the internal and external factors constantly converged and diverged, dispelled and attracted, supported and opposed, pushed and pulled—usually for some discernible reason. And it must be noted that internal controls were always as important as external forces.[11] Emphasizing, then, the enabling aspects of these women's lives rather than the disabling ones might not be so great a leap after all. Translating these women's lives into a model of *socially responsible individualism,* however, may move beyond present historical conceptualizations.

Many people understandably view the concepts of social responsibility and individualism not only as contradictory terms, but as competitive ideals as well. Historians have for a long time limned the tension between liberty (the individual) and social justice (the community). And indeed it is often necessary to remove oneself from one's community to gain the experience that allows or enhances personal development. Privileged Americans are famous for occasionally "dropping out" of society in order to "find themselves."[12] But the developmental process undertaken by these women (or, seen another way, the process that overcame them) was a social rather than a private matter—one in which parents and grandparents, teachers and preachers, community leaders and community lessers worked together, quite consciously, to enhance individual development in a manner that regularly demonstrated, frequently demanded, and often yielded individual postures of collective consciousness and social responsibility.

Across the three generations represented in this book, the basic processes and consequences of socialization changed but little. That persistence is related to the nature of culture itself: social and cultural traditions are by definition persistent. Moreover, persistence is not the same as stasis; cultural persistence is, indeed, quite dynamic. It is a manifestation of multigenerational efforts to produce (and reproduce) particular results. And as one sociologist has noted, the idea "that social and cultural continuity do not require explanation, obliterates the fact that both have to be recreated anew in each generation, often with great pain and suffering."[13]

This is not to say that there were no changes in the conditions of life for these three generations of women: there were many, some small and some large. And often even small changes affected individual strategies and outcomes, as this book documents. Still, it is probably true that "to change culture in any fundamental way, one must transform many things at once."[14] At the very least, many things must change. And during the segregation era not enough changes occurred to affect the worldview of the people studied here. Quite possibly the sweeping changes necessary to alter the construction of gender this narrative describes were not possible until some time after the "death" of Jim Crow. To be sure, the world wars, migration, woman suffrage, the mass production of the automobile, and any number of other important national events had some impact on the lives of black women. Yet great as those events were, they either were not felt consistently enough or were not yet consequential enough when the youngest generation of women reached school age—around 1940—to alter family and

6

community strategies for enabling these children. This book does, however, reveal that the women's responses to that socialization were affected by time and place (the pattern was generational) and changed as circumstances dictated.

Few enough women are included here that at least some become familiar figures in the narrative even if they were not well known during their lifetimes. It is in looking at these lives from many different perspectives that their true significance emerges. I have attempted to examine these women in their full social context: as daughters, wives, mothers, students, workers, professionals, activists, African Americans, women, and African American women. As much as possible, I have considered the economic, political, and social circumstances of the individual women and the groups they represented, placed the individuals and the groups within the larger society, and showed the relationship among the three types of circumstances. In my effort to describe, as far as possible, one vision of "what a woman ought to be and to do," I hope, at least, to contribute to the current reenvisioning of African American women's history.

• • •

The book is divided into two major sections, and they are very different in form and intent. The first part, focusing on the period from the 1880s to the 1930s, concerns the childhood and adolescent years for most of these women and explores how family, education, and community processes and people defined, demonstrated, and functioned to imbue these children with a tradition of womanhood bound tightly both to high individual achievement and to social responsibility—that is, socially responsible individualism. These first chapters are indirectly about the women themselves and more directly concern three of the social institutions of which they were a part and the processes by which people within the institutions sought to influence how the women would eventually define their place in society.

The narrative starts with the child-rearing strategies developed within individual families, strategies explicitly designed to produce self-confident, high-achieving, socially responsible adults. The next chapter, focusing on community, demonstrates how these children were connected to others beyond their families in ways that not only enhanced their own development but also cultivated in them a worldview in which they were partly responsible for the development of others. Focusing

7

on formal education, the third chapter shows how schooling processes reinforced many of these family lessons and extended the earlier socialization regarding collective consciousness. All together, in theory and in practice, the educational programs "completed" the women's preparation for meeting the challenges and opportunities that existed beyond the protective environments of home and school where they came to adulthood.

The second part of the book explains the impact of this socialization. Focusing on the 1890s to the 1950s, years encompassing at least part of the working lives of all of the women, it addresses paid and unpaid work in the public sphere, paid and unpaid work in the private sphere, and personal public work done to achieve full professional status. Chapter 4, though focusing on work within the home, is not confined to unpaid work or to family domestic responsibilities. It concerns productive and reproductive work for the benefit of families, public and private factors influencing the nature of that work, and how reproductive work in the home could be both public (community) and private (domestic). Chapter 5 addresses the very particular aspect of public work involving the women's professional status. Individual women in all the fields considered sought to gain, maintain, or enhance their professional status by making a commitment to the service ideal, by pursuing education beyond that provided by their families, and by organizing with other professionals. The narrative closes by defining, in chapter 6, a larger dimension of public work, revealing the full (individual and collective) ramifications of the earlier socialization. In this instance public work was not limited to paid work, and unpaid public work was not necessarily charity work. The women worked for a wage when necessary and where possible, and they worked toward the development of the African American community in either case. And finally, after nearly three generations, their work took them beyond their own community and into the larger white society.

The interpretations and conclusions of this book rest upon such evidence as has survived. Extensive collections of papers for black women in these professions are a rare find. The very existence of sources for these women means that they were in some ways extraordinary and not necessarily representative of all black women who worked in these professions. At one end of the spectrum are the very few women, like Mary Church Terrell, whose life stories are recorded in a variety of published and unpublished sources. At the other end are the vast majority for whom no manuscript materials and few documents of other sorts exist. For those in between these two groups—women who were not famous but were not completely unknown—there are a few manuscript collections scattered around the country, and, more frequently, among other sources, there exist oral histories and published and unpublished biographies and autobiographies.[15]

Certain characteristics of all these materials—not simply those representing conscious reconstructions (e.g., autobiographies and oral histories)—require that historians approach them with care. First, women whose public lives, at least, did not reflect idealized community images are unlikely to be among those whose papers were sought out by archivists or whose life stories were recounted by biographers. And, second, purposely or not, people representing themselves frequently reconstruct idealized images.[16] It is important to note, therefore, that some stories are no doubt embellished and many others concealed; that life stories reconstructed after mostly successful, productive conclusions are no doubt shaped as much by the outcomes as by the original experiences; and that in those few instances where evidence clearly demonstrates that women acted selfishly or insensitively, even to the point of endangering other members of the black community, those examples should stand as evidence of behavior that must have been more widespread. Still, the available documents portray facets of the women's lives, part of their perceptions of themselves and others, and what they saw as important enough and appropriate enough to reveal.[17] As I have searched for common patterns I have tried to use all this material carefully, questioning what seems to warrant questioning while accepting what the women represented as their lives.

There are, however, other limitations in the sources. First, most of the archival records I used illustrate the important public roles these women assumed but provide fewer details on the private sphere. Adding to this imbalance, in oral histories women too often, no doubt believing that their public work was most important, did not comment at all on their private sphere work. Also, some of the black professional organizations the women participated in had long histories, and the members kept and preserved extensive organizational records, whereas others were not even created until the 1970s. In short, it is not possible to document all aspects of any of these women's lives. But as incomplete, fragmentary, or otherwise unsatisfactory as some of the sources are, they represent what we can know. And, taken all together, sufficient archival and bibliographical sources exist so that it is possible to determine patterns and re-create the worlds in which these women lived.

A major conclusion of this book is that within the African American community there existed a construction of gender that was deliberately designed to enable women to transcend what has often been perceived by scholars as the multiple disabling factors (for black working women) of race, class, and sex.[18] The strategy involved encouraging and providing for high levels of achievement and then linking that individual success to community development. To be sure, there was much that African American women could not do because they were black, female, and from working-class backgrounds as they sometimes were. But as literary historian Erlene Stetson and others have pointed out, "Too often the apparent powerlessness of a group obscures its real power."[19]

These women are members of several social groups too easily characterized as helpless, hapless victims of a tremendously hostile society. And, indeed, they lived in a racist, sexist, and economically stratified world. But their upbringing helped convince them not only that they could cope with that world but also that they could combat many of its defeating elements. Though in hard reality they could not be or do anything they wanted to be or do, as parents and teachers coached, what is at least equally important is that the children were told they could, and almost everyone involved operated as if it were true.

Collectively, their story is not very different from the characterization of the life of librarian Clara Stanton Jones in a 1971 Dallas newspaper article: "It is an epic of struggle and stubbornness, reverence for education and achievement, and a religion which offered . . . sometimes the only salvation in this life."[20] For these women collectively, however, "religion" was not entirely otherworldly. It included an inspired faith in their own ability to foster positive change in their lives and the lives of others. That self-confidence was firmly rooted in their earlier socialization as children in families, reinforced regularly by their educational and community mentors, and mandated by the needs of a client constituency that had few others to whom to turn.

PART ONE

WHAT A WOMAN OUGHT TO BE

"Aim always to attain excellence in character and culture": CHILD-REARING STRATEGIES

As children begin preparing for the societal roles they will hold as adults, family members provide their first lessons on the social and cultural values of the groups of which they are a part.[1] The processes by which parents and others convey those values and traditions are largely self-determined, but the interpretation, the articulation, and the actualization of those expectations are conditioned by many factors, including some that appear to lie beyond the direct control of the individuals involved. That is, fortitude, good character, ambition, and a variety of other personal qualities that parents regularly encourage in their children enable some to achieve more than others. But for African American women who achieved personal and professional success during the Jim Crow era, racism, sexism, and the consequences of economic stratification easily rendered individual means and efforts insufficient in the personal struggle for self-development. For these women self-development sometimes required a collective effort, and the key to their successfully compensating for normally constraining conditions and ultimately overcoming them lay in that communion and in an upbringing in families where the first lessons taught emphasized the importance of working hard and of preparing for, and expecting, success.

This chapter is therefore about the child-rearing strategies undertaken by the families of these women. Parents anticipated the complex range of conditions that could impede their daughters' futures, and consequently the child-rearing processes reflected some thought about traditional public sphere constraints, private sphere responsibilities, personal attributes, and community expectations. Using a formula that emphasized appropriate behavior, dedicated preparation, hard work, and community consciousness, family elders espoused a work and success ethic that was more than a symbolic recipe for maintaining the status quo. They intended that these daughters escape the traditional occupational traps most black women had to endure, and they expected the daughters to make some difference in the lives of the many people in their communities who did not enjoy the advantages that they did.

With few exceptions—one being Mary Church Terrell, the daughter of a millionaire—African American women have had to work for a living. Therefore some aspects of child rearing were particularly individualistic. Whether or not parents preferred to see their daughters enjoy lives of leisure or at least lives free of wage-earning duties, they understood that the economic circumstances of black Americans made it unrealistic to assume that one's child, because she was female, would escape those responsibilities. Black women's incomes were often critical to the family economy.[2] Parents also knew that without formal education their daughters would have few alternatives to working as domestic or agricultural laborers.[3] The economic and sexual exploitation of black women in these occupations was well known to them, so to ensure that that would not be the lot of their daughters, those mothers and fathers who could do so provided their daughters with as much education as possible—sometimes at great sacrifice. Parents deliberately encouraged the pursuit of courses of study that would lead to higher occupations, and they pushed the children to be self-confident, independent high achievers. These parents were neither unrealistic nor irresponsible in rearing their daughters in this way. Nor had they misread society's cues about the social and economic options available to black women. They simply insisted upon distinguishing between what their daughters were capable of doing and what they might be allowed or expected to do.[4]

Public expectations were, however, very important. Parents understood that if their daughters were to receive the best and the most opportunities available, they would have to be extremely circumspect and never give even the slightest hint of impropriety, otherwise they might be negatively typecast and raise doubts about their abilities and fitness to serve in professional, educational, or other public settings. Administrators who made hiring decisions would not employ a person of questionable character. And equally important, if the women were not morally upright, self-controlled, and community oriented, the black community they were to serve would also reject them on the grounds of being incompetent despite formal training and for being unacceptable role models for the children of the community. The Reverend James Preston Poindexter, the first black member of the Columbus, Ohio, board of education, put it succinctly: "Parents of colored youth, like parents of white youth, demand that those appointed to teach their children shall have the requisite educational qualifications; be pure in their lives, orderly in deportment, devoted to their work, and successful, because capable and devoted."[5] Because teachers were important vehicles for children's advancement, parents from less privileged backgrounds, who had high aspirations for their children too, but fewer means of achieving them, found these qualifications especially important. Thus, to obtain a position and to succeed in the higher service occupations, more than self-confidence and formal education was necessary; one also had to be respectable.

But enhancing employment options was not the only reason to maintain respectability. Parents also emphasized such expectations simply because they wanted their children to be well behaved, and they wanted people to know that their children came from good homes—that they themselves were people of good character. And even here the emphasis on respectable behavior went beyond the general concern most parents had for the family image. Because they lived in an environment in which the exploitation and abuse of black people were commonplace, parents also hoped that extremely upright behavior would ward off dangerous attention and counteract the negative stereotypes of African Americans that were common throughout white America.

Finally, as important as educational preparation and respectability were, character was a critical accompaniment, and it involved more than demonstrating good manners. By working to develop character, child-rearing strategies went beyond individualistic concerns to encompass the needs of the community. A person of character possessed the kind of self-confidence that enabled her to trust her own judgment and not be diverted from personal goals by interests contrary to her own. But character also involved being respectful of others and even committed to them. That commitment was demonstrated in a willingness to address situations not necessarily of one's making—the demonstration of loyalty, for example. It required understanding that committing oneself to struggle was not a self-centered quest for martyrdom but the "acceptance of vocation." And perhaps most of all, character depended on being responsible in several ways: demonstrating "loyalty in action," being accountable to oneself and others for one's actions, and assessing situations accurately enough to define one's actions accordingly (otherwise one's actions could be irresponsible). A responsible woman was capable of viewing negative experiences as only a part of a whole, and she also knew that accepting those negatives represented neither "resig-

15

nation" nor "running away from struggle" but was simply a matter of recognizing reality. In short, character involved the possession of particular "moral qualities," the ability to make decisions responsibly, and the acceptance of certain "social roles." During child rearing, efforts at character development often appeared to be simple instructions on good manners, but the habits parents sought to instill in children could lead to their becoming self-assured, community-conscious, socially responsible adults.[6]

Altogether, then, while recognizing and maneuvering against the vulnerabilities entailed by being black and female, parents designed child-rearing strategies that would help to ensure the personal, academic, and professional success of their daughters. These strategies reflected concern for the equally important aspects of formal schooling, respectable behavior, self-assurance, self-discipline, and social responsibility. Parents believed these traits were the keys to success in both the private and the public spheres. And as a consequence of such upbringing, their daughters were partly prepared not just for work but for professional positions, activism, and leadership roles.

• • •

Norma Boyd's parents, Jurell and Pattie Bullock Boyd, migrated to Washington, D.C., soon after their marriage. They left their North Carolina home around 1880 in part because of the limited educational opportunities available there for the children they planned to have. The Boyds eventually had three daughters, and ultimately each one gained a solid education: Norma, who became a schoolteacher in the District of Columbia, graduated from Armstrong High School and Howard University.[7] Norma's education, however, began in her home, long before she started her formal schooling. Her upbringing in this regard was not very different from that of other women included in this book—their parents all expected them to become accomplished public achievers.

Some of the first lessons parents taught were those specifically aimed at generating regular, unselfconscious, respectable behavior. Lessons initially involved simply learning the importance of saying "thank you," "excuse me," and "please." Cleanliness and a neat appearance were important complements to politeness. Gossiping and unnecessary borrowing were unacceptable behaviors. And woe betide one caught eating on the street. If children were ever inclined to defy these little lessons, there were much larger issues than individual choice and personal consequences to consider. For as Norma Boyd's mother reminded her children—and it was not an uncommon strategy—their manners reflected not only their own character but that of the entire family. Because, Boyd learned, everything she did reflected her home training, she always had to behave in a manner that told people she came from a good home. Mrs. Boyd's conveying the lesson in this context provided a powerful incentive to learn it and abide by it. That is, Boyd's choosing to disgrace herself was one thing; disgracing the whole family was not a choice she had a right to make.[8]

Parents taught and reinforced lessons in graciousness, thoughtfulness, and character development in a variety of ways. When, for example, Constance Fisher informed her parents that she might receive an award for her work in the YWCA Conference during the 1920s, Isaac Fisher insisted, "We are proud of all the fine things you have written about the Conference. . . . But your mama, Auntie, and I want you to know that the thing we are proudest of is that you have grown so much in bigness of spirit, that nominated for one of the greatest honors that can come to a student, you can say that another girl is the one to whom the honor should go. You cannot lose with such a spirit as that."[9]

Even when Archibald Grimké served as American consul to Santo Domingo from the middle to the late 1890s, he continued to instruct his daughter Angelina through the mails. Archibald regularly reminded Angelina to respond to people who had written letters to her, to thank people for favors that they had provided, and to keep in touch with old family friends. Because Angelina was left in the care of her uncle and aunt, Francis and Charlotte Forten Grimké, Archibald also instructed his daughter to be a comfort to them. In one instance he begged her: "Do my darling learn to be kind and thoughtful and unselfish," which he described as the most beautiful virtues a person could have. As he worked to make certain that Angelina would not become an undue burden to those who had so generously agreed to care for her in his absence, he also hoped that she, like other "nice girls, white and colored," would always behave respectably.[10]

Parents' occupations rarely caused the kind of physical separation the Grimké family experienced, but because families often sent children away from home for formal schooling, separation was not uncommon. The physical distance between the student and her family regularly precluded quick parental responses to all but emergency situations; therefore it was important for children to learn to provide for their own needs correctly. They had to learn to eat sensibly in order to prevent ill health. They had to learn to shop economically, thus avoiding unnecessary expenses. And they also had to learn how to dress tastefully and wisely to prevent both physical infirmity and social embarrassment. Parents wanted to encourage self-reliance and maturity in their children, and, therefore, they did not hesitate to remind the daughters of their own obligations in these matters. When Angelina Grimké asked her father for money to buy new clothes, he simply reminded her of how privileged she was to have all she had, and he added, "If you look shabby, it will be your own fault."[11]

Angelina Grimké's efforts to obtain extra money from her father were rarely successful. While attending school in Massachusetts in 1898, she asked him for five dollars for a new winter outfit in addition to the five dollars he had already sent her. He agreed to send it only if she were willing to accept it in exchange for her train fare home (to Washington, D.C.) for the Christmas holiday. Three months later Angelina tried again—for a new spring dress. This time, along with her father's refusal and his suggestion that she do the best she could with what she had, Archibald added, "There is no better way to learn the great lesson of self help and self support than to learn how to make old things take the place of new and how to keep new things from getting old." When Archibald refused to send extra money to his daughter, he usually cast his refusal in the context of not being "a rich man." But his point was larger than that. In one instance Angelina had borrowed fifty cents from a schoolmate, which no doubt her father could have repaid. But instead he insisted that she learn to live within her means (she had a quite liberal allowance of fifty cents a week); that she experience the misery associated with indebtedness; and that whenever she got into debt, she "make it her first aim to get out." Over and over, he advised her to "practice a wise economy." After all, he noted, the judicious use of money was a virtue.[12]

Some parents, however, did readjust their expectations when their daughters appeared unable to live within previously agreed-upon budgets. When Miriam Matthews left home in the 1920s to attend the University of California at Berkeley, her parents at first made one bank deposit at the beginning of the school year for her expenses. But either they later became unable to make such sizable deposits or they found she could not budget the money properly. They subsequently made a smaller deposit at the beginning of each semester for her initial expenses and sent her a monthly allowance.[13] Portia Washington Pittman was apparently never able to live as a student within her allowance, and her father was rarely able to hold to his position that she do so. Portia no doubt knew that with his well-known name she could sometimes sign for her purchases and have the merchant send him the bill. When she charged some of her expenses in this manner in the spring of 1904, Booker T. Washington paid the bill he received, but he chided Portia: "I very much prefer that you not make bills before consulting with either me or your mama." And he added, "It is not a safe plan." It is possible that Washington's remark represented a subtle threat not to pay Portia's unauthorized debts in the future, but more likely than not, Washington was alluding to his popularly known position that indebtedness was the first step back into slavery. After Portia moved to Germany in 1905 to study music with Martin Krause, she informed her father that she could live comfortably on seventy to eighty dollars a month. He sent seventy, but not to her. He sent the money to the Kolonial Wirtschaftliches Komitee, where she could withdraw it as she needed it. This way she would not have all the money at once, and maybe she would even be thoughtful about when to ask for it and how to spend it.[14]

For some children, thriftiness and even deprivation were regular conditions of life rather than character-development lessons in self-denial, delayed gratification, and self-control. Most parents encouraged fiscal conscientiousness simply because they could not afford to support the children more extensively than they already did. Having their children in boarding schools was often a financial burden to begin with, and the children had to do their part not to make it worse. Therefore Beulah Hester never expected money from home while she was a student at Hartshorn Memorial College in the early 1900s, and she did not ask for any. She never expected to go home for the Christmas holiday, either, and was grateful for the pair of shoes her parents sent each Christmas instead. The shoes, and the one new dress she received every spring, probably deprived her siblings at home of something. Mabel Northcross's family was equally poor, but she was fortunate enough to live at home during her initial education, and when she studied nursing at Meharry Medical College in Nashville during the 1910s, the school provided uniforms, housing, and a small stipend after her probationary period. Her parents, however, sent her "a little change" from time to time, but more often they sent fresh vegetables from their home garden in nearby Paducah, Tennessee. Because she was an older student living in a situation that allowed (or required) her to prepare her own meals, the produce from home enabled Northcross to feed herself and, probably, fellow nursing students too.[15]

Lessons related to moderation, especially in personal consumption, were significant even when the family's economic circumstances already precluded excessive and wasteful consumption. For those with substantial means, thriftiness was a way of maintaining those resources even as external conditions changed. For those who had little, a Spartan lifestyle for a few more years was a small price to pay for an education, which could change their material condition dramatically and perhaps permanently.[16] Whether intended or not, an important consequence of this short-term austerity was that many of these children did not live significantly better than those for whom they would later serve as role models. And additionally, the conditions under which many of the women would later work would require extensive experience in making something out of what others perceived as nothing.

Other important lessons concerned general social intercourse, and they were not nearly as simple as the lessons related to thriftiness. After all, at some point even a child could see the results of economizing and saving money. But there was not always a tangible by-product of "being nice." And the lessons could be completely confounding. First of all, they often required that the girls be respectful of people who demonstrated no respect for them. This must have been a difficult lesson to grasp, particularly in cases where the culprits were real villains—people who had learned that it was not necessary to respect black people and that it was in fact acceptable to mistreat them. Children had to learn that it was most important to maintain their own dignity in these instances, thereby demonstrating superior character, and to interpret affronts to their dignity as the shame of the offender. Maintaining a posture of respectability despite the insult was an act of self-affirmation, and the ability to affirm oneself in the face of personal affronts was critical to the ongoing process of self-development.[17]

Children learned that being nice to people who shunned them proved their own moral superiority: they had not lowered their standards to those of the offensive person. And there is also some logic in the idea that demonstrating such self-control before people who were offensive might somehow reform those people. But comprehending the mandate not to associate with certain people who had *not* insulted you could be, for a child, even harder. Often there were classmates, neighbors, and even family members whom parents identified as people of bad or questionable character. Parents did not want their children to pick up unacceptable habits or have their reputations damaged by associating with such people, and so children had to learn the importance of "reputation." They had to protect their own by being aware of others'. If these apparent contradictions—being nice to people who were not nice to them and not associating with people who had not directly offended them—were difficult to understand or to accept, the latter lesson was at least tempered by the fact that children were also taught to treat all people respectfully. A person of character recognized and respected the humanity of all people, even those who had different lifestyles and with whom she should never associate.[18]

Despite the extensive lessons in appropriate behavior, children still sometimes misbehaved. And often the misbehavior represented too great a threat to ignore. Although Archibald Grimké was living outside the United States at the time of some of Angelina's transgressions, he came to a rather drastic conclusion in response to "the [negative] influence which Washington [was] exacting upon [her]." He removed her from her aunt and uncle's home. There is no evidence of just what Angelina had done to provoke her father's response, but when Charlotte Forten Grimké informed Archibald that she could no longer care for Angelina because of her persistent bad behavior, Archibald decided to find a school where, as he put it, all her best qualities would develop. He sent Angelina to Carleton Academy in Northfield, Minnesota, and he advised her in the process that rather than burdening herself with guilt and shame, she should "turn over a new leaf" while she was still young. "Mama Day," a family friend, similarly advised Angelina to start working immediately to regain people's confidence.[19]

The point of these parental efforts was to make it unnecessary to *enforce* a particular standard of behavior. Parents sought to make the behavior part of an unconscious individual condition. Where the efforts were most successful, children conformed to their instructions concerning comportment even when out of the direct reach of their elders. Some reported that they "minded" their parents simply to please them.[20] Others, however, understood the larger importance of internalizing these standards of behavior: their safety was at stake. The personal risks were especially evident when children traveled alone.

In the 1890s Julia Smith often rode the train from Washington, D.C., to Massachusetts, where she visited relatives. And each time her parents carefully instructed her to remain in her seat until her aunt or grandmother came for her. Realizing that their daughter might act on her own once out of their sight, however, as further protection, Smith's parents left her in the care of a Pullman porter who was a family friend. Julia's rigid adherence to her prior instructions made the porter's work somewhat difficult. Probably wanting literally to *care* for Julia, or even to entertain her during the long journey, when the passengers were transferred to a ferryboat the porter tried to persuade her to come outside and look at the water. Staid little Julia reminded him that her instructions were to stay in her seat, which she did, with her packed lunch, baby doll, and name/destination tag.[21] Undoubtedly Julia's parents had impressed this behavior upon her to make sure she did not wander off and get lost after arriving at her destination or become a nuisance to other passengers during the trip. But such obedience was especially important to the safety and self-assurance of black children for other reasons too. They might easily and unintentionally attract the attention of not-so-friendly white people or others who might harm them. Although children regularly find hypothetical examples unfathomable, this lesson was very important because such situations occurred with frightening regularity.

As a child in the late 1860s, Mary Church Terrell was traveling by train with her father when he left the first-class car to smoke. While he was away a white conductor tried to move Mary to the "colored" car, a second-class coach. Terrell recalled her effort to explain the incident to her mother.

I assured her [that] I had been careful to do everything she told me to do. For instance, my hands were clean and so was my face. I hadn't mussed my hair. . . . I hadn't soiled my dress a single bit. I was sitting up "straight and proper." Neither was I looking out of the window, resting on my knees with my feet on the seat (as I dearly loved to do). I wasn't talking loud. In short, . . . I was behaving "like a little lady" as she told me to do.[22]

"Ladylike" behavior could not always save one from danger in a society in which many whites demonstrated little respect for black people in general, but without "proper" behavior the dangers would certainly be intensified, the chances for abuse increased, and the opportunities for advancement diminished.[23] Consequently, whenever childish transgressions occurred, parents and guardians acted quickly and firmly. And as Angelina Grimké's relocation to a boarding school suggests, even physical separation did not preclude a direct and dramatic response from family members. Children had to learn to adhere to certain behavioral standards whether or not their parents were around to observe what they did.

Angelina Grimké was not so easily controlled. She left the Cushing Academy campus without permission one day in 1897, and her father, still out of the country but convinced that she should remain in this school, was limited in how he could respond. He insisted that there was no reason for her going to Boston during the school term, but he cushioned his chastisement by adding: "Please do not do it again, my dear little girl." Angelina's uncle Francis, her temporary legal guardian, reacted much more fiercely, ordering her "once and for all" never to leave school again without his permission. He also made his instructions known to the principal, who ultimately had to enforce the directive.[24] Archibald and Francis were undoubtedly concerned for Angelina's safety, but, equally important, they were concerned that her action might be seen as an indication of bad character. A well-reared minor—especially a girl in the late nineteenth century—had no business being away from home or school on her own authority.

The link between behavior (real or imagined) and the kinds of opportunities parents sought for their daughters was genuine. If no other reminders were as clear, throughout the late nineteenth and early twentieth centuries, college catalogs explicitly stated that, in addition to a solid academic record, good character and a spotless reputation were prerequisites for admission. Ever mindful of this fact, when Booker T. Washington sought admission for his daughter Portia to the New England Conservatory of Music in 1903, he assured the manager in writing: "My daughter has been well raised, and I think you will find that she will not be, in any respect, offensive; nor will she give you any trouble in any regard."[25] But neither Washington's fame, his daughter's preparation, nor his assurances about her character earned her admission to the school. The school's failure to admit Portia was not her fault, however; she was prepared to be both a good student and a "good girl." Responsibility for this mischance lay with the school, and Portia did not have to carry any burden of guilt for not living up to the standards set by her family.

Family standards of respectable behavior also included Victorian ideals of restraint regarding matters of female sexuality. Although the public image of black women lay beyond their control, parents still expected their daughters to work to project a flawlessly upright appearance. The negative public image was rooted in slavery when owners and overseers sexually assaulted enslaved women and then referred to

CHAPTER ONE

them as lascivious. The myth of black promiscuity died hard and remained a point of contention well into the postbellum period as white
people continued to perpetuate it, often to justify their own actions.[26]
Cognizant of racist and sexist slurs, parents emphasized the importance
of disproving the sexual myths and stereotypes and insisted on sexual
self-control and, thus again, the demonstration of respectability. Adhering to this code of morality would, however, do more than protect the
individual, family, and race from embarrassment. A breach of these
practices, whether or not it resulted in a premarital or early pregnancy,
could easily eliminate the professional opportunities for which the parents were preparing their daughters.

Recognizing that young black women were especially vulnerable
to sexual abuse and hoping to ward off lecherous attention, parents
reared their daughters not to present themselves in sexual or sensual
ways. And the concerns with sensuality sometimes resembled traditional
fears parents display regarding the maturation of their children. Archibald Grimké, for example, absolutely refused to buy Angelina an evening gown for Christmas in 1897 when she was seventeen. He wrote
forthrightly that she was a schoolgirl, not a society woman. Mamie Garvin Fields's mother disapproved of the first shirtwaist Fields made in
school just before the turn of the century because it was too "woman-
ish." In the 1920s Miriam Matthews, then in her middle teens, could
wear "rice powder" and "pale pink pomade lipstick," but neither she
nor her girlfriends were allowed to wear real lipstick, rouge, or any
other makeup until they were almost out of their teens and well into
their college careers.[27] Parents hoped to control their daughters' physical appearance and consequently to influence other people's impressions and treatment of them.

At the same time that parents insisted their daughters not present themselves in ways that might be interpreted as sensual, they also
understood that black girls did not have to *do* anything to "attract" the
kind of attention that resulted in sexual abuse. For that reason, parents
also worked to keep children out of situations where others could take
advantage of them. One eminent source of danger was white males,
who might not only victimize these daughters, but against whom black
families had no recourse. Consequently, though the brothers of the
women almost always worked during the summers to help pay for their
schooling, the girls were not allowed the same opportunity because the
jobs most accessible to them entailed domestic work in white people's
homes or in hotels.[28]

There were too many "possible dangers sometimes associated with that sort of work," according to Septima Clark's father. Clark's mother similarly believed that "the man of the house, or delivery boys, or even men on the street" could imperil Septima's safety. Both parents thought white men regularly "tempted" or forced black girls into illicit relationships: they knew of many local examples, and furthermore, they were aware of the history of such exploitation. The only acceptable solution for Septima was to work for pay during the school year as a baby-sitter and light housekeeper for the black woman with whom she boarded.[29] Jane Edna Hunter, who was not so fortunate, had no choice but to take a job as a waitress and chambermaid in a South Carolina hotel while in her early teens. She was regularly terrorized by white male patrons until her aunt rescued her and found her a job picking cotton.[30] Lucy Mitchell, who consistently searched unsuccessfully for summer work during the 1910s, needed only to look at her own family history to see why she could not work in New England resorts as her brothers did. Her grandmother, for whom she and her mother were named, had given birth to two children whose father was a patron in the hotel where she worked as a chambermaid.[31]

Although parents were extremely conscious of the sexual exploitation of black women, they also accepted that their daughters were sensual and even sexual beings. Rather than deny or ignore this as some Victorians did, they acknowledged the possibility of their daughters' consenting to a sexual relationship and instituted safeguards to prevent it. Before the turn of the century, Booker T. Washington went so far as to dispatch his daughter's escorts from Tuskegee whenever she had to attend a school event in Massachusetts that required one. To be sure, his "appointing" Portia's dates was in part designed to protect their (especially his) privacy, but Washington's action also made these young men not only responsible for Portia while she was with them, but directly accountable to him. Some years later, when the summer home of Frances Grant's family became a gathering place for black students, mostly young men attending summer school at several area universities, her father sold the house and bought another one "beyond the ten-cent trolley," putting his daughters out of reach of these young men. Until well into the twentieth century, girls were not allowed to date in couples until they were eighteen. Boy-girl parties were chaperoned, and girls had to dance with each other until they were about sixteen. For Ethel Ray Nance these were always "matinee dances," held during the daytime. If these rules regarding social interaction suggest that the daughters might have become willing participants in a heterosexual relationship, they also imply that white males were not the only cause for vigilance; black males were also suspect. Ultimately, in addition to enforcing family rules on work and social interaction, parents had to hold the girls responsible for their own behavior and sometimes even for that of their male friends.[32]

Girls accepted the seriousness of their parents' rules about socializing with boys, and when they did not abide by those rules, they worked to conceal their "misbehavior." Beulah Hester did her brothers' chores when they were growing up lest they tell their parents that she accepted candy and notes from boys at school. Sarah Webb Rice accepted the candy that her friend, Mac, regularly brought to her, but rather than taking it home she always hid it under the steps of a vacant house on the way from school. And Septima Clark literally panicked when she discovered blue dye from her future husband's uniform on her white shirtwaist after kissing him. Septima knew her mother would think she had no business being so close to the young sailor and feared that her mother might even question her morality. Septima not only was twenty-one years old at the time, she was engaged to marry the man. Still, she understood that what would matter to her mother was that they were not married yet.[33]

There is almost no way to know the extent to which these women had detailed talks with their parents about sex. But apparently accepting notes and candy from boys, dancing with them, kissing them, and even wearing makeup represented, for a young girl, dangerous steps toward sexuality. Parental expectations prohibited such public demonstrations, which threatened aspirations for the future as well. Ultimately, even if parents generally used softer terms—Beulah Hester's mother said, "I'd rather see you in your grave" than have Beulah disgrace the family—the pressure to conform to the family standard, and the daughters' need to conceal apparent deviations from it, are nonetheless obvious.[34]

· · ·

Despite the plans for higher education and public careers, and perhaps in preparation for marriage, traditional norms of domesticity were also important aspects of respectability. In fact, knowing how to perform mundane domestic tasks was not enough; these women learned that they should do them well. Beulah Hester's mother taught her to "Wash on Monday. Iron on Tuesday. Mend on Wednesday (be-fore putting the clothes away). Thursday . . . begin your cleaning. Finish on Friday. [And on] Saturday . . . do your cooking."[35] When Portia Washington Pittman returned to Tuskegee from Framingham Acad-emy after finishing grammar school in 1899, her stepmother made her enroll in the dressmaking course at Tuskegee. Upon Portia's return to Massachusetts to attend Wellesley College in 1901, a writer for the Indianapolis *Freeman* reinforced gender-specific expectations by noting her ability to fulfill them.

For college she dresses very plainly, in a gray skirt and jacket and wash shirtwaist. All of them she could make with her own hands if necessary, for last year she devoted herself to an industrial course at Tuskegee. Besides being a practical dressmaker, she can trim a hat or bake a loaf of bread equally well, for she has also taken the courses in millinery and housekeeping.[36]

Hard work and self-sufficiency were important cornerstones of respectability, and therefore the reporter was probably also making an important statement about class and work ethics, reinforcing ideas on the dignity of labor for less affluent readers. One might, after all, expect that because of Portia's class background—her parents' household al-most always included domestic workers—she would not be prepared for and might even be exempted from performing domestic tasks. Yet the article insists that she could perform this labor herself, and the readers of the *Freeman* should suppose she did. Historian Sharon Har-ley suggests other important reasons for the emphasis on domesticity. Among them are the control women had in their homes compared with their usual paid workplaces and the status that being a good home-maker conferred even if one did not have a high-status job.[37] Consider-ing that the *Freeman* had a sizable working-class readership and that these women's public careers were not guaranteed, Harley's conclusions might very well apply here. Equally important, however, domestic abil-ity, especially hatmaking, baking, and sewing, prepared these women to earn an income without leaving their homes if they were unable to obtain work in the professions.

Portia began training for domesticity long before that year of courses at Tuskegee. She had been performing domestic work in her home at least since becoming a teenager. At the age of thirteen she confided to her father that "the hardest scolding I ever got from mamma was because I did not get the children's [her younger brothers'] room cleaned up fast a nough [*sic*]." And two years later, after enrolling at Framingham, her stepmother insisted she do her own washing and ironing rather than pay to have it done. On that occasion Portia appealed to her father again:

I don't see how I am to get time. We get up at six eat breakfast at seven clean up after breakfast then I practice [piano] until school time we are let out at 11.30 then come home study until lunch after lunch go to school from school to practice then go for a walk with Miss Moore come home get ready for dinner. After dinner read, sew, etc. Now you have my day's work.[38]

Portia probably succeeded in convincing her father that she just could not do any more. But after leaving Framingham, and at her stepmother's insistence, she spent a year studying and performing domestic work at Tuskegee, as the *Freeman* reporter noted.

Expectations regarding domesticity could sometimes be extensive. Theresa Lee (Connelly), a close friend of Angelina Grimké's who also became a public school teacher, privately bemoaned her responsibilities.

As you know and I only to[o] well know and realize fully, we have no domestic. So that thankless and unending job is thrust to my door. I have spurned it, but it returns, and rather than have my spurns returned again I take it with drooping head, listless eyes. . . . This morning, . . . I was forced to rebel but was subdued. . . . I have made all the beds but Mr. G[rimké]'s and my own . . . but alas! there is so much more for my bedraggled hands to do. My mother says Genevive's room, the parlor, library, and dining room must be swept today and she can not do it but they must be done today.[39]

Lee was, of course, also complaining because *she* had to do this work when the family could afford to hire domestic workers, and therefore her comments reflect class concerns. But that she was expected to learn and perform the household chores despite the family's economic circumstances makes the emphasis on socializing daughters to perform a set of domestic chores especially clear.

Angelina could have complained as strongly as Tessa did, for Angelina was responsible for carrying out domestic work for her father even when he lived outside the United States. He once sent her two pieces of string representing the length and width of a pair of curtains she was to make and mail to him. Surely the consul's request did not mean he could not get curtains where he was: this was probably one means of maintaining their family relationship even though they were separated. Archibald's request also reflected his interpretation of

Angelina's domestic responsibility to the family and his interest in knowing she could fulfill it. Angelina was in this regard a dutiful daughter, making curtains, bed linens, and tea aprons and sending them to her father a thousand miles away.[40]

• • •

None of these children learned and expected to fulfill the traditional family obligations because parents saw domesticity as the only or the most important role their daughters would undertake as adults. Instead, the model of womanhood held before the children was one of achievement in *both* public and private spheres. Parents cast domesticity as a complement rather than a contradiction to success in public arenas. And it was, of course, a wise thing to do, since most black women historically had to work in both spheres. Thus these daughters did not grow up expecting to choose between the two; they were to be competent domestic workers in their own households and independent, self-sufficient, public achievers as well. To make certain public achievement was attainable, education, broadly construed, was critical and designed to develop and maintain individual self-esteem. No words of encouragement were spared in the effort to shore up the youngsters' self-confidence, because these children would face both racism and sexism in the public sphere. Unless they were carefully prepared for it, prepared not to allow such confrontations to thwart their development, they might not succeed as professionals and would never become community leaders.

Most often the efforts were small ones, though they could have profound consequences. For example, whenever Beulah Hester suggested she could not do something, her mother insisted that if it had ever been done before by anyone, then her children—daughters included—could also do it.[41] But once in a while the steps parents took to assure their children of their self-worth were dramatic. Miriam Matthews was living in an integrated neighborhood in Los Angeles when the film *Birth of a Nation* was released. Neighborhood Armenian children teased the Matthews children, called them derisive names, and taunted them with the movie posters, which portrayed grotesque caricatures of African Americans. When Mrs. Matthews learned of the incident, she took Miriam to the children's home to talk with them and their parents. According to Matthews, her mother took them to task:

You should be thankful that you are in America where you don't have to flee for your life or be beaten to death by the Turkish people. You should show your proper respect for people who have been American citizens for generations, and are your superiors in education and income.[42]

Undoubtedly Mrs. Matthews' response represents an extreme to which most parents could not go, and consequently they had to find other ways of achieving the same end. In fact, had the Matthews family still resided in Florida, where Miriam was born, her mother's response would have been irresponsible and dangerous. The objective here and in all such cases was to make a particular point to the children, whether or not it could be made to the offender. But to protect the children's self-esteem safely, some parents merely reassured them that no one was better than they were except those whose conduct was superior.[43] The elders cautioned their children not to allow other people's problems with race to become their own. And often when the daughters encountered a situation that had explicit racist overtones and parents could not respond in any other way, they simply advised their daughters to ignore other people's prejudice. In giving this advice, however, they were not ignoring the problems and the impact they had on the daughter's lives. They acknowledged the restrictions resulting from racism and fought against them when possible, but they also recognized that often there was little they could do to alter other people's attitudes and behavior. In those cases, parents focused on teaching their daughters to respond in a manner that would not stunt their own development. Dwelling on such negativity was disabling, whereas assuring children of their worth and abilities was empowering.

Children often faced racism in the very environments parents selected because of traditions of safety and hospitality. The schools the children attended, for example, were presumed to be places where they could develop personally and enhance their career prospects without threats to their physical or emotional security. But racism existed in some of these schools, and the girls had to face it without being incapacitated. When Angelina Grimké encountered such a confrontation at the Boston Normal School of Gymnastics in 1899, her aunt's response included a rationale for it and a way around it. She wrote:

Tell us exactly what the situation is there and if, as we do most earnestly hope, you are more pleasantly situated and find the prejudices not so great as you had supposed. In such a large school, in New England, too, there certainly must be some friendly ones [white people]; and you and Tessa [Theresa Lee (Connelly)], being together, can afford to ignore any unpleasantness which I suppose must always exist in the minds of some.

When racist incidents disrupted Portia Washington Pittman's stay in Europe, she assured her father that "it is all good experience for me, and I know human nature much better than ever before." When she later reported specific incidents to him, he insisted that she not allow other people's problems to cause her to lose sight of her goals.

I think you will make a mistake if you . . . let your mind dwell too much upon American prejudice or any other race prejudice. . . . If one gets in the habit of continually thinking and talking about race prejudice, he soon gets to the point where he is fit for little that is worth doing.[44]

Throughout the late nineteenth and early twentieth centuries, race relations in America became worse rather than better. Although the number of lynchings began to decline after the turn of the century, race riots in which white people attacked black communities became more common at the same time. In North Carolina in 1898, New York and Louisiana in 1900, Atlanta in 1906, Illinois in 1906, 1908, and 1917, Texas in 1917, and two dozen states in 1919, hundreds of African Americans lost their lives as victims of race riots, and white perpetrators destroyed millions of dollars worth of black-owned property. The Progressive movement for social justice was slow to extend to African Americans, and respectable behavior and individual self-confidence, important as they were, would not protect black women from racial violence or systemic injustice. But parents still believed (or hoped) that along with these behavioral conditions, formal education would help to place their daughters beyond some of society's dangers.[45]

Many parents undertook the tremendous personal and economic sacrifice of sending their children away to private boarding schools.[46] Most could not afford European or even New England schools, but with some effort they could take advantage of schools nearer home that also had traditions of preparing black students well.[47] Albert Rivers worked his farm in the evenings and worked in a lumber mill during the day so he could afford to send his daughters (he had no sons) away to school. Eunice Rivers Laurie's educational career represents something of an odyssey that reflects the deep interest parents held in their children's education and their unwillingness to accept a form of schooling they viewed as inadequate. Neighbors criticized Albert Rivers for sending twelve-year-old Eunice from their Jakin, Georgia, home to a Fort Gaines, Georgia, school (about fifteen miles away) in 1911. But Rivers insisted that the schools open to black children where they lived could not adequately prepare Eunice for the future (at least not the future he had in mind for her), and equally important, Eunice's uncle was principal of the Fort Gaines school, and her father therefore knew she would come under the influence of black mentors. She remained there until she was fourteen, when she developed typhoid fever and had to return home. After her recovery, Eunice's father sent her to continue her education in Thomasville, Georgia, where she remained for three years until Mr. Rivers withdrew her upon discovering that all her teachers were white. He sent her next to Tuskegee Institute, but when he learned that Eunice was enrolled in the industrial arts program, Rivers convinced her to pursue a course of study that would prepare her to make a better living for herself. She transferred to the nursing program, from which she graduated in 1922.[48]

Several months before Angelina Grimké was scheduled to graduate from Cushing Academy, her father insisted that if she did not accept the "grand opportunity" to continue her studies (presumably by going to college), he expected her to go to trade school. He reminded her that she was nineteen years old (in 1899) and had "no more time to waste." It was his responsibility to see that she could support herself, he added. (She subsequently enrolled at the Boston Normal School of Gymnastics.) Although Portia Washington's stepmother made her enroll in domestic arts courses at Tuskegee, her father also insisted she take academic courses, in particular, chemistry under the great scientist George Washington Carver, and German under a new professor who had been lured away from Hampton. In the early 1900s Beulah Shepard Hester's mother withdrew her from Lincoln Academy, a good private Congregational school in King's Mountain, North Carolina, because she believed that Beulah received preferential treatment from her teacher and consequently was not academically challenged there. After Hester enrolled at Hartshorn Memorial College in Virginia, intending to specialize in music, her mother curtly informed her that as long as her father could afford it, she would take the regular academic course *and* music instruction, because a career in music might not enable her to support herself. And when the Minor Normal School in Washington, D.C., refused to admit Julia Smith because she was under the traditional admission age, her father, believing she was prepared for the coursework and that delaying her enrollment would only inhibit her development, successfully sued and gained her admission at the unprecedented age of sixteen. Henry Beard Delany put the issue of going to college in less personal terms. After his daughter Sarah graduated from St. Augustine's normal course in 1910, her father stated simply, but profoundly: "Daughter, you are college material. You owe it to your nation, your race, and yourself to go." He also advised her not to accept a scholarship but to "make [her] own way."[49]

Whole families often relocated to gain access to good schools for the children. Eula Wellman Dunlap's family moved to Kings Mountain, North Carolina, in 1897 when they heard of the opening of Lincoln Academy. Norma Boyd's family moved from North Carolina to Washington, D.C., before the turn of the century to take advantage of educational opportunities. And Miriam Matthews's family not only moved from Florida to California in the 1910s, in part to have access to better schools, but once settled they used the address of relatives living in a different district so they could enroll Miriam and her sister in *the* school they thought was best. Barbara Miller's family moved from Chattanooga, Tennessee, to Louisville, Kentucky, after her aunt wrote urging them to come because Louisville had a free public library for black residents.[50] And even more astounding, when the families could afford it and deemed it necessary, they maintained two households part of the year for the sake of good formal schooling. Mothers and children lived in one city (sometimes outside their home state) during the school term while fathers remained at home where they were gainfully employed.[51]

African American women who became a part of the professional class therefore came from families in which education was not only desirable but also attainable. Despite parents' willing sacrifices, however, daughters faced many limitations because of the admission policies of white schools and the unavailability of acceptable (and sometimes any) black schools. Thus where the children went to school was not always completely within parents' control, but where they could choose, they did. They made it clear that they wanted the best they could provide for their children, and they expected the children's best efforts as well.

The first-generation women in this study (born between 1858 and 1883) often attended prestigious northern academies including Antioch, Framingham, Oberlin, Carleton, and Cushing for their early schooling. If they came from more modest financial backgrounds or remained in the South for their early schooling, they went to prestigious private, church-affiliated black schools. The next generation, born between 1884 and 1909, more consistently attended public elementary and secondary schools if they lived in Washington, D.C., or farther north. If they lived in the South, they went to private, church-affiliated black schools. The youngest generation, born between 1910 and 1935, attended public and private schools, always segregated in the South and often segregated in the North. The private southern schools were the same ones or similar to those attended by women of the generations before them. But by the time this third generation entered secondary school, between the late 1920s and 1940s, there were many more black public schools available from which they could choose. The pattern in higher education is similar. The earliest-born women regularly attended private white northern and black southern schools; the middle generation more often attended well-established private or independent black colleges; and the youngest women attended more public schools, black and white.[52]

Rather than reflecting changes in the educational interests of the families, the choices made by parents and their children suggest their different economic situations, changing racial admission policies of traditionally white schools, and the development of black public and private school systems throughout the South. The oldest women grew up at a time when prestigious private white schools in the North regularly admitted a few black students; but equally important, the parents of some could afford to send them there. Not only did the girls attend exclusive grammar schools and prestigious colleges and universities, but two of the earliest-born women continued their education in Europe for two years, studying languages and music. Parents of the second generation could not so easily afford to send their daughters to those same white schools, but by this time (roughly 1905–20), white school admissions policies had become more racially restricted anyway, and there were more black public and private schools available. Southern-born women frequently did not have the luxury even of segregated public schools where they lived until well into the twentieth century, and where public schools were available, they were often grossly underfunded and consequently not up to the standards of the parents' aspirations for their children. Parents who could not afford to relocate their whole families or to send their daughters north sent them to nearby private schools for primary schooling. These children usually also stayed in the South and went to private black schools for their normal and college degrees. The only noteworthy (consistent) exceptions were those wanting to pursue nursing, who often found more opportunities for good training in northern cities. The family economies of the youngest generation were almost consistently better than those of the generation before them, but they were not as solid as those of the well-to-do families of the first generation of women examined here. Still, for the most part after the 1920s they received their early education in the now-available black public schools. The improving family economies coupled with the opening of white public colleges and universities to black students by the 1940s did, however, affect their higher-education choices more consistently, and as was the case for many of the earliest-born women, many of the youngest women went to traditionally white schools in the North for their college degrees. When they did not go to white schools, they chose elite black southern colleges and universities, public and private.[53]

Even within restrictions imposed by the larger society and by family finances, parents were very particular about where they sent their daughters to school. The midwestern and New England schools that some attended were "radical" institutions of a sort. Oberlin College, which Mary Church Terrell and several others attended, was the first college in the country to admit black and female students—not only recognizing black women's right to higher education but also suggesting a belief in the women's ability to achieve it. Administrators of Eastern women's schools such as Radcliffe, Smith, and Wellesley prided themselves on maintaining institutions where women students could and would achieve and fully develop their leadership potential. And faculty and administrators at black institutions of higher learning such as Spelman, Howard, Fisk, and Talladega and (then) normal schools including Hampton and Tuskegee stressed the development of black male and female leaders who would return to their communities and serve as successful examples of the "bootstrap" philosophy while working to provide similar opportunities for others. In every case, schools chosen by the students and their parents maintained traditions that the parents respected and recognized as potential reinforcement for the values they had worked so hard to instill in the youngsters at home: values related to respectability, self-worth, high achievement, and social consciousness.[54]

But as confident as parents were about the schools they chose, they did not leave education entirely to the teachers. They worked with their children at home to augment their formal schooling. Often those "lessons" were traditional: parents read with their children, helped them with homework, and took them to museums and theaters. But sometimes the efforts went far beyond traditional exercises and served to reinforce the girls' confidence by suggesting the boundlessness of their capabilities. For example, when she was only fourteen years old Angelina Grimké's father urged her to study languages—French, German, *and* Spanish. In another instance Grimké wrote to his daughter that he thought she would like the novel *Pompeii*, but he cautioned her not to spend all her time reading fiction: "History, biography, and works of travel, etc., etc., you must learn to like" so as not "to be like every Tom, Dick, and Harry . . . of the mentally weak and empty headed simpletons of the feminine world." Angelina's father constantly urged her to study hard and to be a credit to herself and to him. And on one occasion, after receiving a letter from her principal saying she was ill, Grimké remarked that he would be very upset if she were only making excuses to avoid doing her schoolwork. A few weeks later he warned her: "Do not let the precious time slip away from you [but] instead, have something to show for all the expenses of your education. Do not in anything be content with mere mediocrity, but aim always to attain excellence in character and culture." When Grimké informed Angelina that his biography was to be included in an edition of the *National Cyclopaedia of American Biography,* he added: "I hope that someday my little girl will be entitled to a place in the *National Cyclop[a]edia* also by the side of others of the same name."[55]

Parents continued to provide this type of nurturing and encouragement even after their daughters were well established in their college programs or professions. Constance Fisher's father made no gender distinctions when he expressed his desire to see her achieve as highly as she could. After Constance established herself independently of her parents' household and began making her way through a graduate program at Western Reserve University during the 1920s, her father reminded her:

May I repeat my desire to have you continue a daily reading of some good paper? The habit has meant so much to me that I cannot be satisfied until I have made certain that my own daughter for whom I want the highest success possible is having the advantage of one element of my own preparedness. If there is no money for a paper I shall try to deny myself something else so that you may have a paper regularly.[56]

Archibald Grimké similarly chose his moments to remind Angelina of how much she was capable of doing. At one point in the early 1900s it appeared she might not be reappointed to her position as an English teacher. On realizing the threat to her employment and her self-esteem, Archibald urged her to be as comfortable in mind and body as it is possible for you to be under the circumstances. Do not be cast down whatever happens my dear. . . . I hope of course that you will get your appointment, as you ought to get it. But if you do not, why then, *you must show the stuff, the real woman's stuff of which you are made.* Think seriously of following a literary career and begin to work hard to make a success of it. . . . You have the talents to make a name for yourself in some direction in literature. Think of this whether you get your appointment or not, and keep your balance [and] your sanity.[57]

The fight with her principal lasted more than two years, after which Angelina was finally able to transfer to the M Street School. The whole incident was a tremendous blow to her self-confidence, and as soon as her father realized it, he responded:

I know there is no one in the Armstrong [school] who knows the subject as well as you do. . . . You must not let that fellow rattle you and make you lose faith in yourself. Don't let anyone in that school or anywhere for that matter do so. . . . Look up and not down Little girl and never say die.[58]

A disagreement with a supervisor could easily wreak havoc with one's ability to perform, but day-to-day situations more frequently threatened to do damage. An unprepared student, an uncooperative patient, or one's own bad judgment regularly caused confusion. Preventing and overcoming these menaces required skills—the kind emphasized at home and in school and perfected only by the rigors of work.

Finally, if the education and socialization of these women involved more than "finishing," the ramifications also went beyond economic independence. Parents encouraged their daughters to secure their own futures, but parents intended that the children use their education and their subsequent positions—paid or unpaid—in a socially responsible way.[59] These children were, as Isaac Fisher noted about Constance, "reared in an atmosphere of social service," and likewise, their own education was to benefit the group (the race), which by and large was less fortunate than they were and generally without enough advocates. Fannie Dell Jordan's mother influenced her daughter's "choice of a calling" and aspirations for community service by telling her stories of great and generous teachers who provided all they could for their young pupils. She urged Fannie "to be like these good teachers . . . and let the stories of [your] good works be told to other little children." Detroit librarian Clara Jones recalled that "it was accepted that my four brothers and sisters and myself would all go to college to help our race." She added, "That was the way everyone thought in those days." When asked if she resented having to attend the Louisville Normal School instead of area white schools, Susan St. Clair Minor responded: "We really didn't have time to think of anything ugly, and if you did you always had your parents . . . to remind you that you were working for your race." Clara Jones's grandfather, a former slave, delivered the same message in powerful and explicit terms. Before Clara left home to attend college during the 1930s, her grandfather reminded her: "You're going to get your education, and its not yours; you're doing it for your people."[60]

Where parents did not articulate their children's responsibilities to the larger group, they demonstrated the lesson with profundity. Archibald Grimké helped to create the Washington, D.C., branch of the National Association for the Advancement of Colored People (NAACP) in 1912; William Henry Ray, Ethel Ray Nance's father, organized the Duluth, Minnesota, branch in 1920; Robert Church's endeavors in nineteenth-century Republican politics are easily documented; and the abolitionist tradition in the families of numerous other women also demonstrates social responsibility.[61] Beyond all this, parents regularly helped to finance, build, and maintain schools, hospitals, orphanages, and libraries.[62] Since they often possessed the means to provide such services for their own families, their actions demonstrated their assumptions about social responsibility. Close attention was not required to note the example and to absorb the lesson.

• • •

Though these women were products of a racist and sexist society, they were also products of strong family traditions that prepared and encouraged them to resist, wherever possible, the constraints the larger society sought to impose on them. The foundation for resisting societal constrictions was a process begun during childhood in which parents emphasized that if the daughters maintained a posture of respectability, acquired appropriate training, and developed the ability to manage public and private roles effectively, they could achieve both enviable private lives and laudable public careers. This particular worldview was critical to individual development because despite respectability, educational preparation, high self-esteem, supportive families, and an empowering socialization, there were still social, economic, and political factors that limited the choices black women could make in their lives.

Yet despite the obvious constraints, because they learned that they had it in their power to live full, meaningful, and productive lives, as adults they would work within the race-, class-, and sex-stratified system, pushing at its boundaries and establishing themselves as community leaders. Other aspects of these women's experiences no doubt also reinforced the idea that they could succeed.

Individual women's family histories are suggestive. Washington, D.C., schoolteacher Julia Smith, who was born in 1885, had four maternal great-aunts: one taught French to wealthy white women, and one of the other three, all of whom taught school, was among the first black public school teachers in Washington, D.C. Of her five paternal aunts, one was the first black public school teacher in Boston, and another (her aunt Florence, who lived with Smith, her brother, and their parents) was a Washington, D.C., public school principal for forty-two years. Another aunt was an accomplished graphic artist, and her aunt Georgiana was a successful mezzo-soprano concert artist. Mary Church Terrell's father's wealth is well known. He was born a slave but was allowed to work on the riverboats of his owner, who was also his father. The business acumen he gained in that activity contributed to his becoming a millionaire as a free man. Though it is less well known, Terrell's mother, Louisa Ayres Church, was a very successful businesswoman before her husband made his fortune. In fact she purchased their first home, and probably a significant portion of Robert Church's investment capital came to him when he acquired a portion of Louisa's assets when they divorced. Miriam Matthews's father owned a successful painting business in California, but while he performed and supervised the physical labor, Miriam's mother ran the business. (Miriam's sister pursued a business career and eventually became a high-level banking executive.)[63]

The social distance the families traveled, especially those of the first generation, undoubtedly also contributed to the boundless world views that these women developed in terms of their own futures. Mary Church Terrell's parents were born slaves and as free people became important community leaders. Portia Washington Pittman's father, a former slave, became one of the most influential men in the country during his lifetime, and her mother and stepmothers were equally well known for their work in social reform and community development. Angelina Grimké's father and her uncle Francis, also former slaves, received formidable educations and had impressive careers. Her aunt Charlotte was among the first group of northern women to go to the South during the Civil War to start schools for the freed people. Many of the parents and grandparents of these women were former slaves, and within a short time after winning their freedom, the families moved from a state of illiteracy and poverty to having educated, professional daughters.[64]

Across the generations, geographic mobility might have had a similar impact. Many of the parents were "exodusters" of one form or another in that they picked up their families, their households, and their lives and moved because they believed they could live better somewhere else. Mabel Staupers's father came from Barbados to New York in search of a better life for his family. Charlemae Hill Rollins's father took his family from Mississippi to Oklahoma Territory to start anew. Miriam Matthews's family moved from Florida to California. And Joyce Cooper Arkhurst's grandfather pulled up stakes and took his family from the southern United States to Australia in anticipation of a better life.[65]

Any of these factors was significant enough to have had a major positive impact on the lives of these women, and taken together they were absolutely powerful. The women's general family histories encouraged—consciously and unconsciously—mobility, self-improvement, self-determination, and social responsibility. And their own upbringings impelled them to be high achievers and to seek out opportunities for themselves. It was easy for these children to believe, even erroneously, that they could not fail. At the very least, to borrow Mamie Garvin Fields's comment about how profoundly her people assured their children: "If not utterly convinced by their assertion, we children were certainly impressed by their conviction."[66] But however convincing parents might have been about their daughters' potential, the children's ability to develop it ultimately depended on a complex set of conditions ranging from their own respectability to access to formal schooling and the availability of work options. Few individuals or families were able to create all the necessary conditions, and so it was essential that they depend on other people who shared their goals and had some ability to help reach them.

"The daughters of our community coming up": DEVELOPING COMMUNITY CONSCIOUSNESS

As Pattie Gilliam Shepard made her way past members of the 1912 graduating class of Hartshorn Memorial College, her daughter Beulah, a member of that class, heard her whisper, "Lord, help me." Without notice, the president of the school had called upon Mrs. Shepard to say a few words. Caught completely off guard, Shepard, who had always expected Beulah and her siblings to face undaunted whatever circumstances arose, would have to prove her own mettle. She began by telling a story about a tall building in New York that was sinking on one side. Investigation revealed that the building had a faulty foundation. Using the story to urge the graduates to secure their own foundations, Mrs. Shepard cautioned them that college had not prepared them for everything they would face in their futures. She advised them that they could find the foundation they needed in their families and churches—in other words, in communion. The rousing applause that Hester reported her mother received for her brief oration suggested that the graduates were, by experience, already converted.[1]

Beulah Shepard Hester and her peers had just completed one of the most traditionally private and individualistic endeavors that people ever undertake. The learning process, though certainly not complete without a variety of social exchanges, traditionally requires focusing on one's self. And the successful graduate of an ideal and effective program can think for herself, provide for herself, and fulfill her potential. But, of course, individual self-development has never been completely removed from social traditions, community support, and public pressure. Many individual decisions, even the ability to make decisions, are often rooted in community considerations and expectations. The process by which these women came to experience life so profoundly and so positively was no different. It was a consequence of both individual and collective needs, desires, expectations, efforts, and abilities. Family members, friends, teachers, and the exigencies of day-to-day life effectively bound the self and society in both pragmatic and idealistic ways. Consequently these women were as much products of communities as of marriages and families; and community values and traditions were as much a part of their foundations as those demonstrated in their families. Sometimes the two were indistinguishable.

Community in this instance was more than a neighborhood. Interests, rather than buildings and borders, determined membership. Community therefore defied boundaries and tended toward dispersion rather than concentration. Community was also more than a romantic metaphor for racial solidarity. Composed dynamically of a diverse group of people, it was a social institution or an arrangement of people who possessed a common understanding of history, mutual interests in the present, and shared visions of the future for the group and all its members. But community was based on more than philosophical impulses; it was also rooted in activism—theory balanced with practice. Members of the community provided a tangible system of operations designed to help produce these accomplished women. Thus community was both a product and a process—a sociopolitical entity that was the product of collective consciousness and a process for producing that consciousness as well. As a consequence of this configuration of social interaction, and because of participating in it, some of the "daughters of [the] community coming up" made their way a little farther along the highways and around many inevitable obstacles.[2] When the community operated at its best, it fostered communion—a feeling of belonging and of becoming part of, rather than an appendage of, the group.[3]

This chapter moves from showing how parents, with the support of others, worked to educate their daughters broadly so as to ensure respectability, self-assurance, general preparation for public and private work, and social responsibility to a more detailed discussion of the process by which community consciousness evolved in those women. First of all, the very process of achieving a formal education was enhanced by family and friendship networks that provided concrete examples of social responsibility. Second, the women's local communities—people known to them and unknown—contributed to their individual development. And third, community people also worked to develop and maintain institutions that contributed to individual and community development even when they could not or did not need to take advantage of the institutions themselves. Finally, this chapter also explains how parents regularly went beyond preparing their own children for self-sufficiency and high achievement by working to increase the opportunities available to the community at large, thereby providing their own children with more examples of social responsibility. Building schools where none existed; supporting hospitals, orphanages, and old folks' homes; and providing scholarships for young people, among many other endeavors, had a profound impact on the texture of community life. And as these processes unfolded, those who benefited most directly, to the extent that they eventually returned the favor for the benefit of others, exemplified both the product and the process of community.

. . .

In the introduction to *Lemon Swamp and Other Places: A Carolina Memoir*, Karen Fields writes poignantly of traveling as a child with her family in a "self-sufficient" "capsule"—a car containing detailed maps, lots of food, and even water for the radiator in case they needed it. The family traveled in this manner because, Fields noted, "from the time we passed the whites-only Marriott Hotel, just across the Potomac, to the time we at last turned off U.S. 1 toward Charleston," they did not want to risk the humiliation of being denied service if they required it during their journey.[4] Black people traveling long distances during the Jim Crow era regularly took it for granted that they would not be served at many establishments, whether in the North or the South, and consequently they overloaded their automobiles before setting out on their journeys, in anticipation of all types of roadside emergencies.

But reaching their destinations sometimes required more than one day of traveling; sometimes they wanted to attend church, sorority, or professional meetings that lasted several days; sometimes they sought to take extended vacations; and sometimes they simply had destinations that their financial abilities did not allow them to reach directly. They required places to stop over. Situations like these provided children some of their earliest lessons on the importance of community consciousness and social responsibility as people regularly reorganized their households to accommodate the sometimes weary and anxious travelers. John W. Davis, president of West Virginia State College and president of the National Association of Teachers in Colored Schools during the 1930s complained about the way in which "the better homes of Negroes in all of our metropolitan centers are too often called upon to serve Negroes who travel as a 'substitute hotel.'" And it was both unfortunate and sometimes inconvenient that this was the only safe way for African Americans to travel. But black people's homes had served as "Do Drop Inns," as Norma Boyd characterized her childhood home, for generations, and this would continue to be the case for some time to come.[5]

Some people did not complain, but marveled to their children about the way people graciously took them in. Isaac Fisher wrote to his daughter Constance that when he, her mother, and a family friend left Minneapolis for Hampton, Virginia, in the fall of 1936, they drove to Chicago, where they spent the night in a hotel. The next day they reached Columbus, Ohio, where they "found a splendid welcome at Burrell's house," and Burrell's family "would not accept pay." They drove on to Boyce, where they spent the next night in the "home of a relative of Burrell's father. [And] here again, they absolutely refused to have any pay for our lodging and board." On the following day they finally made it home. Traveling rural Ohio roads and mountainous West Virginia and western Virginia terrain before federal highway projects made such travel easy mandated frequent stops, and the Fishers were traveling in a vehicle with malfunctioning headlights that drained the car battery whenever used for too long a time. But they, and all the North Carolinians who stopped at Norma Boyd's home and worked for a while in the District of Columbia before continuing on to New Jersey, were glad for the reliability of these formal and informal networks. And the children observed and were occasionally reminded of their importance to black people's mobility, upward and otherwise.[6]

Families also consciously reorganized their households to create certain advantages for the daughters. Although these adjustments appear simply to be practical solutions to specific problems, they also taught the children important lessons in social responsibility while addressing a variety of more subtle parental concerns. Because of the relative wealth the Grimké family enjoyed, they provide a useful example of the ways practical (though not economic) *and* philosophical considerations influenced the structuring of households. When Archibald's work took him out of the country, Angelina's living with her aunt and uncle served more than the obvious needs. This shared-household (multifamily) arrangement endured after Archibald's return to the States and suggests his interest in compensating for his perceived inability to undertake some aspects of his daughter's upbringing. Considering that so much of child development was gender specific in the late nineteenth century, sharing a household with Charlotte Forten Grimké in particular ensured that Angelina would be appropriately influenced by a woman's insights and example. Charlotte was someone Angelina could rely on when she needed or preferred a woman to turn to. Charlotte could teach Angelina those things related to domesticity and femininity that mothers normally taught their daughters and that were so important at the time. And equally important, Charlotte was an acceptable female role model. She not only was one of the northern teachers who had gone to the South before the end of the Civil War (in her case, in 1860) to teach free black children, women, and men, but she was also a published poet and writer, a family woman, and a race advocate.[7]

This decision to join another household had much to do with the fact that the child was a girl, who, in her father's mind, required a woman's influence in order to develop properly. Possibly Archibald Grimké believed he could not be all a daughter needed in a parent, even when he was at home. At the very least, the general social constructions of gender at the time made it seem imperative to have girls reared primarily by women. Although Grimké no doubt accepted contemporary constructions of gender roles and therefore believed domestic tasks, including child rearing, were female responsibilities, a new wife or even a sensitive housekeeper could have discharged these duties. But there was no assurance that the woman chosen would see to Angelina's upbringing as Grimké wanted. Thus the choice he made for Angelina—to share a household with Charlotte and Francis—ensured that Angelina's development would be conditioned by the values her father held and shared with his sister-in-law and brother.[8] Of course such reorganizations sometimes occurred for the benefit of male children too, for they faced some of the same limitations as their sisters in preparing for the future. But it is equally clear that in seeking to provide a nurturing community for all their children while they were growing up, provisions parents made for boys and girls were sometimes different.

Booker T. Washington remarried twice after the death of Portia's mother in 1884. Portia was not quite a year old when her mother died, and before and between her father's second and third marriages (in 1885 and 1893), Portia's maternal grandmother, her aunt, nursemaids, and select female members of the Tuskegee faculty lived in the Washington household at various times to help care for her. Washington's third wife, Margaret Murray, a schoolteacher, clubwoman, and activist, was fearful of taking on these child-rearing responsibilities. She admitted, among other things, that she did not even know how to dress

CHAPTER TWO

a child. She worried about her already tense relationship with Portia and feared "being thrown with her for a lifetime."[9] Interestingly, by the time Washington proposed to marry Murray, he also had two sons who were even younger than Portia and therefore presumably more "needy" of traditional mothering than an older—indeed, oldest—child might be. The implication is, of course, that Washington, or if necessary his brother, also on the Tuskegee staff, or some other man he selected would share the responsibility of bringing up his sons. Clearly his intended wife, and before her other women, were perceived as more suited to supervise Portia's development.

Household reorganizations like those experienced by the Grimké and Washington families, though often based on family connections, should not be reduced to mere manifestations of personal obligations based on ties of blood, because kinship alone did not enable people to rear these daughters to be self-confident, high-achieving, socially responsible adults. In some instances kinfolk, even parents, could not provide the desirable conditions. Angelina Grimké's mother, for example, found it impossible to create the kind of community she believed Angelina should have. Sarah Stanley Grimké, who was white, left Archibald Grimké before Angelina was four years old. At first Sarah agreed to share financial support and custody of Angelina, but the next year she suddenly announced that she was assuming total financial responsibility for their daughter and that Archibald would no longer have any legal rights regarding her. Two years later, however, Sarah reversed herself and sent Angelina to live permanently with her father. Sarah Stanley wrote to her ex-husband about their daughter:

She needs the love and sympathy of her own *race* which I am sure her father still has for her, but which is impossible for others to give. My own family kind and anxious as they are to do right, do not. Neither is it possible for them to give her the *love she requires to make her good* and *happy*, and a child cannot be good unless it is also happy. It is almost impossible for her to be happy with me, try as I will, because she is getting old enough to see and feel the thoughts of others, which the difference in race and color naturally engender regarding her.[10]

Although the example above suggests the difficulty that even parents experienced in their efforts to create an appropriate environment for their children, this particular failure was not due simply to a difference in race. The successful efforts of some white educators during this time to create a comfortable community for black students are too well known. But what is more important here is that Sarah Stanley believed she could not provide a social setting for her daughter's development that would be to the child's advantage, and she made arrangements to send Angelina where her needs would be met.

Many family and household reorganizations aimed at providing an education for the girls. Although the external (societal) condition of not having easy access to adequate schools forced families to develop an internal response, personal values dictated that response; external factors only conditioned it. That is, it was a given that the children would go to school; at first they simply had to leave home to do so. But having made decisions early on that their daughters would attend school, even the wealthiest parents needed some support if their goal was to be achieved. Where local schools were not accessible or adequate, families regularly had to look beyond their own means. And because of the way the community functioned, they usually did not have to look far for others who stood ready to assist.

Because of commitments to social responsibility, leaving home to go to school usually did not entail isolation. Parents and friends found or created in those educational environments the comfort, safety, and support—the communion—they would have provided for their daughters had schooling opportunities been available locally. For some children, that meant attending institutions to which their parents already had some formal connection, social or professional. In these instances they had some knowledge that a supportive environment existed. For others, it meant calling on known and unknown persons to provide the support the children required. The individuals and families who came to their aid, though often "strangers" to the students, were extensions of the original community, for which providing opportunities for black women to achieve was an important goal.

Mary Church Terrell moved in with the Hunster family in Yellow Springs, Ohio, after she left home at the age of six to attend kindergarten at the Antioch College Model School. Yellow Springs, a small town with black people comprising approximately 16 percent of the population at the time, was a community in which racial difference was not looked upon with hostility. Black and white people regularly boarded in the same households, and some of those homes were owned by African Americans. In 1870 the community had two fifty-year-old black churches that were well supported. And the Hunsters provided a family life for little Mary Church as well. The Hunster children, all considerably older than Mary, "adopted" her as a baby sister, and Mary took pride in her role as a messenger who delivered love notes between

"Miss Sallie," the schoolteacher daughter, and her future husband. Edward R. Hunster, the family patriarch, indulged Mary by regularly allowing her to accompany him on the wagon ride to a distant farm to collect fresh cream for the day's dessert. His wife, Margarite, a homemaker, completed her housekeeping tasks with Mary trailing behind her reciting poetry. Terrell later recalled that Mrs. Hunster was always sure to praise her oratorical efforts, whether she performed well or not. It is no wonder that Mary quickly took to calling them "Ma" and "Pa."[11]

Beginning in the eighth grade, Mary went to Oberlin High School and boarded in the town with the elderly widow of a black physician. When Mary enrolled in the senior class of Oberlin College Academy she moved onto the campus, where she stayed until graduating from college in 1885. During her college years Mary either had a private room or had black roommates. She regularly visited and received visits from friends, traveled with them, and participated freely in a variety of school activities.[12] She recalled her experience at Oberlin fondly.

Terrell's experience of leaving home so early for her education was unique. None of the other women, most born significantly later than she and none from such wealthy families, left their hometowns for preprimary schooling. But regardless of when and why they left, they went where there was some assurance that they would find community.

Angelina Grimké returned to Massachusetts in 1897 to continue her schooling because Washington proved, in her father's view, to be an unacceptable environment for her. Archibald not only was already familiar with the type of schooling his daughter would get in Massachusetts, but he also knew people there who would help provide a supportive environment. Angelina sometimes boarded with the Joseph Lee family when she attended school in or near Boston during the 1890s. Joseph Lee and Angelina's father were old friends, and Joseph regularly referred to Angelina as one of his "best girls," along with his own daughters. He usually addressed her in a manner that was doting, affectionate, and fatherly. Joseph's daughter Tessa (Theresa) was for a while Angelina's best friend. And even when Angelina did not live with the Lees, she often ate meals in their home when she was in the area, celebrated holidays there, and attended recreational and political functions with the family. Although a disagreement between Christina Lee (Joseph's wife) and Angelina resulted in her leaving the household,

Angelina flourished there during her adolescent years. And when she did not find this level of support on the school campuses, there was some comfort in having the Lees and other family friends nearby.[13]

Indicating the way formal and informal connections operated and the importance of them, Angelina, after being in a train wreck en route to Boston in 1911, wrote to her father from the Bridgeport, Connecticut, hospital:

This is where Fred Harley lives. He is Gussie Harley's brother. Do you remember them in Boston? Well, he has been here twice. He is awfully kind. He wants me to go to his home and rest up a bit before I go on to Boston. A Miss Cobb, a young lady from Washington, is here at the Harleys, and she came here yesterday and then went downtown and bought me a dress and some shoes. You know I was dressed in my kimona and lost my dress and shoes . . . [in the train wreck].

People from Boston have been very kind. Mrs. Wilson telephoned that she would come on here and get me if necessary. Fred says that if I do not feel able to go from there alone, Miss Cobb will go on with me.[14]

The support Angelina experienced after her accident was based not merely on general sympathy and humanitarianism, but on commitments to her family and to friends of her friends. "Mrs. Wilson" was probably Mary Evans Wilson, a civil rights activist with whom Angelina had previously roomed for a short time and who knew Angelina's family well. Mary Wilson's husband, Butler Wilson, was a prominent attorney and had previously coedited a Boston newspaper with Archibald, and the two men were later law partners.[15] Obviously Fred Harley was the brother of a woman Angelina knew, and their friend Miss Cobb apparently had not known any of the Grimkés before this incident. Such direct and indirect connections regularly made it possible for some to carry out personal plans, fulfill individual aspirations, overcome various incapacities, and circumvent daily obstacles.

Septima Clark joined a family that lived across the street from Avery Normal Institute when she left home around 1910 to attend the school. And although she worked for the woman with whom she boarded, she apparently never felt like a servant. Eunice Rivers Laurie left her home to attend an elementary school where her uncle was the principal. When Laurie went to Thomasville, Georgia, for secondary school (1903–8), her father placed her in the care of several older girls from their hometown who had been enrolled for some time. Laurie later recalled: "They took me under their arm . . . took care of me, and watched me, and reared me."[16] Her remarks indicate the importance of seeing beyond the practical use of these arrangements. The older girls did more than shuttle Eunice back and forth between home and school. It is true that some students, like Clark, could not afford to live on campus, and others, like Grimké, were not always allowed to, so alternative arrangements were necessary. But parents sought the arrangements (and even when they were economic, they were also social) that supported their children best.[17] Their choices made the difference between their children's flourishing, as Laurie, Terrell, Grimké, Clark, and others apparently did, and merely surviving.

Portia Washington Pittman's experience of gaining a formal education suggests the difference the environment made for some children. Her family's prominence opened many doors for her, and she attended schools and studied where her parents had institutional connections. Her first stepmother, Olivia Davidson Washington, was a graduate of Framingham State Normal School in Massachusetts, and that, coupled with her father's prominence, no doubt made it easier for the school to admit her in 1895. In 1902 Portia became the first black student ever admitted to Bradford Academy, and the vast influential network to which her father belonged was evidently a deciding factor. In fact Alice Freeman Palmer, a member of the Board of Trustees at Tuskegee Institute, was also a member of the board at Bradford, and before her marriage in 1887 Palmer served as president of Wellesley College, which Portia also attended just before enrolling at Bradford. While Portia studied music in Germany, her guardians were officials of the German Colonial Society (GCS), who had an old connection with her father. At one time the society regularly sent African students to Tuskegee Institute, and when the GCS considered building a school in Togo, Washington was one of their chief consultants.[18]

The arrangements for Portia's living, however, were very different from those of the other women described thus far. Her father's and her stepmother's connections to these people were more professional or institutional than personal. And even where they were personal, they were evidently not sufficiently developed, or circumstances had changed significantly since their formation. Portia never became connected in any real way to a community, and not finding the community she needed may have adversely affected her development. At Framingham State Normal School, where she enrolled in 1895, Mary Moore, a white English teacher, acted in loco parentis, but Portia lived in a single dormitory room, having no friends and only an occasional visit from Moore's niece. Her classmates did not bother to get to know her until they discovered her musical talents, and then they usually only wanted her to play the piano for their dances. In 1901 Portia enrolled at Wellesley College as a special student, but she never quite adjusted to that environment. Partly because of pressure from the parents of southern students, she was not allowed to live on the campus, and she did not last a year there. Newspaper writers who opposed her father's prominence and his philosophy of racial accommodation (by African Americans) speculated that either the racist atmosphere drove her away or she received failing grades. Apparently she did fail some classes, and her failure was partly attributable to the fact that many of the students refused to let her participate as a member of their community, and as Booker T. Washington's daughter she was unable to locate in or develop another one. When Portia later went to Bradford Academy, she lived in the only single room on the entire campus, but students at Bradford accepted her more readily, even electing her to the student government association during her second year there. Portia was relieved and excited that "everyone" at Bradford was nice and that she easily "made good friends among the *best* girls." She successfully completed the course at Bradford in 1905.[19]

Still, Portia's letters to her father reflect the difficulty she had in becoming part of a community while in school. She often wrote home about school-related trips that other girls were about to make or had just completed. And even at Bradford she regularly complained of being "nervous all the time."[20] Being a black child in a (sometimes) hostile white environment was certainly enough to make one nervous, but Portia's living conditions were even more constrained than those of other black women students because her father was Booker T. Washington, and anti-Washington press corps members watched and reported every move she made, hoping to discover some news they could use to embarrass him. (Washington implied that what they did not find, they made up.)[21] The daughter of a man whose public reputation seemed to hinge more on his advocating segregated vocational education for African Americans than on any of his other endeavors, Portia attended white college preparatory and liberal arts schools between 1895 and 1905. And the black anti-Washington press attempted to make her presence in the white New England schools a national scandal. Coupled with her necessary isolation because of the media, she also had to endure persecution from some of her classmates who personally objected to her presence because she was African American. Yet when one newspaper reporter (friendly to Booker T. Washington) asked Portia about racist snubs she incurred at Wellesley, she diplomatically responded: "The [white] southern woman's feeling about social intercourse with colored people is a thing beyond her control. Education has not been so effectively directed to this weakness of hers that she is able to overcome it."[22] Almost in character, Portia made these problems the other women's, not hers. Unfortunately, these other women's problems prevented her from living on the campuses, participating in dormitory life, enjoying the full range of school or college experiences, and altogether situating herself within a comfortable, supportive community.

Women who were older than Portia was when she went north to school, especially those born a generation after her, had more alternatives as young women and as African Americans. Coming of age during or after the 1920s, they had more independence and even as daughters were able to decide or to influence the decisions about where they would eventually study. Additionally, there were more acceptable institutions from which African Americans could choose. In the 1930s Clara Jones decided for herself to leave the University of Wisconsin (Milwaukee) where, she said, the twenty-five or so enrolled black students lived so scattered throughout the city (probably because of the scarcity of boardinghouses that accepted black students and the lack of on-campus housing for them) that she rarely saw them. Coming from St. Louis, a city with a large and active black community, Jones found the Milwaukee environment unacceptable. She acknowledged the limitations that segregation imposed on her lifestyle in St. Louis, but what impressed her more was that there were always friends around, and beyond personal friends, St. Louis offered a rich black social life that she had come to take for granted. Jones transferred to Spelman College in Atlanta, which she no doubt believed would provide an environment comparable to what she had enjoyed in her hometown.[23]

Concerted and detailed efforts went into families' decisions about schooling because education was so critical to future endeavors that it could not be left to chance. But people also sought assurances of safety, comfort, and communion in leisure pursuits. In most cities, northern and southern, black entrepreneurs operated hotels and boardinghouses specifically for black travelers who were not accepted at or not interested in lodgings at white-owned or white-operated establishments. Some of these black-owned facilities were well known for the comfort and company (usually reported as "the culture") they provided for their patrons.[24] Still, parents made other arrangements for having their children accommodated. They depended on specific individuals

52

they knew. This was true even when the children were old enough to care for themselves.

Portia Washington Pittman tried to assert her independence when she was twenty-one years old by arranging her own plans for Easter vacation. In 1904 she decided to visit friends in New York City, and by the time she informed her father, she had written to the proprietor of a reputable boardinghouse in Harlem and was practically ready to go. All she needed was her father's approval. Instead of his approval, she received a counteroffer to stay in Brooklyn with the family of Fred Moore, then publisher of the *Colored American Magazine* (and later publisher and editor of the New York *Age*). Washington wrote to Portia: "How would you like to go to Brooklyn, N.Y., and spend the time in the family of Mr. Fred Moore? He is a very nice man and has several very nice daughters. Perhaps you have met them. If you go to New York at all, I prefer you to be in the home of some family with whom I am acquainted rather than at a boarding house."[25] Portia ultimately accepted this offer.[26]

Booker T. Washington probably knew people who lived in nearly any city Portia might have been inclined to visit. For certain, while she was making her arrangements to travel and study in Europe, and even after she was there (1905–7), Washington kept her informed of African Americans also traveling abroad and how she could locate them.[27] But more important, because of the process of community, it was not always necessary to know people personally: the community functioned in such a manner that it was often enough simply to know someone who knew someone else. When Julia Smith and her friends traveled during their youth around the turn of the century, for example, they carried calling cards and letters of introduction from people who knew them from a variety of settings. These letters were addressed to specific others along the way so the women could be suitably accommodated. Frances Grant, born almost a generation later, described a similar circumstance, saying, "I could start at Boston and go straight down to Washington and Virginia, and in every city find people who knew me and my friends, and drop into an established social pattern of acceptance and a certain amount of physical and material comfort." Such travel arrangements persisted through the mid-twentieth century, and the connections were with people who understood their obligations to these children and their parents. The hosts had to provide not only a place to eat and sleep, but a safe, responsible, and supportive environment; they were in temporary charge of the young travelers' physical needs and safety, personal reputations, and general education. To provide anything less constituted a threat to the young women's futures and a violation of community expectations.[28]

· · ·

The experiences described thus far reflect a number of expectations about accommodations used in preparing these daughters for adulthood. Although the expectations undoubtedly reflected and encouraged social responsibility, they were based in part on privilege in that they primarily concerned education (formal and informal) and travel. The families of Grimké, Terrell, Grant, Smith, Pittman, and others represented here had substantial financial means and the social connections to enhance children's opportunities, and where they did not possess the necessary patronage themselves, they had friends who did. This "friends of friends" interaction strengthened community relationships, fostered the fulfillment of certain desires, and reinforced the impulses behind them.[29] This experience did not occur simply because the women were black, or female, or largely middle class. It was possible only because of persistent efforts by many black Americans to realize and maintain community.

Still, the community described thus far was one that, as it evolved and functioned, invigorated a kind of exclusivity that could, if not balanced, make it impossible to experience community beyond such class-based connections or "lifestyle enclaves."[30] Less-affluent families no doubt also wanted to provide or enjoy the "broadening" that education and travel confer; they simply had fewer resources, and sometimes, on account of that, different expectations. For them sharing households, food, and child-care arrangements was a matter of survival, not an indication of privilege. How was it that relatively privileged women who were preparing for futures as professionals came to be part of the same community as those less able to achieve? How were the apparent class divisions bridged so that a community based on more than residence, color, economic status, and access could emerge?

It is true that relatively elite African Americans regularly kept some distance (socially) between themselves and their less-advantaged brothers and sisters. The more privileged people held their private parties, sequestered their children to keep them away from those they perceived as "toughs," and sometimes spoke disparagingly of their "less cultured" neighbors when in their own cliques. On occasion they even blamed "the folk" for their being unable to enjoy the privileges their status should have brought them in the larger (white) world.[31] In spite of these postures, however, the communion that sometimes existed between the groups is equally apparent. They were bound by the same yoke of history, and they could see their futures in tandem as well.

Scholars have described the communion that emerged as race consciousness, as the manifestation of a national identity, and even as race nationalism. Social scientist W. O. Brown described the phenomenon in 1931: "The race conscious posit their race as an entity to which they must have obligations. They have a conscience about this race. They must serve it, fight for it, be loyal to it. To the outsider, the race of the race conscious may appear to be an imaginative construction, but to the initiated, the race is a reality, in a sense, a personal experience."[32]

There is no simple explanation for the formation of this type of collective consciousness, though a system of slavery based at first on nativity and then on perceptions of race surely encouraged among non-enslaved African Americans an ideological identification with those who were enslaved. And soon after freedom came to some four million slaves, black codes and then Jim Crow laws guaranteed that social, political, and economic stratification would be the rule rather than the exception for African Americans as a group. But whatever the situation was for individual people—and circumstances varied widely—it was not only possible but imperative that if the most privileged members of the group did not control the manifestations of status and privilege that differences in class, color, region, sex, and "previous condition of servitude" encouraged within the group, they at least had to control the *meaning* of that status and privilege in the daily organization of life and work. In that context individual privilege quickly came to be linked with social responsibility, and by that process class divisions were regularly, if not easily, bridged.[33]

Not a few of these women saw that process at work, and it affected their lives directly. The change in state laws that allowed Septima Clark to return from the Sea Islands and teach in Charleston and Columbia, South Carolina, schools was the result of such a philosophical position and practical effort. A small group of black citizens of Charleston coordinated a petition campaign that ultimately involved hundreds of people, garnered thousands of signatures, and forced the General Assembly in 1919 to allow black women (and men) to teach in the black city schools, where until that time only white teachers could work. The leaders of the movement noted, "We, the undersigned committee . . .

are not a self-constituted committee of a few educated Negroes of the City of Charleston, but we are the chosen representatives of the petitioners, namely of more than 10,000 adult men and women of the Negro race in the city of Charleston." Black Mississippians in 1920 presented a petition to their state legislature designed to give "heads of families having children of educable age" the power to create schools. As the state laws existed, only "qualified electors" had the right to create schools, and because of racist voter registration restrictions, too many black Mississippians were disfranchised. At the time, literate black residents over twenty-one years of age in Mississippi totaled almost 300,000, but no more than 850 black people voted in any state election between 1920 and 1930. The petition also called for a compulsory education law, a black probation officer, one black person on every board of trustees that supervised black schools, wage equity for black teachers, and night school classes "whenever one-fifth of the resident citizens of a school district petition . . . or when fifteen or more persons between the ages of fourteen and fifty years express their desires to attend." There were only seven signatures on the document, and all seven were identified as "taxpayers," that is, property holders and, presumably, registered voters.[34] The petitioners were addressing the state legislature not solely because of personal or family needs but rather because of their perceived responsibility to the larger group.

Black journalists were especially adept at encouraging this kind of shared responsibility. In one case black Atlantans' response to the urgings of local black journalists contributed to the creation of a powerful public interest organization—spearheaded by women of the Neighborhood Union—that forced Atlanta school administrators to address their generations-old policy of neglecting black schoolchildren. In 1913 at least 1,000 black children were shut out of public schools there because of overcrowding, and 5,000 others attended only three and a half hours a day because all the black schools went into double (half-day) sessions. That same year, the city council proposed a $3 million bond issue, half of which was earmarked for schools. Of the proposed $1.5 million, only $37,000 was allocated for black education, and that was designated for school repairs. At the insistence of the black press, black voters defeated the bond issue, and conditions continued to worsen. By 1915 more than 4,000 black children were closed out of the public schools, and partly because of these bad conditions, parents who were able sent their children to private schools. Given the blatantly racist treatment, probably little cajoling was necessary to convince them to work to bring about local changes.[35]

A writer for the Atlanta *Independent* helped bind the community further by later insisting that "the educated Negro, in common with the uneducated man, . . . come out of his shell and . . . discharge his duty to the community." Taking direct aim at various benevolent, beneficial, and social organizations, the writer continued:

The Independent would like to know what the Twenty-Seven Club stands for, the Nine O'Clocks, the Twelve, the Fine Arts Club, the Graduate Club, the Omega Psi Phi, the Alpha Phi Alpha, the Kappa Alpha Psi, the Phi Beta Sigma, and the Business League, if they do not stand to contribute to the better life of the community. . . . What we want is [for] every church, every school, every club, every movement in Atlanta to rise up in righteous indignation and protest against the abolishing of our night schools because of the mismanagement and incompetency of the present Board of Education.[36]

Black Atlantans subsequently organized the Citizens Committee on Public Education to lobby for equitable education funding. The committee comprised people from all walks of life. Members of black PTA units, church congregations, fraternities, sororities, social clubs, and public housing tenant associations joined with the Servicemen's Center Clubs, the Servicemen's Mothers' Clubs, the Atlanta Mutual Building and Loan Association, local sections of the Brotherhood of Painters and Decorators, the National Association of Letter Carriers, and the Upholsterers, Furniture, Mattress, and Bedding Workers to push, ultimately successfully, for a new black high school.[37]

Throughout the country and across time, black newspapers played a critical role in creating and maintaining this collective consciousness. Without neglecting individual achievements, local and national black newspapers regularly reported on the progress the race achieved through collectivism, while encouraging more of the same. The importance of this print medium in developing community consciousness cannot be underestimated. The *Chicago Defender* alone had a daily circulation of over 200,000 in 1915, and more locally oriented publications quickly reached distant places by railroad (and railroad porters) and riverboat. People who never subscribed to the papers read or heard the news they carried while visiting beauty and barber shops, pool halls, club meetings, and church gatherings. Moreover, the Associated Negro Press, created in 1919, made it possible for the same stories to be printed in dozens of papers around the country at the same time. Ultimately, whether writing about the construction of a community building, the performance of a play, the graduation of somebody's daughter, or the employment of her sister, newspaper reporters expressly promoted social responsibility and race consciousness.[38] Sociologist E. Franklin Frazier, in his famous *Black Bourgeoisie,* charged that black newspaper writers so exaggerated black achievements that they merely "creat[ed] a world of make-believe."[39] And without question, the information delivered through black newspapers was sometimes filtered to present an idealized picture of the community. But ideals *are* effective motivators.[40]

Reporters described in detail the successful collective efforts to raise money for individual and community development. For example, in 1915 readers of the Norfolk *Journal and Guide* learned that members of the Negro Organization Society in Virginia had coordinated a statewide tag-sale day that netted almost $1,300 for the support of a tuberculosis sanatorium. Local people in Tampa, Florida, undertook "many a fish fry and many a chicken supper, all sorts of money-raising schemes" to finance the building of a school during the depths of the Great Depression. Nine county PTA units in North Carolina organized themselves in 1938 and held "fish fries, barbecues, banquets, baby contests, and musical programs," netting $974 to support a single black high school. And Kansas City *Call* readers learned in 1938 that black Mississippians in Lafayette County had completed a school "with no county [or] state aid."[41] People of very different abilities contributed to all of these efforts, and by these and other processes, schools, hospitals, and orphanages were built, teachers' and nurses' salaries paid, books bought, and libraries opened.[42]

The development of these important community institutions was a critical part of the process of community. Here the connections between the more and the less privileged are especially obvious. Parents who could not afford to send their children to distant schools, for example, needed local institutions, and they received considerable assistance in developing them from those who could support their own children more extensively. These were not simply acts of charity, providing for the more needy; they were a matter of developing the infrastructure of the community and community itself. Differences among the participants were celebrated in some instances and deliberately minimized in others, but all forms of support were valued.[43]

A writer for the Dublin, Georgia, *Courier* missed the mark in a

1931 article when he related what was supposed to be an amusing anecdote about local efforts to open a black school. He noted that "an old colored woman who helped found the school fund" began the program celebrating the opening of the school by reading the minutes of various meetings held over the years and the names of all who attended each meeting. The reporter continued:

The Negroes had been making up money for six years, but the old lady had kept the name of every person who had contributed so much as five cents. What is more, she had the names of those who had not contributed anything.

The entire audience smiled when she would read out that Sister Jones gave 10 cents and Brother Brown nothing; Brother Thomas 25 cents and Sister Green nothing.

As a method of getting the cash it must be rather effective. It must be embarrassing to read six years later that you attended a meeting and didn't put anything in when the hat went 'round.[44]

It is certainly possible that the community project historian intended to embarrass those who gave no money, but other interpretations of her report are just as plausible. Perhaps those who had no money supported the effort simply by being present. They might also have provided the physical labor to build the school. Whatever the case, keeping and calling the names of all who attended the meetings was a testimonial that they *did* contribute to the effort whether they gave money or not.[45]

Although sociologists regularly posit homogeneity as a criterion of community, black people who identified with one another on various levels historically constituted a diverse group. In the context of community development, the conditions of their lives that ordinarily divided them became less important.[46] The petition drives of Mississippi and South Carolina residents noted above are useful examples. But an especially instructive one is the construction of a school in Jonesboro, Arkansas, in 1927. Each person's task had to be pragmatically assigned because most of the workers held other paid jobs that they could not neglect. The electrician strung lights over the site so that others could work into the evenings, often until midnight. Schoolteachers and their students scraped old mortar off the donated bricks. They and other residents hauled the used material to the vacant lot that the black community had recently purchased for the new building. And when actual construction began, those with some building skills (including the principal) became working supervisors for volunteers who required on-the-job training. The unskilled workers were male and female, young and old, college-trained professionals and unschooled laborers, but they all were committed to building a school. In a deliberately and perniciously stratified society, collective action was critical to individual and community development, and in the pursuit of such ends, everyone, even children, had a role.[47]

These examples of collective consciousness, social responsibility, and difference (and unity) in communion suggest how the young women of this book came to be similarly inclined. But as important as these examples are in showing this was commonplace, other examples touched the women's lives more directly. One obvious factor that helped bind them to a larger community was the persistence and pervasiveness of racism. Another was the collective nature of the way the young women gained the preparation necessary to achieve the public roles they later attained. Third, the women's families regularly demonstrated their own community consciousness and social responsibility by helping to provide for others who could not help in return. And finally, as the youngsters worked to complete their education—even as they were being generated as products of the process of community—they were consciously influenced to become part of the process too, the system of operations by which the goals and desires of the group would be fulfilled. When these women assumed the roles for which they had been prepared, if the process was successful, they would assume some responsibility for sustaining it. And if they had any uncertainty about how to do so, they had only to look to examples provided by their families, neighbors, and friends.

Racial violence, which often disrupted family life, kept these women connected to those whose lives were less advantaged. Many incidents had occurred before the women were born or before they were old enough to remember them, but the stories became part of the family lore that they learned as soon as they were old enough to understand. Mary Church Terrell's father was attacked in his business in the 1860s, she said, by Irish rioters who resented his success and wanted to teach him a lesson and make an example of him. In addition to vandalizing his business, they shot him in the head and left him for dead.[48] Klan members threatened Eunice Rivers Laurie's father's life during the 1910s because he was "living too well." Later, because they believed he had abetted the escape of a black man accused of shooting a white police officer, they returned and attacked his home. He moved the family into a rented house until it was safe for them to return. Lucy

Mitchell's multiple-household extended family reorganized in the 1920s when Florida Ku Klux Klan activities endangered their lives. The initial attack was against Mitchell's uncle, who owned a movie theater and a restaurant that served the black public. Later the Klan attacked Mitchell's own home, and black men from the community moved in to guard the house and defend it; the women and children moved out for several weeks until the harassment subsided.[49] Even one of Portia Washington Pittman's escorts was brutally beaten by a railroad conductor during an 1895 trip back to school in Massachusetts. And if Booker T. Washington's assistant—and Washington was a visiting friend and regular correspondent of the railroad company's owner—was not safe (and we can be sure that Portia's escort was a model of decorum), then no black people were.[50] While these subjects were coming of age, such acts of persecution were numerous, varied, and not unique to a particular time or place. In fact, racist attacks occurred regularly throughout the country, and rather than being somewhat insulated by their relative status, these families were often particular victims of the violence and hostility. Not only did such incidents make it impossible for them and their daughters to separate themselves from other African Americans who had not accomplished as much, but in many instances community members came to their aid, defending the families and protecting their property.

The racism that pervaded American society touched the children's lives even more directly. Mary Church Terrell was too young at the time to understand why the train conductor harassed her when she and her father traveled. The general inappropriateness of the act rather than its racist implications baffled her. As a college student, however, she fully understood the racist source of inappropriate acts, although she could still be confounded by their being perpetrated against her. Mary's experience at Oberlin College had been a pleasant one. There was a visible and active black community in Oberlin; the white community was for the most part idealistic; black students found the community open to them; and Mary was a good and popular student, accepted by her peers and her teachers. When she left the community there, however, she also left the insulation it provided against racism. She went to New York one summer in the 1880s, excited and eager to find employment, to put her training to good use, and to fulfill her idea of the Protestant work ethic she had learned so well at Oberlin. Not long after arriving in New York, however, Mary returned home frustrated.

Prospective employers to whom she had been referred by employment agencies repeatedly declined to hire her upon discovering that she was black.[51]

Angelina Grimké and Portia Washington did not have to leave school to encounter such painful incidents. By the time they enrolled in northern schools of similar reputations, their classmates felt free to demonstrate racist behavior. Historian James M. McPherson has argued convincingly that many of the white schools that admitted black women during the nineteenth century had been so thoroughly infused with the abolitionist spirit in their early years that administrators demanded there be no discrimination against black students. By the turn of the century, however, few of these same schools were still under the influence of "the abolitionist legacy" and consequently conditions for black students deteriorated dramatically.[52] Black students in the public schools of the South, where only white teachers taught for a time, regularly endured racist insults. In fact, Mamie Garvin Fields believed one of her white elementary school teachers carried a parasol just to keep the young black scholars from getting too close to her.[53] Conditions did not change qualitatively in southern public systems until black schoolteachers gained employment in them. Undoubtedly it was for that reason that many of these women pursued even their elementary schooling in private institutions.

The connections among members of the community were not all based on emergency responses to life-threatening situations, nor were the arrangements for their daughters only responses to traumatic and direct confrontations with racism. The connections reflected long-term commitments that included broad, regular participation in the process of preparing these young women for professional futures. People had welcomed these daughters into their homes because despite how privileged some of these women appear and were, many could not complete their formal schooling and develop their potential without assistance. But equally significant, in a few instances the community helped finance their education by providing "scholarships."

Lula Catherine Jordan McNeil, a member of the first graduating class (1923) of Huntington High School, the first black high school in Newport News, Virginia, recalled: "My people [black residents of Newport News] wanted me to teach," and so they took up money and helped to finance her education at the normal school in Petersburg. They expected Lula to return to the community when she finished and to teach others, which she did for several years before returning to school in

1931 for a degree in nursing. After working one summer to earn money for the fall school session, Jane Edna Hunter almost lost the opportunity to go when the person who was to pay for her train ticket failed to do so. Hunter's school year was saved when about twenty friends and neighbors, who had proudly come to the train station to see her off, took up a more than sufficient collection. Historian Adrienne Lash Jones has characterized their generosity as evidence "of their faith in both the education process and the young woman."[54] These acts also demonstrated the belief, shared even by those unable to fulfill it for themselves or their children, in the importance of preparing others for responsible public roles and in providing opportunities for that preparation. They might also suggest how these women represented both the products and the process of community. People collected their money and sent these daughters off with the expectation of the daughters' returning and providing similar opportunities for others. Only if the women remained active parts of the process of community could they fully exemplify its success. But even if they did not return, their individual achievements still raised the status of the community a little bit more, and though disappointed, their supporters could still be proud and appropriately count the women's accomplishments as their own.[55]

Reflecting the importance of these individual opportunities to the community at large, Lucy Mitchell recalled vividly that the entire local community worked to support the Daytona Normal and Industrial Institute for Colored Girls (now Bethune-Cookman College) when she was a student there during the 1910s: through various projects they raised money to help to pay grocery bills and teacher salaries. And clubs, churches, and other organizations throughout the country also held fund-raisers to support "Mrs. Bethune's school." Probably most of the people who contributed could not afford to send their children to the private school for more than a few months a year or for a few years, if at all; but together these people could and did provide enough support to keep the school solvent so that others, more able, could take fuller advantage of its programs.[56] Eula Wellman Dunlap recalled that on "Community Day" in Kings Mountain, North Carolina, all the black people in town came out to help with the physical upkeep of Lincoln Academy and its grounds. Women emptied bed ticks and washed them, men hauled in wagonloads of straw, and women restuffed the mattresses. Children carried pillows, fetched drinks of water, and did whatever else they could manage, and though they dared not ask, they also wondered if grown folks realized that children sometimes got tired. Throughout the year, women made sheets, pillowcases, quilts, and gowns that they stored at the school in case anyone in the neighborhood became ill or otherwise in need.[57] Here, too, most of these people had no children in Lincoln Academy, since the students, like Beulah Hester, were primarily boarders from out of town. Kings Mountain had a free public school for its essentially working-class black residents. But these residents nevertheless supported Lincoln Academy because of its role in the development of black children in general.

In a similar fashion, the women's own families worked for the development of children other than their own. John L. Dart, Susan Dart Butler's father, sent Susan and her brother to Washington, D.C., to attend public school, then to the private Avery Normal Institute when they were in Charleston, and later Susan attended Atlanta University. But Dart also used part of his wealth to found the Charleston Normal and Industrial Institute in South Carolina in 1894 to provide some education for black children who were closed out of the local public schools. Although John Dart probably earned a small income from this service, he used his own building (and other resources) to create this school, and he also opened his private library to black residents who could not afford to buy books and had no other facility available, whether or not they attended Dart Hall.[58] Charlemae Hill Rollins's father, Allen G. Hill, moved his family from Mississippi to Oklahoma just after the turn of the century, then found there were no schools in Beggs, Oklahoma. But rather than simply teaching their daughter, Rollins's father built on his property the first school to exist in the town, and with no pay Rollins's mother taught all those who wanted to come until they could obtain a better-trained teacher. Eula Wellman Dunlap's father had the economic wherewithal to move his family to Kings Mountain, North Carolina, so that Eula and her siblings could attend Lincoln Academy. But soon after he arrived and purchased mountain property near the school, he and other community folk donated work days to build a pipeline to bring water down from underground springs on his property to the school. Dunlap's uncle and grandfather, longtime residents of Cleveland County, were among twelve men who built the first "public" school for black children there in 1872. They each donated two weeks of labor to construct the building and make furniture, and then each one contributed two and a half bushels of wheat and $2.50 a month to pay the white teacher they hired and to maintain the building. Beulah Shepard Hester's parents operated an orphanage in North Carolina for some time without pay. Although these families' endeavors stand out, many others contributed to local efforts to feed the hungry, house the homeless, clothe the ragged, and further develop the community in general.[59]

Parents worked hard and directed much of their energy toward creating and taking advantage of opportunities that would enhance their daughters' futures, but they did not work at the expense of the rest of the community. Many of them seemed to take for granted that those who were more able to facilitate individual and collective development bore responsibility for those who were less able. Their efforts at institution building would be easily understood if all had possessed resources like those of the wealthiest families. That is, one might expect Robert Church, a millionaire, to undertake such ventures, and he did fund a public park, a city auditorium, and numerous other institutions for black people in Memphis. But even the poorest families were also involved. Until Eula Dunlap was nearly grown, her clothes came primarily from missionary barrels shipped from the North. Similarly, Sarah Delany remembered getting only one new outfit before she was able to work and buy her own clothes. Her family shopped in "the mission store" where they bought second-hand apparel. Beulah Hester's family, while running an orphanage, could not afford to pay all her schooling expenses. She earned much of her tuition at Hartshorn by taking work classes, breadmaking in particular, in which all of the school's bread was baked. Sarah Webb Rice, who taught in the rural schools of Alabama during the 1920s, came from a family that often had only bread and gravy to eat for weeks on end. Still, her mother helped feed and clothe others, even after losing their family farm and other personal property because Rice's father had mortgaged it to start a school and was later unable (even with community assistance) to repay the loan.[60]

African Americans as a group frequently demonstrated this collective consciousness: however important individuals were, their real social status was based on their connections with the larger group. This "consciousness of kind" was reflected in thoughtful, deliberate processes of community building that combined the construction of schools, libraries, orphanages, churches, and other institutions with efforts to develop human consciousness as well.[61] In both kinds of endeavors the process was designed to produce women and men who could symbolize the power and potential of the group. Black newspapers, the most significant medium for disseminating information to black people far and

65

wide, played a central role in crystallizing that collective consciousness by suggesting appropriate political postures, ridiculing people whose positions seemed to threaten group development, and exalting, often beyond what circumstances warranted, both everyday and extraordinary examples of social responsibility. Social responsibility, living not solely for oneself but for the advancement of the group, was a common way of life during the Jim Crow era.

• • •

It is common knowledge that within black neighborhoods, people regularly cared for each other's children, feeding them when necessary, disciplining them when circumstances warranted it, and in general reporting the children's activities to their parents on a regular basis. It is clear in such examples that these actions did not reflect an inability of the parents to care for their own, but rather the general responsibility that adults felt for protecting and providing for the children of the community. Such characterizations, however, have rarely gone far enough. They almost never extend beyond the neighborhood, and rarely have they gone beyond the most obvious day-to-day, practical attention to children's backyard and sidewalk activities. But children's place in the community encompassed far more than those important but limited concerns and included large and concrete visions of individual and community development.

Because of those visions for the future—group goals, in effect—the community helped to reinforce family values and traditions and contributed to the development of its children. When young women had to travel far from home for schooling, community people provided them with shelter and all that the word implies. When children needed financial support to pursue their education, people who hardly knew them often contributed to the cause. And whether or not they gave directly to individual children's educational funds, local residents helped construct and maintain schools so that many might have the advantage of an education. Even when young women had no need for community support to pursue their education, the community helped provide for them as they traveled for business and pleasure. And if some children never needed to take advantage of any of these forms of assistance, community members still regularly and sagaciously provided instruction in social responsibility by demonstrating an unmistakable ethos of mutuality. Truly these were "daughters of [the] community coming up." Their upbringings and their futures were not wholly determined by capricious white people who controlled state and local governments, school boards, philanthropic agencies, and vigilante groups. And also, these young women's futures were too important to the community to be limited by individual family resources. People other than the parents regularly assumed some responsibility for feeding, clothing, housing, schooling, nurturing, and protecting these daughters as their own.

On completing their education, in addition to serving as good examples of the consequence of individual effort, ambition, and ability, these young women also represented one of the best traditions of the community. The nature of the schooling they received, however, was critical to how they actually developed once they left their families. Often the educational process was designed to enable them not only to think for themselves, provide for themselves, and fulfill their potential, but also to become community leaders who could enable others to fulfill the same conditions for themselves. But because leadership almost always renders individuals both a part of and apart from the masses, the women's teachers, like their parents and community advocates, trod a delicate path to make certain that these students could balance their roles as leaders of and members of the group or as examples of both the product of individual striving and the product and process of community.

"We are not educating individuals but manufacturing levers":
SCHOOLING REINFORCEMENTS

Janie Porter Barrett's upbringing was very different from that of the other women included in this book. She did, like some of the rest, grow up in a multifamily household; but she and her mother did not share the house with kinfolk. The other family in the household of which they were a part was white, and Janie's mother worked as their domestic servant.[1]

This arrangement had both advantages and disadvantages for Janie. In terms of material comfort, her early upbringing was quite privileged; she was reared in a household that bespoke "refinement and ease." Janie's mother and her mother's employers easily provided food, shelter, clothing, and many of life's luxuries. The white employers also allowed Janie to be taught along with their own children, and so she was probably far better educated than the average black child growing up in South Carolina during the 1870s. But that is probably as far as the advantages went. The employers also assumed control not only over the life of Janie's mother as their live-in domestic, but over Janie's life as well. And when the time arrived for her to go away to school (probably when the white children moved into a traditional school for the rest of their education, which Janie, because of her race, could not attend), the white woman of the house decided that Janie should pass for white and enroll at one of the prestigious New England schools. Janie's mother defied her employer, took control over her own life and her daughter's future, and sent Janie to Hampton Institute.[2]

Janie's early education undoubtedly prepared her well for the course that was in place at Hampton in 1881, but socially and politically she was less well prepared for attending the black industrial/normal school. She found the living conditions at Hampton to be crude and the food to be equally bad. But more important, Janie was totally unprepared for the intense socialization process that pushed students to commit their lives to serving the black community. Janie quickly tired of being drilled by Hampton faculty and administrators on "her duties to her race." And she, at first, endured the weekday indoctrination by looking forward to Sunday, because, she said, "On Sundays, I didn't have to do a single thing for my race."[3]

This chapter focuses on the schooling process that black women underwent between the 1870s and the 1930s at schools that were heavily influenced, from their founding and in their development, by Christian missionary principles and community development impulses. The schools include Oberlin College, a private white coeducational evangelical school during the nineteenth century; Howard University, an independent private black university; Hampton and Tuskegee Institutes, private black normal and agricultural/vocational schools; and Spelman, Hartshorn, and Talladega Colleges and Fisk and Atlanta Universities, private black schools that were heavily supported by missionary associations from their founding. Spelman and Hartshorn might also be set apart because they were single-sex colleges.[4]

As different as these schools might seem on the surface, they were very similar in their missions and in certain aspects of their development. They were designed to cultivate or further develop a Christian (communal) spirit in the students; to instill leadership qualities in them; and to prepare them to use their training—moral, mental, and manual—to go into any community and establish themselves as useful members. These schools were founded in the wake of international evangelical revivals; during American women's movements to establish permanent public sphere roles for middle-class women; or during early efforts to establish recently freed men, women, and children as full participants in the American mainstream. In one way all the schools were products of reform movements, and as they encouraged reform, they prepared young black women for public work and reinforced family and community interests related to self-development and social responsibility.

Oberlin College, however, was unique in many ways among the schools these women attended. From its founding in 1832 Oberlin was coeducational—the first private coeducational boarding school in the country; soon after its opening black students were admitted; and significantly, the college was founded along with the community of Oberlin, Ohio, as an idealistic, if not a utopian, society. Philo Penfield Stewart of Sherman, Connecticut, one of Oberlin's founders, wanted to create an institution "where study and labor should be combined, and the whole establishment conducted upon such principles of thrift and economy, that enterprising students could defray all their expenses by their labor, without any detriment to their progress in study." The school's cofounder, John J. Shipherd of West Granville, New York, wanted to plant "a community and school where their ideas of Christian living and education could be realized." He sought to create a place where "worldly influences should be excluded, and where gospel principles should prevail." It was also important to Shipherd that community members subordinate individual interests to the common good.[5]

Although Oberlin stands out because of the number (four) of women in this volume who matriculated there, several of the black schools these women attended had important connections to Oberlin and other well-regarded private white schools. Founders of Hartshorn and Spelman Colleges, for example, consciously patterned aspects of their programs after the elite white women's schools in New England.[6] Mary Tefft, a Hartshorn teacher from 1891 until 1913, was a graduate of Wellesley College.[7] As late as the 1930s there was a heavy concentration of Mount Holyoke graduates (five out of twenty-five) on the staff at Spelman. Spelman's president at the time, Florence Matilda Read, was herself a 1909 Mount Holyoke graduate.[8] Fisk, Howard, and Talladega were designed to give black students an education equal to that provided at leading institutions where white men studied. Most of Howard's early black male faculty members were graduates of Ivy League schools, and many of the first faculty members at Fisk and Talladega were graduates of Oberlin, Radcliffe, and Wellesley. Talladega's first two principals or presidents, the Reverend Henry E. Brown and Albert A. Safford, were Oberlin graduates. And one of Fisk's founders, Erastus Milo Cravath, president of the school from 1875 to 1900, was an 1857 graduate of Oberlin.[9]

Perhaps more important than the "pedigree" suggested by similarities to white schools and the connections black school staffs had with them, all these schools for black students except Tuskegee were directed until well into the twentieth century by people connected to missionary societies and who represented, according to historian James M. McPherson, a part of "the abolitionist legacy." According to McPherson, the passage of the Fifteenth Amendment was only a partial victory for the antislavery activists. The larger struggle involved preventing the " 'social persecution of men on account of their color.' " The former antislavery activists sought to accomplish this (and to respond to "the sordid materialism of the Gilded Age") through religion and education for black *and* white southerners.[10] The abolitionists' emphasis on education and leadership development meshed perfectly with the interests of the freed community. In fact, when the white missionary educators arrived at these southern locales to undertake their work they often simply stepped into a process of school development already begun by the black community.[11] Yet the impact of the missionary support, material and symbolic, should not be underestimated.

The missionary/abolitionist spirit that had such a profound influence on the structure of black postsecondary education was in one way quite egalitarian. The activists, for example, regularly espoused the argument that black people were inherently equal to white people and that acquiring formal education would both prove that equality and help to consolidate it. As industrialists and philanthropists poured money exclusively into vocational education for black people, Malcolm MacVicar, superintendent of education for the Baptist Home Mission Society, which helped to support Spelman and Hartshorn Colleges, insisted that "it is one thing to give to young men and women such industrial training as will fit them to earn successfully a good livelihood; and yet quite another thing to imbue them with a missionary spirit, and fit them to be instructors and leaders of others. The latter . . . should be the chief, if not the only, work of the Home Mission Schools."[12]

Representatives of the American Missionary Association (AMA), which supported Talladega, Fisk, and Hampton, similarly noted the importance of higher education and leadership development among African American students. The Reverend George Hall, reporting on the AMA's southern work in 1902, concluded: "The most difficult problems confronting the Negro, and this nation as well, in relation to that once enslaved race, are to be solved largely through the influence of Christian leaders raised up from among themselves." Another writer, commenting explicitly on Fisk University, insisted that "capacity not color, Christianity not caste, is to decide the question as to the kind of education a youth is to receive. . . . [The students graduating from Fisk] are to be the leaders of a people sorely needing leadership." And the Reverend J. G. Merrill, president of Fisk from 1900 to 1908, concurred: "It is the purpose of the Faculty to send forth no one who is unworthy of confidence or incapacitated to be a leader of those who have never had the opportunities afforded at Fisk." Altogether, the prevailing viewpoint among the missionary workers, black and white, was that black students must receive the same training as that available in white schools. One missionary insisted: "No more, and especially no less."[13]

As much as the missionaries, most of whom were white, insisted that African Americans were equal to whites, and as concerned as they were with leadership development among black southerners, they were also often paternalistic and even racist in their pronouncements.[14] These negative assumptions had as much influence on the schools' programs as the positive assumptions. H. S. De Forest, for example, an earnest worker in the education of black people as president of Talladega College (1879–96), described one consequence of slaves' having had to steal in order to eat. "It is probably true," he remarked, "that our colored brethren will take more chickens from the roost and make less noise about it than any other class of men on earth." Armory H. Bradford, president of the AMA at the time, wrote in 1905 that "the vices of heathenism, with few of the virtues of civilization, may be found in the 'Black Belt.'" And when the Reverend David O. Mears addressed the 1876 AMA annual meeting, he quoted "a few passages from that truth-loving magazine, *The American Missionary*": "'Lying, stealing and licentiousness seem irretrievably fastened upon these people by their centuries of bondage.' 'Gross darkness and the lowest forms of vice and sin are well nigh universal.' 'They practice their religion and their vices together, the one about as much as the other.'" Mears approached his conclusion: "We here briefly recapitulate the undeniable facts. Five millions of our citizens, as a rule, are ignorant and immoral, and without the necessary means to obtain an education. Left to themselves, they will assist in making the nation just what they are." While each of these men attempted to balance his remarks by noting that such conditions were a consequence of material deprivation and learned rather than innate, their remarks were nonetheless rank at best and racist at worst.[15]

The missionary educators also came to attribute the postbellum politics of "redemption" to the alleged faults of the freed people. The activists concluded that the formerly enslaved African Americans had not had proper training in the "responsibilities or duties of citizenship," which caused white southerners to "fail to meet this unpleasant state of things in a Christian way." The missionaries, however, had a plan for resolving that problem. They would "go among these men and train them for their civil duties."[16] William Hayes Ward, longtime editor of the abolitionist paper *The Independent*, suggested the qualities he believed would matter most by saying that education, temperance, thrift, and Christianity would have more impact on black communities than would civil rights laws. Others added that *when* black people became virtuous citizens, military protection would not be necessary in order for them to vote.[17] Undoubtedly many black people living in the post-Reconstruction South agreed that if they were hard workers, better educated, morally upright, civic-minded property owners white racists might stop harassing them. But most freed women and men probably would not have agreed that their being trained in a particular way was more important to maintaining their freedom than legislation and federal troops. Undoubtedly, many also disagreed with the assumptions about their character that underlay the abolitionists' conclusions in the first place. The freed people did, however, agree that education was vital to their practical efforts to vote, to work, to acquire and protect property, and to develop their community. And for that reason, however paternalistic (and even racist) some of the missionaries' ideas were, the ends at first seemed to more than justify the means.[18]

The abolitionists' and missionaries' ideas about the process and product of formal schooling reinforced the traditions of these women's families and communities in yet another way. They all sought to build character.[19] Although school administrators' directives to students about character development paralleled lessons from parents and community leaders, the particulars of the two sets of instructions were not always the same. Not surprisingly, the objective from the point of view of school administrators was explicitly Christian character. And consequently, whereas parents' efforts at character development involved teaching the daughters how to bring all their powers under control, the Christian ethic that brought with it the same charge described character as self-control, demonstrated best by a submission of control—to God's will. Parental efforts to develop self-confidence in their children were bolstered by the Christian mandate to have faith—the kind that only children of God could have. Parents told their children they could be anything they wanted to be, and school administrators reinforced this by insisting that not only were high aspirations admirable, but fulfilling them was part of God's plan. The Reverend James Bond, a graduate of Fisk University himself, exhorted students at his alma mater "to be strong because of what you are to be." They were to be "strong men and women" and "the advance guards" in "the regeneration of the race." Because of "what God intended that [they] should be," they were to "find a path or make one."[20]

The students' charge, in the secular jargon, to accept social responsibility was reinforced, in Christian terms, by their "duty." Accepting Christianity as a personal philosophy required them to live their lives for others. They were not simply to work to bring about equality, justice, and a better standard of living for their people, which was the practical hope of their families and communities, but more broadly they were to work to establish the kingdom of God on earth. Those able to live by such an ethic, like Moses, the students were told, possessed "adequate, competent, broad-visioned, unselfish, altruistic, native leadership."[21] Not a single student needed to worry about her ability to live up to these ideals, because as the parents put it, individual conscience, not color, was the key to living this socially committed life. And according to the Christian teachers, the key was the quality of the soul, which was also "independent of physical features."[22]

There was still another parallel between the Christian context and the worldly one. In the more popular tradition, students learned that the whole race was often judged by the condition of a few. In the Christian context they learned "that each man's freedom is wrapped up in the opportunity and freedom of every other." In one way, none of them could possibly be free if any of them were not, and in the other way, all the members of the race would rise or fall together. Thus in the secular and in the sacred contexts, these women's obligations to work with and for those who were less fortunate would not situate them in the workaday world exclusively as privileged public charity workers. They would work, in every way, for themselves as well. Their sacred salvation and their secular survival depended on it.[23]

The "abolitionist legacy," then, with all its faults, still reinforced black family and community traditions that encouraged self-confidence, high achievement, leadership development among individuals, and individual service to the larger community. And though the colleges and universities that benefited from missionary support, including these, began with little more than an elementary class, they were founded in the context of a much grander mission. As they developed full normal, college, and university programs, one idea, articulated best in the *Lincoln Institute Worker,* was always kept in view: "WE ARE NOT EDUCATING INDIVIDUALS BUT MANUFACTURING LEVERS."[24]

The schooling process by which these levers would be manufactured was decidedly Christian, laden with value judgments about "refinement" and "culture," suffused with ideas about "the dignity of all respectable labor," and explicitly directed toward producing socially responsible individuals. The Reverend D. E. Satterfield, a black repre-

74

sentative of the AMA, went so far as to note that it was not even necessary that the young students understand precisely why they were undergoing such a process. As with the earlier lessons transmitted in their homes and communities, the students were simply supposed to accept and internalize these lessons. Satterfield hastened to add, "When they are advanced enough to understand it, we must teach them what it means, and what depends upon it."[25] But in fact by the time these young women began their professional education, many of them were already well versed in the ethic of socially responsible individualism and experienced in carrying it out. Many had seen examples and heard advice similar to that given to librarian Clara Stanton Jones by her grandfather: the value of their schooling lay not only in the individual accomplishment that it represented for the student and the subsequent personal advantages it might allow, but rather the real value was in the potency it represented for the community at large.[26] Altogether, the schooling process provided especially effective reinforcement for family and community values regarding what a woman ought to be and to do.

• • •

Before Fressie Bell of Atlanta, Georgia, ever set foot on the campus of Tuskegee Normal and Industrial Institute, she had earned a reputation as one who "fills her place promptly, efficiently, and regularly, not as a girl, but as a mature business woman." The members of Atlanta's Union Baptist Church commended Miss Bell to the principal of Tuskegee as "a young woman very different from the average." At the time of her application for admission to Tuskegee, she was already "pianist for both church and S. S. [Sunday school]; . . . chairman [sic] of a committee to raise money to pay for the S. S. piano; . . . an active worker in raising funds to pay for the church"; and a helper "in every other way possible in furthering the Christian work of church and community." In undertaking a course of study at Tuskegee, Fressie Bell might learn much in the way of educational theory or domestic science, but considering her established record of public work, school officials at Tuskegee would not teach her much that she did not already know about community service or social responsibility. As further evidence of the community tradition from which Bell came, although her letter of recommendation was signed by the Sunday school superintendent, he strengthened its authority by noting that it was written "by order of the entire Sunday School and Church" membership.[27]

CHAPTER THREE

Partly because of the application process that required letters of recommendation from respectable community people, and also because of historical traditions, these daughters were not sent to schools by their parents alone; they were often sent by their communities.[28] In sending the daughters off to historically black institutions, those involved had specific ideas about the schools' and the students' sometimes shared responsibilities. Charlie Mae Crawford, for example, had already "been well trained by Godly parents," according to the Reverend James Brown of the First Congregational Church of Anniston, Alabama. But the Reverend Brown, Crawford's "friends, and her church, expect that with the advantages [provided at Tuskegee] she will be a most useful woman in the uplift of our people." J. R. Philpot of Loachapoka, Alabama, was certain that, considering Consula Bradford's already demonstrated abilities, her further training at Tuskegee, would "cause her to be of more service to community and race." And in recommending Sarah Moore as "one who will be obedient, faithful, ladylike and Christian while under your care and keeping," the members of the Pensacola, Florida, Sixth Avenue Baptist Church noted that they were paying for Moore's schooling because she had proved herself "deserving," and, furthermore, she was "faithful to church and community work for the uplift of the race." They expected "that by hard study and careful training, that when she shall have been given the command by your school to go out into the world and hang up her shingle as a servant to her race and the world, she will be [an] honor to her church, a credit to her community, a defender of her race, and a general benefactor to mankind."[29] Family and community expectations regarding the purpose of formal schooling and these young women's subsequent public work were obviously extensive. And the school programs meshed perfectly with those expectations and served in a mighty way to address them.

The published goals of the schools were among the first indications of how those extensive expectations might be fulfilled. By 1899 the practical, intellectual, and idealistic objectives of the educational program at Spelman College were united clearly in its mission statement: Spelman administrators intended to build character by training the head, the hand, and the heart. The faculty would "send forth graduates who shall be home-makers, educators, leaders in social reforms, church workers, servants of Christ."[30] Hartshorn Memorial College officials added that the nature of race relations demanded that schools develop black leaders who could work among their own people.[31]

The push for educational programs that would enable black

women to help lead the community forward was not limited to all-female schools or those supported by the Baptist societies. Schools supported by the AMA—Hampton, Talladega, and Fisk—and black normal/vocational school administrators at Hampton and Tuskegee were similarly inclined. Before the turn of the century, Fisk University officials sought to make Fisk "a great center of the best Christian educational forces for the training of the colored youth of the South, that they may be rightly disciplined and inspired for leaders in the vitally important work that needs to be done for their race." By establishing a normal department, Tuskegee staff members expected that when their students assumed their work in the public sphere after graduation, they would "become the real leaders of their communities, and thus bring about healthier moral and material conditions."[32]

This emphasis on leadership development was not accidental. By the standards and desires of its own members, the black community before the turn of the century had not moved far enough beyond the shadow of slavery to rest easy. In fact, between 1876 and 1900 it had been pushed backward. And few black southerners as individuals had either the economic wherewithal to pursue private schooling or the political clout necessary to demand and achieve access to public institutions. Consequently many African Americans believed that those most able to pursue formal schooling had to be prepared in the process to help those who were less able. In support of that tradition, school administrators consciously designed their programs "not to give some education to a large number but a thorough training of the most serviceable kind to a picked company who will then become examples, missionaries, and helpers to their own people."[33] This thorough training included the reinforcement of social behaviors that would command respect and allow leadership to develop, the pursuit of traditional academic courses, opportunities to practice the application of that newly gained knowledge, intensive training in community work, and for women students, a good amount of coursework and practice in the domestic arts. By their manual, mental, and moral training, these young students were to become women of character and culture. And as such they would, theoretically, do whatever work they could to enhance the quality of life in their communities.

Training in the domestic arts was a very important part of the formal schooling the women undertook even at the liberal arts colleges and universities. Women at Atlanta University first pursued these courses in the classrooms, then practiced in several dormitory rooms designed to simulate a traditional home. But before the turn of the century the university began planning to construct a special cottage where girls would live, twelve at a time, to study and practice the households arts. While they resided in the cottage, in addition to their regular studies, they would receive basic and more intricate domestic training in "cooking, washing, sewing, the care of rooms and furniture, . . . entertaining guests, and the thousand and one little things that contribute to the making of a well ordered home." Both normal and college students at Spelman took domestic courses. And here too, by the early 1900s all seniors, five at a time, lived in the Practice Cottage and assumed full responsibility for all the housecleaning, meal planning, and food purchase and preparation.[34]

Hartshorn officials insisted that no one take this emphasis on domesticity to mean they were training domestic servants, for they were not. They sought to prepare each young woman for work "at the head of her own family, and for the teacher or missionary at home or abroad." In the eyes of the school administrators, "the taste and idea of domestic elegance . . . [could] endow their possessor of whatever rank with an undefined power always possessed by the well bred cultivated woman." Thus practical and idealistic imperatives influenced this aspect of the school program. Whereas parents had simply wanted their daughters to be capable of taking care of their own homes, school personnel—believing that some forms of women's leadership were not overt but rather operated by example—held that well-trained black women could also lift up the black community through the example they set in maintaining clean, orderly, and well-cared-for homes and families. By the same means, the homemakers might improve external perceptions of the black community. Furthermore, school officials realized that for many of their students, their "wealth must be their economy," and so students had to be prepared to work in their own homes in a disciplined, economical, and efficient manner. Ultimately, whether these students' futures would involve working exclusively in their own homes, setting up their homes as examples for others, or actively teaching the household arts, by their own abilities, efforts, and actions they could help prove to those in the larger society who were not already convinced that the black race was rising.[35]

For many outside observers and actual participants, however, the best evidence of the community's rising status was intellectual achievement. Therefore the academic component of the school courses was of great importance. Accordingly, Henry L. Morehouse, field secretary for the American Baptist Home Mission Society in the 1890s (and executive secretary 1879–93 and 1902–17), noted that the programs at Spelman and Hartshorn were designed to create not "superficial feminine accomplishments" but real intellectual women.[36] Morehouse and other school supporters insisted on having curricula, textbooks, and teachers equal to those in white schools, and ultimately they flattered themselves as being creators of institutions comparable to the white New England women's schools.[37] Spelman, like Mount Holyoke, was founded, maintained, and managed by women. And besides their all being single-sex schools, their curricula were similar enough that the comparison was legitimate. That is, despite white public observations at the turn of the century that classical study was wasted on black students who would likely end up in nonprofessional work, the college course at Spelman included two or three years of Latin and Greek; a series of mathematics courses including algebra, solid geometry, and plane trigonometry; science courses including physics, chemistry, geology, and astronomy; and a social science curriculum that included logic, mental and moral philosophy, sociology, and ethics. Students also took English courses (in grammar, composition, literature, and rhetoric) and some form of religious study (English Bible, Old Testament, New Testament, and Christian evidence) every term. The college course in place at other schools was very similar.[38] And even after curriculum modernization, black schools held on to the classical program, and some merely added scientific, literary, and liberal arts programs.[39] Although that practice eventually made the black institutions appear backward, it nonetheless proved the abilities of black students and prepared them to compete favorably with white students whenever the opportunity arose.[40]

Tuskegee Institute was, at its inception, the State Normal School at Tuskegee, Alabama. The program, which at first did not exceed traditional grammar school courses, was designed to provide broad-based, general preparation for women who would settle throughout the rural South and provide basic education to the millions of African Americans who would otherwise not see the inside of a classroom until the 1910s and 1920s, when, with the support of private philanthropy, the common school movement reached the rural South; or even until the 1920s and 1930s, when public (tax-dollar) support became more available. Therefore, in 1881 (before the normal course was actually in place) Tuskegee's "language" courses were limited to elocution, reading, spelling, grammar, and composition. The mathematics curriculum

CHAPTER THREE

included only arithmetic, geometry, and algebra. And the social and physical sciences included basic courses in geography, history, zoology, botany, chemistry, and natural philosophy. Music and physical education, courses taught in the common schools by the "regular" teacher, were also part of the required coursework.[41] Once the normal course was in place, the most significant change in the curriculum was the addition of methods (pedagogy) courses.[42]

Women who gained their normal diplomas at Tuskegee (and at Hampton, Tuskegee's parent school) were not to be satisfied with them alone, however. Graduates were advised to continue to study, to earn their higher degrees, and to maintain their places as community examples and leaders. To support this effort, long before it was possible for Tuskegee and Hampton to staff a regular college curriculum, both schools offered summer school programs for the common school teachers who held normal diplomas and certificates so they could work all year, save their money, and pay for the summer college courses.[43]

Hampton and Tuskegee administrators never maintained any illusions as to the purpose of their early work. They were not concerned with preparing black students to compete with white graduates as equals and across the occupational spectrum. Rather, they were preparing black students, very practically, to earn a living in the South and to improve the conditions of life for black southerners in the process. For male students this required, according to the administrators, agricultural or vocational industrial training; for women students it required normal or vocational industrial training. Tuskegee and Hampton did not introduce regular degree-granting college programs until 1927 and 1922, respectively. By then the professionalizing of teacher education and the higher standards of accreditation demanded the reorganization.

Scholastic achievement, whatever its character in time and place, was substantive evidence that the community was rising. But the successful completion of these sometimes rigorous academic programs was not enough to guarantee wage-earning opportunities and important public or leadership roles for the graduates. Beyond college degrees and normal diplomas, the graduate had also to possess good manners and high moral standards. And to whatever extent these were important for the black community in general, they were especially critical for black women because, as one writer in the *Fisk Expositor* noted (and the general public conceded), "The place occupied by woman is said to be the best test of the real advancement of any race or people." Because according to white society slavery had had an even more demoralizing and degrading impact on black women than on black men, all could easily concur that "the future of the colored race in this country depends upon the virtue, intelligence, industry and heroic self-reliance of the women." In 1900 Gertrude Hadnott, a member of Fisk's 1903 class, accepted that view, and she was among a great number of people who believed that the black woman "alone has the power to uproot ignorance, break down prejudice, and solve for us this great race problem."[44]

The widely held view of women as socializers of men and children served to place the burden of changing evil social conditions on those who were least responsible for them. That fact, however, had little impact on the process of and rationale for encouraging a certain type of social behavior among the students in these schools. Teachers and administrators insisted that practicing good manners could affect the esteem others would grant the young professionals after their graduation and therefore enhance their ability to gain paid public positions, if necessary or desirable, and public leadership roles whether paid or not. Practicing good manners might also influence the deportment of people around the graduates and thereby contribute to the uplift of the community. But perhaps even more important, the "good" behavior of the graduates could enhance the community's development because the more upright they were—the school staffs maintained, in accordance with the parents—the more likely it was they could break down the prejudice of white people.

In one form or another, writers regularly expressed the idea that "liberty for the Negro people, already given in name yet long delayed in actual experience, shall be realized when the moral force of educated [black] men and women . . . shall compel the unprejudiced regard of white people. Intelligence, combined with moral excellence and spiritual insight, will surely win the conflict with ignorance and prejudice, irrespective of the different colors of the faces of the contending hosts."[45] The perceptions and behaviors of white people were always important considerations in formulating school programs for black students. But rather than concern themselves with the potential improvement in the behavior of white people, observers rationalized more frequently that black people needed to behave a certain way because "every white man stands on his own merits, but every colored man is acting not for himself, but for his people."[46] If for no other reason than this, students fortunate enough to gain formal higher education had to toe the mark in the process.

Although all these young women arrived at their schools with extensive training in manners and morality, school administrators worked as if they were starting from scratch. Published statements reminded students to remember to say "thank you" and "if you please" when asking or receiving a favor; they were not to be loud in public; they were not to ridicule others; they were not to take the best of anything for themselves but to leave it for elders, parents, teachers, and others in general. Clean teeth, fingernails, and clothes and combed hair were not simply a matter of hygiene but a reflection of good manners. And because the students' every action revealed their manners, good or bad, they learned that "the ways you look, the ways you speak, the ways you act, the ways you move, the ways you eat" should always remain at the forefront of their consciousness.[47] Some schools even sponsored student societies for the purpose of transmitting lessons in good manners.[48]

A few observers, including students, took this everyday concern with courteous behavior to a much higher level. A *Hartshorn-Union Journal* writer remarked that "the very genius of politeness, lies in the fact that we treat every man as if he were perfect." A nineteenth-century writer in the *Spelman Messenger* noted that in public "the truly polite man . . . is quiet, unobtrusive, putting on no airs, nor hinting by word or manner that he deems himself better, richer, or wiser than those about him." Another student equated politeness with integrity. "The loud, the blatant, the arrogant, are never to be trusted." In this student's view, arrogant and ill-mannered persons could only be viewed as selfish; they could not possibly have the interests of the race in mind.[49]

The use of alcohol, tobacco, and profanity were high on the list of unacceptable behaviors, and card playing and gambling were also "immoral or opposed to true culture." School officials sometimes developed hierarchical systems of scale whereby particular offenses "against the welfare and happiness of all" were assigned demerits, and upon accumulating a certain number of them, the student was warned, suspended, or expelled. Students accumulated demerits for any of the offenses listed above, and for stealing, fighting, or violating any of the other rules, designed by school staff in part to allow a close watch on students' activities.[50]

Until the 1920s boarding students had to attend religious services every weekday, and special services on Wednesday evenings and Sundays. School personnel regularly inspected students' rooms for neatness and cleanliness, and they restricted letter writing and "inspected" both incoming and outgoing mail. Administrators designated recreational hours during the week and on Saturdays, but at all other times students were to direct their attention to serious study and service work. They could entertain friends during specific hours on Saturdays only, in public rooms, and with a chaperone (sometimes even when the visitors were of the same sex). No student could leave campus for any reason without permission; girls could leave *only* in the company of one of the "lady teachers"; and students could not travel, even during the holidays, without the written request of their parents. During holidays, if they did not stay on campus, students could remain in the city where the school was located only if it was their home, parental permission notwithstanding. The regimentation that resulted from the elaborate codes of behavior was designed, according to administrators, not to discourage "all spontaneous life and action," but rather "*to develop spontaneous life and energy under self-control.*" In that way, they believed, they could reduce the prevalence of "engines with full head[s] of steam, with no engineer[s] and off the track."[51]

The rigid codes of behavior and other aspects of the schools' administration are often attributed solely to puritanical values among the many white missionary teachers. But parents often shared these traditions and chose these schools precisely because of the discipline enforced there. Finding programs as structured as these gave them and their daughters a kind of insurance against exposure to some of the dangers that black girls faced in less controllable public environments. At these schools, the girls would be substantially insulated from hostile encounters with whites, potential sexual abuse, too early experiments in (hetero)sexuality, and whatever "bad examples" might exist in the communities from which they came. So important were these controls to the parents that when V. W. Barnett, a single parent from Montgomery, Alabama, learned in 1920 that his daughter wanted to come home from Tuskegee because of disagreements with her boardinghouse keeper, Barnett appealed to school administrators to find her a room on the campus because, he noted, "I should not like to have her come home[,] for Montgomery is no place for a motherless girl unless it were possible for her father to be at home." A Fisk parent informed school officials in 1916 that her daughter had been reared in a "somewhat strict home" and that she had too much freedom at Fisk. Thus school administrators' efforts to maintain strict discipline were as much a consequence of parents' interests as a reflection of the missionaries' values or their concern for the public image of the school. But no doubt for all these reasons, whenever a student's behavior did not come up to expected standards, school personnel readily decided to "cast the bad [student] away." The administrators acknowledged that "parents who send unspoiled children away from home into the care of strangers, expect that they will not be thrust into the companionship of those who will lead them into evil. For the sake of the good, the bad must be put away. To save the pure, the corrupt must be rejected."[52]

In the spring of 1920, the beginning of the decade of the general "revolution in morals and manners," Robert R. Moton, principal of Tuskegee Institute, suspended Pricilla Buchanan "for being in company with a young man without permission, and for leaving the dormitory pretending to be going to Bible Class," when she had actually met the man in a classroom and visited with him for five or ten minutes. Moton wrote to inform Buchanan's mother of her daughter's suspension and to request the girl's train fare for her trip home to Washington, D.C. Mrs. Buchanan and her brother tried to convince Moton to reverse the suspension because there were only six weeks left in the term and Mrs. Buchanan did not have the money to send for her daughter. But their pleas fell on deaf ears. Moton subsequently wrote to Pricilla's father in Pittsburgh, instructing him to remit the transportation costs. Pricilla Buchanan had to go. She had broken several important rules of the school, in each instance raising questions about her morality and character. She not only had met alone and secretly with a young man, but also had skipped Bible class, which all students were required to attend, and she had lied to school officials. Any one of those acts was a serious infraction, and together they made her presence at the school intolerable.[53]

It is not clear that Tuskegee officials were harder on women than men when it came to "moral offenses." In fact a male student was suspended in January 1920 for kissing a woman at a New Year's night social. But even lesser offenses committed by women students sometimes resulted in the drastic suspension. For example, Tuskegee officials also discovered in 1920 that Florence Hall was "carrying on indecent correspondence with a young man," and she too suffered immediate suspension. Moton advised her mother simply: "You can understand, I am sure, that we cannot allow young people to remain here who fail to conduct themselves in a proper manner." Not being with the young man, as Pricilla Buchanan had been, did not reduce the seriousness of this offense, for as a Hartshorn staff member noted in 1912, the year Beulah Hester graduated, secret meetings and love notes between male and female students represented the kind of "lovemaking" that "renders high scholarship or lofty character or sound religion impossible." Thus the censoring of incoming and outgoing mail, from the administrators' perspective, was not meddling but a matter of protection.[54]

Parents supported these stringent measures because their daughters' (perhaps also the family's, and sometimes the community's) futures were at stake. The economic sacrifice of the family and sometimes the community, and the hope that they invested in the young women, made it difficult to suffer the failure of the student owing to indiscretion, naïveté, or even self-will. Consequently it was not unusual for parents to encourage this discipline and also to request official reports on how their daughters were holding up under it. Willie Mae Guidry's aunt advised Tuskegee officials to "see that she writes only to homefolks." Mrs. Fobish was paying for her niece's course and therefore assumed the right to point out to the principal, "I don't want her to write to young men as she is not old enough and it may detract her thoughts from her studies." W. H. Drew, of Waverly, Virginia, wrote for an official report on his daughter's progress "in her studies and deportment" because, he added, "I am anxious for her to make good." Parents of Fisk coeds regularly informed the president that their daughters were under no circumstances to receive male company.[55] Coeducational school administrators no doubt felt more pressure than women's school administrators to "guard" the girls intensely, and probably for that reason, Howard University men and women students did not take their meals together until the 1890s, twenty-five years after the school's founding.[56] Talladega College did not hold its first mixed dance until 1928, more than sixty years after its founding, and no doubt even then school officials feared a scandal would result.[57]

That Hartshorn and Spelman were women's schools did not eliminate efforts to control the potential development of (or opportunities for) expressions of heterosexuality. Spelman and Hartshorn were very close to all-male schools, but men and women students did not often socialize together. Spelman students enjoyed socials and other entertainments every Friday night, and only at the end did Morehouse men visit for "a few minutes." When Hartshorn women and Virginia Union University men met for various activities, Hartshorn administrators wrote, "our girls will be cared for, and not subjected to excessive exposure."[58] Administrators at the women's schools defended their watchfulness by saying that "this separate education is not [designed] to secure present safety by an oversight so strict, and a separation from temptation and from the opportunity of evil so complete, that wrong doing becomes impossible." Rather, they sought simply to guide the youngsters through their first encounters with the world beyond their homes.[59]

To help their students behave in ways dictated by the administrators and parents, Spelman and Hartshorn officials urged students to join the White Shield Society, which worked to develop a "purity of heart, which shall manifest itself in conversation, dress, and conduct." The White Shield Pledge required students:

1. To uphold the laws of purity as equally binding upon men and upon women;

2. To be modest in language, behavior and dress;

3. To avoid all conversations, reading, art, and amusements which may put impure thoughts into my mind;

4. To guard the purity of others, especially my companions and friends;

5. To strive after the special blessing promised to the pure in heart.

Hartshorn, officials claimed, had "the Largest White Shield Society in the World."[60]

The White Shield Pledge held each person responsible for her own behavior and that of her friends. But whether or not the young girl could control the behavior of those she encountered, she had to know how to recognize "bad company" and keep away from it. Fisk University officials encouraged their students at the start of the 1888 school term to cultivate strong self-will and not to be negatively influenced by people around them.[61] Hartshorn administrators took a more positive approach by publicly announcing that some of the hometown friends of their students would no longer associate with them because the students had come under the influence of Hartshorn discipline. The administrators also boasted of "the power of their straight-laced" girls.[62] But Hartshorn officials also offered practical advice similar to that offered at Fisk. On the importance of good company, good habits, and good character, one administrator wrote: "The young person who begins the year with the determination to keep clear of all bad company and to seek the company of the best, and only the best, is starting on the up grade. . . . He who puts good habits and good character and a good conscience before money or pleasure or show is walking the upward road."[63]

The white administrators, in particular, believed that their ultimate success in developing black students' leadership abilities depended on having total control over their students' lives. For that reason many educators expressed a decided preference for boarding rather than day students because it was not possible to control "the habits and associations" of those who lived at home. One missionary teacher lamented, "It is with heavy hearts [that] we often times watch our scholars returning to their homes in the evenings, for we know that there everything tends to overthrow the religious teaching received during the day." Anna Cahill, a Fisk University faculty member, concluded that the only solution to the "depraved" condition of the black woman was to "take her early away from the home . . . [and] transplant her to as good a Christian home as our schools will afford." Faculty at all the schools believed it was important to "educate . . . the youth away from their old associations," but some, like Atlanta University officials, were more subtle and perhaps more sensitive to the students' family responsibilities and economic abilities. Atlanta University regulations simply required every student to "spend at least one year in the school family [on campus], where day after day he [sic] may come into friendly association with other students and with the teachers." The teachers, the writer reminded the readers, were products of the best training available anywhere.[64] Tuskegee officials were even more practical. They were simply grateful for whatever time they controlled their students. Tuskegee staff people did not worry about boarding or nonboarding status and were glad when students enrolled even for one term because, most agreed, even a little exposure to their program was better than none.

Obviously the teachers regularly overestimated their own importance and underestimated parental influence on the good behavior demonstrated by these students, who for the most part arrived at the schools with values not terribly different from those held by the teachers themselves. Chlora White, an Atlanta University graduate, and probably other students too, reminded her educational mentors that "the principles of right were very early taught around my mother's fireside" and that they were only "nourished . . . by those whole souled philanthropic instructors under whose care I was placed."[65] But school officials nevertheless worked as if the students' only hope was the rigorous discipline enforced at the school. And as long as the young woman was at school, administrators enforced all the rules, including those designed to protect the student from public white harassment and those designed purely to maintain order on campus. In some instances students were subject to the school rules even when off campus and when school was not in session.[66]

The extensive regulations also covered the way students dressed. While making the point that cleanliness and neatness were much more important than cost and style, school officials were determined to make certain that their students dressed sensibly and "tastefully," because they knew that people's appearance sometimes made a statement about them before they could speak or act themselves.[67] School rules ranged from establishing a strict dress code that required uniforms to elaborate regulations detailing what clothes were not acceptable. Wherever the individual school fell along the spectrum, administrators wanted their students to be seen as cultured from the moment their presence was noticed.

Tuskegee Institute students had to wear uniforms. This regulation addressed a number of concerns. First, it helped reduce the expense of schooling for the parents, many of whom were quite poor. Uniforms might also have protected the students when they were in town, if white residents granted them a higher status than that generally accorded to local black citizens. As long as students were in their uniforms, school administrators could spot them in an instant if they were off campus without permission. And importantly, uniforms (and quasi-uniforms) often reflected a very conscious effort on the part of school administrators to reduce the obvious evidence of class differences among their students.[68]

Hartshorn officials did not include detailed clothing regulations in their catalogs. About the most they ever said was in the 1925–26 issue: "Students should dress for health and comfort, and not for show. Special dresses for special occasions are not necessary. This Institution does not wish to encourage expensive dressing." Since there had been no such statement in the nineteenth-century catalogs, this admission, such as it was, was probably a precaution taken to counter the influence of 1920s women's fashions, which emphasized flamboyance and sensuality.[69] In the intervening years, however, an occasional article appeared in the *Union Journal* that focused on how a Christian woman should dress. "Dress reveals character," one such article announced. It condemned vanity as selfish and flash as frivolous. The author acknowledged that it was wise to dress so as to flatter the body and conceal imperfections, but after a mention of the popularity of corsets, the Hartshorn article warned readers that any woman who dressed in a way that could injure her health was "unfit for grave responsibilities."[70]

Spelman College administrators, on the other hand, after considering but not instituting uniforms in the early 1890s, persisted in detailing an elaborate dress code until the 1920s. They urged the parents of the students to support their efforts to eliminate extravagance and to "develop a taste for simple, suitable, and healthful clothing" in their daughters. They recommended clothing that was "quiet in color, style and material." "Loud, inharmonious colors, extreme styles, and inappropriate materials are always in poor taste." They insisted that "cultured and virtuous" women did not wear "much jewelry, cheap jewelry, clothing that is injurious to health, and showy and immodest styles and materials." Spelman students had to wear lace-up oxfords or similar buttoned shoes. They could wear only "strong [thick], black cotton stockings." Special school programs required "plain white cotton waists and dark skirts" or white wash dresses with no fancy trim. And probably also to demonstrate taste, culture, and modesty, students could not wear "thin crepe or silk, net, lace, all-over embroidery, or any other transparent waists." Skirts could not "be too short or too narrow, and necks are to be high enough to avoid any appearance of immodesty." Graduating seniors could have one special reception dress, and the president had to approve it. It would not receive approval unless it met all the criteria above. Not until the late 1920s was the dress code at Spelman so simple that students had some personal choice about what they would wear—as long as their choices conformed to what the school staff defined as good taste.[71]

Given the economic, political, and social strife that the black community faced between the late nineteenth century and the 1930s, all this attention to clothing might seem inane.[72] But in the minds of teachers and administrators (and parents too) the actual appearance that these women made could help or hurt them in their efforts to establish themselves as community leaders and to address large community problems. The future professionals could never expect to convey the values they wanted the larger population to adopt if they did not "look the part" themselves. The administrators believed they needed to eliminate the preferences of the "less cultured" for fancy clothes and bright colors (which, significantly, many were not allowed to wear as slaves and subsequently were unable to purchase as cash-poor recently freed men and women). Where the administrators were not fighting actual preferences, they hoped to defy stereotypes that white people regularly held about black people.[73] In the most extreme situations, "tasteful" appearance, "dignified" carriage, and "cultured" bearing—along with good manners and high morals—might save the young professional's life. More likely, however, such conditions would regularly spare her from routine insults, such as being called "auntie" by some unknown white person. And equally important, when these students assumed their professional positions in the black community, plain dressing would help mask the sometimes great economic gap between them and their clients.

The schooling process that many black professional women undertook at least through the 1930s went far beyond the pursuit of academic courses. The reinforcement of good manners and high moral standards, a "cultured" appearance, and Christian character was just as much a part of being prepared for leadership, and many school officials believed it was more important. It also bears repeating that the purpose of the schools was not merely to create a body of individuals who would achieve success by the material standards of the day. Whether they eventually commanded a good steady income or not, the graduates would be better situated to gain individual acceptance by the white society. And perhaps more important, women who established themselves as learned and respectable people would be better able to create the circumstances that would allow them to bring the rest of the community along. The graduates could, in effect, become part of the "highway through [the] wilderness" by which others could travel in their journeys toward individual self-sufficiency and, as a group, toward community development.[74]

• • •

Supporters of the higher education of black women regularly hailed the development of a "new and improved type of womanhood" that was destined to change the course of the race. And the prognosticators expected that by undertaking broad educational programs that went beyond academics, these students would become representatives of that "new" style. The Reverend T. J. Morgan, writing for the widely circulated Baptist *Home Mission Monthly* and hoping to create broad sentiment in favor of this educational mission, reminded his readers, including the students, that the women he described—the type of women the students should be—possessed an "enlarged capacity for culture, a truer self-consciousness, a keener sensitiveness, purer and loftier aspirations, and greater possibilities of achievement."[75] He believed that people who possessed those traits were different from the masses, and that was precisely his prescription for preparing young black women to work to the best advantage of the larger group.

The moralizing and proselytizing through which the educators conveyed the importance of culture and character development regularly helped both to join the students with and to set them apart from the people they would ultimately work to serve. In fact the language the administrators used to make their points about scholarship, manners, and morals did not in itself distinguish these students from the larger black community. The point was that those who studied hard, accepted the indoctrination, and practiced the preaching *would* become distinguishable from the masses and perhaps even become their leaders.[76] Still, although these women's schooling could easily encourage community (class) divisiveness, because the rhetoric was so profoundly rooted in the service-oriented missionary tradition, or in "talented-tenth" doctrine from the perspective of the black community, the women could just as easily remain community oriented.[77] This mixed message—rendering a person part of and apart from the group— bombarded the women from several directions. Missionary benefactors pushed it. Official school publications and programs reinforced it. And visiting lecturers drove the message home.

"The race must be lifted up . . . by leaders who are on a higher level—lifted from above—as every race has been that has risen to higher civilization," insisted a *University Journal* writer. According to a Spelman student, as long as they remembered "to have regard to the masses rather than to the classes," they could maintain their connectedness to the larger group, and by this process their work efforts could be most successful. "You cannot expect to have much influence over one whom you look down upon," Atlanta University's president reminded the 1911 graduating class. "If you are by your work of the brains to help make life worth living you must heartily respect and honor the workers with the arms who make life possible."[78]

At a time when most Americans over eighteen years old were not high-school graduates, vanity and self-absorption could certainly develop among those who accomplished more, but regular advice encouraged the students to overcome such perils in the process of attaining that education. "Privilege must always be translated into terms of responsibility, or else it will become shackles to your feet and chains to your hands," the Right Reverend Charles H. Brent told a group of Howard University students in 1910. "The very moment privilege comes to us," he added, "we ought to use it so that it will be a benefit to others."[79] One visitor advised Spelman students not to allow their education to make them selfish, aloof examples of "superficial and unworthy dilettantism." They could either finish school, go home, and become, in the words of the Reverend J. C. Austin of Chicago, "the belle of the town and have every one looking up to [them]" or, he told the young women in 1928, they could return to their hometowns and "be of as much service to all as possible." Students were to "feel the pressure of that responsibility for others which your education has distinctly placed upon you." The Reverend Samuel V. V. Holmes put Atlanta University's 1912 graduating class on notice: "Your culture is not a pedestal upon which you may stand to invite the admiration of the crowd, but an instrument by means of which to serve your community." Invoking a biblical parable, he added, "It is the leaven with which you are privileged to leaven and sweeten the communities." In short, the graduates had to "roll up [their] sleeves, gather [their] knowledge, and get down to the task of lifting that man" who dwelled "in the most profound depths." To do this work most effectively, one writer advised them to "throw off all shackles of egotism."[80]

Students undoubtedly felt the tension inherent in balancing their individual advantages against perceived community responsibilities. But transcending class and status differences was not necessarily difficult. In addition to their earlier socialization in homes and communities that encouraged social responsibility, many of the women came from families who could afford their daughters' education largely because the schools provided "self-help" (later called work-study) opportunities.[81] Moreover, for a time the schools themselves were so poor that they could stay open only because the students' own contributions were so extensive.

Most of these schools first met in church basements, in private homes, or in abandoned Civil War military hospitals and army barracks; and in the early years the students bore as much responsibility for developing the physical plants as did missionary societies and local people.[82] The Jubilee Singers, for example, a student chorale, raised money for Fisk University, and beginning in the 1870s, not only financed the construction of several major buildings but also saved the school from bankruptcy. During Tuskegee's early history, male students (with supervision) built all campus buildings, and women students helped raise funds for the construction materials and subsequent maintenance. Students at Spelman contributed to the "Improvement Fund," which financed the school's heating system, sidewalks, and classroom building repairs. And in nearly all the schools students sold items made in "fancy needlework" classes to support the institutions.[83]

This important student labor was the schools' first and most dependable endowment. It not only allowed the advancement of the schools, but it also taught students in a very practical, though sometimes exhausting, manner how important individual efforts were to the development and maintenance of the community. In the early years students carried wood and coal for heating and cooking, lit the fires in fireplaces and stoves, and removed the ashes from them. Across time, they cleaned all the public areas of the school—dining halls, kitchens, lounges, and classrooms—and also the rooms of the teachers who lived on campus. They prepared and served the meals, and where the schools provided the students' linen, they helped in the laundry rooms. Beyond the drudge work, however—the sweeping, mopping, dusting, bed making, washing, and ironing—students also provided services to the schools and their classmates that equipped them with important marketable skills that could, in the future, be more highly remunerated than housework. At Hampton they made the uniforms that other students purchased more cheaply than similar items available in the public markets. And at all the schools, students staffed the printing offices and produced school stationery, catalogs, campus newspapers, and other subscription publications.[84]

Even after the institutions became more financially stable and less dependent on student labor for their survival, school administrators maintained programs to ensure that students continue to think of the community. They did this in part by continuing to require all students to work on campus at least one hour a day without pay. This compulsory labor saved the school some expenses in wage labor and thereby saved the parents from having to pay higher tuition. It helped discipline the students to work whether they wanted to or not and to work at tasks that might not please them should it become necessary in the future. Equally important, school administrators intended that this hour of manual labor reinforce the idea of the dignity of all honest work, with the aim of encouraging respect for those who performed manual labor. The symbolic and actual importance of the campus work, however, was in providing a model for developing and maintaining a community beyond the campus grounds.

School administrators judged the success of their programs by "the services rendered to the people of the communities where these young folks go to live and labor."[85] And since they judged success not only by the number of graduates produced or the school's own relationship to the black community, but also by the future work of the students, the students had to be fully prepared to take up community work upon graduation. Since evidence indicates that many students arrived at their schools with this knowledge and experience, in some cases the schooling process only reinforced the connections between them and the larger community. But whether the student already possessed this orientation or not, the schooling process for encouraging it also demonstrated a work ethic that was collective. It concerned not simply the individual gains that would come as a consequence of having more knowledge, better manners, high morals, and good character, but also the group advancement that would ensue as the women put that total education to proper use. To whatever extent the traditional aspects of their schooling made these women different from the black communities from which they came, such a work ethic as this would help keep them in touch— even if from above.[86]

Rhetorically, this idea was easily and frequently imparted. Official American Missionary Association resolutions on the development of Hampton Institute, for example, noted that the school would not train "teachers as to put them out of sympathy" with the people of their communities. Mary Tefft, conscious of Hartshorn's goals beyond educating individuals, wrote, "It seems very necessary that these girls, who plan to work for their people in years to come, be . . . kept in touch with those for whom they are to labor." And during a commencement address at Tuskegee, Channing Tobias, then senior secretary of the Colored Work Department of the YMCA, encouraged the students not to allow any set of circumstances "to dim within you the consciousness of your national family status."[87] School administrators insisted that their students' success or failure depended "not so much on how well they have mastered the subject mater [sic] required of them" but on "their willingness to make themselves a part of the great life with which we shall find ourselves surrounded."[88] School programs allowed extensive opportunities for applying these day-to-day lessons, and more often than not this practical application took the form of working, without pay, among the people who lived in areas surrounding the schools.

All of the student organizations were at first service organizations, and even after the development of academic clubs and Greek sororities, service organizations remained a central part of the students' experience. Hartshorn Memorial College, from its founding in 1883 until its college program was transferred to Virginia Union University in 1928, sponsored two missionary organizations. Members of the Rachel Hartshorn Education and Missionary Society raised money to furnish rooms in school buildings and to support black women missionaries in Africa.[89] The Hartshorn Home Workers worked in the city.

Members of the Hartshorn Home Workers canvassed the city of Richmond on Sunday afternoons, visiting the sick and poor, reading the Bible to area residents, praying with them, enrolling and teaching the children in Sunday school, and distributing food and clothing. A few years after the organization's founding, members began volunteering at the city almshouse, where they performed similar work. And by 1900 they had organized a weekday program in which they taught community boys and girls to sew. In all these venues, students also provided lessons in temperance and morality.[90] Hartshorn Home Workers did their work so well that they eventually had to stop making appointments for home visits because some people began to leave home or not answer the door if they learned in advance that the Home Workers, in particular, members of the prayer meeting committee, were coming.[91] Other families, however, found the "alley school" classes taught in their backstreet homes by Hartshorn students to be a blessing.[92]

All the schools had comparable campus organizations. The Circle of King's Daughters, which existed at most of the schools, was a public benevolent organization, and at Hampton "every girl upon entering the school [automatically became] a member."[93] Christian Endeavor societies existed on every campus at various times up to the 1940s, and student members raised money to pay the tuition and fees of their neediest classmates, bought food and clothing for those in need in the larger community, made "plain garments" and quilts for inmates at local reformatories, and taught community children in Sunday school and secular school programs.[94] During Christian holiday seasons, regardless of the organization, students intensified their efforts.[95]

The students' work in the community was sometimes a formal part of their coursework and thus required for graduation. Hampton Institute might have surpassed the other schools at this in that by the early 1910s it offered a formal program called Training in Community Work that was designed to prepare students to address "the perplexing and almost unsolvable problems" that would confront them upon graduation. The program description also promised to "prepare the students to relate their special work to the needs of the communities in which they are to live." Students in the Training in Community Work program took classes in education, economics, sociology, religion, literature, and science. They also had to perform "actual work in the neighborhood, in homes and gardens, in night schools, clubs, churches, and other helpful social activities." Administrators reorganized the program between 1913 and 1915, and it appeared in 1915 as two fields of study: Religious and Social Services Training and Neighborhood Work. The programs placed the students in community Sunday school classes, jails, poorhouses, old people's homes, and other "public" institutions. School officials expected that "the majority of the students at some time in their course [would] help in this work" whether or not it was their major field of study. And some version of this neighborhood work remained among the school's programs for the next ten years.[96]

Fisk administrators had always expected their students to work as volunteers in the local community, but upon establishing a social science department in 1910, they extended the scope of that community work. Students in the social science department at first assisted at a local settlement house as part of their degree requirements. By the end of the next decade, the school supported a community training center for church workers. And ten years later Fisk operated its own community settlement house with a "People's College" for adult education as well as a "Children's Institute." By the 1940s Fisk faculty had developed a rural-life program to train rural residents to lead in the development of their communities. One important result of the work was the establishment in 1946 of a rural leadership school in Hardeman County, Tennessee, where groups of Fisk students alternated working for six weeks at a time.[97]

Tuskegee's community work programs were an integral part of the whole school's campus life. To take one example, by the early 1920s small groups of students took turns living in the Rising Star Model School for community adults, a five-room house located near Tuskegee's farm. The students were responsible for maintaining the house, the yard, and the gardens while also keeping up with their academic work. Moreover, the programs developed around the Rising Star Model School included a six-, seven-, or eight-week night school, depending on when the harvest season ended, in which the students, with the help of professional staff members, taught community people farming and home-improvement techniques. Unlike dormitory rooms, the Model School house never functioned as a private residence for the students who lived there; it was a community center dedicated to public programs all year.[98]

Because of the likelihood of their working in extremely neglected rural areas when they left school, normal students at Tuskegee were prepared much more extensively than prospective teachers in other programs. The school's Rural Extension Program took students off the campus very early in their educational careers, and through it male students and faculty helped people in the surrounding area to build schools while women teachers and students helped organize local people into clubs to maintain and extend the work that would take place in those newly built schools. Practically from its founding until an adequate public school system existed in the region surrounding Tuskegee Institute, the school offered basic education courses, including literacy classes, five nights a week, on the campus and off; students taught these classes. Tuskegee Mothers' Clubs involved Institute teachers and students in work with community women for the improvement of "their homes, moral life, and in the general upbuilding of the community through the school and the church." Tuskegee's Health Center, instituted in 1921, was open on the weekends for free public lectures, and though students were not part of the center staff, they were responsible for the Girls' Health Club and the Boys' Health Club, auxiliary programs established for the same purposes. The Moveable School, a mobile unit for which Tuskegee gained national acclaim, traveled throughout the county carrying an agricultural expert, a social worker, and a public health nurse. They addressed a variety of community concerns and provided students with another important example of reaching out to the community to work wherever their labor was needed.[99]

Atlanta's Gate City Free Kindergarten Association, which by 1912 included five institutions throughout the city, developed out of Atlanta University's Oglethorp Practice School (kindergarten through eighth grade), where normal students completed their practice teaching.[100] University personnel had always been involved in community development efforts, but in the 1910s the school's Board of Trustees issued a formal statement urging the staff to use every opportunity "to correlate its work with the needs of the community." After that announcement, normal school courses continued to provide basic content and pedagogy, but they also gave special attention to "problems peculiar to the common schools of the south." Faculty reorganized all history and sociology courses to focus on the economics, history, and social condition of African Americans. Sociology courses subsequently required "lab work"—fieldwork in the black community—and students' theses addressed the history, current conditions, and development of black people and their communities.[101]

The organization of community work took on similar formal structures even though the schools were in demographically different environments. The area around Tuskegee Institute (Macon County, Alabama, and its environs), for example, although in better shape than comparable rural southern counties because of the presence of the school, still showed the ravages of being a neglected black-belt county in terms of public services. But Hampton, though some might have considered it the hinterland of Norfolk or Newport News, was not an isolated settlement. Yet Hampton Institute's community work program not only was extensive but also had been institutionalized for some time before it was possible to pursue a degree in social work in most schools. Fisk and Atlanta Universities and Spelman and Hartshorn Colleges were in three of the South's most populous cities. Their students too engaged in similar public work, though in the case of Hartshorn and Spelman it was intensive rather than extensive. Thus, notwithstanding the contemporary and subsequent debates between advocates of classical education and vocational programs, both types of schools shared this public mission. Black communities were to benefit from the existence of these schools, and people everywhere were to profit from the training of the students as they spread out over the country to live and to work.[102]

Many of the students tested the effectiveness of their education before graduation, by teaching during the summer in rural schools. Credentialing standards for teaching there were lower than most urban school requirements, and until the 1920s many rural schools regularly met only in the summers. Thus normal and college students were particularly able to take advantage of this situation. Equally important, since the salaries for students were lower than those offered to fully credentialed teachers, local administrators were eager to use the students. Those who sought summer school positions usually needed the money to continue their formal schooling in the fall, but school administrators still solicited full reports from them as if the work were a required course. Sparing few details, they used those reports to teach other students a great deal about the field of work that awaited their arrival.

Summer school teaching provided students a more authentic practicum for future public sphere work than student teaching in campus model schools. Away from the campus, students could not so easily control their work routine or environment. One Atlanta University coed arrived at her school to find an open grave in front of it, with a drawing of a coffin and a note advising her to "leave the place within an hour and a half," which she wisely did. Other students had no problem taking up their work, but they battled local landowners to get children in school, because in the cotton districts, reported one teacher, "every child that can must work." Still others, after having performed the work, fought school commissioners for their wages, often paid in vouchers that could not be redeemed for cash until some later date. Students regularly sold them at a loss in order to have school tuition in September. They all struggled to compensate for inadequate buildings and supplies (if they existed at all) and too little time with the students to do enough good. But whether they would eventually work in the North or the South, in rural or urban communities, in common school classrooms or social settlement houses or public health institutions, they were bound to find facilities, supplies, and salaries that were grossly inferior to those provided in comparable white communities. Consequently, the reports of making nothing into something (wood planks into blackboards), of plying a trade as if nothing mattered except finishing the job one undertook (even if one did not get paid), and of performing work for which one was not hired (because someone had to do it) were arrestingly prophetic.[103]

If after academic courses, school community work, summer wage work, and the general spirit of service that enveloped the entire educational process there were any doubts as to the work these women were being trained to do, school officials had one more strategy. They solicited reports from former students and graduates about their endeavors, reported them in school publications, and used them in various ways to keep the enrolled students mindful of the fullness of their future responsibilities.[104]

Sometimes the accounts were short and simple. Perhaps the point was simply to encourage those still enrolled to use every possible means to keep at their studies. In 1883 students at Fisk learned that "after a pleasant year's labor at Corinth, Mississippi, [in order to afford her schooling] Miss Bracker is again in school." Leonora Bowers was teaching near Nashville in 1888, and "as her school is only a few miles from the city, she, through the kindness of the professors, comes in on Saturday and recites her lessons." Mabel Chase, more fortunate than some of her "sisters," had graduated from Fisk and been admitted to the Music Conservatory at Oberlin College. And G. P. Williams, who graduated in 1895, was teaching in Evansville, Indiana, in 1896 and was reported to be "very dignified" in her work.[105]

Soon the accounts of former students' activities became more consistently extensive as school officials threw aside all semblance of subtlety. Sallie Waugh McBryan, who had graduated from Freedmen's Hospital (Howard University) after leaving Spelman, reported that she spent the next several years nursing "in white families for a living, and among the colored poor for the good I could do." Ida (Burton) Jones graduated from Spelman in 1891, was married, and had two children by 1897. The reporter noted that her "two daughters speak well for their training, even though the mother's time has had to be divided between home cares and the needs of the community." Selena Sloan, of Spelman's 1888 class, taught until 1893, at which time she married. Since that time, the reporter noted,

Temperance, health, Sunday School and church work, free kindergarten, social purity, parent-teacher clubs, in fact, every kind of movement for the betterment of her race [has been] worthy to receive her encouragement and aid. Her latest effort is teaching in the public night school where hard-working men and women, who have not had their chance, are now receiving the inspiration and help of a woman who is there because of the good she can do.[106]

Similar accounts were passed on to coeds at other schools. Editors of the *Southern Letter* always solicited reports from former Tuskegee students, and in 1897 Bessie T. Roane wrote back that she arrived home (at the end of the school term) on May 28, Friday evening, began work on Monday, May 31, and did not stop working for thirty days except for Sundays. Miss R. A. Mickle, an 1878 graduate of the Normal Department at Fisk, was teaching in Marion, Alabama, in 1885, and Sunday was no day off for her. She taught school during the week, conducted Sunday school for children and adults, and was involved daily in the work of converting souls. Mrs. J. A. Tyson, who graduated from Tuskegee in 1885, spent 1906 teaching and helping to raise money—to build a church, to buy an acre of land for a school, to build the school, and to insure it for $500. The church and the school building were fully functional when the Tuskegee report appeared.[107] Abbie Smarr Woodward (Spelman 1890) had married and had several children by 1901. But Spelman administrators boasted: "Besides caring for a family of little ones, she has taught school eleven years, and has made herself busy in all Christian work, being assistant superintendent of the Sunday

School, Bible class teacher, president of the Education Society, and Secretary of the Epworth League."[108] These and other graduates were also passing out whitewash and paint to get "the homes of the people . . . up to the place where they could be." They were boarding students in their homes so the youngsters could attend school. They were cleaning up public property around the schools and planting trees, shrubs, and flowers. And they were organizing their own students to undertake all manner of family and community work. They were, in the words of one woman, keeping after the people all the time.[109]

Clearly, some of the schools' graduates were fulfilling the mission of their education in ways that no doubt made their teachers proud. When Spelman faculty members visited one of their graduates in 1908 to see that she was living up to her charge, seventy pupils lined up in front of the cottage to meet them, and the teacher (the former student) was standing on the porch. After exchanging greetings, they all marched into the school "to the beat of a tiny drum." All the students were from the rural community and yet, the visitors marveled, their "books, pads, and pencils were not lacking, nor was there one untidily dressed." Inside the schoolroom, "the floor was scrupulously clean; the windows were glazed; there was a fire in the hearth." The teacher taught regular school during the week and Sunday school besides. She had sent several girls to Spelman for more extensive education so that they could better "help the community." And though this was a "government school" (public school), black people in the community paid for the (unspecified) extension of the term. They had also bought the land on which the building stood and were raising money to build or buy a better schoolhouse. This teacher, the Spelman representatives reported, was "loved by her people and held in respect and favor by the white residents of the town." As she had "identified herself with the life of the community for over eighteen years," she was doing all she had been trained to do.[110]

• • •

It was nearly impossible for Janie Porter Barrett to leave Hampton Institute with the same tired attitude with which she had arrived because the program there was explicitly designed to prepare her not only to become self-sufficient but also to work for the race. Unlike Barrett, however, many of these women knew when they left their homes that they were on a mission. The mission involved self-development *and* racial advancement. Their families and community members, by example and by instruction, had already made it clear that they should prepare to assume broad social responsibilities whether or not they earned an income, and in addition to domestic responsibilities if necessary. And ultimately, after the total educational process these women underwent in their homes, communities, and schools, they would have shamed everyone involved if they had done anything less than all they could after graduation to serve the larger community. Some of their schools were located within sight of old slave pens and auction blocks, and their teachers reminded them of that fact. Even beyond 1900, entire graduating classes were composed of children of formerly enslaved women and men. Therefore the graduates represented the future and the hope of the race. If ever they weakened in their struggle to achieve the education made available to them or in the work they subsequently undertook, they were encouraged to pray not to have easier lives but to be stronger women; not "for tasks equal to [their] powers," but "for powers equal to [their] tasks."[111] Their schooling had prepared them for some of the worst of circumstances, and if, in the midst of it all, the grand objectives of their education escaped them, they could at least gain inspiration from the example of their missionary teachers, whose sacrifices had been as great as theirs would be.[112]

By the 1930s, however, several important changes were under way in the schooling process for the women of this book. One of the changes concerned where they pursued their professional or higher education. They more consistently gained access to public white schools; they regained access to the private white schools that others had attended before the turn of the century; and more women pursued their studies in black public schools as well. In short, beginning in the 1930s the choices made by these women and their families about schooling fit no particular pattern (until one examines their graduate education).

There were other important changes as well. The "new Negro," not necessarily of the type the missionary teachers regularly announced would develop as result of their programs, had fully evolved, and the post-1920 students reflected this. They rebelled against the rigid discipline, unacceptable food, courses they believed were irrelevant, excessive work details, and the fact that most of their teachers and administrators (except at Tuskegee and Howard) were white. Unlike their predecessors, who were perhaps too grateful for their opportunities to protest the less-than-desirable conditions that often came with them, students enrolling during and after the 1920s more regularly expected and demanded something different.[113] It is safe to say that by this time the communities from which they came were doing the same.[114]

These later students were not necessarily less committed to social responsibility than earlier students had been, but they were much more independent. With more knowledge of, if not direct connections to, post–World War I race riots, Garveyism, and the Harlem Renaissance, their view of the purpose of formal schooling was somewhat different from their predecessors' in at least one regard. They insisted that their teachers teach them *how* to think rather than *what* to think.[115] Details from the life of Clara Stanton Jones, who enrolled at Spelman College during the 1930s, suggest that they were still being told by their families and communities that they were getting their education for the benefit of the race, but they were no longer willing to accept the old evangelical program in its specifics. It would no longer be sufficient for school administrators to teach them to use their education and positions to "leaven" the rest of the communities with a view also to gaining favor with white citizens. "Proving" their worthiness to white society, an important basis of the early school programs, was not, in the main, these students' concern. They were inclined to *expect* more equitable treatment for their communities and responsible mainstream positions for themselves from the beginning.

But as was true for those earlier women students who paved the way, the schooling process—including coursework, character development, and community work—still saturated the later graduates of traditionally black colleges with the importance of socially responsible individualism and of *earning* a favorable place in the American mainstream. It was a process that did not operate differently from their upbringing to that point; it simply reinforced the traditions set forth in families and communities, which encouraged self-development, high achievement, community consciousness, and social responsibility. Upon graduation, these women were simply more able than before to "achieve greatly," to "watch their standards grow," and to "bear [their] womanly responsibilities."[116] The real test of the effectiveness of these combined efforts at socialization, however, was yet to come.

Epilogue to Part One

"And right here comes danger for the young student. Conscious that he [*sic*] has been well prepared and that many others have not been so well trained, unless he is well-poised, unless he is fortified with the strength of character and sense of relative values which make *all other things equal* [to] the breadth of his mental horizon, he is likely to conclude that there is but one position he can fill and do justice to his superior training and that is the position of leader.

"But let us not deceive ourselves. This young graduate is not yet a leader, although he has been prepared to win leadership; indeed, it may be that under stress of the trial to which the world will subject him, it will be proven that he has within himself none of the heart qualities which with mental equipment make leadership possible. He is a carpenter with a splendid kit of tools in his hand, but he has not yet builded a house; a sculptor with chisel and marble, but he has carved no statue; a painter with subject, brush, paint, and canvas, but he has painted no picture; a musician with organ and score before him, but he has produced no deathless symphony; a physician in the midst of his laboratory and theories, but he has snatched no dying patient from the power of the grave. As the Lord liveth, . . . we shall not follow him until he has builded a house, carved a statue, painted a picture, played his symphony, or made the dying to live again; and until he does some of these things, he must be content to march in the ranks with us.

"More than this: if he build a house or paint his picture or sing a song that we may call him great, although we followed him yesterday, we shall forsake his lead tomorrow; for we follow no leader, permanently, who believes himself entitled to our homage. . . .

"When we say, therefore, that the purpose of the college and the university is to train leaders, we do not mean that we are seeking to train a body of scholars who 'love the uppermost rooms at the feasts' . . . but we are striving, rather, to prepare scholars like Saul of Tarsus, who [asked] . . . 'Lord, what wilt thou have me do?' And this question means a willingness to serve wherever and in whatever capacity service for the common good is needed, whether giving commands or obeying them."

From Isaac Fisher, "Training for Leadership—What Is Meant by the Phrase," *Fisk University News* 8 (1917): 1–6, Constance Fisher Papers, Tuskegee University Archives, Hollis Burke Frissell Library, Tuskegee, Alabama. Isaac Fisher was director of publications at Fisk University when this article appeared. Constance C. Fisher, his daughter, was a professional social worker from 1924 to 1978.

PART TWO

What a Woman Ought to Do

"About this time, I began to consider what hopes I had for my people. As an educator who could slightly influence a few conditions for Negroes especially in my county, I began to consider the problems seriously. My philosophy about this matter is still developing. But my attitudes concerning racial issues began then to be crystallized. Before, they had been vague. I had realized that my people suffered, were discriminated against and were often treated brutally and even lynched. I faced discrimination daily and had occasionally been shocked and hurt by incidents which happened to me. But I "wore the world as a loose garment," took practically nothing seriously for long stretches, and enjoyed idealistic and rather barren academic mental gymnastics. I had paid slight attention formerly to racial matters in light of my doing something about it. But Jeanes work sobered me. I began to think as a responsible adult. It brought me face to face with matters which challenged me. I began to develop a sense of social responsibility.

"After working with suppressed and cheated tenant farmers, knowing of their thwarted longings and realizing their hopelessness, a great desire took shape within me to help people of the rural South. I attended conferences in and out of the state of Georgia. I heard issues discussed. I began to weigh the issues for myself. I did not worry too much so that I hesitated to do "first things" before I *decided* on my philosophical stand. There were too many elemental things which needed to be done regardless of what I believed. People needed food, shelter, education, fuel, sanitation, clothes, and other things, whatever philosophy anyone had. However, as I planned to help on elemental phases, I soon realized that the *how* of getting such things was definitely a part of my philosophy. So I had to come to grips with it.

"What did I want for my people and how did I want to help them? I wanted them to acquire some economic security. I wanted to help them acquire education which would enable them to choose and to achieve in fields of work and in sections of the country best suited to their economic and social needs and their talents and interests. I wanted to avoid helping them in any way or encouraging others to help them in ways which developed or increased their dependence on paternalistic treatment. I wanted to see them given a chance to live as adults and I wanted to help them to be ready to so live when the opportunity came and to help hasten its coming. I wanted to do things which would hasten the acceptance by government of its responsibility in connection with Negroes, especially in the South. (I could not, however, accept the tenet of having a group doing altogether without certain necessities until the responsibility was accepted by these agencies. . . .) I wanted to help my people and myself in particular develop an understanding of our race and its fitting into the scheme of things which would give us a faith and pride in ourselves so that we could accept ourselves and others as being Negroes—Negroid—without being apologetic about it. Other beliefs took form also but these sort of guided my actions as I worked with my people."

From Catherine J. Watkins Duncan, "An Autobiography," MSS, b. 409, Rosenwald Fund Foundation Papers, Fisk University Library, Special Collections, Nashville Tennessee. This autobiography was not written as a part of an application for Rosenwald Fund fellowships. Instead, Duncan wrote it more than a decade after having held two Rosenwald fellowships and after becoming so well known for her work in rural black communities that the Foundation officials asked her to write it for them. The paragraph breaks above may not be consistent with Duncan's organization.

"I am teaching school here . . . [but] I find it rather hard . . . with my housekeeping": PRIVATE SPHERE WORK

As children, many of these women were given to moaning and moping and wringing their hands about having to perform domestic chores, but parents pushed them to master the tasks anyway, and at least through the 1920s, their teachers cut no corners in this regard either. They lived at a time when gender roles were tightly prescribed, and neither intense personal desire nor exceptional individual ability in other areas excused many of them from carrying out household routines.[1] They were also women who had learned that their communities deserved as much of their attention as their families. The support they received to go out of their homes and to work for the race made no small difference in their having the ability to perceive these public and private ventures as complementary rather than contradictory. As they took their places in the professional world or continued their pursuit of professional training, they regularly received reassurances that they were following the correct path.

"We shall expect great things from you when you return," Booker T. Washington wrote to his daughter Portia in 1906, after she had settled into her routine as a music student in Germany. "Greatness," however relative the term, was a general expectation of those whose advantages had been as abundant as these women's. Just after Constance Fisher accepted her first job as a social worker in 1924, her father sent her money for clothes—clothes befitting her new professional status. He wrote for himself and her mother: "We are with you in your determination to 'look the part,' since you are so determined, also, to act the part of the fine woman we have wanted you so much to be." Charlemae Hill Rollins's husband imagined that she must have "covered [her]self with glory" when she lectured in Europe during the late 1950s. And when she went to Oslo in 1962 to present the Jane Addams Peace

Book Award, he predicted: "It will be a grand success because you have everything at your command, and you are quite capable of doing anything that you attempt." Finally, showing the encouragement some received for seeking nontraditional public roles, immediately after Booker T. Washington died in 1915 ("Peace rest his soul," Thomas Church paused to pray), Thomas urged Mary Church Terrell to "go after" the presidency of the coeducational Tuskegee Institute. Thomas insisted that she could "deliver the goods better than he [Washington] did" and that she should start right away to gather support among her friends. With high self-confidence, sufficient preparation, and resplendent moral support like this, what could these women *not* be or do?[2]

High achievement beyond domesticity was certainly *possible* for women who were able to find this kind of support. But moral support from family members and educational mentors was not enough; there had to be both public and private structural and logistical support as well. Even if black women desired to work as professionals and were prepared to do so, they had to be *allowed* to. Before the 1930s they rarely had problems pursuing these occupations in the South because public administrators regularly ignored many areas of public need. But in the North, both racial discrimination and the higher credential requirements limited their options for paid public work. Undoubtedly it was for these reasons that schoolteacher Amelia Perry Pride frantically began to search for work for her husband in Newport News, Virginia, when he started contemplating a move from their home in Lynchburg, Virginia, to Long Island. She knew that as a black normal school graduate it would not be easy for her to find acceptable paid work in New York, and in a most telling remark Pride added: "There are no negroes in Patchogue for me to work on, and unless I am working I would not be satisfied."[3]

Equally important, regardless of what educators had said and family and community members implied, domestic duties and public commitments more often than not did represent conflicting demands on women's time, energy, and ability. Public responsibilities complicated the already burdensome household routines, as Janie Porter Barrett indicated in a letter to one of her former Hampton teachers in 1893: "Where there are two babies and a husband and a house to look after it keeps me busy, and I have tried to do a little teaching this winter."[4] Moreover, in the days before electric heating, cleaning, and cooking equipment was widely used, water had to be heated, groceries bought, and wood and coal "toted" almost daily. In rural southern communities this did not change appreciably until the 1950s. And even after "modern conveniences" reduced the time needed for one domestic task or another, as historian Ruth Schwartz Cowan has demonstrated, expectations increased so that the housekeeping chores had to be done more frequently, using up the time and energy the technology was supposed to save.[5] Besides cleaning, cooking, and sewing, many women had to care for children, their own and others, and they sometimes had parents and other aging relatives to look after as well. Ultimately, even when the women readily accepted the family and community responsibilities, a variety of conditions easily frustrated their ability to fulfill them.

• • •

After all the training that had suggested (even insisted) that women maintain orderly homes, work for a living if necessary, and work for the race in all circumstances, most women found it nearly impossible to carry out the total mandate, and upon marrying many of them gave up the professional careers for which they had prepared. Mary Church Terrell left her teaching position after she married Robert Heberton Terrell in 1891. Portia Marshall Washington Pittman did not work for wages for several years after her 1907 marriage to William Sidney Pittman. When Septima Poinsette Clark's husband left the navy in 1920, she too gave up teaching. And Florence Edmonds left her nursing career in the 1920s upon marrying; Lucy Mitchell gave up a teaching position during the early 1930s just before giving birth to her first child; and at the end of the decade, Clara Jones left her work as a librarian shortly before the birth of her first son.

The obvious cannot be trusted in these cases, however. It is true that matrimony and motherhood had a significant effect on women's ability to attend to public—especially paid—work, and occasionally they were the deciding factors. But public policy and public tradition complicated the impact of matrimony and motherhood for many women. Despite all the previous training that centered on women's obligation to perform both public and private sphere work, the prescription did not reflect the many factors that could make it nearly impossible to do. Personal ambition, previous intensive socialization, and economic need, however, made it equally difficult for women to limit themselves to one arena or the other. And so each woman had to devise a strategy that would allow her to fulfill personal, family, and community roles within her particular situation.

Florence Edmonds's perception of the public climate for black professional women in Pittsfield, Massachusetts, cut her nursing career short after she married William Baily Edmonds and they moved from New York City back to their Massachusetts hometown. Upon relocating, a move William insisted on, Florence determined that Pittsfield was not "ready for a black [registered] nurse" and made no attempt to obtain a professional position. She assumed full responsibility for cooking and cleaning and for nurturing the four children they eventually had. With children, however, William's wages as a janitor in department stores and bank buildings were not sufficient to support the family comfortably. Yet Florence's obtaining a position commensurate with her training seemed impossible, and no doubt the work most available to black women—domestic work in white women's homes—was equally unacceptable. She therefore had to find a way to earn an income while remaining in her home. Ultimately she took in sewing, increasing both the family income and her domestic work.[6]

For the next fifteen years Florence Edmonds pursued the double duty that black women so often undertook without leaving home. She carried out the traditional work that women regularly did for their own families, and she performed paid domestic work for others. Not until her youngest daughter entered high school in the 1940s did Edmonds decide to move back into professional nursing, and by that time not only had her home environment changed—her daughters were older, required less of her attention, and could assume some household duties—but the public sphere had changed too. The United States had entered World War II, and the wartime shortage of nurses made it easier, or even necessary, for public officials in Pittsfield to employ black registered nurses. Edmonds enrolled in a refresher nursing course and moved back into her chosen profession.[7]

Although marriage led Florence Edmonds to quit her position as a visiting nurse in New York City, that alone did not cause her to leave paid professional work altogether. Her perception of the traditions of public employment was the decisive factor. For other black women it was neither perception nor tradition but actual policy that made them modify their work upon marriage. And whether or not public tradition or policy affected their ability to move in and out of certain types of paid work, as the Edmonds example suggests, women made the adjustments necessary to fulfill their different responsibilities as they saw them.

Beulah Shepard Hester's movements into and out of the public work force were affected by more complex circumstances than Edmonds faced. The work Hester had to perform in the home was also more complicated. She started her career as a schoolteacher in North Carolina in 1912, and in 1918 she married a poorly paid Baptist minister named William Hester. Living in the South, where there were teaching positions "reserved" for black women (most consistently in rural areas), allowed Hester to continue to work in her profession, and World War I–era conservation programs soon brought her a better-paying position as a demonstration teacher/extension agent to the rural black community. About one-third of William's salary of twenty-five dollars a week went for a room and the use of the kitchen in someone else's home, but as soon as the Hesters found a house they could buy they left their cramped, nonprivate quarters, and Beulah's earnings became even more critical. The addition to the household of William's sister, a Bennett College student, increased the family's financial needs, and as long as the sister was there Beulah's domestic workload was more extensive as well. She was fortunate because her sister-in-law insisted on helping with the housework, but her presence increased the consumption of food, fuel, and the like, and Beulah's income helped to pay for the difference. The Hesters then took in a boarder, a Bennett College secretary, who shared a room with William's sister. The new boarder undoubtedly improved the family's economic situation, but because she paid to live there, she did not have household duties. Beulah and her sister-in-law had to prepare all the meals, so one prepared lunch and the other cooked dinner, and they divided the housecleaning tasks as well.[8]

When considering Hester's subsequent work routines, her education becomes ironic. As noted earlier, when she enrolled at Hartshorn in 1908, her mother would not permit her to take only the music course, as Hester wanted to do. Mrs. Shepard believed her daughter might not be able to earn a living (if she had to) with such narrow preparation, and for that reason, Hester had to add the normal program to her course of study. But it was musical and domestic skills that she turned to when she could no longer teach. In 1924 her husband became the pastor of a Boston church, and they moved to Massachusetts. Taking advantage of family and friendship connections, they first sublet the home of a couple formerly from North Carolina who worked out of town as live-in domestics for wealthy white New Englanders during the summers. When the couple returned home in early September, the Hesters moved into a much larger house than the two of them needed or perhaps could afford. The larger house required Beulah to perform more domestic work, simply because of its size, but also, in order to afford the house more comfortably and have some money of her own, she began to give private music lessons, which took time away from the domestic work. They also took in student boarders, which multiplied the amount of domestic work Beulah had to do. Besides cooking and cleaning for herself, her husband, and his niece, who had come to live with them, she also prepared the students' meals, cleaned up afterward, and did their laundry. In addition, she performed the public functions of a minister's wife and a civic-minded woman—visiting the sick and elderly, raising money for the church, and organizing church and community programs. Her husband's pastorate might have provided a decent living, but affording the large and expensive (by North Carolina standards) house exceeded his financial ability. Well prepared to teach music and to do domestic work, and probably believing the undertaking would be easy because she would not have to leave home to do it, Beulah Hester came under great stress from the extensive unpaid public and paid private work. She eventually had a nervous breakdown.[9]

Parents and teachers alike had insisted that domestic training for these women was designed to enable them to care for their own homes, set an example for others, and train others. But all too often, when these women's families fell on hard times, the domestic skills they had developed at home and in school allowed them to earn a living and helped avert economic disaster. Sometimes musical training, also a regular part of women's "finishing" until the early twentieth century, similarly made a critical difference in their families' material comfort. Musical ability and domesticity also gave black women some measure of control in meeting financial needs because neither one required them to leave home in order to earn money. Ironically, after preparing so intensely for paid public positions, carrying out family responsibilities regularly resulted in the inversion of what was common practice: black women's paid work often was conducted in the private sphere, and their public work regularly remained unpaid.

Portia Washington Pittman probably represents an extreme, but not uncommon, example of black women who had to combine paid and unpaid public work with paid and unpaid private work. Portia and her husband, William Sidney Pittman, moved from Tuskegee, Alabama, to the Washington, D.C., area after Sidney had a confrontation with his supervisor at Tuskegee Institute, where he was employed as an instructor. Sidney at first made a good living in Washington as an architect, and so housewifery for Portia did not necessarily limit her to cooking, cleaning, and caring for the three children she and Sidney had between 1908 and 1912. Sidney's income at first afforded domestic workers in the home, so besides running her household Portia devoted considerable time to escorting her famous father whenever he visited the city, to giving concerts to raise money for the higher education and professional training of young black scholars and artists, and apparently to chicken farming. Even when her second son, Booker, was extremely ill soon after his birth in 1909 and required special care, though "undergoing such a trying strain [as to be] in great danger of breaking down nervously," Portia had a full-time wet nurse and a full-time nurse who performed much of the work associated with the child's care.[10]

Eventually Sidney's contracts began to dwindle, the family's finances became seriously strained, and Portia needed to earn an income. Adhering to middle-class traditions, she at first gave private music lessons in their home. Unlike Florence Edmonds, Portia would have had few problems finding a professional position in the Washington, D.C., area, both because it was common for African Americans to hold such positions there (although she could not have taught in the public school system as a married woman) and also because of her father's influence. She was responding to other pressures, social and domestic—namely the convention that married women of the apparent upper classes did not work for wages and the misplaced pride of her husband, who would not have it known that he was unable to "take care of" his family. Portia abided by Sidney's wishes, even though her obtaining more lucrative public work could have eased their burdens considerably. And throughout their stressful financial situation, her father sent presents to the children and money for the household. Portia continued to give private music lessons and to "pray each night for work to come [to Sidney] for the sake of these little folks of ours."[11]

Sidney's inability to earn a living in the District of Columbia and his increasing frustration caused him to move the family to Dallas. After another good start, his work faltered yet again. Although Portia started by giving private music lessons again, she also took on several public jobs, first directing church and school choirs and later working as a full-time music instructor in the public school system. Getting beyond Booker T. Washington's sphere of influence, one of Sidney's reasons for moving the family to Texas, also released Portia from more rigid East Coast gender conventions, and pursuing paid public work therefore was easier for her. But unfortunately her efforts to help support the family by working in the public sphere brought on a tragedy in the classical sense. As she traversed the city, working in a variety of jobs, she earned an excellent reputation as a music teacher, a chorale director, and a performer. The more successful she became, the more moody, depressed, and less able to earn a living Sidney became, and the more Portia needed to earn an income. Enmeshed in what seemed to be a cycle of professional regression and unable to cope with some or all of the implications, Sidney became violent. Portia left him and moved back to Tuskegee, where she became part of the Institute faculty. She lived in one of the dorms until teaching private students provided enough money to build a small house near the campus.[12]

Although Portia Washington Pittman's work history is an important example, it was probably rare that black women could not pursue paid public work because of their class image. Rather, racist employment patterns regularly locked them out of the public work force, and social pressures on women to assume primary responsibility for organizing, supervising, and performing the work of the home also had a significant impact. But for these women, whose careers embraced a number of transitional social and historical periods, there was at least one other factor as well—their character as migrants. Although most black migrants saw northern and urban migration as a move to enhance personal and collective social and economic status, and many indeed moved "from fields to factories," black professional women— schoolteachers in particular—were not as fortunate. The higher certification requirements maintained in northern and urban areas easily pushed them out of the professional class.

Beulah Shepard Hester, a normal program graduate, was unquestionably caught in this situation when she and her husband moved to Boston. Septima Clark's relocation from South Carolina to Ohio had the same effect. Moving from South Carolina to Charlotte, North Carolina, probably had the same impact on Mamie Garvin Fields's employability as a teacher. And though Portia Washington Pittman's training qualified her to teach in black Alabama schools had she needed to work for pay there, it was not enough for teaching in the District of Columbia (even if her husband and local law had permitted it). Portia's degree from Bradford was essentially a higher normal degree (as was Beulah Hester's Hartshorn degree), and although school officials from Bradford certified that her coursework was equal to two years of college, she had to work for less than a full salary in Dallas.[13] She made up the financial shortfall by continuing to offer private music lessons and by directing church and community choirs. Altogether, where family economies had been based partly (or potentially) on professional women's earnings, migration regularly caused the family standard of living to drop precipitously because of the wives' unemployability in their professions and the higher cost of living in the new cities. To help offset the decline in living standards, some women, including Florence Edmonds and Beulah Hester, took on private paid work. And some, like Portia Pittman, managed paid public positions, paid private work, and unpaid public and private work as well.

Between 1890 and 1954, few black women were relieved of the necessity of earning an income. But among those socialized as the women in this book were, even that privileged position did not eliminate their obligation to work in the public sphere. They had been conditioned to believe that not to contribute to the public good was to waste their lives. Not to assume or create community work options for themselves, whether paid or not, would have been to deny their missions and the important roles as community leaders for which they had prepared. And the more skills, training, or preparation they had, the truer this was. Not to use their advantages for the advancement of the race was deemed selfish and even traitorous.

Mary Church Terrell stands out as one who neither needed to earn an income nor had to work within her home. Her husband's high-paying position and later her own inheritance from her father afforded her the luxury of employing domestic workers and not working for wages. Nevertheless, she believed that she had to work in the public sphere. As a young adult she had expressed her eagerness to put her work ethic into practice. As a mature woman both economic factors— wanting certain things only if she could pay for them herself—and the social/political requisite of working to advance the race moved her into the public sphere.[14] After local laws forced Terrell to give up her teaching position when she married, she was enabled, partly by her family wealth, to circumvent some of the traditional obstacles that married black women often faced and that regularly led them to do paid work in their homes. Unlike most, Terrell was able to create an alternative paid public position for herself. Using her formidable education, her reputation as a civil rights advocate and a community leader in education, and her financial security, she pursued a career as a public speaker. People wanted her to speak at their events, and she could afford to pay her initial expenses to accommodate them. She and her husband had no children for nearly a decade after they married, so she was not encumbered, at first, by child-care responsibilities. But even after the birth of their daughter, Phyllis, the Terrells could afford to pay domestic workers. And perhaps even more important, Robert Heberton Terrell was willing to and, especially, capable of keeping the household running smoothly in Mary's absence.

While Terrell traveled as a public lecturer, she regularly experienced anxiety about her absences from home, but she felt free to instruct her husband on every little detail she wanted him to attend to. "How I miss you all this beautiful sabbath morning," Terrell wrote while traveling and speaking in the Midwest in 1900. "I enjoy very much doing this kind of work because I really feel that I am putting the colored woman in a favorable light at least every time I address an audience of white people, and every little bit helps. . . . But it is a great sacrifice for me to leave my house, I tell you. It grows harder and harder every time I leave." Terrell explained that she had traveled so much when she was younger that it no longer appealed to her. She continued to do it only out of "a sense of duty to [her] race." That by this time she had a young child (the first to survive out of four pregnancies), probably also made being away for long periods emotionally difficult. But she managed the separations in part by remembering why she had to work—for the benefit of the race, black women in particular. It was especially important, however, that she could expect Robert to take care of their "dear little sweetheart of a baby" and to follow the extensive instructions she regularly sent him. In one letter Mary asked Robert to tell her mother that the housekeeper did not pack her "nicest white undershirts"; to read one section of the letter to Mrs. Church; to take care of her papers and letters; to keep their daughter, Phyllis, out of her (Mary's) papers; to open her mail and forward the important items; and to store the rest in particular places, all of which Robert apparently carried out.[15]

Probably only because of support like this was Terrell able to maintain a career as a public lecturer despite being married and having a child under five years old. At one time Terrell had a veritable support corps in her husband, her mother, and their housekeeper, but it was still Robert who organized the household work in her absence. Even when she took her children with her on various trips, mostly vacations, Mary sent her detailed instructions to Robert.[16]

Because of Robert's attentiveness, Terrell more than once was able to help find a new house for the family even though she was out of town during the search. Robert mailed real estate advertisements to her, she identified the houses that interested her, and he visited the properties before she was able to see them. In one instance, after they settled on a house and bought it, Robert supervised the moving while she was out of town, and he assured her that he was carrying out her "orders." Promising to write every day until everything was settled, he even apologized because "things were in such a turmoil the last few days of your stay that we could not hold a family council behind closed doors for several hours so that the children might get some idea of what it means to break up a home."[17] Because Robert worked to keep Mary involved in the household although she was often absent, one might conclude that the biggest event that Mary Church Terrell missed (besides the housework) while working out of town was the electrification of their home.[18]

Mary and Robert adopted Mary's niece, also named Mary, and as she and Phyllis grew up, their mother's attention and detailed instructions to Robert increasingly concerned them, rather than her clothes, mail, and other personal items. In one instance she attended the National Purity Congress in Columbus, Ohio, and heard incessant details about young girls and boys who had "gone wrong," which made her feel very insecure about not being a traditional homemaker (if not exclusively one). "I do wish I were home tonight," she wrote, "I am dreadfully worried about the girls. I shall never leave them without an elderly woman again. It is not right. It is positively dangerous." Surely Terrell was not suggesting that *only* a woman could care for Phyllis and Mary effectively. She recognized that such a statement questioned Robert's ability to see to his children's safety, and so she qualified her first thoughts but nevertheless went on about her fears: "You will do the best you can," she acknowledged, "but you are a man and you are not at home when they return from school. I am worried nearly to death. I can hardly think that I shall be absent from home another whole week. . . . Over and over again the speakers at the Purity Congress emphasized the great danger of allowing girls the ages of our girls to go around alone. You see to it that Phyllis [the younger of the two] in particular does not walk home with boys. Mother was right about guarding the girls." Then Terrell speculated: "I have been too lenient and lax, I fear, tho' I did it for the best. Please come home *early* and *stay* home till it is time for them to retire."[19]

Although Terrell's family wealth, Robert's attention to detail, and their occasional employment of domestic workers allowed Terrell to pursue a public career as a lecturer, her absences from home did not leave her free of domestic worries. She was, in fact, attending to child-rearing details as if she were still there. Consequently she represents not simply the more common example of a woman's working outside the home and in it as well, or of doing double duty within the home (where she prepared her lectures and articles). For her, domestic work was further complicated by earning an income out of town rather than simply outside the home, and her paid public work was made harder by her assuming some domestic responsibility even while not present in the household. For example, she informed Robert of her instructions to Phyllis regarding male company, to make certain Phyllis adhered to them. She reminded Robert to have Phyllis's violin repaired. She was aware of the clothing Phyllis and Mary needed and advised Robert on what to buy. She told him to have the children watch newspaper ads for hat and shoe sales and to shop for their shoes at a particular store. She also instructed Robert on what the girls should wear to upcoming special events. From a distance, then, and with Robert's help, Terrell was still counseling, shopping for, and clothing her children, and in general seeing to their upbringing.[20]

For many years Terrell's most concentrated time with her children came during the summers when they were out of school, and she cut back her lecturing to accommodate them. They regularly vacationed at Oak Bluffs (Martha's Vineyard), which she viewed as an ideal place for the girls because there were no "temptations" or "evils" there. She saw to it that they learned to swim, and she indulged them in their "daring stunts" in the water. Probably because she spent so much time apart from the children, she made certain the girls were deliriously happy during these excursions. In one instance she concluded that if they were any happier, "they would expire from pure joy."[21]

The vacations, however, were not always "pure joy" for Terrell. Although this was a different kind of work, vacationing with children nevertheless required work, especially since this was when she compensated for not being with the children more often. During one of those summer vacations (at Opequon) in 1909, Terrell discovered that Phyllis, then in the seventh grade, could not read well. Terrell had another task to do: "I try to be as calm as I can when I give her her reading lesson, but she is enough to try the patience of Job," Terrell wrote to her husband.

I feel certain that no child in Washington passed to the seventh grade knows so little about reading as Phyllis. Bless her dear little heart. She is the sweetest piece of humanity that ever lived. I feel like a criminal when I think how I allowed her to run wild nearly six weeks last summer without requiring her, forcing her, to read everyday as I am doing now. I have tried to use as little force as possible because I feared I would make her hate the sight of a book. . . . But now I see she dislikes to read because she actually doesn't know how and doesn't have the remotest idea how to spell out a word so that she can pronounce it.[22]

Several years later when Robert received a letter from Phyllis (then a student at Oberlin) with no spelling or grammatical errors, he immediately sent a report to Mary, adding the commentary: "Progress."[23] And even after Phyllis was a grown woman, her mother continued to instruct her in English and to correct errors in her letters.[24]

Neither Terrell nor any of the other women who continued to work outside the home after having children could have carried out all these responsibilities without substantial assistance.[25] No doubt for that reason—the lack of assistance—and also so as not to have to work in white women's homes, Beulah Hester and Florence Edmonds earned money during part of their lives by taking on more work within their homes. But Robert Terrell's income as a district court judge obviously allowed many privileges that other women's husbands could not afford, including domestic workers, and moreover, Robert's own proficiency in child rearing and housekeeping is noteworthy. He shared Mary's understanding of the broad significance of her public work and thus was willing to help her pursue it with as much ease as possible. Demonstrating this attitude, while Mary worked in 1920 for Warren G. Harding's presidential campaign, Robert wrote, "It is well for the Hardings to meet a woman like you and [to] get some idea of the caliber and ability of the best there is among colored women." Interestingly, Robert did not know precisely what Mary's job was; he simply knew that it was important both for her personal fulfillment and for the benefit of the race—she was representing not simply herself but all black women—and so he supported her efforts.[26] Still, undoubtedly ingrained with contemporary ideas of women's domestic responsibilities to their children and their husbands, Terrell agonized over being away so often. While her children were young, her fears reflected her own sexual stereotyping—of her husband as a man (unable to care for girls as well as a woman presumably could), her daughters as girls (too naïve to take care of themselves), their "boyfriends" as boys (prone to "taking advantage" of girls, given the right circumstances), and herself as a woman, a mother, and a wife (ultimately responsible for all of them in one way or another). Yet all the while she was a living contradiction of most stereotypes—and Robert was also.

Most married women's work situations fell somewhere between that of Terrell, who could carry on extensive public work with few negative repercussions, and that of the women who gave up paid public work altogether but not all paid work. Lucy Mitchell noted that marriage and parenthood came first with her, but "career drives had a place whose needs could be met with skillful planning and cooperation of the spouse." Mitchell married a young Harvard Law School graduate who had finished his undergraduate work at Talledega College a few years before she did. She had taught school in the South before joining him in 1923 when they married, and holding a bachelor's degree, Mitchell was able to continue teaching school in Massachusetts during the first few years of their marriage. After their first child was born, Mitchell attempted to devote her attention to the home, but she soon became bored with domestic duties alone. Consequently, in 1932 her husband encouraged her to go back to school, and he assumed more of the housework and child-rearing responsibilities so she could do so comfortably. Mitchell divided her time between her husband, housework, children, and graduate work at Boston University. And just before completing her master's degree in 1935, she accepted a paid public position in a kindergarten where she could take her children with her.[27]

The husbands' physical support made the difference in married women's ability to achieve outside the home without disadvantage to themselves and their homelife. Clara Stanton Jones, like Terrell, was fortunate in that her husband was cooperative, increasing or decreasing his domestic responsibilities as his wife varied her public sphere work. Clara Jones took part-time positions in libraries after her children were born during the late 1930s and early 1940s because, she said, "I wanted to be a good wife and mother as well as a good librarian." She decided to resume her career full time during the early 1940s, and the family moved from Louisiana to Detroit when she accepted a position with the Detroit public library system. Her husband was a professional social worker in Louisiana when she received the job offer, but they agreed that he would be able to find work in as large a city as Detroit and that he could even go back to graduate school there. Arriving in Detroit as a black professional couple in 1943, however, made both of their public jobs more stressful and time consuming than they might otherwise have been. Clara was at first assigned to public relations, and Detroit had just experienced one of the most violent civil outbursts the nation had seen. She had to relinquish even more of the child-rearing and household responsibilities than she had anticipated to cover all the public roles she had to step into as librarian, public relations specialist, and community activist. Her husband, whose social work assignments undoubtedly also intensified, took over whatever tasks she gave up.[28]

In their own time, Robert Terrell, Joseph Mitchell, and Albert Jones would not have been seen as merely fulfilling their own duty to their families and households, as they might now be seen. They were taking on the work of their wives as the women relinquished it. Cooking, cleaning, child rearing, and the like were traditionally women's work, and though some men supported their wives' public work by assuming private domestic tasks, others were anxious to see that their wives did not turn their backs on household work that social norms dictated wives should do.

Fostine Riddick made a determined effort to carry on paid public work in spite of her husband's attempts to confine her to the home. And her experiences represented a significant aberration from most others' in several important ways. She had no children, her family was not exceptionally wealthy, and her employers were willing to keep her on after her marriage. But her husband did not want her to work for wages. Riddick gave up her position as a nurse anesthetist after her late 1930s marriage to Henry Riddick, and for two years she stayed home, she said, learning to cook, giving parties, and gaining weight. But after "two years of complete housewifery" Riddick was bored, so she sought a resolution. She found part-time employment as a nurse anesthetist at a nearby children's hospital, and she worked there two mornings a week for nine years (1943–51) without her husband's knowledge. As far as he knew, the only paid public work she performed during the first ten years of their marriage was the occasional short-term private-duty nursing she accepted after convincing him that the patients had searched the entire city without finding another nurse available and that she had a moral duty to help those in need. Otherwise Riddick confined her *acknowledged* public work primarily to unpaid church and community projects. Through the Lindenwood Beautiful Group, for example, she petitioned the city for paved streets, gutters, and sidewalks; planted flowers and trees all over the neighborhood; and seeded and tended public vegetable gardens wherever the organization could find a vacant lot with a cooperative owner. Not until 1957 did

125

Riddick resume a full-time paid public job with her husband's knowledge.[29]

By her own admission, Riddick despised housekeeping, not just housework. In all likelihood it was equally difficult for her to forgo the kind of public work role for which she had prepared and presumably desired. That is certainly suggested by the extremes she went to in order to maintain a public wage-earning role. She not only worked for pay without her husband's knowledge for many years, but after he retired from his job with the United States Postal Service, she tried to join the navy. Her education qualified her as an officer, and Riddick hoped she could take her husband as her dependent wherever she had to go for basic training, and that eventually she could return to an assignment in the naval hospital at Portsmouth, Virginia, near their home. Riddick had worked it all out in her mind, but for reasons she never revealed, none of it came to pass. Perhaps she was already over the navy's maximum enlistment age or failed to pass the physical examination. Maybe in the mid-1950s the navy did not need nurses. It is not unreasonable to suspect that her husband opposed the scheme. Other people certainly did, because they feared this would be a first step toward leaving her husband permanently. Whatever the case, in 1957 Riddick went to work at the Norfolk Community Hospital with her husband's approval. Perhaps this was their compromise—an alternative to her joining the navy.[30]

Fostine Riddick's plight is indeed an interesting one. Although she had no children, her husband did not want her to work for pay outside the home, at least as long as he was employed. In every other respect he seemed to be a cooperative partner, though his cooperation resembles paternalism. When Riddick went to New York to work on her master's degree during the 1950s he, by then retired, went with her. He drove her to school, helped with her research, and was an attentive listener whenever she needed him. It seems, then, that Henry Riddick subscribed to an old tradition (which was becoming less and less influential in general, and which had never been a real tradition among most black families) wherein the wife of a "good" husband did not need to work for pay. But of course Riddick worked to fulfill not financial needs, but personal ones. She apparently could have lived in reasonable comfort without her earnings. Where married women worked for wages despite the luxury of not needing to, usually the family's obvious wealth averted spousal insecurity over public speculations on the family's financial condition. But though the Riddicks lived in what historian Earl Lewis recently described as one of the most affluent black communities in Norfolk during the 1920s, Henry Riddick did not overcome his insecurity until his wife was well into middle age.[31]

. . .

Single women who had lost their husbands to divorce or death did not combine private and public work any more easily than those with unhelpful spouses or hostile local public traditions. Whereas, for married women, holding a paid, public position was a small miracle, for formerly married women, maintaining the domestic traditions became a major feat. Domesticity for them was difficult to uphold not because they did not want to do the work or because they lacked support within the household, but because their economic situations were so precarious that they could not afford a house of their own, and sometimes neither could they afford to rear their children.

Septima Clark's economic status as a widow with a child, teaching in poorly paid positions in historically neglected regions of the South, made it nearly impossible for her to do more than the extensive paid and unpaid public work for which she felt responsible. Clark pursued a rigorous routine during the 1920s—not only teaching in a traditional classroom but also attending to a variety of other public needs. But soon she was stunned by her son's running away from their boardinghouse mistress to come to his mother's school, two and a half miles away. Clark had never had any reason to doubt that her son was in good hands during the day, but she had not anticipated the trouble he could get into on his own. Because his baby-sitter, as a boardinghouse keeper, had innumerable responsibilities besides child care, the likelihood of Nerie Jr.'s getting into mischief was greater than Clark had suspected. Although no harm came to the child, the event was shocking. Unable to afford other child-care arrangements, Clark decided to send him to Hickory, North Carolina, to live with his paternal grandparents.[32] Because she missed him, however, and wanted to mother him directly, after a few years Clark sent for him again. But he was growing fast, and she could not afford to feed and clothe him. Moreover he was a big boy, and a rough one at that; he regularly damaged the landlords' property, and Clark had to pay after each accident. After trying three boardinghouses in an effort to live more cheaply, and having already been reduced to eating cheese and crackers herself so she could feed him balanced meals, she gave up and sent him back to his grand-parents.[33]

Clark's extensive paid and unpaid public work made it impossible for her to rear her child by herself. And the meager wage she earned while Nerie Jr. was young and needed direct supervision made her unable to afford dedicated child-care providers. The small wage also kept her from buying a home, where she could have traded a room for child care. But she could not even contemplate homeownership until teacher salary equalization reached South Carolina during the 1940s, and by then her son was a grown man about to enter the military. A traditional homelife, whether it included children or not, frequently required more than the income available to most black women. Consequently, during most of her teaching career, Septima Clark resigned herself to being unable to rear her child and, for a long time, to being unable to own a home.

Laura Terrell Jones, sister-in-law of Mary Church Terrell, presents another case. She never had children, and her belief that she had lost the chance for domesticity because of her divorce haunted her for much of her adult life. Jones, who taught at Tuskegee Institute for approximately thirty years (until the depression forced school administrators to cut their staff), was legally separated from her husband as early as 1908, though she did not obtain a divorce until 1917. Although childless, she was as bound by financial pressures as Clark was, and more limited by social constraints because of where she worked. Tuskegee Institute officials required single women faculty members to live on the campus because of their important unpaid work as role models for the female students, and probably also to prevent any suspicions from arising about their lifestyle. Their low pay likely precluded their living alone anyway, so this housing arrangement, in effect, became a part of their salary. After nearly thirty years of such a living arrangement, Laura Jones began to reflect on her life, and she reviewed the personal, social, and financial loss that resulted from her divorce. In 1934 she wrote to Mary Church Terrell:

I live so much of my life as Mrs. L. T. Jones—schoolteacher—that to wake up in the morning in a house instead of a dormitory—to realize that the stirring about you is the noise of relatives and not girls from here, there, and everywhere—to be able to put on a house dress instead of school attire—to dawdle over a meal—etc. . . . mean so much.

Jones insisted that she did not want sympathy and that she was thankful for her job. In fact, she commented not on the policies of the school that were partly responsible for her loss of personal freedom, but on her personal status as a divorcée. She wrote:

I hold no brief against life that domesticity was snatched ruthlessly from me. Like all who look back on something denied, I believe I'd have made a good wife, a good mother. I know I love a home [and,] in fact, I might have become one of those tiresome women to whom sweeping, dusting, etc., are veritable rituals. God forbid! As it is, I have lived a very full life.[34]

In spite of Jones's effort not to sound totally dispirited, her remarks are a lamentation, and they reveal another variety of the compression of public and private spheres. The living arrangement at Tuskegee made it impossible to separate paid from unpaid, public from private work. Having to dress immediately after rising suggests that Jones was always in "public"; she never had any privacy. And clearly, she never felt "at home" even though she lived, almost permanently, in the dormitory. Although Jones might have, as she said, lived a full life, the tone of her remarks suggests that she did not believe she had lived a complete life. Domesticity was "snatched ruthlessly" from her when she became divorced. She not only missed traditional domesticity, she missed being surrounded by family—blood kin. She was painfully aware that whether married and with children or not, single women could still have a "homelife" if they could afford a home. But for most women singleness severely limited that possibility.

Divorce, widowhood, and lifelong singlehood (choosing never to marry) easily reduced women with modest incomes and no other means of support to poverty. Laura Terrell Jones might have fallen through the cracks without the living arrangements for single women faculty at Tuskegee—constraining as they were. Portia Washington Pittman and Septima Clark struggled fiercely to remain afloat economically, and usually they hardly managed. Septima Clark might have continued barely to make a living and to roam from boardinghouse to boardinghouse had the teacher salary equalization campaign not reached South Carolina before she retired. And had Portia Washington Pittman not been able to return to Tuskegee upon leaving William Sidney Pittman, absolute, not relative, poverty would have struck her family even sooner than it did. After she gave up her teaching position at Tuskegee because of increasing credential requirements, she moved to Washington, D.C., and lived in extreme poverty until the local Tuskegee Alumni Club discovered her plight in the 1970s and began to subsidize her housing.[35] Marriage almost never ensured financial security for black women, but singleness, in some circumstances, guaranteed eventual poverty.[36]

The threat of poverty, however, did not prevent some women from deciding not to marry. The independence their upbringing had encouraged, even inadvertently, no doubt contributed to their choosing singlehood. Those who chose to remain single did not have to worry about local employment policies that pushed married women back into their homes, or at least out of their professions.[37] Remaining childless could also extend women's options. And their public endeavors would not be impeded by domineering and insecure spouses. But even if women could have been guaranteed that the men they might marry would be perfectly cooperative, they had learned that domestic work was their responsibility, and so whether they worked in the public sphere or not, they—and often they alone—would have had to do it and be proportionately constrained in their public lives by it.

For these reasons Washington, D.C., schoolteacher Norma Boyd was always convinced that marriage was a gamble, and she was not a betting woman. Boyd was never convinced by the rhetoric that posited that domesticity and public careers were complementary. To her mind, marriage unequivocally limited women to the home. She believed that a married woman would (and should) have to give up her career and focus all her attention on her children and husband—that she was responsible for their success. For Boyd, marriage and paid public work represented competing interests, and she concluded that "you can't have your cake and eat it too."[38] Had Boyd married and been typical of black women, she might have learned quickly that domesticity did not preclude a public career. Probably only because she shared a house with her sister, also an urban professional, and thus could afford to pay for domestic workers, was she able to avoid domesticity.

Domesticity was, however, a fact of life for single women who remained in their parents' households throughout their careers (or until their parents died). They, like married women, were obligated to cook and clean. They mended the clothes, papered the walls, answered the doors and telephones, and helped pay the bills. Although they usually were not burdened with child care, they eventually cared for their parents. But whereas children grew up, enabling women to assume more extensive public roles, those who cared for elders saw their caregiving routines intensify over time as their parents and their parents' siblings aged and became more dependent.[39]

Julia Smith's unmarried aunt Florence, a public schoolteacher and principal, lived with Smith's parents for forty-two years. And since Smith never married (and came of age just after the turn of the century), she remained in that household too. The era in which Smith grew up also shaped her role as a dutiful daughter. Even though her brother was a successful, unmarried Massachusetts physician, it was she who cared for the elderly family members. Her father died in 1924 when Smith was twenty-nine, her aunt Florence died in 1926, and Smith's mother died in 1936. Smith helped to care for all of them in their old age, and when her brother became ill in 1947, she resigned her teaching position in Washington, D.C., and went to Massachusetts to care for him.[40]

Although remaining part of their parents' households obligated single women to care for the home and its elderly inhabitants, such women frequently had economic security that divorced and widowed women did not enjoy. Angelina Grimké lived with her uncle and aunt until her father died in 1930, when she was forty-seven years old. Neither she nor Smith ever had to worry about food and shelter. And in a rare example, Grimké amassed a small fortune while she lived with her relatives, no doubt partly because her expenses were minimal, and because she worked where black schoolteachers earned a good living. In 1934, when many working people were struggling to survive, she held $110,000 worth of notes with Swartzell, Rheem, and Hensey Company (an investment firm then in the process of filing bankruptcy). Angelina undoubtedly inherited some of this wealth from her father in 1930, but between 1913 and 1924, she owned (or was buying) several rental properties in Washington, and she had already made other investments ranging from $500 to $2,000.[41] Most single women who lived their adult lives with parents did not fare so well, but neither did they suffer economically like those whose marriages ended early. Domestic work for never-married women was probably a small trade-off for the financial independence that frequently came with it.

Even though they had been prepared for public professional careers, women, married or single, regularly took on domestic responsibilities beyond those required by their immediate families. Mary Church Terrell, for example, not only adopted Mary Church, her brother's daughter, but she also adopted her nephew after his father died. Beulah

Shepard Hester and her husband had no children of their own, but Beulah reared the daughter of her husband's youngest sister. South Carolina schoolteacher Albertha Murray reared two of her brother's children after their mother died. And when librarian Miriam Matthews's sister-in-law died, leaving a two-year-old child, Miriam, along with her mother, moved into her brother's home. Probably Miriam's mother performed the household tasks, while Miriam, who accompanied her brother to PTA meetings, seems to have handled the child's outside needs. Matthews remained in her brother's home for six years, until he remarried.[42]

Murray, Matthews, Terrell, and Hester possessed or created the means to take in children of their relatives. But black women have historically also shared responsibility for the children of their communities, and their efforts to create orphanages have been well documented.[43] Until public or private agencies existed, some black women made room in their households and places in their families for these other children. This was especially common before the turn of the century, and therefore it is more evident among the parents of some of the women studied here. But Amelia Perry Pride, who assumed her public professional work in 1881, practically turned her home into an orphanage—no doubt because Lynchburg, Virginia, had none for black children, who otherwise, according to custom, would have been placed out by public agents.

Pride worked as a social worker, a church worker, a construction supervisor, and a schoolteacher—an all-around community developer. Without doubt her Hampton mentors were proud that thirty years after her graduation, she still readily assumed that "all sorts of things I have to do." Pride wrote on one occasion, "I have put a man and his wife together three times and now they have parted again." But there was no need for her to apologize, for apparently the only work routine at which she had had little success was as a marriage counselor.[44]

In addition to the extensive public work Pride undertook, she fulfilled extensive duties in her home. She was married to a very successful black barber, and she cared for their large home and three sons. Her sons were especially rough little characters, who kept her occupied with sewing and mending "the elbows and knees [that] seem always [to be] out."[45] Pride's child-care responsibilities became even more extensive, however; in addition to rearing her own sons, as she later wrote to another mentor, "I have had three small girls given to me and they keep me busy. Two of them," she noted, "came from bad homes." It is not clear how long Pride cared for these three girls, but later she took in another girl, whose father was white and whose mother was allegedly an alcoholic. One of these children (or another girl) she legally adopted.[46]

Soon after Pride finished rearing her own children and the others she took in, her son died, and she and her husband took custody of their three grandchildren. The girls were not as rough on their clothes as their father had been, but, Pride noted, "they are much more delicate than Carrie or the other girls I've reared and so finicky about their food, and such a care."[47] Throughout her life Pride's domestic routines went so far beyond the care of her own home and children, that an early statement she made about her work pales. In 1888, when Pride had "only" her own children to care for, she wrote to General Armstrong, Hampton's principal, that "I am teaching school here in Lynchburg and my aim is to remain teaching as long as there is a piece of me. I find it rather hard though sometimes with my housekeeping, but then I love my work."[48] She taught school for another twenty-five years. Over that time, she never relinquished any of her paid and unpaid public work, and her private domestic work never ceased but became even more extensive.

• • •

Working effectively in both public and private spheres, whether for wages or not, was never as simple as the women had been taught. Because of the adjustments most of them made in their homelives or their public lives, Amelia Perry Pride stands out for her ability to carry out extensive domestic responsibilities with no apparent assistance and without giving up any of her public work. Most women who were married or had children could pursue the public work they had been trained for only if they had cooperative spouses, domestic workers in their homes, able-bodied live-in parents, friendly local public policy, or older children. If some or all of the ideal conditions were not in place, they could easily work themselves into a breakdown as Beulah Hester once did. Where single women remained members of their parents' households, their situations were rarely as difficult as that of widows like Septima Clark. But the responsibilities that never-married women had to their households, including housework and eventually elder care, were sometimes just as great as those of married women with children. Singlehood therefore did not, as one might expect, guarantee the easy pursuit of a public life. Formerly married women, as a group, did not easily maintain traditional domestic routines, and they found it equally difficult to earn an adequate living as well.

Possessing professional credentials and the potential for relatively high-status employment relieved few black professional women of mundane domestic work, but neither could they, as a group, confine themselves exclusively to homebound productive and reproductive duties. For their own benefit, and for the benefit of the larger black community, African American women also needed to work in and for the public. Though the public work often provided an income, whether paid or not women directed much of this work to higher goals. Addressing the needs of the black community was clearly a primary mission in life, and carrying out that work, as Isaac Fisher's poignant warning to young graduates suggested, was the only way to become a real leader.

But African American women also had to work in another way, purely to enhance their own individual status. A very important dimension of this public work involved seeking social acceptance as professionals and full access to the professional mainstream. As obviously self-serving as this aspect of public work was, such work for credentials and inclusion also had far-reaching ramifications for their communities and the larger society.

CHAPTER FIVE

"It was time . . . that we should be members": PERSONAL PROFESSIONAL WORK

If black professional women had not been prepared for all the details of the public and private work they would eventually face, they had at least been prepared to work hard, broadly, and well to help develop the community and to enhance their positions as leaders in it. They were ready for the highest levels of work available to black women at the time, and if they worked in a particular way, they might achieve high status in their communities as well. But there was a great gap between the status these women could achieve in their communities and the possibilities that existed in the larger society. Beyond their communities, there were many more and higher levels of employment to reach and a social status that seemed impossible to attain. Reconciling this dual status—their high status in their communities and their low status in the larger society—would have been difficult under any set of circumstances, but for African American women during the Jim Crow era the process was further complicated because their careers spanned a period during which new standards developed for determining the public status of many white-collar workers, black or white. Regardless of how well these women had been trained, how efficiently they worked in their homes, and how effectively they served community needs, their standing as professionals, if not as community leaders, came to be shaped by national movements that placed them, as black women workers in feminized occupations, in a precarious position. Consequently, in addition to working for their families and communities, and beyond working simply to earn a living for themselves, black professional women had to work to bridge the gap between the place of some distinction they achieved in their communities and the more ambiguous position in which the larger society held them.[1]

The complications involved in bridging that gap were many.

Each of the occupational groups created national organizations to enhance and protect the status of its members, and racist restrictions at first prevented black women from joining them. And the more extensive, convoluted impact of racial stratification further impeded the black professionals' access. For example, the meager salaries black women earned as professionals inhibited their pursuit of formal education beyond their initial diplomas, certificates, and degrees. This advanced training came to be required for credentialing in most of these fields. Further inhibiting access to additional schooling, most white schools did not admit African Americans, and as late as 1945, only fourteen black universities offered graduate degrees. In 1940 only forty-two of twelve hundred nursing schools in the country admitted black students; twenty-eight were at historically black institutions.[2] And finally, even as state and local government officials established higher and higher criteria for professional status in general, the same officials and black women's employers imposed a lower standard on African Americans, partly to justify paying them less and partly to avoid recognizing their professionalism. It is to these dimensions of work, which relate to black professional women's efforts to raise their external status as public sphere workers, that this chapter turns.

Education was very important in gaining professional standing, but the first generation of women, born between 1858 and 1883, rarely sought higher degrees. They gained their professional status like others of their time, who regularly saw their public work as a "calling." The second generation of women, born between 1884 and 1909, came to maturity during and after Progressive Era movements began to standardize training and licensing procedures and consequently were much more likely to pursue higher education and extensive training. As the new professional standards came to include membership in the licensing or certifying occupational organizations, black women also had to struggle for entry into the larger white groups that defined the standard to the public. Members of the third generation, born between 1910 and 1935, seemed to have an easier time achieving higher education than members of the generation before them. Indeed, because they entered college after the new professional standards were in place, they more often obtained advanced degrees (now deemed professional by the modern standards) before ending or taking a break from their formal schooling. But they too sought the all-important membership in mainstream professional organizations.[3]

Using the National Association of Colored Graduate Nurses (NACGN) as an example, this chapter ends with a detailed examination of the struggle for professional inclusion from an organizational, rather than an individual, vantage point. Although librarians and schoolteachers were involved in similar efforts during the first half of the twentieth century, their organizational histories preclude recreating their collective cases from surviving documents. Some black educators, for example, participated in the integrated National Association of Teachers in Colored Schools (NATCS), created in 1903, which became the American Teachers Association (ATA) in 1942. But for most of the NATCS's history its members were college teachers. Most black primary and secondary school teachers gained their professional identity through segregated state-level organizations.[4] Black librarians never created a national organization until they formed the Black Caucus of the American Library Association (ALA) in 1969. Beginning in the 1920s, however, they organized as "departments" in the segregated state-level teachers' organizations because the ALA did not explicitly remove its racial bar until the 1960s.[5] Black social workers were always included in national organizations, even though in some states they could not participate in local branch activities.[6] Thus nurses were the only one of the four groups of workers to maintain a nationally coordinated, autonomous organization throughout most of the Jim Crow era.

This organized struggle, along with individual histories, suggests a comprehensive campaign to enhance the status of black professional women workers. It was a campaign that was simultaneously personal and public, individualistic and collective. Some of the women's concerns focused on external public images and nationally recognized professional status; they were therefore very individualistic in that they related to higher salaries, better working conditions, and greater employment opportunities. But the women's success or failure had greater ramifications, for racial exclusion affected all black people's lives. As one might guess, efforts to enter the fairly exclusive club of the nationally recognized professional rank came to a climax during the 1940s. When Americans at large cast World War II and the Cold War that followed it as contests with the preservation of democracy at stake, black professional women, in turn, looked at the segregated organizations and announced, "It [is] time . . . that we should be members."[7]

• • •

Although there were several among the first generation of women who completed bachelor's degrees before beginning their careers, their degrees alone did not confer professional status. Possessing a college degree before it was required for working in these occupations more readily reflected class background. Thus Mary Church Terrell, Judith Ann Carter Horton, and Julia Hamilton Smith, all of whom earned four-year college degrees while still dependent on their parents, were easily recognized as women of the upper classes. When they accepted their first teaching positions, most people interpreted their actions in terms of pursuing a "vocation" or "calling."

There were strong parallels between answering a calling and demonstrating character, discussed earlier. Work as a calling implies public responsibility. To "take up a definite function in a community" involved responding to community needs and reflected a moral bond between the worker and the work. The value of the work in this instance was determined not by the income it earned but by the good it accomplished.[8] Thus, in the tradition of most professionals of their time, women of the first generation could best achieve a high public status as workers by responding well to their callings.

Anna DeCosta Banks, a graduate of Hampton Institute (1891) and Dixie Hospital (1893) and a South Carolina native, like many black professional women of her generation, fulfilled a variety of work roles. Beginning in 1896, she worked as head nurse at the Hospital and Training School for Nurses in Charleston, created because black physicians could not practice and black women could not study at the City Hospital Training School. Banks also supervised the nursing students and coordinated their training. She raised money to help pay for the institution, and to feed the residents and heat the building. Banks became the visiting nurse for the Ladies' Benevolent Society (LBS) in 1903, and beginning in 1912, local black residents who held policies with the Metropolitan Insurance Company of New York City were added to her list of clients.[9]

True to the tradition of pursuing a calling, Banks implicitly rejected any notion that she worked for pay and suggested by her actions that her aim in life was to be of service. In speaking about her paid work for the LBS Banks usually, though always briefly, alluded to her reputation. When officials of the Metropolitan Insurance Company announced that they were satisfied with her work and would continue to use her as their representative, she simply noted it as a matter of fact. In a rare instance, she boasted that local physicians had concluded that her service shortened their patients' recovery time.[10] That the LBS, a white women's organization, paid her for more than two decades to attend black and white patients was an obvious testimony to her good work.

But when Banks commented on her hospital work, which rarely paid a salary, she took a decidedly different tone. Almost consistently, commentary on this work was religiously symbolic. Just after Christmas 1898, for example, in noting that she could not afford the traditional holiday meals for the residents of the hospital school, Banks recalled Prov. 15:17: " 'Better is a dinner of herbs where love is, than a stalled ox and hatred there with.' " Some years later, as Robert R. Moton prepared to leave Hampton Institute for Tuskegee, she offered her support for his move while summarizing her own accomplishments: " 'I have planted, Apollos watered, but God gave the increase.' Each of us have a certain work to do; but the help must come from God."[11]

Five years after Banks began working for the LBS, the group's annual report described her as "judicious, tactful and experienced"; as "skillful, capable and tenderhearted"; and perhaps most important, as one who "unlike one of her predecessors, would never abandon the society during an epidemic."[12] The characterization of Banks hinted at the stereotypes of black "nurses" and of nurses in general, but it also suggested Banks's status as a public sphere worker—skilled, but more important, selflessly devoted to the public good.[13]

Women who worked as "social workers" during these early years regularly described their undertaking in ways that paralleled meeting the obligations of one who was called. Janie Porter Barrett, for example, who briefly "retired" from schoolteaching upon marrying Harris Barrett, was called back to public service after realizing the danger faced by children playing in the streets, and she opened the Locust Street Settlement House. Lugenia Burns Hope, best known for her role as cofounder of Atlanta's Neighborhood Union social settlement program in 1908, was similarly moved. Immediately before starting the Neighborhood Union, Hope found that one of her neighbors had been ill for some time. Unfortunately, when she discovered the woman's condition, it was too late to seek the help that might have saved the woman's life. Louie Shivery, the first recorder of the Neighborhood Union's history, wrote: "Deeply grieving that at their very door and under the shadow of the College [Morehouse], a poor woman could sicken and die probably from the want of such womanly care as the neighbors could have given had they known, the College women said, 'this should not be; we should know our neighbors better.'" Jacqueline Rouse, Hope's biographer, notes that Hope concluded that "the incident occurred because of the 'absence of neighborly feeling.'" Hope was moved to action; she and other neighbors organized the Neighborhood Union.[14]

Hope, Barrett, and Jane Edna Hunter, founder of the Phillis Wheatley Association in Cleveland, Ohio, as well as other women who embarked on careers in social (settlement) work before and soon after the turn of the century, were moved more by social conscience than by social science, which guided the actions of later social workers. Their callings legitimized their efforts as public sphere workers, and how effectively they worked helped to determine their public standing. Even Anna DeCosta Banks, who entered the workforce when people were just coming to accept nursing as a "legitimate" profession, found that her personal reputation as a professional was conferred as much by a work ethic of self-sacrificing devotion as by a nursing diploma.

The ease with which women of the first generation crossed occupational lines suggests that perhaps only for nursing were there fixed educational standards in place. Almost half the women of this generation established public careers outside the fields of their training. Both Judith Ann Carter Horton and Susan Dart Butler, for example, were trained to become teachers—Horton in the academic department at Oberlin, from which she graduated in 1891, and Butler in the normal program at Atlanta University, from which she graduated in 1908—but both became librarians because of local community needs. Sarah Collins Fernandis and Janie Porter Barrett, 1882 and 1884 Hampton normal graduates, similarly moved easily from schoolteaching into social work. Jane Edna Hunter trained as a nurse but became a social and community worker. And Mary Church Terrell moved from the classroom to the public lectern. The women's moving into an area of work different from their prior training certainly reflects the broad-based nature of their schooling and its emphasis on practical application and individual adaptability. But the phenomenon also suggests fluid or even nonexistent occupational boundaries that allowed professional status to be determined by the demonstrated commitment to one's calling, which was sometimes different from one's formal training.[15]

Black professional women of the first generation were not unique in their mission to serve the public and respond to community needs. Even after the establishment of rigid credentials in all the occupations, working for the common good remained a hallmark of professionalism. Moreover, the socialization process that nearly all the women had undergone as children and young adults had already inculcated an ethic of social responsibility. Consequently not the service ideal but advanced education—the necessity of having it and the process of gaining it—most clearly distinguishes one generation from another. Toward the end of the century, educational requirements for entering these occupations became the subject of great debate. And though the higher standards did not become fixed until the 1930s and 1940s, these early discussions influenced the actions of many women who were determined to maintain leadership roles as professionals.

Black professional women were concentrated in teaching until well into the twentieth century, and, predictably, over half of the first-generation women studied here were normal school graduates.[16] Through the nineteenth century, normal school curricula were heavily weighted with moral and mental philosophy coursework that emphasized religious (Protestant) values. And students in normal schools were often isolated from other advanced students in order "to ensure dedication to teaching as a calling." They were also set apart from the liberal arts students because the normal course required only a common school (eighth grade) certificate for entry, whereas the liberal arts program required a high school diploma. But in 1908 the National Education Association (NEA) proposed that normal school admission require a high school diploma, and the national transition from (two-year) normal schools to (four-year) teachers colleges began shortly thereafter.[17]

Until after 1920, work as a librarian required even less formal training than common school teaching. Melvil Dewey instituted the first formal library school training program at Columbia College in 1887 (Columbia College School of Library Economy), and it was only a three-month course of lectures. Between 1889, when Dewey's school moved to Albany (becoming the New York State Library School), and 1919 several library training schools opened, however, and the first real professional standards for training were established in 1915 when library educators organized the Association of American Library Schools and established relatively strict criteria for membership. Potential members would have to require a high school diploma for admission to their programs, offer a one-year course of technical and professional training, and have a staff of at least four including two faculty members who were trained in a library school. Most training for librarianship, however, still occurred in libraries, not library schools, and so in 1924 the American Library Association created a "permanent Board of Education for Librarianship" to develop and oversee training standards. When Judith Ann Carter Horton and Susan Dart Butler established their libraries in 1908 and in 1927, most librarians, like themselves, were self-taught or, at best, trained by apprenticeship. By the 1930s, however, working as a public librarian would require much more formal training.[18]

Although women who assumed responsibility for "social" work have historically come from among America's most privileged people and have therefore been relatively well educated, the field of social work, like librarianship, at first required no formal school course. The first "social workers," associates of the Charity Organization Societies (COS) beginning in the 1870s, coordinated the local distribution of private philanthropy and tried to improve the plight of the poor. The job of the "friendly visitors" from the COS was to provide "friendship and, through the example of [their] superior social position, moral uplift." The visitors suggested housekeeping hints, provided employment counseling, and administered aid (money) only as a last resort. The first formal schooling program, a six-week summer course sponsored by the COS of New York, began in 1898, almost a decade after Barrett founded the Locust Street Settlement House. Known first as the New York School of Philanthropy, the program was extended to a one-year course in 1903–4, and it became a two-year course in 1910, when the program became known as the New York School of Social Work (now the Columbia University School of Social Work). But even as educators established more rigorous schooling standards, leaders in the field concluded in 1930 that social work was still hardly more than " 'a craft in which expertness is acquired primarily through practice or supplemented by some schooling concerning the character of which social workers have vague and indefinite ideas.' " Indeed, the American Association of Social Workers, formed in 1921, did not accredit its first school until 1927. Beulah Whitby and Constance Fisher, both of whom graduated from college during that decade, completed courses in social work.[19]

The field of nursing therefore stands out in that by the 1890s a two- or three-year nursing diploma was already a professional certification, distinguishing those who held it from practical nurses and nursemaids. The emphasis on education in nursing, consequently, first concentrated on standardizing the training rather than encouraging higher degrees. Graduate nurses, first trained in hospitals, received their training in exchange for working in the institution. Consequently, across the country, instruction was inconsistent and difficult to standardize because the student's first obligation was to work rather than to study. But Progressive Era nursing educators resolved that "educational standards" rather than "hospital economics" should be the basis of nurses' training, and they gained some control by advocating state licensing laws. The New York State licensing law, passed in 1903, allowed the State Board of Regents (which supervised higher education) to create a Nurses Board of Examiners. The purpose of the board was to set educational standards for admission to nursing schools, to establish minimum standards for nursing education, and to design the nursing examination and the registration process. The New York bill, the most extensive in existence at the time, did not require nurses to adhere to the Nurses Board's program in order to practice, but noncompliance precluded their adding R.N. after their names. Although no state passed a mandatory licensing law until 1938, ambitious nursing students and those who intended to become leaders in the field paid close attention to the changes their professional peers were advocating and based their training on those recommendations.[20]

The changes under way were not lost on black professional women. Five of the seven first-generation women who became teachers graduated from normal programs (only one went on to complete the bachelor's degree). Of fourteen second-generation women who became schoolteachers, seven came directly from college programs. Those normal school graduates whose initial credentials did not hold up in the new era either returned to school for more training, as Septima Clark, Barbara Simmons Miller, Mamie Garvin Fields, and Susan St. Clair Minor did, or left the field altogether as did Sarah Webb Rice.[21]

For some of the second-generation women, attaining higher education was a slow process. One could easily get the impression that many of them were not deeply committed to advancing themselves and their communities in the ways that more education and higher-level credentials would allow. Missouri nurse Mabel Northcross, for example, took more than two decades to complete a bachelor's degree in nursing. And South Carolina schoolteacher Septima Clark required almost thirty years to complete her bachelor's degree. But the delay was not because they lacked commitment. Whereas first-generation women worked their way through normal school and nursing courses as "self-help" students or came from families that could easily afford their pursuit of college degrees, some second-generation women did not have the same advantage. Moreover, educational standards changed after they left their parents' care, and those who later pursued higher degrees had to combine the effort with their regular paid work and sometimes care for families as well. Whether working as a nurse or a teacher, a social worker or a librarian, anyone who did not keep up with the changing standards dropped out.

Fostine Riddick was one who temporarily left her profession as national standards changed. She had been trained as a nurse anesthetist at Tuskegee/John A. Andrew Hospital during the early 1930s. When the occupational classification of nurse anesthetist began to break down and more extensive training and degrees in the area of anesthesiology became common, Riddick quit her job. Until she returned to school in the 1950s, she worked only as a short-assignment, traditional private-duty nurse. And upon completing a bachelor's degree during the mid-1950s and a master's degree in 1963, Riddick was qualified for entirely different, supervisory, work.[22]

Whereas Fostine Riddick's professional dilemma had much to do with her highly specialized area of anesthesiology, Septima Clark was caught in one more typical for black professional women. Upon graduating from Avery Normal Institute in 1916, Clark's diploma (and certain test scores) entitled her to a state teaching certificate, and she went to work in the Sea Island schools. At the time, black public school terms were half as long as white school terms (67 days versus 133 days); black teachers earned less than one-third the annual income of white teachers ($112.31 versus $383.39); and they taught almost twice as many students as white teachers taught (64 versus 36). Louis Harlan, an early historian of the southern school system, characterized the situation as "inequality as a higher law."[23] Two-tiered credentials were included in that inequality, for in South Carolina school administrators maintained different standards for African American and white teachers.[24] Thus Clark's normal diploma was acceptable in South Carolina even during the 1920s; and that was about as much as South Carolina officials were willing to pay for at the time.

Whether or not the southern school system required the additional credentials or would pay a black teacher for having earned them, Clark had seen the requirements in northern (Ohio) schools and determined that she would complete the bachelor's degree. But earning a substandard salary and being a single parent limited her and helped make her pursuit of higher education seem haphazard. She took occasional courses at North Carolina A & T State College, South Carolina State College, Atlanta University, Columbia University, and Benedict

College. The bachelor's degree she earned in 1942 (from Benedict College), more than twenty-five years after completing the normal diploma, symbolizes her commitment. Furthermore, Clark then immediately enrolled in a master's degree program at Hampton Institute and completed it in three summers. Despite the constraint of having to work for a living during the regular school term, the "speed" with which she earned this graduate degree reflects her new freedom from domestic obligations to her son, who by then had enlisted in the military, and her higher income that resulted from the NAACP's successful salary equalization suit.[25]

The piecemeal approach to obtaining a higher education (beyond what their parents provided) is apparent among nurses too. Mabel Northcross, a Missouri nurse, took courses at Southern Illinois, Columbia, and Indiana Universities; the Universities of Michigan and Chicago; and the Chevalier Jackson Bronchoscopic Clinic of Temple University, among other schools. Northcross, who earned her nursing diploma in 1919, did not finish her bachelor's degree at New York University until 1946.[26] But unlike Septima Clark's teaching certificate, Northcross's nursing diploma from Meharry Medical College was an acceptable credential for nurses anywhere, then and for decades to come. Her pursuit of the nursing degree therefore clearly reflected her own ambition rather than changing external standards. But just the same, legal proscriptions against integrated education, like those Septima Clark faced, affected the way Northcross had to pursue her degree.

Northcross's desire for higher training could not be fulfilled in Missouri. First, most of the nursing programs in the South offered only the diploma, which she already held, and most of the institutions that offered the degree did not admit black students. Northcross chose to attend programs that allowed black students to participate fully, and she also wanted experience in a variety of areas. She therefore first took courses in one area and then moved on to another school to study another specialty. Equally important, Northcross's work ethic as well as her finances prevented her from leaving her job to study full time. She pursued coursework only when she had accumulated enough vacation time and sick leave. Had nurses had a summer schedule that released them from direct institutional duties as teachers did, Northcross no doubt would have completed her degree much sooner. Instead, twenty-seven years passed between her receiving the nursing diploma and the bachelor's degree.[27]

Nurses, especially in the South, also met another obstacle to full professional status that teachers sometimes faced. Southern state officials regularly maintained a racial double standard in nurse registration and licensing, holding black nurses to lower criteria than white nurses had to meet. Yet the nurses' situation was not exactly parallel to that of the teachers. Some state officials gave black nurses an examination different from the one administered to white nurses, and some officials did not test black nurses at all. The southern double standard reinforced the stereotype of black women as "natural" nurses. Jim Crow policies implied that there was nothing special about these women, that their brand of nursing was no different from that of generations of black women "nurses" who had wiped the noses and washed the diapers of many white children.[28] With little sympathy from southern public administrators, African American nurses braced themselves for a protracted battle to change the unequal policy.

In the one case for which some documentation exists, Ludie Andrews, a 1906 graduate of Spelman College and a principal organizer of the nursing program at Grady Hospital in Atlanta, worked for ten years to have state officials require registration for black nurses in Georgia. The state board in Georgia examined and licensed white nurses by national standards, but black nurses could not sit for the same exam and therefore did not have equal credentials even if they met all other qualifications. Perhaps to put an end to Andrews's efforts, state officials offered Andrews her professional license. But Andrews was not in this battle solely for her own benefit, and she refused to accept the bribe. Through sheer persistence, in 1920 Andrews's efforts finally paid off. The Board of Nurse Examiners began to allow black nurses to take the same examination white nurses took. Local NACGN members immediately organized "coaching classes" to make certain that black nurses would pass the test.[29]

When it was common knowledge that black professionals did not meet the same qualifications as white workers, it was easy to assume that the black workers were not as capable and therefore not "real" professionals. Economic opportunities were at stake too, for if state laws "excused" black women from meeting certain standards, the same statutes disqualified the women from certain jobs. Equally important, women who could not meet the regular professional standards because of their own shortcomings could be a threat to the health and safety of the black community they were supposed to serve. Thus there were compelling reasons—personal, professional, and community based—

for black women's pushing individually for more advanced training and for organized efforts to have the new standards applied to everyone. Still, family obligations, racially restrictive school policies, disparate credentialing traditions, and limited personal finances were powerful forces that sometimes brought long delays in black women's qualifying for full professional status.

Some women found ways around these obstacles. Family responsibilities, for example, could be flexible: husbands might do more at home, as Joseph Mitchell did so that Lucy could return to school. And children grew up, which allowed Septima Clark to gain more education and allowed Florence Edmonds to pursue higher-paid work. With enough effort, disparate licensing policies could be changed, as the Georgia nurses witnessed. And even while access to institutions of higher learning remained limited, there were always some accessible programs—even if one had to move far from home, as Fostine Riddick did, to take advantage of them. Beginning in the 1930s, women able to surmount these normally inhibiting conditions also found public and private programs that made it possible to surmount the financial limitations and to move all the more quickly toward gaining higher professional status.

Estelle Massey Osborne, one of the "younger" members of the second generation, received Rosenwald Fund money to attend Columbia University's Teachers College in New York for her bachelor's degree in 1929, only seven years after receiving her nursing diploma from Homer G. Phillips Hospital in Missouri. Rosenwald Fund representatives saw "leadership potential" in Osborne, and she took advantage of their sentiments and insisted that if she were to become a real leader in her field, then "certainly education had to be fundamental." Osborne completed her bachelor's degree in 1930 and her master's in 1931.[30] A National Youth Administration program enabled Mary Elizabeth Carnegie, a member of the third generation, to complete her bachelor's degree at West Virginia State College. Carnegie, a 1937 graduate of the Lincoln School for Nurses (New York), was working at John A. Andrew Hospital in Tuskegee, Alabama, when she learned of the opportunity. She recalled, "It was my chance to go to college, and I went." She graduated from that program in 1942, and the very next summer she went to Teachers College at Columbia University on a Public Health Service grant.[31] Beulah Hester, a 1912 normal graduate (and a member of the first generation) was not lucky enough to have the support of organizations like the Rosenwald and Rockefeller Foundations, and she left teaching after she and her husband relocated to Boston. But at about the same time that Osborne and Carnegie, supported by private philanthropy, enrolled in degree programs, Hester enrolled in the Simmons College School of Social Work after persuading the bursar to accept payments of twenty-five dollars a month. She was still paying the installments when she graduated in 1933.[32]

Black professional women were not guessing about what they needed or wanted in the way of education. In addition to understanding the value of the education in their work, they were aware of changing trends in their fields and intended to be prepared for them. One 1930s nurse, capturing the temper of the time in an application for a Rosenwald Fund scholarship, emphasized the difference between the "old-time" nurses and women like herself:

A decade or so ago, the words "Nursing Education" were seldom, if ever, used. . . . "You learn by doing" was the accepted theory, and so probationers "as green as the grass of the countryside" from whence they came were sent on the wards to learn how to be a nurse by the "trial and error" method. . . .

Today the trend is toward higher education in all professional fields. Nursing, being among the youngest of the professions, was among the last to recognize and stress the need of college preparation for its students. . . .

I wish to help solve that problem [of the undereducation of nurses] or at least make a contribution, as a result of wider experience and knowledge. . . .

I have set myself a tack which only through broader education can I accomplish.[33]

Without exception, the third-generation women completed the higher degrees while still under their parents' charge. In this way they more closely resemble the more privileged women of the first generation, and indeed, their socioeconomic background was generally higher than that of the second generation. But equally important, they began their postsecondary education after the modern professional standards were firmly in place, so even those who became teachers enrolled directly in college courses rather than normal courses, which by this time were practically extinct. Moreover, the "oldest" two members of this generation, who were nurses, graduated from hospital schools, and the very "youngest" was the first (and obviously only) one to enroll, from the beginning, in a college of nursing. She was also the first to enroll initially in a fully integrated nursing program.[34]

. . .

Most of these women expressed extraordinary concern about being fully prepared for their jobs. They constantly sought education, or "preparation," as they termed it, through formal schooling, conferences, and workshops. That additional education enhanced their status in the public sphere in general and the black community in particular. It might even have boosted their earning potential and their employability. But beyond the personal advantages that education and professional employment allowed, the women also saw themselves as public servants whose main concern, they said, was not how much money they earned or how many hours they worked, but how well they served their clients or contributed to the common good. Miriam Matthews, one of the "youngest" members of the second generation, for example, said she found community service a privilege and a responsibility. And she added that she worked not simply to make a living but also to improve the life of her community. When Ollie Jewell Sims applied to the Rosenwald Fund for a fellowship to study for a master's degree in public health nursing during the late 1930s, she wrote in her application, "I believe that this more widened experience received through such preparation would prepare me properly and more adequately to serve in a greater way." Then she thanked the foundation for providing her "the opportunity to submit my plan for fuller service." Mabel Staupers reported that when she graduated from nursing school in 1917, she earned three dollars a day for ten hours of work. Implying that the work brought rewards other than pay, Staupers noted that nursing was not the kind of work one did for the money.[35]

Despite being poorly paid compared with white professionals, black professional women still earned much more than less-skilled black workers earned. And that fact could make the women's retrospective comments seem dubious. But this seemingly unstinting commitment to service was shaped and perhaps mandated by their "preparation." Even had they not been exposed to the particulars of "professional culture," which involved recognizing the work as having social significance beyond the salary it earned, their socialization in schools, communities, and families had already emphasized this service ideal. If the women did not believe it, even if they secretly resented it, this is still the line they would have articulated. Too many cultural traditions—family, school, community, and professional—prevented their saying anything else.

The relationship between these women and the black community they served was not one-sided. The black community was the first to grant the professionals their high status. Schoolteachers readily recalled that their word was never questioned when they reported to the parents of their students. And during the 1920s Florence Edmonds had no fear of walking New York City streets after dark to reach her patients, because her nursing bag and uniform were her passport. Julia Smith similarly remembered that when she visited the homes of her students in Washington, D.C., between the 1910s and 1940s, she had to walk through some of the toughest neighborhoods in the city. But when people saw the schoolteacher approaching, all the swearing and roughhousing stopped.[36]

The recognition of their work and their status was sometimes much more formal. For example, a hospital administrator praised the "initiative, imagination and creative thinking" that Sadie Peterson Delaney, a hospital librarian, used in aiding patients through bibliotherapy. Black sororities, the National Council of Negro Women, and the National Urban League also recognized Delaney's work. The Booker T. Washington Business Association of Detroit awarded Beulah Whitby, a social worker, its highest achievement award. Detroit's West Side Human Relations Council honored librarian Clara Jones for outstanding community service. And in 1951 Mabel Staupers received the NAACP's prestigious Spingarn Medal.[37]

People beyond the community for and with which the women worked also recognized their important contributions, underlining the shortsightedness of the professional organizations that continued to exclude African Americans. Sadie Delaney stands out in this instance. For her work with hospitalized veterans, for example, the Lions Club honored Delaney with "the lion's roar" during a special ceremony, and a unit of the Veterans of Foreign Wars gave a testimonial dinner in her honor. One physicians' association made her an honorary member. Library journal editors and conference organizers solicited papers from Delaney. International library groups sought her help and commended her work. The warden of San Quentin Prison wrote to her for information on bibliotherapy that might be applied to prisoners. The Rosenwald Foundation solicited a list of books that Delaney thought should be in all Rosenwald schools. She was also the subject of one of Eleanor Roosevelt's "My Day" radio programs. And *Look* magazine featured Delaney on its "*Look* Applauds" page in 1950.[38]

But in spite of advanced training and all the recognition from within and outside the black community, full professional status continued to elude most black workers. By the 1930s, membership in the national occupational organizations was required for full credentialing, but the national organizations generally had no room for African Americans. There were rarely any written policies that prohibited black membership, but in practice black associates were excluded from branches of the ALA, the American Nurses' Association (ANA), and the NEA until the 1950s and 1960s. Black professional women were, however, active in comparable black organizations designed to benefit the communities and the professionals, and included in the important work of these organizations was a drive to break down the racial barriers to mainstream organizational membership.

Black teachers formed their own state-level organizations in Kentucky and Georgia in 1878, in Alabama in 1882, in Virginia in 1888, in Florida in 1891, and in Arkansas in 1898. There was a black teachers' organization in almost every state in the South by 1900, and the Alabama organization, at least, acknowledged the hierarchical salary scales and charged men one dollar a year for membership while women paid fifty cents. One role of all the organizations that was perhaps even more critical for black than for white professionals (because of limited schooling opportunities) was the education they imparted. One author noted that the Louisiana Education Association "made every effort to keep the Black teachers abreast with new developments and techniques in education through educational articles in the journal and by sponsoring various educational workshops throughout the state."[39]

Black librarians organized much later than the teachers, but they did so for the same reason. Since there were few black librarians in the country before there were places where they could work, they never formed an independent group until they were accepted as full members of the ALA and established the Black Caucus within it. Before then they organized as divisions within black state and national teachers' groups. The librarians' division of the Virginia State Teachers' Association worked to "provide incentive for the members to engage in continuing education" and to promote the value of library service to students, teachers, and principals.[40] In Georgia they sought to improve and expand library service, to promote the "professional growth and development of librarians," and to work with other professional groups to promote child welfare. Black Alabama librarians also had their own organization, and they regularly sent representatives to ALA meetings "in order to keep abreast of national professional activities."[41]

Black women recognized the educational, social, and political value of belonging to professional organizations. Mabel Staupers joined the NACGN in 1916 when she was a senior nursing student. When

Estelle Osborne went to Freedmen's Hospital in the 1930s as the first education director in the nursing program, she insisted on time off to attend professional meetings as a condition of her employment. Not only did Mary Elizabeth Carnegie attend all the conferences she thought would benefit her, beginning in the 1930s, but, she added, "I always dragged my students to everything. I'd just pack up the car and take them with me. I thought that was important too." Florence Edmonds became active in the Pittsfield (Massachusetts) Visiting Nursing Association as soon as she began to practice there in 1945. And Gloria Smith, who graduated from Wayne State University College of Nursing during the mid-1950s, immediately began attending the meetings of the ANA, which had just opened its doors to all black nurses.[42] Most of these women, however, were in the paid workforce at various points during the segregation era and so were limited to black organizations and excluded (in varying degrees) from the activities of the larger white groups.

As difficult as the circumstances were, existing proscriptions did not destroy the women's desire to participate in these national groups. Mary Elizabeth Carnegie, a diligent NACGN worker from the beginning of her nursing career in the 1930s, began to pay membership dues to the white Florida state nurses' association in 1948, the first year African Americans could join. Because of segregation, however, she could not attend the meetings until several years later. Fostine Riddick joined the Tidewater (Virginia) Association of Colored Graduate Nurses as soon as she moved to the area; she could not join the white Virginia Nurses' Association at that time, but she became a member of the ANA as soon as the racial barriers came down. Barbara Pickett became a member of the Kentucky Library Association (KLA) as soon as she qualified for membership and the organization accepted African Americans, but KLA officials "discouraged" black librarians from attending conferences by holding meetings at segregated hotels. Suited up with all the required professional credentials—and a good bit of courage and self-esteem—Pickett attended some of the meetings anyway. Barbara Simmons Miller, also a Kentucky librarian, was not so accommodating. After her reservations were "mistakenly" accepted for one KLA meeting, one of the organizers arranged for her to stay with a local minister instead. Miller refused to go. Septima Clark attended interracial teachers' conferences in South Carolina when black and white teachers had to sit in separate sections. And Eunice Rivers Laurie went to professional conferences when "there weren't but four of us

Negro nurses [there]." They braved the meetings, avoided the meals, and "had very little to say, but [they] would be there." As the white organizations lowered racial barriers, even partially, black women became as active as circumstances would allow. From their point of view, the advantages they might gain from attending the meetings outweighed the unpleasant circumstances under which they had to attend.[43] A few women, however, eventually made a personal crusade of opening up the white organizations to all black professionals.

Sadie Peterson Delaney was one such woman. She graduated from the College of the City of New York in 1919 and immediately enrolled in the New York Public Library School. She completed the one-year program and accepted her first professional position at the 135th Street (Harlem) branch of the New York Public Library in 1920. In 1923 Delaney relocated to Tuskegee, Alabama, and became a librarian at the Veterans Hospital. Although she developed an international reputation over the next two decades, like most other black professional women she endured the racist snubs of white professional organizations in the United States. In 1947, however, Delaney was elected to the Hospital Division of the Council of the ALA, and it seemed that Jim Crow was giving up his reign.[44] Further evidence of change came to Delaney in 1950 or 1951 in an invitation to join the Alabama Library Association. But although the invitation came directly from the organization's president, as soon as a new president was installed the next year, Delaney's membership was revoked. The new president, Mabel E. Willoughby, explained: "At a meeting of the Executive Council, April 15, 1951, it was decided that the President (1950–51) had acted without authority in extending you an invitation to join the Association. In view of this decision we considered it only fair business practice to return to you the dues which you had remitted." President Willoughby assured Delaney that the association was considering "enlarging its membership" and that they would keep Delaney apprised of their decision. Meanwhile, Willoughby concluded, "We ask your patience."[45]

The Alabama Library Association did come to a fairly quick conclusion early the next year. They recommended that black librarians in Alabama start a new, all-black library association. In response, Delaney wrote to her good friend Clyde Cantrell, a white librarian at Alabama Polytechnic Institute, that she hoped the movement to start a separate organization could be stopped, adding that "the Alabama Library Association had no right to suggest" it. She reminded Cantrell that black nurses, dietitians, and physicians throughout the state now had access to formerly all-white professional associations and that the state librarians' associations in Kentucky, Texas, Mississippi, and Virginia were desegregated too. To her mind, the Alabama association's decision was "not in keeping with the times [or] with the principles of their profession." And she added, "With America advocating democratic principles and emphasizing them, it was time that here in the state . . . we should be members."[46]

Two years later Delaney tried again to join the Alabama Library Association. The organization's secretary responded with a familiar tune:

As you know, the Alabama Library Association has as yet not opened its membership to Negroes. I am sure you realize the problems involved in Alabama in contemplation of such action. The association is divided in its willingness to admit Negroes to membership, and partly as a result of the laws of the state of Alabama, which would prevent the admission of Negroes on terms of genuine equality, the group not willing to admit Negroes as members has succeeded in having its way. The Executive Board has been studying the problem and its members feel that the situation will in time be changed, but it is the overwhelming opinion of the Board that any insistence at this time on Negro membership, or even Negro visitation at the meeting, would result in more friction than it would be worth, would be embarrassing to both races, and . . . would serve only to set back such progress toward integration as has already been made.[47]

Although it was not possible to tell in Alabama, real progress had indeed been made. Even though the American Library Association did not constitutionally denounce racial exclusion until 1969, it had been accepting black members directly since the 1940s. Delaney had even become a member of the national group's council. By the 1950s ALA officials made conscious decisions to hold annual meetings "in a setting in which the personal rights and dignity of all ALA members will be respected." The Southeastern Library Association (SELA) had also desegregated. When Delaney inquired in 1956 whether black librarians could attend upcoming meetings in Roanoke, Virginia, the program coordinator responded that SELA members had, in fact, chosen to hold the meeting in Roanoke so that "Negro members could attend with the minimum of embarrassment." The Virginia Library Association had been desegregated for nearly a decade, and therefore black librarians could attend meetings they hosted. Because of local policies, however, black conference participants could not sleep in the conference hotel or take their meals there. But SELA officers had enlisted a local black librarian to make alternative room and board arrangements for all who needed them.[48]

Sadie Peterson Delaney's chief professional goal during the 1950s seemed to be knocking down the wall of segregation in the Alabama Library Association. She had proposed to retire from her position in the Veterans Hospital in 1951, but for no apparent reason she changed her mind.[49] That was, however, the year that she gained and then lost her membership in the Alabama Library Association. Delaney labored, with little assistance, to open the doors; probably other librarians, black and white, did too. But perhaps they failed because their campaigns were individual, making them seem less urgent and less threatening to white groups. Black nurses, on the other hand, beginning in the 1930s, mounted a nationally organized campaign for inclusion and full professional status. And they were ultimately successful.

•   •   •

The national emergency created by the Second World War made the work of health care professionals in general a critical component of the national agenda. And the popular and official wartime rhetoric that condemned Nazism and fascism made the exclusion of any care providers a national embarrassment. Black nurses, who had labored for professional status while sidestepping the issue of membership in the ANA (by advocating the acceptance of the National Association of Colored Graduate Nurses as an alternative certifying organization), used the extraordinary political circumstances to take aim at the ANA itself. Individual women were important in the nurses' efforts to achieve public recognition as full professionals, but their ultimate success was based on a collective effort.

Estelle Massey Osborne, president of the NACGN from 1934 to 1939, wrote one of the first official requests for the ANA to change its policy. In 1937 Osborne, on behalf of the NACGN members, wrote to the director of the ANA:

The professional status of the Negro Nurse in the South is greatly handicapped by the lack of opportunity to affiliate with the American Nurses' Association.

To this end, we are recommending that the Board of Directors of the American Nurses' Association consider the following plan:

In every Southern State where custom forbids the joint organization of the two groups [ANA and NACGN], we suggest that the American Nurses' Association recognize the Negro state organization, if it meets the American Nurses' Association state requirements, as the necessary medium through which the nurses may obtain membership.

We further recommend the appointment of qualified Negro nurses as members of standing committees of the American Nurses' Association. We feel that such participation will be mutually educational and helpful.[50]

The first response to that request, dated four months later, was ambiguous. The secretary of the ANA noted that the association already had a policy on both of Osborne's recommendations. She said, first of all, that the ANA recognized only one state nurses' association and that there were provisions for membership through that state association. On Osborne's second recommendation, the secretary responded that standing committee members received their appointments directly from the Board of Directors "unless otherwise provided for" and that those committee members "are appointed because of their particular fitness to serve on the committee to which they are appointed as members."[51] In a very disheartened response, Osborne informed the secretary of the NACGN members' disappointment with the ANA position because state organizations were not likely to admit black nurses without an explicit national policy welcoming all qualified nurses regardless of race. And as a parting shot, Osborne juxtaposed the ANA position to a horrifying image: "In the face of such policies, I seriously wonder how many 'good Americans' shudder at the acts of Hitler."[52]

Understanding fully the potential effect of broad-based community support for stimulating social change, NACGN officers then called on their Advisory Council for assistance. The council was an auxiliary organization of attorneys, college presidents, civic leaders, physicians, and other public health professionals created by the NACGN to promote their causes. In the fall of 1939, representatives from the ANA, the National League of Nursing Education (NLNE), and the National Organization of Public Health Nurses (NOPHN) met with NACGN Advisory Council members to discuss public health and professional issues. At that meeting, an NACGN representative asked members of the other groups to speak briefly on their organizational objectives. After the three presentations, Osborne surmised that their goals were perfectly consistent with those of the NACGN. Then someone asked if any African Americans served on the boards of the organizations. The representative from the NLNE responded that state leagues nominated board members, and "if several states sent in the name of a Negro representative she would be elected." But black nurses could not join the League in southern states because they could not join the ANA. And so it went, in the same vicious circle.[53] NACGN officials continued to inform their southern members in particular that there was still no way for them to join the ANA. But Staupers also wrote to a Virginia constituent that "it is no fault of ours and we have to continue hammering this point home to our white sister nurses until some plan for membership is developed for all of our nurses in the American Nurses' Association."[54]

ANA members were, however, beginning to budge. At a 1938 meeting they had authorized sending questionnaires to members "asking their attitude toward the Negro nurse" in the ANA. And at the 1939 interorganizational meeting, the representatives of the four organizations (NACGN, NLNE, NOPHN, ANA) agreed to establish a "Joint Conference" of representatives of the groups to explore ways black nurses could be fully integrated into the American nursing mainstream.[55]

NACGN advocates gained an important forum in the Joint Conference meetings, where they kept NACGN issues in the forefront. They advocated opening more postgraduate programs to black nurses, eliminating disparate salary scales for black and white nurses, and accrediting all qualified nursing schools in order to eliminate substandard programs. At one meeting Alma Scott, an ANA representative, proposed inviting black nurses to special public health training institutes "in those states in which Negro nurses are not accepted into membership in the State Nurses' Associations." And Mabel Staupers, NACGN executive secretary from 1934 to 1946, approved the suggestion but also noted "that for a Negro nurse to obtain certain jobs, an institute was not enough qualification."[56]

At the next Joint Conference meeting, in October 1940, NACGN Advisory Council member Frances Williams forced the conference to address directly the ANA's foot-dragging, which inhibited black nurses' acceptance into the armed services. Mary Roberts (ANA) reminded everyone that black nurses had proved their usefulness during World War I, and apparently her point was that their time would come again. But Williams responded emphatically: "I think it is wrong to presume that the patterns that we followed in 1917 are the patterns of action that will be used in this situation of 1940. Defense in 1940 rests partially on different and new legislation and will be administered by new personnel. It is my feeling that in thinking and working for defense it is now recognized that men must experience the democracy which they are called on to defend and to die for." Williams was challenging the Joint Conference to take a stand for the inclusion of black nurses. She also, incidentally, had to ask for a rewrite of the minutes of the meeting to include this short speech and another that she made during the meeting.[57] Still, except for the inclusion of NACGN representatives on the Nursing Council of National Defense, NACGN requests continued unheeded.[58]

By 1942 the ANA Board of Directors had a new president, and NACGN officers made their appeal again. They urged that black nurses who were excluded because of racial barriers in state associations have access to ANA membership through the NACGN, as had happened with the American Red Cross and the National League for Nursing Education. But Staupers phrased the request poorly and gave the board a loophole. The request began with the conditional: "'If and when alumnae association membership is eliminated,'" and consequently "the board voted to defer action on this matter until and if the contingency mentioned in the statement from Mrs. Staupers arises."[59]

NACGN nurses had worked for thirty years and established a secure position for themselves before directly confronting the ANA. Still, the ANA refused to accept them. But in a bold move in 1945, a move no doubt encouraged by a new military policy of enlisting black nurses with no numerical limit, NACGN officers sent an announcement to ANA members that represented a dramatic change from their earlier position. For the first time, they demanded full, front-door admission to the ANA rather than admission through their own black organizations where state ANA chapters refused to admit them. The NACGN request insisted:

The burning political question regarding the nurse draft has placed in the hands of the profession a new opportunity of becoming a potent force for world unity. It offers a great challenge to the profession for the removal of policies which prevent the full use of our nursing facilities on our civilian and fighting fronts. . . .

The time has come for the total mobilization of nursing services without limitations. This can be accomplished primarily through your cooperation by accepting [black nurses] to membership and making available to your members factual information by Negroes in nursing, and by making known to the American public your desire for integration without the limitations which now face nurses because of race, religion, sex, and nationality.[60]

Considering the new Army Nurse Corps policy, black nurses' exclusion from the ANA became a great embarrassment even for many white nurses. Consequently, in response to yet another NACGN request, ANA representatives met with NACGN officials "to discuss the question of ANA membership for Negro nurses in states where they are not admitted to membership in the state nurses' associations." At that January 1946 meeting NACGN officials requested: "THAT the Board of the American Nurses' Association be requested to give individual membership in the ANA to Negro nurses from states which do not now accept them to state membership, and THAT it [the ANA board] recommends to the By-laws Committee the consideration of such amendments in order that it be appended to the call of the meeting of the next House of Delegates to assure its adoption." The discussion that followed the proposal was a good one. Some participants asked how black nurses would be represented in nominating ANA officers, since they would have no state affiliation and the nominations for national officers came from the state offices. Others questioned the impact of black nurses' having to pay for two memberships (NACGN and ANA). Black nurses countered that the NACGN was to fold once the ANA made provisions for including them, and therefore the double dues would be only temporary. One ANA member suggested that black nurses be admitted to the ANA but also continue to work in the NACGN. And yet another opposed integration altogether and suggested that the ANA commit some of its resources to strengthening the NACGN instead.[61]

ANA representatives ultimately agreed to present the NACGN recommendations to the ANA House of Delegates meeting in September. At that meeting in Atlantic City, New Jersey, the ANA House agreed that "colored nurses who are eligible should be accepted as members in the ANA and in their state associations wherever possible and that this House of Delegates requests [that] the Board of Directors of the American Nurses' Association find a way to give colored nurses membership in the American Nurses' Association and to bring that recommendation before the next convention." The ANA Committee on Constitution and Bylaws spent the next year revising its regulations so the group could comply with the House of Delegates' order.[62]

NACGN members continued to hold conferences as a separate organization, but with a foot finally in the door, they were no longer to be satisfied by mere membership in the ANA. The NACGN met late in 1946 or early in 1947 and prepared a report for the ANA that began by stating current NACGN objectives. Primary was "furthering the integration of the Negro in the main channels of nursing." They noted that nursing associations in ten states still refused to admit black nurses, but said they were willing to be patient. The two recommendations they added, however, suggested that their patience was wearing thin. The first was that the ANA "take the necessary steps to absorb the functions now carried by the National Association of Colored Graduate Nurses." The second was "that sufficient Negro personnel be provided to interpret the needs of the Negro people to the entire staff and membership of the American Nurses' Association, and to continue to stimulate work among Negro nurses."[63] Mabel Staupers later summarized the new position on integration: "Integration goes . . . beyond the courtesy of membership. It must be a complete working together for the good of the profession and the people it serves. Negro and white nurses must accept the challenge and demonstrate to the world that women can and will make Democracy work."[64]

The ANA Advisory Council subsequently split on whether they could "absorb the functions of another organization" without going through the long process of obtaining House of Delegates approval. But they did request more information from the NACGN—a detailed account of the group's functions.[65]

By June 1948 the ANA House of Delegates had finished revising the organization's bylaws to allow black nurses direct membership, and they demonstrated their new commitment to integration by employing NACGN nurse Elizabeth Ann Edwards as an assistant executive secretary of the ANA. Shortly thereafter they elected Estelle Osborne to the Board of Directors.[66]

With its mission nearly accomplished, the NACGN began preparing to go out of existence, but officers kept reminding ANA members that simple desegregation would not be enough and that there had to be a complete "consolidation of services for all Negro nurses in the United States under the aegis of one national organization, the American Nurses' Association." The officers also demanded a fully integrated ANA staff and black nurses' participation "in the total program" of the ANA.[67]

The ANA ultimately did agree not only to desegregation, but also to assuming the functions of the NACGN. Based on NACGN goals, this obligated the ANA to work to end discrimination in nursing in general, to help develop leadership among black nurses, to recruit black students to nursing, and to fulfill the other interests of black nurses and the black public.[68] Appropriately, in 1949 and 1950, ANA personnel appointed NACGN representatives to all the national nursing committees organized by or administered through the ANA, and members of the two groups activated an Intergroup Relations Program.[69]

Finally, NACGN officers turned to concluding their business. In 1950 they arranged to donate their equipment and furniture to other agencies. After extended legal consultations, they agreed to place all their papers that concerned work with the ANA in the ANA office. They arranged to keep all financial records in private storage. And they deposited the rest of their papers in the Schomburg Center for Research in Black Culture. As a final act, President Mabel Staupers encouraged NACGN members to write their local organizational histories and send them to the Schomburg Center, to continue to pursue courses in "parliamentary procedure, public speaking, and leadership training," and equally significant, to form local clubs among themselves, their "husbands, sweethearts, and relatives," and other laypeople to continue to promote the cause of nurses and nursing.[70]

At the January 1951 NACGN biennial meeting in New York City, Staupers, now president, announced the dissolution of the organization. Newspaper headlines and news releases heralded the completion of the historic merging of the NACGN and the ANA. Significantly, one writer noted that "it marks the first time as far as could be ascertained, that an important organization composed predominantly of the nation's largest minority voted itself out of existence because much of its work was accomplished."[71]

From all accounts, the final NACGN meeting was a real celebration. Walter White reported that it was the first "funeral" he had ever enjoyed, for "instead of being lugubrious the obituaries were gay and congratulatory. The quite lovely corpse handed out thank you scrolls to individuals and organizations which had helped and cooperated with the late departed. Then stripping off its sable shroud, the corpse promptly marched into a new life of greater usefulness."[72]

For forty-three years, leaders of the NACGN had worked for the same things as other professional group members. They sought registration, licensing requirements, and quality training. But additionally, they worked toward an end that few other professional groups had to strive for—inclusion in existing organizations. Their exclusion from ANA membership suggested that they were not real professionals, and yet many of the black women were better educated than their white counterparts. Estelle Osborne, for example, reportedly the first nurse, black or white, in the Washington, D.C., area with a master's degree, at first could not belong to the District of Columbia branch of the ANA or the National League of Nursing (later the NLNE).[73] Osborne and the other members of the NACGN were professionals long before the ANA accepted them as full members, but their lack of affiliation suggested to the public that they were not. Other members of the ANA knew better—knew that black women were not members because they were black, not because they were unqualified. But that knowledge had no impact on ANA policies until the 1940s, when NACGN members, like other black professional women, began their own campaign to break down the barriers. On gaining membership in the ANA they finally had full credentials by the professional standards of the day.

· · ·

After the turn of the century, individuals who worked in areas that required extensive formal education sought organization in part to promote and maintain what they perceived as their special status. Members of the organizations established the criteria for participating in the professional arena, and those criteria included standards in training, licensing, service, and ethics. Only by meeting those guidelines did a person achieve public standing as a professional.[74]

Except for nurses, these issues were not critical to the first generation of black women studied here, or for others who worked in the feminized professions before the turn of the century. Their commitment to providing a service and their skill at doing so determined their status as public sphere workers. Subsequent generations, however, faced more institutionalized standards, and so beyond the commitment to public service, they had also to respond to changing educational and organizational expectations.

The parents of these black professional women and their educational mentors had undoubtedly prepared them to be the best they could be in their chosen professions, and the women regularly pursued additional higher education to achieve that standing for themselves. But as national occupational organization leaders scrambled to create a privileged place of some power and authority for their members, black professional women found themselves left out. Whether or not African Americans were viewed as professionals depended on the legal, social, and political climate when and where they worked. Not having the proper education, position, or commitment could certainly keep them out of the nationally defined professional class; but meeting those qualifications did not automatically let them in.

Gaining entry to mainstream professional ranks required the women to undertake this largely hidden layer of unpaid, personal public work. And their eventual success brought important advantages in terms of wages and work options. But ultimately the public work of black professionals went beyond concern for their individual status. They had been groomed, to borrow from Walter White's NACGN "obituary," for "greater usefulness": prepared, beginning in childhood, to fulfill expectations beyond the needs of their families and themselves. Although "greater usefulness" took on different meanings in different times and places, the women's understanding of the idea is best illustrated in the evolution of the public work they performed for the direct benefit of the communities where they lived and worked.

"Working for my race in one way or another ever since I was a grown woman":
PUBLIC SPHERE WORK

A 1915 publicity brochure for the Locust Street Settlement House in Hampton, Virginia, quotes Janie Porter Barrett: "What our people need . . . isn't to be told to 'go ahead' but to 'come on,' and we must know it and say it and help them to follow."[1] While explicitly designating herself as one of the leaders and others as followers, Barrett struck a balance in that remark between a person's leadership and her responsibility to the community—a philosophy clearly demonstrated throughout Barrett's public work history. She had graduated from Hampton Institute in 1884 and taught school in Georgia for a few years before returning to Hampton and marrying Harris Barrett in 1889. After repeatedly noticing girls playing in the street, she and her husband agreed to take money they had squirreled away for installing indoor plumbing in their home and use it to create a safe place for neighborhood children to play and a base from which to "improve the homes, as well as the moral and social life of the community." Thus the Locust Street Settlement House was born. After first establishing a girls' club, true to her Hampton training, Barrett designed and instituted a broad, continuing program for all age groups and both sexes, including classes in homemaking, child welfare, poultry raising, cooking, canning, and traditional academic disciplines in the evenings for adults.[2]

By 1915 Barrett was a veteran in the area of community development and about to launch her project to create a training school for black girls who had been judged delinquent by the Virginia court system. Then Margaret Murray Washington, director of Women's Industries at Tuskegee Institute and the widow of Booker T. Washington, offered her a principalship at Tuskegee. Barrett probably discussed the offer with a variety of people before she made her decision, but ultimately she declined the position. She told Hollis Frissell, then principal of Hampton Institute, that Washington's letter "makes me wish that I could be in two places at once. I should be glad to serve at Tuskegee, but I know I am going where I am needed [most?] and though the undertaking is most difficult, it isn't impossible, and if the friends[will stand by me, this Home School will be, in time, a tremendous power for good."[3]

Undoubtedly Barrett intended this letter to inform Frissell of her good reputation among well-known and respected individuals in the field of race work. And of course Booker T. Washington was Hampton's most famous student and Tuskegee its most notable offspring. But the letter also demonstrated the effectiveness of Hampton's educational process. That is, despite Barrett's irresolute beginnings as a Hampton student, one who at first looked forward to Sundays because no one compelled her to do race work on the Sabbath, she was now converted to the school's emphasis on social responsibility. Frissell could be proud of Barrett's commitment, and Barrett, in this modest way, could boast of her acclaim.

The position as "lady principal" at Tuskegee would probably have brought more predictable work and been a more financially rewarding job than undertaking the creation of a new institution, but Barrett's decision about where to work did not depend on wages. It did not have to at first, for her husband was employed in the Treasurer's Office at Hampton. By the time Washington's offer came, however, Barrett was a widow, yet she still did not hesitate to take on the responsibilities of the experimental and as yet financially unsupported "home school."[4] In fact it might have been precisely because of the opportunity for leadership that she chose founding the school over the Tuskegee offer. As already noted, women teachers at Tuskegee were intensively supervised, not only because they were expected to be full-time role models for the female students, but also because most employees had to serve the institution in several capacities, not all of their choosing. Indeed, only a few years earlier Ruth Anna Fisher, a 1906 Oberlin College graduate, was forced out of her position at Tuskegee the same year she arrived because she did not cooperate when the administrators attempted to extend her obligations beyond the academic department to include work in industrial education. In calling for her resignation, Booker T. Washington also charged that she "absolutely refuse[d] to have any part in Sunday School work."[5] Barrett, in directing her own program, would not have less work to do than Washington expected of Fisher, but she would gain a number of privileges, including independence. She and many other African American women regularly chose such positions because of their personal interests. But equally important, they saw needs that no one else was filling, their earlier upbringing led them to take some responsibility for other people in their communities, and they believed they were fully qualified to fulfill the demands of leadership positions.[6]

This chapter explores the ways black professional women assumed their public work responsibilities. It was a dynamic process in which women (sometimes) gained incomes, served community interests, developed leadership roles for themselves, and regularly challenged local, state, and national policies. Although significant changes occurred in the nature of their work roles because of demographic, political, and economic events, it is in their public work that their earlier socialization regarding individual status, collective development, and social responsibility is especially evident.

A vital distinction emerges, however. Just as black professional women's private responsibilities included both paid and unpaid family and community work, and their quest for professional status was public yet very personal, it is possible also to distinguish between the women's "work" and their "jobs" in the public sphere. Their "jobs" reflected bureaucratic occupational categories and the responsibilities they entailed. Their "work," that which they defined for themselves, however, far exceeded those categories, often was unpaid, and, ultimately was not performed exclusively for the benefit of their employers.[7] Considering that much of these women's socialization had been designed to prepare them not only to provide whatever services the community needed but also to situate themselves where they could ultimately gain admission to the American mainstream, individually and for the black community, the public work they performed had important ramifications beyond their own status and even beyond the community's practical needs. The higher imperative was a moral one, which, in the form of an ethic of socially responsible individualism, had far-reaching consequences for American society as a whole.

• • •

Bolstered by ambition, training, and the high expectations of their families, communities, and teachers, women like Janie Porter Barrett showed no lack of self-confidence as they moved from their roles as students to their roles as workers. Black professional women in the workforce between the 1890s and 1920s were aware of the reform impulse stirring throughout the country and actively encouraged it. But they were not typical reformers, working for zoning laws and building codes, attacking "the system" and hoping to change it to the advantage of the amorphous "masses." These women were also working, perhaps less obviously, for themselves.

Even had they not been taught so rigorously that they must work for the advancement of the race, black professional women could hardly have done otherwise, for they understood that white Americans rarely distinguished between the black middle classes (people like themselves) and lower classes. The personal frustrations this generated among relatively privileged women are keenly apparent, as are the women's elitist tendencies, in their insistence that white Americans judge African Americans not by their worst examples but by their best, and not by their failures but by their possibilities—that is, not by those they most obviously worked to serve, but by themselves. There was no doubt in their minds that for them to be seen individually as they wished to be seen and to have the privileges they wanted for themselves, the economic and social conditions of the group had to be changed.[8] The women began their careers, then, intending to make a positive difference in the lives of others, working toward community development and thereby gaining for the black community the higher status in society it deserved, and establishing themselves as leaders and as public servants in the process. The manner in which they proceeded depended on actual conditions. And for the most part, in the early years (roughly 1890–1920), it meant not simply going into schools, libraries, social welfare institutions, and public health facilities to take up the work, but also, as leaders and servants, creating these institutions themselves.

Black professional women began their work by reenacting some of the lessons from their own childhoods. They began with attempts to instill in other black people the manners, morals, and tastes, in general, that might promote mobility. Since one of their goals was to move the group closer to, and even into, the American mainstream, this "uplift work" seemed to be an important first step.

Much of this work focused on the condition of black people's homes. The professionals understood that outsiders regularly transformed this essentially private matter of individual choice or ability into a public issue and held it up as evidence of the character of the inhabitants. That is, a poorly kept home, in some people's minds, reflected the residents' character defects rather than economic deprivation or some other problem. But the women's work also included institution building and community development. And though without a doubt it was through this development work that some women's leadership roles materialized, incomes were gained, and status was enhanced, the importance of this work went far beyond the individual advantages that resulted. In light of the consistent failure of government agencies to provide adequate public services to black citizens, black professional women's efforts were also designed to move the community beyond "the shadow of slavery," where the politics of the post-Reconstruction Jim Crow period sought to keep them.

As recent graduates of seminaries, normal schools, and colleges, black women often created social settlements where they provided basic services, coordinated race uplift work, and developed other public institutions. Sarah Collins Fernandis, a Baltimore native and an 1882 normal graduate of Hampton, decided "to set up her little refined home" in the most deprived section of Washington, D.C. From her home, she and her husband instituted "a day nursery, kindergarten, branch library, various clubs among the children of the neighborhood, and a mother's club." Fernandis's philosophy of life, incorporating a sense of responsibility to others, led her "to look up and lift up." She hoped "to make [her] life a contradiction to the idea that a Negro is low and groveling in sentiment and purpose," and she also hoped that her less fortunate neighbors would follow her example. Fernandis distributed paint and flower seeds throughout the neighborhood to encourage community beautification. She had "her ragged little boys club" members saving their pennies with the goal of buying new suits for themselves for Christmas. She believed, as did most settlement social workers, that "only as we can raise the standard in the home can we hope to lift the neighborhood and the race," and that is how she shaped her work. She furnished her own home "so simply that no one in the neighborhood need hesitate to aspire to copy" her. And whenever a neighbor visited Fernandis's home, the visitor "carrie[d] away with her some hints about food, values, or neatness and order that possibly will help her in her own standards."[9]

Settlement houses were centers for coordinating community development and examples of community development as well.[10] Social settlement workers organized traditional school courses; programs for economic development; domestic/vocational training; and lessons in morals, manners, and appearance.[11] One of the best-known settlements, the Neighborhood Union that Lugenia Burns Hope helped to create in 1909, was, like most others, organized for the

moral, social, intellectual, and religious uplift of the community and the neighborhood; . . . to establish lecture courses that shall instruct and help the mothers of the neighborhood in the proper care of themselves and their infants; . . . to unite our efforts in breaking up dens of immorality and crime in the neighborhood; . . . to encourage wholesome thought and action in the community by disseminating good literature among the young; to encourage habits of industry by establishing clubs for cooking, sewing, millinery, manual training and general homemaking; to keep a census of the community by which we may know the full status of every family and individual therein; [and] to provide . . . harmless and beneficial sports and games for the young of the community.[12]

The activities carried out through the Neighborhood Union included but went beyond uplift work, and neither was it simply charity work; it was unmistakably community development. The founders of the Union were women who saw themselves as part of a neglected community that was in distress. It was economically, socially, and politically deprived and suffering all the consequences of such deprivation. As members of that community, the founders felt partly responsible for correcting those ills. And so they worked to develop and improve the community infrastructure by instituting a wide variety of educational programs, a public health clinic with a full-time paid nurse, and social service projects directed by a college-trained social worker. Moreover, the Neighborhood Union was not simply an idea that better-off and better-educated women instituted to provide for the less advantaged. Poor and working-class people were also members of the Union, and they were equally responsible for its efforts: the founders deliberately structured it to require broad participation. They divided the city into zones, zones into neighborhoods, and neighborhoods into districts. Each entity had a director (zone chairwomen, neighborhood presidents, etc.), and a board of managers composed of those directors governed the Union. In this way a variety of community people, across classes, shared the responsibility for meeting local needs, individual and collective. The Neighborhood Union's intended beneficiary was not simply the vague, unidentifiable masses. Its intended beneficiary was the whole community.[13]

The void created by shortsighted (at best) politicians and the resulting segmented society helped to define the Neighborhood Union's work. Streets were in bad condition, open sewers were not exceptional, streetlights were rare, and crime and disease flourished. No public agencies in the city effectively promoted black health care, recreation, and safety. City administrators made no allowance for playgrounds, boys' and girls' clubs, or social workers for black youngsters.[14] Prior training within educational institutions and the black community encouraged those who were most able to take a lead in addressing this neglect, but the women who assumed leadership roles anticipated, encouraged, and received the help of people who were often less able but equally interested.

Establishing these community centers in black neighborhoods was distinctly different from, for example, Jane Addams's efforts through Hull House. Addams and her colleagues were deeply concerned with improving the conditions of life for the urban immigrant community in Chicago, and in creating Hull House the reformers developed an institutional base for this effort. But from the very beginning Addams was also preeminently committed to designing an acceptable public lifestyle for middle-class single white women who regularly found themselves limited in their public lives by a restrictive construction of gender roles. Addams wanted to create a place that would allow for the independence of some of these women who did not want to remain dependent on their fathers. Although Hull House was a center from which workers could address the social ills generated by the new industrial order, it also fostered these women's independence without evoking a serious challenge to prevailing assumptions about their "place" in society. Workers at Hull House transformed charity work for white women into social work. They became, to borrow a term from social work historian Roy Lubove, "the professional altruist[s]."[15]

African American women who created settlement houses throughout the South did so from the beginning to change the conditions of their own community life. And not only were they already trained for the work, but because of their prior socialization they had always expected to do it. The institutions they created became the centers from which their efforts could be coordinated and rendered more effective. Barrett in Virginia, Hope in Atlanta, and many other black women throughout the South were already married by the time they undertook this work. Thus they did not create these work roles to circumvent an unacceptable community construction of gender for privileged single women. In fact, black women who were able to succeed in both private and public endeavors represented a community ideal.[16]

Consequently, in 1933 the Neighborhood Union and the larger black community in Atlanta celebrated the fact that "being the wife of the illustrious educator, John Hope, the builder of his home, the mother and rearer of his children, did not exclude from the vision of Lugenia Hope the possibilities of making her life more significant to the lives of her neighbors and her neighbors' children." At the twenty-fifth anniversary celebration of the Neighborhood Union, the speaker noted that Hope was "in the front ranks of constructive accomplishment not because of the achievements of her illustrious husband, John Hope, but standing steadfast upon her own feet because of her own efforts and powers of leadership."[17]

Hope was not alone. For while being wives and mothers, educated black women were still expected to work for the race, and it was typical and acceptable for them to develop careers whether they married or not. Had money for this work been available from the beginning, they would have been wage earners too. But with or without a salary, black women regularly created careers as professional social service workers and community developers. Although Hope became the best known of the Union women, and though her fame did in fact derive partly from her being married to John Hope, what is more impressive is the number of other women who similarly worked for the community and their own families while also working for wages in a distinctly different capacity.

Social service centers were only one of the institutions that came out of the women's efforts at community development. In the South, where most African Americans lived, there was no public library that admitted black patrons until the Louisville Free Public Colored Library opened in 1906. Most efforts to create libraries before and even long after that were private ones. And the pattern of creating libraries was no different from that for social services in general.

One of the early community efforts to provide free reading materials to the black public began in 1913, when Aaron McDuffie Moore, the first black physician in Durham, North Carolina, opened a library for black residents (only the second in the state) in the basement of White Rock Baptist Church. Most of the library's first patrons were members of the congregation, however, and since White Rock was probably the wealthiest black congregation in the city, its members were the people most likely to have books in their homes already. Because Moore's intention was to provide this service for the community at large, he enlisted John Merrick, a prosperous black barber who had recently purchased a lot on the corner of Pettigrew and Fayetteville Streets, the heart of the black community. In 1916 Merrick and Moore constructed a $2,400 community building on the lot, housing the library and an upstairs apartment for the first librarian and her mother. And in 1918 Merrick, Moore, and other black residents chartered the Durham Colored Library Association, a mutual association whose members devoted their energies to providing reading materials to the black public at no charge and to raising literacy levels in the community. Although the library came to receive tax funding, beginning with thirty dollars a month from the city in 1917 and twenty dollars a month from the county in 1918, it did not become part of the Durham County Public Library System until 1969. Before that time, however, those who created and supported it called it the Stanford L. Warren *Public* Library, and three generations of black women, including (Onie) Ray Moore, the wife of Moore's nephew, began their professional careers there.[18]

Black women did not in general possess the capital necessary to provide public services as some black propertied or professional men did; the women had to depend, from the beginning, on broader community resources.[19] Though Janie Porter Barrett at first transformed part of her home into the Locust Street Settlement House, when she created the Home for Girls at Peake Turnout, she relied on black Virginians and particularly black clubwomen for support. The Virginia Federation of Colored Women's Clubs, of which Barrett was a founding member, purchased the farm where the school was built.[20] Oklahoma schoolteacher Judith Ann Carter Horton, an 1891 Oberlin graduate, used her position as president of the Excelsior Club, a black women's organization, to raise money for a public library in Guthrie, Oklahoma, and a school for black juvenile delinquents.[21] Black male physicians and dentists arranged for the construction (or purchase) of the Colored Hospital and Training School for Nurses where Anna DeCosta Banks worked in Charleston, South Carolina. But it became Banks's job to raise the money to pay for the facility, to support the students in training there, and to feed the patients. Local churches and private citizens apparently provided the bulk of the five-hundred-dollar yearly mortgage payment. And community people, cash poor especially during the winter, also regularly sent hens, turkeys, cakes, barrels of potatoes, baskets of fruit, and other food.[22] Before Susan Dart Butler opened her father's private library to the black public on a permanent basis, she held dances, concerts, and parties to raise money for lumber to repair the floors, paint to refinish the walls, and shelving to organize the books. The library opened in 1927 with two tables and twelve folding chairs.[23]

Butler had studied to be a schoolteacher. When she finished the normal course at Atlanta University in 1908, however, local laws prohibited black women from teaching in the public schools of Charleston, so to teach in South Carolina she would have had to leave home and work in the rural counties. Alternatively, she could have created some other opportunity for herself. Whether in an effort to do so or not, Butler subsequently went to Massachusetts to the McDowell Millinery School, and she remained in Boston until 1915, having married Nathaniel Lowe Butler, a successful realtor, in 1912. The Butlers moved to South Carolina in 1915, and until 1920 (the first year black women could teach in the state's public city schools), Susan Butler earned an income working out of her home as a milliner. One day, an Avery Institute coed came to her home and asked to borrow several books to complete a school assignment. The incident prompted Butler to move into another area of work. She decided to open a library for black public use in Dart Hall, the site of her late father's school. Butler, however, was not simply creating a position for herself. In fact, she stayed on only until the city assumed responsibility for the services in 1931, even though as owner and donor of the building (not to mention a member of a prominent family) she probably could have continued to work there for a salary. Instead, she gave up that work when the city took it over and went back only when Julia McBeth, the librarian hired by the city, became ill and had to leave. While Butler worked there, however, she arranged for Mae Purcell, a city-paid library assistant, to take periodic leave to complete a professional course in library science and earn her degree. Butler worked to develop this institution, raising money, acquiring books, and rehabilitating the building. Once people began to use the library widely and it became too expensive for her and Charleston clubwomen to maintain by themselves, Butler leased the library to the city for one dollar a year on condition that city officials maintain it for black public use.[24]

African Americans had a history of creating public service institutions and then leasing or donating them to their local governments. For two generations already, throughout the country but especially in the South, black people had bought land and donated it to the city or county for the construction of schools, or else built the schools themselves before deeding them to "the public." The success of these early efforts suggested that this was one way, and for a time the only way, to gain tax support for black institutions.[25] Public officials were much more inclined to take over an existing facility and support it minimally than to build one from scratch. Thus, in a rather clever exchange, sixteen years after its founding the Neighborhood Union sold its public health clinic to the federal government and in return obtained a lease on an office in a new federal public housing project (to be built in an area that encompassed the old Union clinic site) for their other community work, perpetual maintenance of the building, and security services. Eventually, Butler donated the library, Dart Hall, to the city of Charleston, and Barrett donated the "home school" in Virginia to the state.[26]

These actions in no way meant the women had lost interest in providing the services. Instead, they often could not afford to keep it up. Moreover, as workers and as leaders, black professional women expected not only to provide public services themselves when necessary, but also to cause appropriate public agents to carry out their neglected responsibilities. Donating these institutions to the city, state, or county was a way of seeing that public officials provided the services they ought to have been providing to African American communities all along.[27]

Black women who entered the workforce as schoolteachers around the end of the nineteenth century fared no better than librarians and social workers. Despite education's relatively high priority in government funding of public services, expenditures on public education in the South in general in 1914 averaged $10.82 per white child and $4.01 per black child. By 1930 the dollar amount was up but the white-to-black spending ratio was even more disparate: $42.39 per white child and $15.86 per black child. And only a fraction of black children had access to those meager expenditures. Consequently black women had their work cut out for them in this area too. Many of the early college, normal school, and seminary graduates went directly into rural areas to teach, and as Mamie Garvin Fields recalled many years after teaching in the South Carolina Sea Islands, "being a teacher in the country . . . meant teaching all the time." In these rural communities, black people were regularly unwaged workers—sharecroppers and tenant farmers who frequently ended up in debt after several seasons of work—and this economic deprivation affected the quality of life through and through. A nineteenth-century writer described some such areas as "cotton districts, where all is discouragement and demoralization resulting from debt, mortgaging, renting, and lack of school advantages."[28] Housing was often inadequate; children were regularly ill clothed and poorly fed; and poor health was an easy consequence when, additionally, public sanitation systems did not reach them and public health programs were nonexistent. There was in these communities, however, the proverbial will. Teachers were part of "the way." They knew they were working against tremendous odds because, as Fields noted, "in the eyes of the powers that be, the Negro teachers really didn't amount to much. Neither did the pupils."[29] Nonetheless, teachers and parents went about working to resolve the complex local problems and developing individual children and the community in the process.

Women who had prepared to teach and had accepted (or created) teaching positions upon graduating regularly became settlement house workers themselves *in addition* to teaching regular school courses.[30] In these schools/community centers, teachers taught classes in agriculture and home economics, and they created a variety of community clubs depending on local needs. In Lowndes County, Alabama, schoolteachers in the Calhoun School, through their "extension work," helped black residents purchase over a hundred homes and farms between 1892 and 1916. Judia C. Jackson, who had sold land she inherited in order to build a school and community center, earned such a reputation for her extensive work that the Board of Education required all black Clark County, Georgia, schoolteachers to spend four weeks a year in her school (thereby saving themselves the expense of training their employees). Jackson not only taught basic school courses but also, in and out of school, coordinated programs "to keep the young people in the community, to destroy ignorance and crime, and thereby make desirable citizens upon whom the race and the nation can depend."[31]

It was indeed fortunate that the historically black college and normal/industrial school staffs prepared their students so broadly, for these new teachers regularly found themselves faced with tasks that required more expertise than traditional teacher training imparted. It was quite common for teachers to be sent or called to work at a place where a school did not yet exist, and in those cases, they had to begin by raising the money for, and organizing, the school. Although it is possible that the actual construction of the building was a most atypical activity for women teachers, it was not unheard of. At least the teachers in Jonesboro, Arkansas, apparently did not feel exploited when they became part of the school construction crew once the black community raised enough money to purchase a lot.[32] Moreover, considering that at least one of the two black women's colleges and at least two of the coeducational schools taught carpentry to female students during the late nineteenth and early twentieth centuries, perhaps the construction role was more typical than our ability to document it can show.[33] At any rate Genevieve Nell Ladson, a graduate of the American Missionary Association's Avery Institute, began her work precisely at that point. She recalled: "When I say I built a school . . . I mean I built it, from helping them cut down the trees with my saw, to hammering boards in place."[34] She began teaching in the late 1920s, when annual state expenditures for public education in South Carolina were $5.20 per black student and $52.60 per white student.[35] Ladson and the people who hired her probably had no choice but to build the school themselves if the community was to have one.

Black communities regularly demonstrated a commitment to educating their children, most notably through building schools and hiring teachers.[36] Where local governments appointed and paid teachers, community folk supplemented the teachers' salaries by housing and feeding them without charge or for minimal sums. If local school administrators paid black rural schoolteachers to work for three or four months a year, community people raised money to pay them for an additional month or two.[37] And though many of these teachers lived on a shoestring and probably kept their fingers crossed, hoping for the extra work and pay the community might provide, many found supplementary work, sometimes as domestics.[38] Others, like Mary Lee McCray, budgeted their money during the regular term so they could pay their own expenses during the extended, sometimes unpaid months. McCray was already teaching first, second, and third grade from 8:30 A.M. until 1:30 P.M. without a salary during the summer of 1900 while community people worked to raise money for a school. She informed Margaret Murray Washington that Miss Wright, a leader in the fund-raising effort, "says she may be able to pay me a little money for my Summer work, but I told her I should work this Summer regardless of what she was able to pay, because I usually pay up [room and board] the last of Spring for all the Summer, so [I] have very little money to pay out during the Summer."[39]

Whatever the circumstances of wages and school terms, the community expected and received more work than the "official" school schedule allowed. And in most circumstances, regardless of the type of school, and particularly in the South, teachers did not anticipate the luxury of merely teaching. Nor did they define their work that way. Mamie Garvin Fields had to gather wood for fires, and she organized students to clean the grounds. When children failed to show up for school, she went to their homes to find out why. If they stayed out because they had no clothes, she went to her church, her club, and her friends to obtain the needed articles. When the older and bigger children were embarrassed to go to school with younger ones, she arranged for them to attend an "opportunity school" in the evenings. Upon determining that local girls were interested in sewing, she and Rosalee Brown, a coworker and fellow graduate of Claflin, a Methodist Episcopal school, virtually organized another school, teaching the girls to sew, thereby providing them with a practical trade. To make more food available to the islanders all year, Fields used her own kitchen as a classroom on the weekends and taught parents to can and preserve the vegetables they grew in their summer gardens.[40]

Septima Clark taught in the Sea Islands about the same time Fields did, and her working conditions were similar. For Fields, the school equipment included a bell and a roll book. Clark was more fortunate and received "an ax, a water bucket and dipper, a table and chair, and later, the firewood." In Fields's school students had benches with no backs, and they improvised desktops by kneeling on the floor in front of the benches rather than sitting on them. There are no indications that circumstances were different in Clark's school. Fields and her sister once taught 100 students of all ages, and Clark was responsible, in a three-teacher school, for 135 students three to eighteen years old. Promised Land School, where Septima Clark began teaching in 1916, no doubt represented a route to that state for the community at large, but it was no land of milk and honey for Clark. On top of all the obvious material deficiencies (and Fields noted that while "Joshua f'it the battle of Jericho, [the teachers] f'it the battle of the books" in that at first they had none), school attendance was always sporadic because many students who were able to work could not come until the cotton was picked, which often took until December, and they left again in the spring to start preparing the fields for planting. Yet parents did not always voluntarily take their children out of school to work. Rural school trustees regularly scheduled only a three-, four-, or five-month school year for black students. Women who taught under such conditions had to concentrate their classroom work on providing the basic skills that would enable students to gain as much knowledge as they could on their own. Teachers focused on history, reading, writing, and arithmetic. And they made up some of the missed lessons—those requiring a less structured environment—when they continued their work in the evenings and on the weekends in the community.[41]

After Genevieve Ladson helped construct the school where she taught, her work was not confined to the building. She helped pick cotton, slaughter hogs, grind sugarcane, and harvest tomatoes as she "became involved in the rural life of the people she served."[42] And though some of these rural schools were so isolated that teachers had to take part in community activities if they were to have a life outside school at all, they had already been trained to do this. Working in this way would help them establish membership in the local community if they were not natives of it, and in this more social setting they could have a direct and immediate influence, whereas the impact of their classroom work would not be significantly felt until sometime in the future.

In the more social setting, teachers worked to change what they perceived as backward ways of being and doing among the poor rural people, who often justifiably measured success in terms of a good crop, and for whom day-to-day survival was more important than the not-promised distant future. Parents clearly appreciated the potential value of formal schooling, but teachers had to make it relevant to local ways of life. They advised the parents that formally educating their children would ultimately, even materially, reward them and perhaps even that they—the parents—should want that. Parents, already interested in the education of their children, sent them to school, sometimes irregularly—seasonally, according to the clock of the crop—and teachers took what they could get and worked to enable the children despite the limited exposure to formal schooling.

Occasionally teachers became overzealous in their efforts to "uplift" their rural clients, and in such instances someone promptly put them in their place. Fields, for example, once decided to give her students a lesson in beauty culture, and she washed and straightened the hair of several girls in a classroom demonstration. One mother came to the school to remind Fields of why she sent her daughter there—for schooling, traditionally defined. Fields was imposing her own education on her students, but well intentioned as she was, she had suggested a standard of beauty contrary to that of the local people—or at least of the girl's mother. It was also a time-consuming and impractical standard in the hot, humid Sea Islands, where braiding or wrapping natural hair was much more logical and common. But probably most important, Fields had overstepped an unspoken boundary. Although she saw this instruction as a matter of self-improvement—uplift work—the child's mother did not.[43]

Fields was not alone in such endeavors. Margaret Murray Washington was proud that she and other women teachers from Tuskegee Institute who worked at the Plantation Settlement virtually wiped out "the old plantation habit of 'wrapping'" hair among the women. And while working as a Jeanes supervising teacher in Bullock County, Georgia, Maenelle Dixon recommended to all the teachers under her charge that they discourage girls from wrapping their hair.[44] Rural teachers regularly sought to change other behaviors they viewed as antiprogressive, including expressions of sexuality, superstition, and religiosity, and they saw no harm in trying to change people's traditions.[45] In fact they were only doing what they had been trained to do—bringing "civilization" to the masses, socializing them for acceptability in the larger world, enabling them to be upwardly mobile. But though the women saw these efforts as "uplifting the race," some aspects of the uplift prescription— manners, culture, appearance, and education, all of a particular sort— were laden with value judgments that did not coincide with those of the people the professionals thought needed their help. Thus, in any of these situations, professionals could be powerful agents for racial advancement and community development while simultaneously subverting the values of individual clients.[46]

The professionals' ideas and efforts related to "acceptable" behavior did not usually result in serious confrontations because community people trusted the professionals to do for, to, and with them what was necessary to improve their quality of life. Even when they were not so convinced, they had granted the professionals a certain amount of authority, and it included a certain amount of accountability. Unless there was a major breach of the public trust, there was no confrontation. Conflicts were also kept to a minimum because the professionals were well trained in terms of what was needed and expected of them and in carrying it out without causing offense.

Amelia Perry Pride, a Lynchburg, Virginia, teacher and a graduate of Hampton Institute, made certain she did not refer to the women in her evening canning and preserving classes as servants, even though they were domestic workers, because she knew they would then interpret her efforts as designed to help their employers rather than themselves. (Because Pride wanted them to feed themselves better but also to keep their jobs and to enhance their reputations and her own among local whites, this was in fact one reason she taught them.) She also made certain to dress plainly whenever "I am working among my people," so as not to make them uncomfortable and unaccepting of her (and probably also to suggest how they should dress).[47] Still, the professionals'

179

perceptions of what was needed and what their clients expected were sometimes different, so fulfilling the mission of their education regularly entailed finding the middle ground.

Septima Clark successfully blended her personal and professional goals for community and individual uplift with the goals of her clients. She helped local women tend the sick and prepare the dead for burial, and in doing so she could continue to teach them—lessons in health and hygiene, for example. On Saturdays she often helped neighborhood women with their sewing, and as the women's personal and family needs were met, Clark could also suggest "appropriate" clothing, housekeeping techniques, manners, and the like. She helped men organize fraternal self-help societies and in the process helped remedy adult illiteracy. At first she helped them conceptualize, construct, and then memorize the speeches they would deliver in their new public roles that Clark had helped to create. Eventually they got tired of memorizing their speeches, and Clark took advantage of their frustration and began to teach them to write and read. The men achieved literacy under Clark's tutelage, working in the evenings after the wage-work day had ended and everyone had finished supper.[48]

In Chatham County, Georgia, in 1920, members of the Commission of Colored Women took over a good portion of this adult literacy work. They believed that teachers should not have to continue to work for no pay in the evenings after teaching all day for very little pay. But most typically "moonlight schools," evening schools where people who worked during the day went to acquire some formal education, were staffed without remuneration by the regular day school teachers. These schools were a common feature of southern black people's lives at least through the 1920s, and rather than lament the inadequacies that the schools represented, the students—often parents, grandparents, and older brothers and sisters of the day students—boasted of having "their own" principals, superintendents, and boards of education.[49] In the evenings they celebrated their privileged position and the autonomy that such schools represented. The morning after class, however, these once deprived students went back to underpaid, backbreaking, labor-intensive jobs, and their teachers likewise returned to theirs.

Only after obtaining work in more established, financially better supported school systems, and in locations where public services were available for those who needed them, was it even remotely possible for teachers to focus on teaching narrow course preparations in traditional school settings. But even then they found ways to extend their work to benefit their clients and community. Mary Gibson Hundley, a Washington, D.C., schoolteacher and a 1918 Radcliffe graduate, taught English, French, and Latin at the famous Dunbar High School, whose graduates overwhelmingly attended college. One reason for the high rate of college attendance was that Dunbar teachers voluntarily tutored special advanced classes in most subjects during free periods and after school to prepare students for College Entrance Board exams. Hundley became the coordinator of that work beginning in the 1940s. In addition to coordinating the classes with volunteer teachers, she also sponsored programs to encourage parents to send their children to college, had graduates and their parents speak to students and their parents, and hosted parties for students to which she invited members of the boards of admissions from elite white colleges.[50]

Norma Boyd, a Howard University graduate, began her career in 1912 as a math teacher in the Washington, D.C., public schools. Boyd taught junior high school and was not as concerned with college preparation as Hundley was. Her unpaid public work, however, was also significantly influenced by location. Public officials in Washington had a much longer history of commitment to black education than the rural southern administrators had, and the black public schools in Washington were considered the best in the nation. Boyd's family had moved from North Carolina to the District of Columbia for that very reason. And as a product of the system, Boyd boasted of having been taught math by a Princeton graduate, English by Angelina Grimké, an important writer and playwright, and German by Otelia Cromwell, who distinguished herself by achieving some language training in European institutions and, in 1926, earning a Yale Ph.D. Mary Church Terrell was on the Board of Education in the city when Boyd was a student, and Boyd, aware of Terrell's reputation, adopted her as a role model.[51] A number of factors militated against Boyd's succeeding in being "like Mary Church Terrell." Most obviously, Boyd was not independently wealthy as Terrell was, and when Boyd received her college degree in 1910, many more black women possessed this credential than when Terrell received hers in 1884. And because Boyd never married, she did not have to create an alternative career outside the classroom as Terrell had done in becoming a professional lecturer. But Boyd could and did match Terrell's commitment to assuming broad social responsibilities through her work. And if Terrell noticed the development of Boyd's career, she might have been pleased that she had helped inspire it.

Boyd's work routine was very different from that of members of her "cohort" who worked in less developed school systems. In Washington, D.C., she did not have to teach her students' parents to read and write, sew, or preserve food, though some might have benefited from such instruction. There were already public service programs to address these and other needs, so Boyd could concentrate her work on her students. Still, she structured her classes so as to make the importance of collective responsibility clear to her young scholars. Instead of organizing smarter students in one group and slower ones in another, which might have made her routine easier, she created work groups that included students of differing abilities. Stronger children had to help weaker ones, and in doing so they developed self-confidence and even leadership skills. The participation of the slower students was critical to the successful functioning of the group not simply because better students needed someone to practice on, but because they all needed to learn the important lesson about mutual obligations. Those who benefited from the help of their classmates would someday be able to help others, and they would understand the importance of doing so.[52]

Boyd's main concern as a teacher was seeing "that each child reached his [sic] potential." She insisted to her students that "all things are possible," and she made herself an example by reminding them that her family was not wealthy and that she was never brilliant; she simply had ambition, goals, the determination to achieve them, and support.[53] Yet Boyd did have opportunities that many black people in the city lacked, advantages she sometimes took for granted. After asking her students why school-age black boys so frequently hung out on the street, their response put her back on track. They told her they could not find jobs as easily as white boys could, and this reminded Boyd "that it was the duty of the teacher not only to teach but to [create] opportunities for her children."[54] In a setting like Washington, where black people had regular access to public schools, libraries, social services, and health care, it was easy to assume falsely that people's basic needs were being met. But even after recognizing this, Boyd at first concentrated her efforts on her students rather than the community at large.

The Junior High School Federation of Student Councils, which she founded while teaching at Banneker Junior High School, became a vehicle "to open doors for her students" as others had done for her and to "inspire the children to be ambitious." She used the school's chapter to teach about the functioning of the federal government, and she took the young scholars to public hearings, particularly when Charles Hamilton Houston was scheduled to speak, hoping that these live examples would inspire them "to become a part of the world in which [they lived]."[55] Even though Boyd was a math teacher, she worked to have her students see themselves in the context of a community much larger than their neighborhood. To that end she involved them in activities normally considered part of civics and social studies. Boyd was inclined to work in this way because of her training. She was able to do so because she had the advantage of working in a system with a committed Board of Education, a school with adequate equipment, and an urban economic environment where household economies did not automatically include children's labor and where there was a broad and visible range of lifestyle alternatives. All these factors made it possible for her to focus her paid work on extending, rather than improvising, the basic education of her students.

Clearly, the manner in which teachers worked depended as much on their own abilities and imaginations as on the location and equipment of the schools. In Washington, Boyd could, as a matter of course, take her students to observe Congress, whereas in the Valena C. Jones School in the rural South, students could not attend state legislative hearings; but they still studied government. Their teachers organized the school as a republic, and the classrooms became states with elected lieutenant governors, secretaries of state, judges, police, senators, health inspectors, *and* room, hall, and yard cleanliness commissions. The teachers were advisers of state, and the principal was the adviser of the Senate. The states and the Senate had rights and responsibilities parallel to those outlined in the United States and state constitutions.[56] Unlike those in the Sea Islands and other neglected areas where teachers had so little classroom time with their students that they felt compelled to teach informally while they did community work, urban teachers more easily exposed the students to extracurricular activities that suggested a variety of ways to achieve beyond attaining literacy or a "regular" job.

Bordentown Manual Training and Industrial School in New Jersey was similar to the Washington, D.C., schools in that its founder, the African Methodist Episcopal Church, had an equally historic commitment to the education of black youths. Bordentown students, however, were being prepared for productive, successful, and self-affirming futures in the trades. And though there was no loss in being a skilled laborer, it was still important to enable the students to see their wider potential. One way was to balance the vocational education with traditional liberal arts coursework. Frances Grant, who taught at Bordentown from 1917 until 1954, assumed some responsibility for achieving that end.

Because she was a Radcliffe graduate herself, and the daughter of professional parents (her mother was a college-educated proofreader for a Massachusetts publishing house, and her father was a dentist, on the Harvard faculty for a time, and an attorney), Grant's efforts should come as no surprise. For her, a liberal education symbolized a pinnacle, and in an age when people still spoke of educating the hands, the heart, and the head, it was easy enough for Grant to view vocational education as incomplete. Grant could not accept the built-in limitations on individual development at Bordentown, and she developed a liberal education complement to its industrial education emphasis. As a consequence of her work in curriculum development, students left the school with a traditional liberal education *and* a trade, because the new curriculum required them to earn a four-year high school diploma and a trade certificate too. This new curriculum also included a five-credit course in African American history.[57]

Grant also encouraged students to participate in extracurricular activities, including the prizewinning student newspaper she founded, the *Ironsides Echo.* She organized student theater groups, produced plays, and otherwise created educational opportunities for them. As often as possible, she invited black writers, actors, and activists to the school and gave tea parties for the visiting celebrities, including Nella Larson and Paul Robeson. Grant used these parties not simply to entertain but also to teach the children "how to manage a tea, how to act at a tea, how to dress for a tea, [and] how to conduct themselves with people they were meeting." In addition to providing the students with lessons in gracious manners, Grant's efforts also showed them that their creativity might surpass the jobs they had prepared for through the vocational curriculum; they could also think about becoming writers, actors, or political activists.[58]

Amelia Perry Pride's work was similar to that of the other teachers in that it was broad, often unpaid, and regularly critical to the development of the community. But Lynchburg, Virginia, where she worked, was not quite like the rural South, where most women worked before 1920, nor was it a metropolis like Washington, D.C. It was somewhere in between, and closer to the former. Though Pride's work did not differ greatly from that of others, she may be distinguished by her effort to make certain her Hampton mentors knew that she was living up to her training and their ideals.

Pride had graduated from Hampton in 1879, and in 1882 she gained employment in a Lynchburg school that had been "built by the colored people of the town in 1868." By 1890 Pride was principal of the large school, and her training, the reputation of Hampton graduates, and the manner in which she worked probably influenced her quick promotion. In an early Hampton survey of its graduates, Pride answered a question about students' occupations since graduating by saying she had done "some of everything." In elaborating, she noted that her work roles included "veg. gardening, housekeeping—Florist—rearing poultry—raising hogs—dressmaking—Tailoress—Teaching school—Fruit growing—built houses, supervised I mean—missionary work—temperance work—Sunday school." Perry was also, by then, taking care of five elderly women in a rented house that later became known as the Dorchester Home.[59]

Poverty was as common among black people in Lynchburg as anywhere else, so Pride worked to feed and clothe her students, partly by soliciting donations from local people, Hampton teachers, and Hampton "friends." But she also held evening cooking and sewing classes, teaching children and adults skills that enhanced their employability and their efforts to feed and clothe themselves. Pride's work with the Dorchester Home also went beyond supplying food, fuel, and clothing to the residents—difficult enough during the depressed early 1890s. Because the Virginia legislature had recently passed a law to allow the University of Virginia medical school "to take anyone for the benefit of science" who would otherwise have to be buried at public expense, Pride also had to promise the elders "not [to] let [them] go to Charlottesville." Consequently she had to bury them after they died. In all of her work, Pride taught lessons in manners, dress, and morals, and she reported that her students were very appreciative of her efforts.[60] Amelia Perry Pride was conscious of her reputation as a leader in Lynchburg, and when a Hampton teacher, Myrtilla Sherman, decided to visit Pride's home, Pride sent her the train schedule and added that "anyone at the depot will tell you where the school teacher Pride lives."[61]

Public health nurses, even up to the 1930s, had to define their work in much the same way as turn-of-the-century rural schoolteachers. The nurses generally served people already identified as disadvantaged, and usually their work was done outside a fixed office. Lula McNeil, who worked on the prevention and treatment of typhoid fever and tuberculosis in the Virginia Tidewater area in the 1930s, held "clinics" in churchyards, farmyards, private homes, and wherever else she could. In order to work in the remote "offices," she first had to go to the city dump to gather wood for a fire, warm up the outbuilding, pick up patients, bring them to the "clinic," and then take them home again. She taught midwives how to improvise and sterilize supplies and to deliver babies in as sanitary an environment as possible. Like most public health nurses during this time, she also taught and performed post-delivery care of new mothers and their babies.[62]

In rural Alabama, Eunice Laurie's job involved going from plantation to plantation gathering vital statistics on births and deaths, organizing and compiling the material, and filing certificates. This was work that the Tuskegee graduate designed for herself because at the time there was no systematic way to determine the conditions and public health needs of the rural community in Alabama. Traveling in a van ("the movable school") with a man who taught carpentry, mattress making, and agricultural classes, she also taught sanitation, food preservation, preparation for child delivery, maternity care, and home nursing. In addition to her other work, she unofficially collected clothes, food, shoes, tools, or whatever she had determined her clients needed.[63]

Mary Elizabeth Carnegie performed similar duties in rural Alabama without a salary while she worked as a paid staff nurse at the Tuskegee Veterans Hospital. Carnegie reported that she was bored with hospital nursing because male attendants performed so much of the work. Consequently she "bought a car, had some public health uniforms made, went to the [public] health department, and offered [her] services as a volunteer to . . . the rural community." After Carnegie moved to West Virginia in 1940, she also worked for no pay in a variety of capacities. In one instance she served in a Girl Scout camp as nurse-counselor-business manager-chauffeur. In fact, throughout her two years in West Virginia, where she was studying to complete a bachelor's degree, "much of her off-duty time was given to working with girls in the community and in the city of Charleston. She worked with the Girl Scouts, teaching first aid and mothercraft (a group of deaf and blind girls were [sic] included), and she volunteered to act as nurse for a summer camp for underprivileged girls of the vicinity." Carnegie even "gave up her vacation following graduation in 1942 and served the interests of the camp."[64] Laurie's and Carnegie's work illustrates Rossa Cooley's 1905 tribute to her mentor, "Nurse King," in which Cooley concluded that "nurse," for public health nurses, came "to mean a social worker in the largest sense of the word."[65] Nurses and others became "social workers" because of the obvious needs of the community and because of their own perceptions of the process of community development, for which they were partly responsible.

Jane Edna Hunter did not have to undertake this work in institution building, community development, and social work in order to proceed with the work for which she had been trained as did many public health nurses, "social workers," and rural teachers. In fact, she undertook it partly because of her own problems trying to live and to work as a nurse just after the turn of the century. Hunter moved to Cleveland, Ohio, in 1905 after graduating from Hampton Institute/ Dixie Hospital. And probably, like most migrants who saw the North as a "land of opportunity," she expected to begin work immediately as a graduate nurse. A number of factors, however, prevented her moving so quickly into the profession. First, black nurses could work only on segregated wards in public hospitals, and therefore paid positions for them were limited. Some of those few slots disappeared when white nurses also worked on black wards. The use of nursing students in the relatively small black hospitals and nurse training schools further reduced the number of positions available. And black nurses often could not serve as institutionally based private-duty nurses because many of the people who requested nurses were white. Housing in Cleveland was segregated as well, and many of the rentals Hunter could afford were unacceptable. She moved out of the first place where she roomed after discovering that the owners were involved in prostitution.[66]

Hunter did not find nursing work or suitable housing for some time, but she quickly decided to do something for other "poor motherless daughters of the race" needing help with housing and employment in Cleveland. The Dixie Hospital graduate worked as a private-duty nurse, a cleaning lady, and a laundress to support herself, while also working with a few of her new friends to form the Working Girls' Home Association. They met for the first time in 1911 and pledged to contribute five cents a week and to recruit new members. In 1913 they opened a twenty-three-room building to house single black working women, and in 1917 they opened another with seventy-two rooms to replace it. By 1928 the Phillis Wheatley Association (its name had recently been changed) owned and operated an establishment with 135 bedrooms, 4 parlors, 6 clubrooms, a cafeteria, and a beauty salon. The

Phillis Wheatley Association also ran an employment agency for black women. And Hunter's work provided her an important leadership role.[67]

The northern urban work environment therefore resembled the southern rural situation in several ways. In both environments, black professional women often devised their own work and created the institutions for doing it. And in any case they defined their work roles more broadly than traditional job descriptions in the professions for which they were trained. Professional women worked both to repair and to prevent the damage that frequently resulted from systematic discrimination, and thus their work reflected, if it was not defined by, the neglect of existing public institutions. But equally important, through their work women could and did apply the lessons of their upbringing and training by providing others the wherewithal to move themselves along life's highways. In the process, the women further developed the black community.

• • •

The educators who prepared these women for their public work roles had always believed that good training, hard work, and respectable behavior would eventually gain places within the American mainstream for their students and for the larger black community. And by the beginning of the 1930s it seemed that the professionals, at least, had achieved that acceptance—they were more and more frequently employed in white institutions. But in spite of changing environmental conditions and changing workplaces, these professional women continued to work in their usual ways. For example, ongoing migration and the national economic depression intensified their labors because of the increased numbers and needs of their clients. And though New Deal programs provided a few educated women with more opportunities than they would otherwise have had, negotiating the new bureaucracies on behalf of the black community became an unofficial work role for many. Yet something was very different about their work beginning in the 1920s. As they came to work in these more established institutions, white supervisors began to redefine the women's jobs to include community race work—which the women previously had done without wages and beyond the requirements of their regular jobs—and, also, significantly, race-relations work.

White administrators' new interest in the black community did not necessarily reflect a new sensitivity to the needs of the black public or a new commitment to equity. Instead, in the rural South, the out-migration of black workers portended a dramatic labor shortage that public officials hoped to stop, and the increasing concentration of African Americans in urban centers made providing more public services there seem imperative, especially in light of nationalistic black political movements such as Garveyism (which some government officials considered so dangerous that Garvey was eventually jailed and then deported).[68] Moreover, as scholars have pointed out, the riots that occurred after World War I suggested that public administrators had better pay attention to the changing environment because the major urban uprisings of 1919 were different from earlier race riots in which whites invaded, attacked, and destroyed parts of black communities. This time black people armed themselves and fought back, sometimes beyond the boundaries of their own neighborhoods. The stress and despair triggered by the Great Depression seemed to multiply the "dangers" of having this new concentration of black residents in the city, and the increased visibility and influence in the black community of left-wing labor organizers, socialists, and communists made those "dangers" too great to ignore. Public administrators were at a loss for what to do, or they felt ill equipped to address the needs of these newcomers. With black urban populations increasing exponentially in some locales over ten or twenty years, it was simply expedient to have people within the black community involved in race and race-relations work in an official, wage-earning capacity.

The career of Detroit social worker Beulah Whitby demonstrates how the 1920s to the 1940s marked a turning point in the paid public careers of black professional women. Whitby graduated from Oberlin College in 1920, and after teaching two years in Nashville, she went to work at the YWCA in Detroit. The first major wave of African American migration from the South to the North and the second major rural-to-urban shift had not yet ended. Many of the newcomers arrived without prior arrangements for work or housing, and Whitby's first job with the black branch of the YWCA was to meet trains at the station and direct new arrivals to agencies where they could get assistance.[69] The migration probably also contributed to her obtaining her next position, with the women's division of the Detroit Police Department. By 1931 Whitby was a staff social worker for the Department of Public Welfare, assigned to the city's largest and almost all-black Alfred District. Her caseload was segregated, as was the caseload of every black social worker, but white social workers regularly worked with black clients.[70]

As the number of Black Muslims in Detroit increased, white caseworkers, unable to impose their own values, became more and more frustrated. Muslim converts had dropped their "slave names" and assumed the last name "X." White social workers insisted on issuing relief checks in given (birth) or legally changed names, which the clients refused to accept. The Muslims also sent their children to private, self-supported schools, and individual white social service agents withheld their relief checks for that reason too. The white social workers, however, were treading on questionable legal grounds, and before pushing too far—and in exasperation—they turned the cases over to Whitby. Whitby obtained the Muslims' money in their chosen names and worked to prevent other agency representatives from inappropriately interfering in their lives. Although for the time being she would have worked exclusively with black clients whether they were Muslims or not, her supervisors gave her these cases because of the problems white workers engendered. And though few might have predicted the violent public outbreaks that Detroit experienced in the 1940s, it was still neither the time nor the place to incite hostile race relations. The national economy had collapsed, the population was in transition, and radical fringes, of which the Muslims appeared to be a part, were becoming more and more visible.[71]

At the start of the 1940s, the Office of Civilian Defense employed Whitby as executive secretary of the Emergency Welfare and Evacuation Services. In 1943, however, the year after the first Detroit riot, she became assistant director of the Commission on Community Relations. In this capacity Whitby helped to create the "community barometer," a research tool designed to gauge the volatility of race relations. The community barometer was a system in which police officers, streetcar workers, teachers, public park and playground workers, and many others recorded every racial confrontation they encountered each day. Officials charted all the incidents, from name-calling to fistfights, on spreadsheets, noting time of day, location, provocation, race of the perpetrator and the victim, and several other variables. When the barometer indicated rising tensions (when incidents occurred at a certain frequency), city officials organized "neighborhood jamborees," apparently only in black neighborhoods, that included movies (e.g., *The Negro Soldier*), music, dances, and reasons-for-race-pride-and-self-respect speeches by black community leaders. The jamborees evidently provided an outlet for built-up stress.[72]

The changes in Beulah Whitby's employment and her work routines represent more than the upward mobility of a well-trained black professional woman. Her career began near the end of an era when public services to black communities had to be provided by black institutions lest they not be provided at all. Upon finishing her bachelor's degree at Oberlin College, probably her best employment options were to teach in a black school or to work with the black YWCA. It took the Great Migration to create additional opportunities for her and many women like her. Between 1910 and 1930, Detroit's black population increased nearly 2,000 percent—from just about 6,000 to about 120,000. And it was certain that many of these new arrivals would not easily find work and housing, even had they came in dribs and drabs, which they did not. Most arrived between 1920 and 1930.[73] But more important than the numbers were the attitudes they brought with them. If James R. Grossman's conclusions about migrants to Chicago can be applied more generally here, they arrived in these northern urban centers with expectations of sharing "the perquisites of American citizenship."[74] Their families had survived slavery, and on arriving in the North they had, they believed, escaped Jim Crow. They were ready to vote, to earn a living wage, to send their children to good public schools, and to live in decent housing. But Detroit was not Canaan, and the discrepancy between these newcomers' perceptions of the North as the "Land of Hope" and what they found to be the reality was too great for city officials to ignore. Therefore they hired Beulah Whitby, and women like her, to mediate between those newcomers' expectations and the real conditions of urban industrial life for most African Americans.

When the Great Depression exploded many migrants' plans for really "making it" in the city, black professional women became very important to white public administrators. As working-class black men received pink slips in the envelope with their previous week's wages, and as their wives lost their home-based piecework and went looking for domestic jobs, a new source of hope emerged. Left-wing political activists, who had never before attracted a great following among African Americans, found a more attentive black audience. Black people in larger numbers began to listen to the Left, even if they still would not join it. Communist Party members recognized the great membership potential that black urban dwellers represented during the depression, and consequently the Party, to paraphrase Mark Naison, took the offensive. In New York, Communists aggressively campaigned against racist employment practices, organized relief programs, and launched a well-organized antilynching movement. They were also constantly on patrol for black families who had been "set out" (evicted), promptly moving them back into their homes and coordinating "No Work, No Rent" parades.[75] Earl Lewis notes that in the southern seaboard city of Norfolk, members of the Communist Party "took up residence" in the black community during the 1930s and began to organize residents "around issues that affected them directly—work, hunger, housing, [and] relief."[76] And Robin D. G. Kelley has detailed how black workers in Alabama made the Party uniquely their own.[77] Even the black middle class, treading lightly so as not to offend the National Association for the Advancement of Colored People (NAACP), had to sit up and take notice when the International Labor Defense succeeded in winning a Supreme Court decision to suspend the death sentences of the "Scottsboro Boys" in May 1932.[78] Many black professional women had, to that point, dedicated their public careers to making up the difference between the public services officially provided to black people and those that were needed. Left-wing organizers, however, were advocating full and unconditional equality. Public administrators found the role of the educated, articulate, and relatively conservative professional women workers to be a far more acceptable alternative than that put forth by the radicals.

Thus, in the midst of increased activity among labor organizations and growing activism by communist and socialist groups in the 1930s, as racial protests exploded around the nation and as the Second World War encouraged the United States to present a positive image of domestic race relations overseas, white bureaucrats in various locales and agencies began to recruit black professional women intensely and to focus some of their jobs on race relations. And as Beulah Whitby's career suggests, some women's employment represented a kind of cooptation. They were no longer representing the race in the same way black women did a generation earlier. In their new capacities, black professional women traversed the city, state, and nation representing their employers.

Nurse Estelle Massey Riddle Osborne's work history is not atypical. Osborne had worked in traditional black hospital settings during the late 1920s and early 1930s, but by 1934 the Rosenwald Fund Foundation employed her to work on a public health project that required her to live among sharecroppers in rural areas, organizing agricultural workers and teaching public health and Red Cross classes. She put on plays, organized dances, and otherwise helped create entertainment and recreation in areas that were especially depressed. There is no evidence that the foundation representatives designed Osborne's work to bring just enough relief (or distraction) to the depressed work camps to head off major protests among the workers. But certainly the administrators were aware of the organizing efforts being made among southern sharecroppers and tenant farmers by the Croppers' and Farm Workers' Union, for even if the organizers had been working in secret, the violence perpetrated against them upon discovery was well known. Thus the possibility that Rosenwald Fund representatives designed Osborne's assignments to inhibit the radicalization of workers or even to "protect" them by discouraging their association with Communists cannot be dismissed.[79]

When Estelle Osborne returned briefly in 1935 to traditional hospital work and to representing the National Association of Colored Graduate Nurses (NACGN), she presented papers around the country that addressed the multifaceted negative effects of racism on the black community. Representing the NACGN allowed very different activities compared with representing the Rosenwald Fund. As a representative of the NACGN Osborne could speak directly to the causes of the problems rather than limiting herself to their consequences.[80]

Osborne's nursing career took another turn when the mayor of St. Louis announced in 1939 that he would appoint a black nurse to head the nursing department at City Hospital no. 2 (the black public hospital, later renamed Homer G. Phillips). Osborne reported receiving nineteen calls and telegrams from people urging her to apply for the new position. She did apply, was hired, and began work on 1 January 1940. Conditions in the hospital were so bad—it was in a dilapidated Barnes Medical School building—that the fire department advised all staff members that in case of a fire they should attempt to save no one but themselves. The hospital was a death trap not because of inadequate medical care, but from simple public neglect. Osborne, most of the people who worked there, and their public supporters—most notably attorney Homer G. Phillips—spent much of their time attempting to compensate for the disgraceful conditions and, with little success, trying to shame city administrators into improving matters.[81]

When Osborne left the hospital in 1942, her new paid position related simultaneously to the wartime emergency and to race relations—she went out as a paid consultant of the National Nursing Council for War Service, an agency at least partially funded by the Rockefeller Foundation.[82] Much of what she did was race-relations work—work designed to improve social relations or reduce tensions between black and white people. By her success on one assignment, she might have helped prevent a new series of riots in Detroit. In 1945 Wayne State University was about to file a condemnation suit to obtain property owned by black people in order to build a new nursing center on the land. The Rockefeller Foundation sent Osborne to help smooth over this controversy and to get the land the school administrators wanted. School officials used Osborne as a liaison with black community leaders, whom the administrators apparently had been unable to reach on their own. She also provided the names of black Detroit residents she considered appropriate candidates for the advisory committee of the College of Nursing being organized at the time. University administrators knew that having the right people on the board might prevent future confrontations. It might also mollify a community just defeated in a contest to hold on to its property.[83]

During the 1930s and 1940s public administrators regularly used black women for race work designed to meet the increased needs of the black community and in race-relations capacities to relieve, mask, or eliminate the stress generated by tension-filled interracial public encounters. Even librarians experienced this redefinition of traditional professional jobs. When Clara Jones moved from Louisiana to Detroit in the 1940s to accept a position as a librarian in the city public library system, her first assignment was to work on the Commission on Community Relations. As she went about the city, ostensibly to talk about the library, she had to address race relations—the real purpose of this "extension work." She was also supposed to determine the needs of the people, present her findings to the council, and help to develop public programs.[84]

Social worker Beulah Whitby, nurse Estelle Osborne, and librarian Clara Jones were able to earn a salary for this kind of work, but most women who found themselves engaged in similar activities by the 1940s received no pay for it. Pauline Byrd Taylor, a Kalamazoo, Michigan, schoolteacher, was by 1942 an unpaid member of the Michigan State Committee for Intercultural Understanding. Constance Fisher, a social worker in Minnesota, was on the St. Paul Council of Human Relations. And Thelma DeWitty, then a newcomer to Seattle, Washington, was an appointed member of the Governor's Board of Discrimination. Southern public officials were in general not yet sufficiently moved in any direction, but in 1933 Charleston, South Carolina, public administrators assigned schoolteacher Albertha Murray to the "colored swimming pool commission."[85]

Historically, the manner in which black women worked depended not only on the interaction of family, educational, and community socialization with clients' needs and expectations, but on available resources, the workers' own class biases, their professional training, and employer demands as well.[86] Because of the limited alternatives available for black professionals during the 1930s and early 1940s, however, they could easily lose the balance.[87] When the relative importance of employer demands increased at the same time that paid work alternatives declined, situations could arise that compromised the well-being of the community or some of its members in ways more devastating than the examples above suggest. Eunice Rivers Laurie's work with the Tuskegee syphilis project is a case in point.

Laurie worked intensively and superbly as a public health nurse in Alabama for forty years. During the 1920s and early 1930s she carried out fairly traditional public health tasks, and before she retired from public health nursing in 1965, Macon County officials recognized not only her years of dedicated work in nursing but also her involvement in community development and social service.[88] During the depression, however, the State Health Department Bureau of Vital Statistics eliminated Laurie's job, and she moved on to work at the John Andrew Hospital. After an eight-month stint there, to get off the night shift Laurie accepted a half-time reduction in that position, and a group of public health physicians paid for the rest of her time as an assistant for the infamous Tuskegee syphilis project—a nontherapeutic government research program that, from its inception in the 1930s until it ended in the 1970s, kept almost four hundred syphilitic black males untreated as a control group to elucidate the natural history of the disease. Although Laurie was in a large way responsible for keeping the men in the study and preventing their getting treatment elsewhere—this was a part of her job description—a definitive explanation of her participation is not possible. Her motive for taking the job was probably economic. But once on the job, perhaps her professional training, which mandated that she assume the superior knowledge of physicians and respect their authority, prevented her from seeing the undertaking as a pseudoscientific experiment, as later commentators viewed it. It is clear that because of her professional training and practice she viewed early conventional treatments for syphilis as ineffective and dangerous, and perhaps that helped her rationalize the potential benefits of this project. But Laurie's participation was probably more complex than that; perhaps when the physicians maintained that the study would ultimately benefit the local community, her earlier upbringing—which obligated her to use her position for the benefit of the race—combined with her professional socialization and the order of race and gender relations at the time, making it nearly impossible for her to challenge the white male physicians' claims and ultimately making her a key figure in this notorious affair.[89]

Surely having and keeping a job during the Great Depression was important to many women's individual survival. Because employers often believed that men were primarily responsible for their families' support, they regularly fired women first as the crisis ensued.[90] Consequently the only way for many women to keep paid professional employment was to work in positions that required them to represent their employers more than the race or their clients, as they had done previously. Even Mary Church Terrell, who did not need to work for the income, virtually disappeared from the public lecture circuit during the 1920s. As a lecturer, she was her own employer, still representing the race. During the 1920s she began working for someone else. Her new job saw her employed by the National Republican Committee, recruiting black votes among the newest enfranchisees—women. She worked on the Warren G. Harding presidential campaign, took part in Ruth Hannah McCormick's campaign for a seat in the United States Senate, and in 1932, Terrell was stumping New York for Herbert Hoover.[91]

Though many white employers created or redefined black women's jobs during the 1930s to include race and race-relations assignments, employers still did not control all of the women's work. Black professional women continued to do extensive race work on their own time, in the same socially committed way as before. During the 1930s and after, however, such work as they performed of their own volition tended to move in a new direction. The women no longer aimed simply to repair and prevent damage that resulted from social, economic, and political stratification, as seemed to be their focus up to the 1930s. Their unpaid work became, more clearly, reform work. Moreover, the reform efforts no longer focused exclusively on physical labor in the black community. Although the women's aims continued to include the physical development of the black community, their unpaid public roles took a dramatic turn and came to focus on the larger political economy. They even sought to change it.

• • •

Despite all the paid and unpaid race work that women had undertaken up to this time in the interest of individual uplift and community development, it was clear that these endeavors had only ameliorated the harsh conditions caused by social, political, and economic stratification. And much of the race-relations work that employers later assigned to black women as a part of their jobs was stopgap as well. To achieve widespread and lasting positive changes in the black community and the nation, the women implicitly decided that they not only had to address the immediate needs of individuals and groups, which they had trained so well and worked so hard to do, but they also had to make a concerted effort to break down the system that created and perpetuated such distress in the first place. By the 1930s the women's work beyond their jobs—work they defined for themselves—in the area of individual and community development came to be accompanied more consistently by an important new emphasis. It included an aggressive attack on the real roots of individual and community underdevelopment—institutionalized racism—and not just the consequences of it.

Beyond the enlarged quest for social justice, the Great Depression was undoubtedly an important factor in this new emphasis. Between 1930 and 1933, cotton prices dropped from eighteen cents a pound to six cents. As the earnings of black tenant farmers, sharecroppers, and landowners plummeted, black urban dwellers fared no better because white men and women competed for and received the "menial jobs traditionally reserved for Afro-Americans" in the cities. Half of black urban southerners were unemployed by 1932, and the statistics are similar for northern cities. In Cleveland the black unemployment rate exceeded 50 percent. In Chicago and Detroit, over 40 percent of black men and 55 percent of black women were unemployed. In Harlem the unemployment rate approached 50 percent, and in Philadelphia it surpassed 56 percent. In New York (and probably other places too), "slave markets" appeared where white employers "bought" the domestic labor of black women for as little as fifteen cents an hour.[92] If African Americans were to survive these conditions, changes in the system were essential.

Moreover, as much as the early New Deal programs helped to improve economic conditions in general, they did very little to reverse the devastation suffered by African Americans. The National Recovery Act (NRA) did not prevent employers from releasing black workers, nor did it provide for the enforcement of a minimum wage. In fact NRA codes allowed southerners to use an entirely different wage scale from that maintained in the North. And in the South in particular, agents classified most jobs held by African Americans so as to place them beyond NRA protection, anyway. The Agricultural Adjustment Act led to the withdrawal from production of much land farmed by black tenant farmers and sharecroppers, but they did not receive the bonus paid for its removal. The Social Security Act did not cover domestic and agricultural workers in its pension or unemployment insurance programs, thus excluding two-thirds of all black workers. And decentralization of federal relief distribution organized under the Federal Emergency Relief Act and the Works Progress Administration (WPA) further ensured inequitable treatment for black citizens. Southern administrators of the act concluded that black families needed less money to survive than white families needed, and parceled out WPA jobs to white men and women first. Indeed, many southern politicians saw supporting black men and women through these programs as a waste of good money on people who (because of systematic disfranchisement) could not return the "favor" with their votes. Even the Tennessee Valley Authority, regularly hailed as the most successful of all New Deal programs, systematically reinforced the racial status quo.[93]

Black migration patterns encouraged the women's more aggressive approach to their paid and unpaid reform work in ways other than by increasing need among the general public. Philadelphia's black population more than tripled between 1910 and 1940. Detroit's, as already noted, increased from almost 6,000 to 120,000 between 1910 and 1930, and New York City's black population grew almost fivefold during the same period. Throughout the Midwest and in many Mid-Atlantic states, these newly enfranchised migrants held the decisive votes in local and national elections, giving "liberal" politicians the votes they needed to address the concerns of black citizens with less fear of electoral reprisals in statehouses and city halls.[94] The subsequent American participation in the Second World War, touted as a war against fascism and racism, was not lost on black professional women either. They quickly took the position that the war had to be fought on two fronts, at home and abroad, and that victory abroad would be meaningless without a victory at home. Working to *all* black people's advantage was a major shift among black voters to the Democratic Party during the 1936 election. If black professional women had not previously had the clout or the nerve to aim some of their reform efforts directly at government agencies and agents, they gained it now.

Even on local levels in the South, the women's bold intentions were apparent. In South Carolina, Mamie Fields made a point of informing her school's PTA parents of new minimum wage laws, and she advised them to ask for more pay. They protected her by insisting to their employers that they got this information from newspapers. When local relief administrators did not fulfill their responsibilities to African Americans, Fields threatened to get "the government" (the federal government) involved, and the threat was usually sufficient. Women in Atlanta's Neighborhood Union, after experiencing decades of problems with the administration of black public schools, demanded assembly rooms in black public school buildings, a second black high school in the city, and a second black assistant in the local administration of WPA relief. And Ethel Ray Nance, in a new clerical position in the Minnesota state legislature, helped to organize the Minnesota Negro Council, an organization designed "to help Negroes get jobs . . . [and to get] one Negro in each state department [office]."[95]

Black nurses provided a good example of the new activism when they started a nationwide campaign in 1939 in support of the proposed National Health Act (S. 1620). The bill addressed rural health problems in particular and rural and urban poverty in general. Officers of the NACGN reminded their supporters (whether true or not) that nine-tenths of all black Americans lived in rural areas or in poverty and therefore the nurses had to *insist* on certain conditions in the administration of the bill: equal pay for equal work in all jobs created or affected by the bill (many of them nursing jobs); minority representation on all advisory boards involved in the programs; and public announcements of all program plans before state approval. They also sought a modification in the bill itself to guarantee the equal distribution of funds in segregated public systems. NACGN officers circulated the memo to their state and local affiliates for distribution to every black nurse known to the local officers. The individual nurses were to write to their national (elected) representatives and to raise broader community support through presentations to local YWCAs, YMCAs, church groups, race organizations, and even "the civic and social clubs, the medical organizations, and other nursing organizations" of which they were not members. The memo encouraged the nurses to "talk with every friend you have in your community about your interest in this bill and get them to write." And last, it advised them that "it may take three or four years to pass this act, but the Negro will find himself left out unless he gets into the fight for the passage of this bill now, in the early stages. No one can afford to be idle if victory is to be ours."[96]

Many black women were involved in the effort to convince public officials to create a permanent Fair Employment Practices Commission and in the March on Washington Movement (MOWM) of 1941, coordinated to force federal officials to end racial discrimination in defense industries. Layle Lane, a New York City schoolteacher and activist, was one of the principal organizers of the MOWM, and she was a forceful speaker who predicted more significant problems for the nation if the war did not also "bring the four freedoms" to black people throughout the world. Lane used the column she wrote for the New York *Age* to publicize persistent discrimination in the employment and deployment of African Americans during the war, and she solicited letters from some of her former students, then in the military, to document her claims.[97] Additionally, throughout the 1940s, women in all the professions began their most intensive push for the integration of the professional organizations that were not yet open to African Americans.[98]

Since before the turn of the century, black women had worked for the passage of federal antilynching legislation, but Norma Boyd joined the crusade, she said, after reading in the *New York Times* that southern congressmen had threatened to expose northern members' legislative compromises if they continued to push the antilynching legislation. Legislative blackmail was not uncommon, and in fact, during the 1922 campaign, southern legislators made it very clear that they would start a filibuster and prevent the Senate from accomplishing any official business if their colleagues brought up the bill. Norma Boyd, as far as can be determined, had never been as intensively and directly involved in the family and community lives of her students as had her southern colleagues, who attempted to supply the public services their clients failed to receive from local officials. But living in Washington, D.C., did allow Boyd to fight institutional racism more openly and aggressively than most other southerners could. With no experience and no money, she began to organize a lobby for the passage of a federal antilynching bill.[99]

The old lessons of community support were familiar to Boyd, and she began her work by approaching Dorothy Ferebee, "a powerful woman," in Boyd's opinion, who was then president of Alpha Kappa Alpha, a black women's national sorority to which Boyd belonged. She told Ferebee of her interest in a national antilynching campaign and suggested that local sorority women should pay ten dollars each to have someone lobby congressmen, observe Congress, and report back to them. Ferebee agreed, and they hired a small staff. Boyd convinced her sister, a woman who "was not a joiner," "liked few people," and "didn't have much use for women," to allow them to put an office in their home until the organization could afford other quarters. Then she began to give lectures wherever she could to spread the word about the campaign and increase support for it. The sorority designed and distributed Christmas cards to promote the antilynching law; they sold antilynching buttons; and they printed and distributed special newsletters about the progress (and lack of progress) of the bill and other relevant goings-on in Congress. After several years of working out of Boyd's home, the national organization assumed the expenses of a new office, and Alpha Kappa Alpha's antilynching law lobby, coordinated in part by Boyd, remained functional until 1948. By that time even the NAACP had given up the effort and turned most of its attention to achieving equity in public education—campaigns in which black professional women were deeply involved.[100]

Women schoolteachers knew intimately the impact of the unequal distribution of funds by local officials. But other people also knew that the practice profoundly impeded black individual and community development, and therefore the various public education campaigns became massive efforts. So obvious were the broad implications of the inequitable salaries, for example, that one journalist recommended that black people collectively sue local and state governments for billions of dollars in back pay, since its cumulative withholding had stunted the development of whole black communities and generations of individuals. NAACP officials not only recognized the impact of wage inequity but also knew it was an issue their legal defense team could influence—if community support was strong enough. Not until an important victory in Maryland in 1939, however, was public support easy to gain, for many white southerners saw the NAACP as a subversive organization, and open affiliation often caused black southerners to lose their jobs. But after this Maryland victory, Aline Black, on behalf of black Virginians, petitioned the Norfolk Board of Education for an equitable salary, and the campaign moved forward.[101]

As dangerous as it was for black southerners to belong to the

NAACP, Septima Clark joined as soon as she lived where there was an active branch. She paid her first dues almost immediately upon moving to Columbia, South Carolina, during the 1920s, and she assisted in a variety of local programs that the organization sponsored.[102] It was not until February 1943, however, that the Columbia branch of the NAACP found a plaintiff for a salary equalization suit. People in Columbia, as elsewhere, were afraid of losing their jobs, or worse, if they became publicly connected with a legal effort to change local customs. But after the NAACP finally filed the suit in October 1943, Clark helped collect the affidavits needed to document the case. And in February 1944 Judge J. Waties Waring signed the consent decree that provided for the equalization of South Carolina teachers' salaries.[103]

The illusion of victory was short-lived, however. Since 1939, when Maryland teachers won their suit, a South Carolina legislative committee had been looking for alternatives to equalization. And by the time the South Carolina consent decree was issued, the committee had already devised "an apparently effective merit system" based on National Teacher Examinations. They created a four-tier teacher certification process in which the top 25 percent of those taking the test would get A certificates, the middle 50 percent B certificates, the next 15 percent C certificates, and the lowest 10 percent D certificates, and based salaries on these classes of certification. The committee's four-volume report had also revealed that 90 percent of white test takers (based on pretest results) would get A or B certificates while only 27 percent of black teachers tested would score as well. But no matter; an argument could be made, however contrived, for objectivity, and so this was the route South Carolina legislators took. Clark had no problem passing the exam at the A level, and so she kept her job—at three times her former salary. She also began to tutor black women who had not fared so well.[104]

Among the small number of black women gaining A or B certificates, however, there were apparently still too many agitators, for as public education campaigns among African Americans intensified—to include integration as well as equalization—local officials came up with another strategy for getting some black teachers out of the system. Not long after the 1954 *Brown v Board of Education* decision made segregated public education unconstitutional, the Charleston school board sent questionnaires to all teachers that included questions about their organizational activities. Clark was one of the few black teachers daring enough to admit membership in the NAACP, and consequently the school board fired her without a hearing. Having Septima Clark in a school system in which administrators had no intention of implementing integration was too much of a threat. Clark lost her job and all her retirement benefits after nearly forty years of teaching in South Carolina schools, almost thirty of them in the public school system. Losing that job did not stop her efforts to end systematic discrimination against African Americans, however. She subsequently joined the staff of the Highlander Folk School and continued to work for equality.[105]

In the 1960s, after nearly fifty years of working for community and individual development, Clark wrote, "My participation in [the] fight to force equalization of white and Negro teachers' salaries, on the basis of equal certification, of course, was what might be described by some, no doubt, as my first 'radical' job." She added, "I would call it my first effort in social action challenging the status quo, the first time I had worked *against* people directing a system for which I was working." Clark had, in fact, always worked against the system, even if not directly challenging its leaders. From the beginning of her career on Johns Island in 1916, when she used her own funds to buy chalk and paper for her students, and throughout the thirty years that she taught adults how to read in night schools, she had worked against the system. Clark's mother often feared for her daughter's safety because she recognized how threatening Clark's work was to many white southerners, but it never caused Clark any uneasiness. "I was working for the accomplishment of something that ultimately would be good for everyone," she said, and she pursued her course "not only with an easy conscience but with inspiration and enthusiasm."[106]

Septima Clark's work with large organized efforts to change the system did not prevent her continuing to work in the usual direct way for uplift and for local community development and reform. In 1947, upon completing her eighteenth year as a Columbia public school teacher by day and an adult literacy teacher by night, Clark returned to Charleston to teach seventh grade and, later, remedial reading. On arriving in Charleston, she "went to work, and put others to work" in unpaid community development and reform. She got the old, run-down YWCA building repainted, had a new concrete porch poured, and had the building rewired, all through "500 hours of free labor volunteered by workers of the community." Then she and two local white women paid a visit to the mayor and convinced him to provide a police officer for the black YWCA on program days to prevent young boys from harassing the girls. Clark also convinced the mayor to address the long-term solution for the problem by providing Y activities for black boys because, she insisted, "we should have some sort of program for them that will help use up in a good and positive way the surplus energy that these boys are now using in doing mischief." About six months later, the Reverend Emmett P. Lampkin "was brought to Charleston from Mount Vernon, New York, . . . to have charge of what was called a boys' work program."[107]

Septima Clark gained some fame for her community development work in South Carolina and for her efforts in the larger civil rights movement. And Layle Lane, through her work with the American Federation of Teachers, did as well. But many women carried out their work for social change with much less fanfare. The campaign of Chicago librarian Charlemae Hill Rollins to eliminate racist images in published material is one example. Rollins began her professional career as an Oklahoma schoolteacher, but in 1927 she moved to Chicago with her husband, Joseph, and their young son and went to work at the Chicago Public Library. In 1932 a South Side branch, named for George Cleveland Hall, opened, and Rollins became head of the children's room. Working in this new library in a growing black community no doubt contributed to her decision to send 150 questionnaires to black and white high school principals asking them to list books used in their schools that included material on African Americans. When she received only two responses, she began working on a literature guide that identified material for children conveying positive images of black life. Even though, according to some observers, the resulting guide "helped to raise the level of consciousness [about the] need for more honest portrayals of the Negro and to correct the inequities of limited representations of the Negro in every genre of literature for children," Rollins believed it was not enough. The annotated pamphlet she compiled, titled *We Build Together* and published in 1941 by the National Council of Teachers of English, included only twenty-four books. Rollins resolved that she would help change this situation.[108]

Rollins began what many have described as a one-woman campaign to force publishers to be more accountable for the images of black people in their books. One of her friends wrote to her: "The letter you wrote to P.W. is bearing fruit. Mrs. Poole has written to you, I'm sure, about the two books we have received for review. The Negro reading public is large enough now to make demands on publishers."

Indeed, Rollins exerted enough pressure that several publishers hired her as a paid consultant and adviser to their white authors of children's books about African Americans. Editors at Thomas Y. Crowell sent *Rifles for Wattie*, which would become a prizewinning book, to her for review before publishing it. Rollins reviewed the manuscript carefully, pointing out the many racist assumptions embedded in the text. One line in the manuscript read, "When she opened her vast mouth to grin at him, her teeth reminded Jeff of a row of white piano keys." Rollins referred to the line as "the most objectionable of all words [and] phrases in the book." It must have been a difficult decision to label this line rather than some other as the most vexatious, for there were equally offensive statements throughout the text. About one of them—"He even smelled clean"—Rollins simply noted that the sentence represented "deep down unconscious stereotyping by an author who feels that 'all Negroes smell [bad].' "[109]

While continuing to work as a public librarian, Rollins therefore had a hand in editing many well-received children's books and stories, and several white women writers undoubtedly were successful in part because of her help. Publishers had repeatedly rejected Virginia Cunningham's juvenile account of Paul Laurence Dunbar before Rollins edited the manuscript; then Cunningham was able to sell it. And "everything was wrong" with Florence Means's second book manuscript, according to Rollins. "The characters spoke in dialect at Tuskegee—of all places." The original manuscript, titled *Dark Lillibell*, referred to black people as "negresses" and "pickaninnies." After Rollins's review of the manuscript, Means rewrote it and retitled it *Great Day in the Morning*, and the book was acceptable. Frances Cavanah thanked Rollins for critiquing her story "Little Hiram." And if one example of the public response to the story is any indication of the successful collaboration, shortly after it appeared in *Good Housekeeping*, Mary Terrell Tancil dashed off a note to her mother, Mary Church Terrell, urging her to get a copy of the magazine and to read "Little Hiram," which, she said, was written by a genius.[110]

Rollins, whose career pattern closely parallels that of Augusta Baker,[111] a nationally known New York City librarian, worked for twenty-seven years in the Hall Branch of the Chicago Public Library. She performed the traditional librarian's duties, including checking out books, shelving them, and tracking circulation. But Rollins was also a storyteller in the children's section of the library, and she became an author of children's books as well. She worked to make the Hall Branch

CHAPTER SIX

a place where young people could learn more about African American history and culture. She started library clubs to improve individual reading ability and increase race consciousness. She brought writers Arna Bontemps, Richard Wright, Langston Hughes, and Jean Toomer to the library to lecture. She also took advantage of the generosity of Illinois writers including Gwendolyn Brooks, Doris Saunders, Hoyt Fuller, and Era Bell Thompson. She worked to increase the library holdings related to African American life and history. And one writer gave her credit for creating at the Hall Branch "one of the most complete collections on Black people in this country."[112]

Rollins did not have to spend her time soliciting donations of books as Sadie Peterson Delaney was doing at the Veterans Administration Hospital in Tuskegee, Alabama.[113] Nor did she have to round up a volunteer staff as Susan Dart Butler was doing in South Carolina, although Rollins undoubtedly worked at getting the writers to visit. And Rollins was much more fortunate than Mollie Huston Lee, a Columbia University School of Library Service graduate, who in 1935 was still working to create a public library for black residents in Raleigh, North Carolina, and walking the streets with baskets of books to lend in the meantime.[114] Because Rollins was in an established library that paid her a salary—and no doubt, recent black migration forced the opening of "black" branch libraries throughout the country—she could easily take on race work beyond her job responsibilities.[115] She promoted black writers, demanded ethics and accuracy in publications, edited other people's work, and wrote books herself. But her efforts reflected more than job security. The same social and political movements that motivated employers during the 1930s and 1940s to pay black women to do race and race relations work, enabled and encouraged black women to work, more often without wages, to eliminate racism altogether. Librarians were aware of the important role they could play in the struggle for fair and equal treatment, for eliminating stereotypes from publications, and for preserving and promoting the rich history of African Americans. And that is how they worked, whether or not it fit their job descriptions.[116]

• • •

Over the generations, family members, friends, teachers, and mentors had worked to instill respectability in these women while they were still children. The goal of these socialization efforts, along with formal education, was to imbue the children with the strength of character that would enable them, as they grew up, to undertake whatever challenges life and work might present. Their adulthoods were indeed filled with disrespectful treatment, hard work, low or no wages, and persistently bad working conditions, but they persevered with a vengeance. Starting first with traditional social-service oriented community work, regardless of their occupations and usually in addition to their job assignments, they quickly became involved in community development. And when they realized that community development and race uplift would not get them where they wanted to be as long as they were uplifting only the black race, they went to work on uplifting the white race. Almost prophetically, Mary Church Terrell had written on the needs of white people in a 1905 article titled "Service Which Should Be Rendered the South." Terrell began her article,

When the two words "Service["] and the ["]South" are mentioned in the same breath, one involuntarily thinks of the needs of the freedman and the variety of the ways in which assistance may be rendered the race to which he belongs. . . .

Among the many subjects discussed on the platform, in the pulpit and by the press it would be impossible to name one, on which it is more difficult to express new thoughts than the need of lifting colored people to a higher plane. . . .

There is one kind of service which might and should be rendered the South, however, that is rarely discussed. Generally speaking, the country is blind to the unfortunate mental and spiritual condition of a large number of its citizens, who need civilizing and Christianizing even more, perhaps, than the freedman. . . .

Briefly stated, this service consists in freeing the white South from the thralldom of its prejudices; emancipating it from the slavery of its petty, narrow views which choke the good impulses and throttle the better nature of even its worthiest citizens; teaching them the difference between the highest, purest patriotism and a harmful sectional pride; instilling into the people as a whole a sense of justice which will prevent them from either inflicting or withholding penalties for wrongdoing and crime according to the color of a man's skin; finally, breathing into the hearts of all a compassion and a Christian charity which shall extend even to the despised and oppressed.[117]

Perhaps many of these women knew early in their public careers that they would ultimately have to undertake this type of reform work. By the 1930s or so and in some locations, they began, systematically, to do it. And by the 1950s African Americans began to reap more fully the rewards of these efforts and to engage in them more widely.

. . .

Because of public and private sphere constraints historically imposed on women, scholars regularly demonstrate the importance of studying women workers in such a way as to include their unpaid activities. Black professional women, however, were not constrained in the same ways, and therefore an analysis of their work must consider additional issues. As I have explained, much of the work they did, even while on the job, dramatically exceeded their job descriptions, and that work is subject to misinterpretation. For example, almost all schoolteachers at one time or another supervised student activities after school hours, and this work was understandably a part of the job. At least until the 1930s, however, when local governments began to take some responsibility for eliminating illiteracy, black schoolteachers also saw teaching the parents of their students to read and write as a part of their work, though it was neither written into job descriptions nor financially compensated. It would be a mistake to characterize all of these efforts as (stereo-)typical examples of charity work, because the women perceived their work in terms of responsibility to the community rather than of wages and bureaucratic job classifications.[118] Thus black professional women's unpaid work was regularly neither domestic work nor charity work. It was community development. And when they worked for a salary, their training and their clients' conditions of life dictated that they not see themselves exclusively as schoolteachers, nurses, social workers, or librarians. They had to be whatever the community needed them to be and do whatever the community needed them to do.

Overwhelmingly, they worked intensively with community members to improve the individual and collective quality of life. For Septima Clark, Judia Jackson, Frances Grant, Genevieve Ladson, and others, much of what they did, even as schoolteachers, constituted community development. The people with whom these teachers worked often required the labor of a person dedicated to the whole community. And so the professionals involved themselves in all aspects of the school and community as they worked for the general advancement of the people they served. More understandably, perhaps, social workers also wore the hats of teacher, socializer, and civil rights activist as they took part in the social, political, and economic life of the community. Black settlement houses became centers for studying domestic science and for neighborhood cultural, educational, and intellectual activities. Women in these institutions gathered vital statistics on the black community that informed and justified subsequent public health studies and programs, voter education projects, and even public school activities.

Nurses and librarians could more easily have limited their work to their official job descriptions, but they often did not. An award presented to Eunice Laurie when she retired from public health nursing in the 1960s explicitly described her as a "health adviser, a housing adviser, a financial adviser, a spiritual adviser, and a moral adviser."[119] In a similar fashion, Clara Jones, the Detroit librarian, characterized black librarians' work thus: "Black librarians have never been saddled with the image of the prim, forbidding, 'jailor of books' (to quote Melvil Dewey's scornful phrase). Invariably, [the black librarian] . . . has been . . . an active leader, helper, worker in the community, who was never intimidated by the kind of role required to take the library to the people." She continued, "They have shared their talents . . . with the community as a part of their involvement in civic and cultural life." Vivian Hewett, another librarian, described her work role as "a social worker, an 'Ann Landers,' a public relations specialist, a fund raiser, not to mention the teacher-writer-reference-bibliographer-lecturer bit." Mary Church Terrell could have been summarizing the work lives of nearly all of these women when she wrote to her daughter in 1920: "I have been working for my race in one way or another ever since I was a grown woman."[120]

The way they worked for the race did, however, change over the decades. At first the women worked in traditional social-service-oriented community uplift work regardless of their occupations, whether or not they received a salary, and often in addition to their job assignments. They quickly became involved in community development activities to make up for the neglect by local public agencies. But as a more northern, more urban, and potentially more radical black community began to emerge in the 1930s, these women, while gaining more lucrative employment than they ever had before, began to lose control of their job definitions. They did not, however, lose control over their work. As their employers began to define their jobs to include race and race-relations work, the women began to redefine their unpaid work to include the reform of the political economy. They had, as individuals, finally obtained positions in mainstream institutions and therefore achieved a lifelong goal—some level of acceptance by the larger white society and perhaps even differentiation from the masses. But gaining these positions individually only underlined the extent to which the group remained underserved and excluded. Despite all their intensive paid and unpaid work, focusing on community development and the uplift of the black race was not enough. Consequently, they went to work attacking the larger system of institutionalized racism and, in so doing, began working to uplift the white race.

In their own day, these black professional women served as role models—to the extent that the world was never the same afterward. And like any historical figures who have accomplished much, their experiences can still instruct us.

In particular, their lives provide a useful contrast to portrayals of leadership in terms of national "spokespersons." Insightful and prolific writers, heads of important educational institutions, high-level government bureaucrats, and founders and owners of important businesses have regularly achieved some fame as leaders in and beyond African American communities. Those individuals did not, however, hold a monopoly on leadership. The women of this book touched many people's lives daily as they acted on the socialization that held them directly responsible for changing social conditions. With much assistance from their constituents, they successfully attacked illiteracy; they helped coordinate the building of schools, libraries, hospitals, and social settlement houses; they altered the physical landscape, the material conditions, and the social, political, and economic status of African American communities throughout the country. And as other scholars have noted, they also contributed greatly to the reclamation and reformation of American society at large.[1]

These women did not stumble upon these leadership roles accidentally; nor were they, in general, born to them. But in addition to the important discussion of how they achieved leadership—through an empowering socialization process and a particular understanding of womanhood—and how they experienced it, this narrative also contributes to an understanding of intraracial—community—dynamics. In this case, intraracial dynamics (also, significantly, interclass dynamics) were much more intimate and productive than many portrayals, old and new, scholarly and popular, might lead one to believe.

Our need to understand class phenomena led us, from the

outset, to an examination of what made groups different from one another. Perhaps we surmised too quickly and conclusively that the different places where people fell on our charts and graphs exactly paralleled how differently (and apart) those people led their lives. A study of class structure obviously reveals little about the meaning of being in a particular position. Black professional women derived their status not merely from the material conditions that characterized their own lives but from the extent to which and the manner in which their individual positions affected a larger community. Their interpretation of their responsibilities, determined in part by their privilege and demonstrated in part by their actions, contributed greatly to the status they achieved.

The women of this study, and the people with whom they lived and worked, understood the intricacies of class dynamics. That understanding allowed women who had been trained as professionals to do domestic work when necessary and to feel no shame about it. It allowed for, even called for, people who could not afford to send their own children to college to contribute to sending the children of others. And finally, it allowed black professional women, especially in my first and second generations, to maintain relatively high status positions in the communities where they worked while being housed, fed, and paid, in part or in full, by people considered to be far less privileged. The operation of class relationships in the black community reveals a sometimes ironic material relationship between the groups and calls for more detailed examination.

Among the questions we must ask in that examination are those related to the development of class groups in general. Although we know much (though still not enough) about the creation of a black working class, the details of these women's lives speak directly to the development of the black professional class.[2] Many of these women came from cash-poor, working-class families. The economic conditions of their families therefore cannot unilaterally explain why they achieved higher education. Moreover, for the first generation, movement into the professional class did not depend on their families' having been free before the Civil War, as is a traditional conclusion. Although without a doubt the higher economic class backgrounds of some families had a tremendous impact on their children's life chances, access to schools, the availability of self-help (later, work-study) programs, community support, and probably many other factors worked together to facilitate the development of a post-emancipation professional class.

Questions about the process of professionalization come up here, too. Indeed, in the context of existing scholarship on professionals and professionalization, black professional women present a conundrum. First of all, their experience fits none of the models established to describe how an occupational group achieves professional status in the national arena. These women possessed a relatively high standing within their communities at the same time that people beyond those communities held little or no regard for them. They possessed the general traits established by the professional mainstream as the prerequisites for entry, yet they remained excluded. And their status was not controlled (denied) by their professional superiors, as was usual among aspiring professionals; black women were excluded by their professional peers, their alleged "natural" allies. But second, and equally important, the experiences of these women do not exactly follow the pattern established by scholars who describe the eventual (and total) cooptation of people who were professionals. Black professional women shared in the modern movement to carve out a special place of privilege based on their credentials. But while relishing the status these credentials allowed, they brought to their positions an agenda beyond establishing their own individual prestige. They also worked to raise the status of the race.[3]

Finally, and most obviously, blurring the boundaries between family (private/institutional) and women's (public/movement) history, the experiences of the women studied here make it clear that African American movements for individual empowerment, local community development, and national social change began in families. And most profoundly, they also demonstrate that individualism and social responsibility do not have to be competing ideals.[4]

The lives of black professional women suggest important questions about other groups and fields in American history. But still there are many gaps, some of them glaring, in our knowledge of these women's lives. In spite of intensive socialization and obvious success, some women must have fallen short of the ideal far more often than this book suggests. Similarly, many women were probably crushed under the burdens that they, with some encouragement, assumed. And undoubtedly many African American women in the feminized professions preferred to pursue law, medicine, or some other higher-level occupation but, for a variety of reasons, did/could not. These, of course, are issues that we must explore further. Meanwhile, what can we make of the facts we do have?

• • •

"Marie," a good friend of Constance Fisher's, was among the first black professional women to desegregate the offices of the Cleveland, Ohio, Social Services Department during the 1920s. And even after the completion of the reorganizations, she witnessed a series of shenanigans, conducted by administrators, designed to avoid true integration. When the process of eliminating several district offices and redistributing the work and the workers began, Marie speculated in a letter to Constance that "the powers that be sat up nights figuring out where to send the colored members of the Buck staff." At first Marie learned that the black staff of the Buckeye district would be sent to a new office set up to serve single men only. But members of the NAACP heard of the plan, "and when the smoke cleared away the lists [had been] revised, and five of us [including Marie] were slated for Brdwy [Broadway]," a district that encompassed large East European immigrant neighborhoods and an office that had never used black workers.[5]

Soon after the transfers took place, "one of the 'powers' at Central Office" telephoned Mrs. Sears, the newly appointed black supervisor for the Broadway office, to inquire about her satisfaction with her new assignment, since it would not allow her to supervise "any of her 'own people.'" The administrator also advised Mrs. Sears that if her new office was unsatisfactory in any way, they could send her somewhere else. Marie observed, "'somewhere else,' of course, meant Wilson" (the office now handling most of the black cases from the old Buckeye district).[6] Mrs. Sears made it clear that she had no complaints about her new position, and Marie was delighted that the new boss held fast.

A variety of other incidents continued to nag Marie, however. In one case, a white coworker asked if she was "happy" about her new assignment. In response, Marie reported, "I smiled very sweetly and said that I didn't work to be 'happy' but to eat: my idea of happiness was not to work because I was certainly born for luxury." Marie concluded her discussion about the incident by saying,

It just burns me when a white person starts telling me about being "happy" on a certain job—or in a certain school—and with certain groups. I'm going to do my job well, no matter where I am, and when I get too big for it or to the point where I complain all day and can't stand the way things are run—why, I'll just retire. We've got to put up with white people's foolishness on almost any job that we may have, the only difference is in the amount, and believe me—since I have to work with and for them—I know how to get along with them.[7]

Marie's lengthy epistle (there was much more) evokes much about the historical preparation of black professional women and their achieving the important goal of gaining professional positions in the American mainstream. Marie, like many others in paid public work after the 1920s, came to work "with and for" white people. And she had been prepared for that. Indeed, had the women who queried Marie and Mrs. Sears about their job satisfaction known much about the upbringing of the black women who were just then entering the professional mainstream, they probably would not have asked the questions. In spite of Marie's sardonic "born for luxury" comment, her mother, a Louisiana schoolteacher, worked diligently, as did the families of other women, to make certain her daughter was prepared to take advantage of opportunities like this one as soon as they came along.

That preparation had included not only the best formal schooling obtainable under socially and sometimes economically constraining conditions but also the development of great self-confidence and high aspirations. The possession of these attributes, along with basic good manners and high morality, would contribute to the women's gaining important public positions that might not be available to others who were not as highly accomplished or respected. But family, community, and schooling processes also required the demonstration of character—joining individualistic aspirations to the needs of the larger group. As suggested in Marie's situation, women in the possession of the traits advocated by family, community, and teachers not only could eventually enter the American mainstream but presumably could sustain themselves once there.

Clearly, much of black professional women's upbringing prepared them to work in whatever capacity was possible and necessary: and "necessity" was both individual and collective. For that reason, many of the women examined here not only created the institutions from which they could eventually earn a wage, but they did so with no assurance that the work would actually pay off. Because of the needs of the community they served, those fortunate enough to find existing paid positions regularly had to work in ways that far exceeded their job descriptions. And whether they worked for wages or not, whether in established public institutions or in the "private" ones they created, their work not only sometimes provided an income, but also helped establish them as leaders in the movements to bring the larger African American community into the mainstream. The women's socialization as children assured them that they could achieve all these things if they were properly prepared and appropriately committed.

Still, one could logically conclude that if these women were brought up to believe they could do anything they wanted to do, then they were clearly, and perhaps even deliberately, misled. For in every way they pursued that promise, they met with varying degrees of obstruction. The first limitation was implicit even as they were being prepared for their futures, in that they were being trained as teachers, social workers, nurses, and librarians rather than as physicians, attorneys, research scientists, and engineers. Second, once they obtained the education necessary to pursue the feminized professions, few of them had much choice about where they would work. And third, with their training completed and their positions secured (often created by themselves), they were for a time consistently snubbed by public officials and the existing professional organizations. Those were the hard realities they faced.

But perhaps the larger issues concern why the families, community people, and educational mentors constructed such a democratic promise for these daughters; why the daughters did not succumb to disappointment when it was not realized; and what the implications are of their reconciling the latter with the former. To address these questions, I shall return to a suggestion I brought up in the preface: the idea of perception. The women's perceptions of themselves shaped their lives as much as legal proscriptions, social exclusion, and economic deprivation did. That self-image was deeply rooted in a particular understanding of history and in their own experiences.

These daughters were often the children and grandchildren of slaves. The chief travail of the former bondswomen and bondsmen during their lifetimes was the pursuit of freedom—making the idea real. But ultimately, for many of them, it was not possible to unburden themselves of the "legacies" of slavery. Upon emancipation, they remained in restrictive and oppressive environments, and the promise of freedom—equality—regularly eluded them. True, it was no longer against the law for freed women and men to learn to read and write, as once had been the case. Yet material and political realities, embodied in local laws and customs, continued to prevent most of them from gaining much formal schooling. And for the same reasons, they could no more pursue paid work based on their personal abilities and inclinations than they could have while enslaved. Perhaps what most of them could celebrate most consistently was expressed by Septima Clark's mother. Mrs. Poinsette, who did laundry for white families in her own home for most of her married life, celebrated the fact that "she 'never gave a white woman a cup of coffee.' "[8] Septima's mother boasted that she had never been a "servant," and with some effort she and her husband, who was born a slave, made certain that Septima would not have to be a domestic worker. With little education, less capital, and only half a chance of acquiring either, as was true of many of these parents, they did as Zora Neale Hurston's Nanny did: they invested in the futures of their daughters.

Their daughters and granddaughters were born free, and the elders, having come so far themselves—to some level of freedom, if not equality—could easily believe that these children of freedom could fully experience its promises. They educated their daughters openly, even if they had to send them away from home to do it. And the elders could, theoretically, rightly believe that by virtue of appropriate formal and informal education their daughters could realize the freedom that had eluded them. The daughters' gaining access to formal schooling at all was evidence of the distinct possibility. And so it was most important to prepare their daughters for the leadership roles that were *possible* for those who obtained the right preparation and *necessary* for the benefit of the rest of them. Believing so fiercely in the power of freedom to deliver equality, the elders had only to convince their daughters to believe in themselves. They designed their child-rearing strategies to that end.

The women's teachers were equally compelling in making a point of the women's power. According to the educators, each individual woman, by virtue of her preparation—mental, moral, and, for a time, manual—had the superhuman ability to uplift the masses and to change the whole society. And that was what she had to do.

Working among some of the most deprived people of their communities further reinforced the evidence of these women's actual privilege and potential power. The first generation of teachers taught in schools where the students included two and three generations of the same families. Children, their parents, and sometimes their grandparents were, together, pursuing their letters in the same classrooms because none of them had had the opportunity before. Thus the effective memory of slavery for these women did not have to be shaped by their own enslavement. Elders in their families, communities, and schools actively helped shape memories for them. And, moreover, until well into the twentieth century, as they pursued their work on a daily basis, the persistent vestiges of slavery continued to inform not only the first but also the second and third generations of professionals and to reinforce notions of their own privileged positions.

The women's training and subsequent work thus afforded them a relatively high position in their communities. They accepted that elite status and undoubtedly saw themselves as "different" from the rest of the masses (black and white). But the process by which they achieved their education introduced a balance between their becoming elite and their becoming aloof. A most important manifestation and consequence was the development of a social and political alternative to the individualistic success ethic embedded in the larger society. That alternative was characterized by socially responsible individualism, and with it black women emerged as leaders.

The promise of the parents that their daughters could do anything they wanted to do was undoubtedly an idealistic pledge, but it was not necessarily an unattainable, unrealistic avowal based on cultural myths. It was a democratic promise, but that should not be confused with a promise of democracy. The youngsters knew, even as they went off to school, that America was not very democratic. They at first attended particular schools rather than others closer to home, with well-established programs and well-educated black teachers, because America was not very democratic. With the proper training, however, they would have the ability to help democratize it. Consequently, when they emerged from school they began working to "equalize opportunities" and "prevent handicaps" among other African Americans. It was then that they built schools, social settlement houses, public health clinics, and libraries, and even when they did not have to build or develop them, they worked in them in ways that far exceeded traditional job definitions.

Probably it was *only* because they had been promised that their presence and their efforts would make such a difference in the lives of so many others that black professional women so staunchly endured the restraints they themselves continued to face. As much as family, community people, and teachers advocated education for "the race" as a key to progress, prevailing conventions related to gender remained intact. For that reason, women could achieve, but mostly in particular ways. These women did not stubbornly seek to become attorneys or physicians, although their brothers sometimes did. They were not trained to be domestic workers, but they did domestic work. In accepting these societal constraints, they in one way reinforced the subordinate status of traditional public and private female roles. But the formal education and vocational goals they pursued—in social work, education, librarianship, and nursing—while reinforcing those subordinate roles, kept them from internalizing an inferior status.

Early in life, these women learned that even within the traditionally limiting feminized professions there were important social and political opportunities and obligations. They extended far beyond the individual and her family and included the support of, the promotion of, and the development of the entire community. Thus, these women were groomed from the beginning for leadership, and these professions were the vehicle. When one considers the mighty efforts that families and communities made to maneuver their daughters around various obstacles, and the central role of the schools in producing graduates who could effect change wherever they took up residence, few other conclusions are possible.

Ultimately these daughters realized all that their parents promised. To be sure, the subtle and the not-so-subtle messages that bombarded them on every front led many of them "to want" to be teachers, social workers, nurses, and librarians. But from their perspective, these were not necessarily inferior roles. It was through these professions that they would "uplift" the race, develop the community, gain for it the more equitable place in society it deserved, while creating for themselves important positions as leaders. As their families and teachers had predicted, their fulfilling the requirements that holding leadership positions demanded not only had profound and lasting consequences in black communities, where most of the women began their public work, but their success ultimately put them in positions from which they gained direct access to the American mainstream. Once in the mainstream, they began their uplift and development work again, aimed this time at the white community, and they pursued it with the same zeal that had characterized their earlier efforts.

BIOGRAPHICAL SKETCHES

Amelia Elizabeth Perry Pride (1858–1932) was born in Lynchburg, Virginia, where she returned to teach after graduating from Hampton Institute in 1879. She married Claiborne Pride, a successful barber, in 1881, and they had three children. Pride taught in the Lynchburg public schools for thirty-three years, founded and operated the Dorchester Home (an old folks' home), and was a volunteer Red Cross worker during World War I.

Mary Eliza Church Terrell (1863–1954) was born in Memphis, Tennessee, to Louisa Ayres Church and Robert Reed Church. Both parents were born in slavery. After emancipation, Louisa owned a "hair store" where she styled white women's hair and sold hair care products, and Robert operated a grocery store and became a real estate speculator. The Churches had two children (and after a divorce, Robert remarried and had two more). Terrell attended the Antioch Model School in Yellow Springs, Ohio, Oberlin Preparatory, and Oberlin College (A.B., 1884, M.A., 1888). She studied languages in Europe from 1888 to 1890. Before her 1891 marriage to Robert Heberton Terrell, a Washington, D.C., schoolteacher, attorney, and later municipal court judge, Mary taught at Wilberforce College in Ohio (1885–87) and in the Washington, D.C., public schools (1887–88, 1890–91). After her marriage she became a prominent public lecturer and an author. The Terrells had one child who survived infancy—a daughter named Phyllis, and they adopted Mary's niece, also named Mary. After Robert's death in 1925, Terrell also adopted her brother Thomas's son, also named Thomas.

Janie Porter Barrett (1865–1948) was born in Macon, Georgia, and reared by her mother, Julia Porter, a live-in domestic worker. Barrett graduated from Hampton Institute (normal course) in 1884. She then taught school for two years in Georgia before returning to Hampton,

Virginia, and in 1889 marrying Harris Barrett (Hampton, 1885), cashier for the school. They had two daughters. Barrett founded the Locust Street Settlement House in 1890 and was a founding member of the Virginia Federation of Colored Women's Clubs. With the help of the latter, she also created a training school for delinquent black girls in Peake, Virginia.

Judith Ann Carter Horton (1866–1948) was born in Wright City, Missouri, to recently freed parents. They enrolled her in Oberlin College in 1891. Horton served as a teacher and principal in Columbus, Kansas (1891–92), and in Guthrie, Oklahoma (1892–94). She married Daniel Gibbs Horton in 1894, and they had six children, three surviving infancy. Horton was a principal organizer of the Oklahoma State Federation of Colored Women's Clubs and was president for five years. She also helped to found a state training school for delinquent black boys, a state home for black girls, and a black public library, where she worked part time, unpaid, for eleven years.

Anna DeCosta Banks (1869–1930) was born in Charleston, South Carolina. She graduated from Hampton Institute (normal course) in 1891 and from Dixie Hospital's nursing program in 1893, after which she returned to her hometown. In Charleston she took charge (without pay) of the Hospital and Training School for black nurses that had just been created, while also working as a full-time visiting nurse for the (white) Ladies' Benevolent Society. She was married to Isaiah Banks and reared an adopted daughter.

Lugenia Burns Hope (1871–1947), the youngest of seven children, was born in St. Louis, Missouri, to Lousia M. Bertha Burns and Ferdinand Burns, a carpenter. She attended high school in Chicago and, after graduating, took a variety of classes there at a number of schools including the Art Institute. She married John Hope in 1897, and they eventually settled in Atlanta, Georgia, where she became involved in settlement house work and John served as president of Morehouse College. They had two children.

Angelina Weld Grimké (1880–1958) was born in Boston, Massachusetts, to Sarah Stanley Grimké, a writer, and Archibald Grimké, an attorney. Archibald and Sarah divorced while Grimké was young, and she was reared by her father, his brother Francis, and sister-in-law Charlotte Forten Grimké. Grimké completed her secondary education at Carleton Academy in Northfield, Minnesota, and Cushing Academy in Ashburnham, Massachusetts. She then completed a three-year normal course in 1902 at the Boston Normal School of Gymnastics. Grimké taught English in Washington, D.C., first at the Armstrong School and later at the M Street School (Dunbar). She was a published poet and playwright.

Jane Edna Hunter (1882–1971) was born in South Carolina to Harriet Milner Hunter and Edward Hunter. After a break in her schooling following the death of her father, the assistance of two black Presbyterian missionaries enabled Hunter to complete roughly an eighth-grade education at Ferguson-Williams College (in 1900). After a brief marriage ended in divorce, she attended the Cannon Street Hospital and Training School for Nurses in South Carolina and Dixie Hospital and Training School in Hampton, Virginia, from which she graduated in 1891. (Several decades later, she attended college at Western Reserve University and earned a law degree from the Cleveland School of Law at Baldwin-Wallace College.) Hunter moved to Cleveland in 1905 where, in 1911, she founded the Phillis Wheatley Association, an institution very much like a YWCA in that it provided living accommodations and employment referrals for single black working women and sponsored a variety of public programs. Hunter was executive director of this important institution until 1946.

Portia Marshall Washington Pittman (1883–1978) was born in Alabama to Fanny Norton Smith Washington and Booker T. Washington, both of whom graduated from Hampton Institute. Washington's father was the founder of Tuskegee Institute, and her mother, who died in 1884, was a homemaker. Washington was educated at Tuskegee, Framingham Academy (now State College), and Bradford Academy (now College). She also attended Wellesley College for one term in 1901, and she studied music in Europe from 1905 to 1907, under Martin Krause. In 1907 she married William Sidney Pittman, an architect, who at first taught at Tuskegee and later owned architectural firms in Washington, D.C., and Dallas, Texas. The Pittmans had three children. Portia taught music in her home in Washington for a short time, and after the family moved to Texas, she directed church choirs, taught music in the public schools, and gave private music lessons. She separated from Sidney in 1928 and returned to Alabama, where she taught music at Tuskegee Institute until the late 1930s and in her home until 1944. In 1949 she returned to Washington, D.C.

Beulah Shepard Hester (1883–1981) was born in Oxford, North Carolina. Her father was a Baptist minister who founded and directed a large orphanage, and her mother was his business assistant. Hester attended private church schools (Congregational and Presbyterian) for her primary and grammar schooling. She graduated from the normal program of Hartshorn Memorial College in 1912. Hester was a county demonstration agent in North Carolina after graduating from Hartshorn, and she worked in that capacity even after her 1918 marriage to William Hunter Hester, a graduate of the National Religious Training School at Chautauqua (now North Carolina Central University). They moved to Boston in 1924. Although Hester eventually became a prominent social worker in the Boston area, for about the first ten years after moving to Massachusetts she worked primarily in her home as a boardinghouse keeper and a piano teacher. She received her bachelor's degree from the Simmons College School of Social Work during the 1930s. In 1971 she returned to Oxford, North Carolina.

Julia Hamilton Smith (1885–1980) was born in Washington, D.C., to Julia Luke Brooks Smith and Hamilton S. Smith. Her father was a Boston University graduate (1879), an attorney, a dentist, and a special examiner for the United States Bureau of Pensions. Her mother was one of the first black schoolteachers in the Washington, D.C., public schools. Smith graduated from the M Street School (Dunbar) in Washington, the Minor Normal School, and Howard University. She taught school in Washington, D.C., for approximately forty years, retiring in 1947.

Ruth Anna Fisher (1886–1975) was born in Lorain, Ohio. She graduated from Oberlin College in 1906 and worked as an instructor at Tuskegee Institute for part of the next year. She subsequently taught at the Manassas Industrial School in Virginia and in the public schools of Indianapolis, Indiana, and Lorain, Ohio, between 1907 and 1918. From 1921 to 1940 she worked as a researcher in British archives, first for the Carnegie Institute and then for the Library of Congress. From 1940 to 1947 and 1950 to 1956 she worked at the Library of Congress as a manuscript librarian.

Norma Boyd (1888–1985) was born in Washington, D.C., to Pattie Bullock Boyd, a homemaker, and Jurell Boyd, a livery operator who also worked as a domestic servant to wealthy white people. Boyd, one of three children, attended public high schools in Washington, D.C., graduating from Armstrong High School in 1906, and she received her bachelor's degree from Howard University in 1910. She taught in the Washington public schools from 1912 until 1948.

Susan Dart Butler (1888–1959) was one of five children born to Julia Pierre Dart, a former Washington, D.C., schoolteacher, and John Dart, an educator and minister who attended Atlanta University and graduated from the Newton Theological Seminary (B.D., 1882). Butler graduated from Avery Normal Institute, a well-regarded private school in her Charleston, South Carolina, hometown, and Atlanta University (normal course, 1908). She then attended the McDowell Millinery School in Boston. In 1912 she married Nathaniel Lowe Butler, a Boston realtor, and soon thereafter they moved to Charleston. The Butlers had one child. In 1927 Butler started the first public library in Charleston for black residents, and she worked there and maintained it herself until 1931, when she leased it to the city for one dollar a year. She took occasional library science courses at Hampton Institute during the 1930s, and was eventually rehired by the city of Charleston. She retired in 1957.

Mamie Garvin Fields (1888–1987) was born in Charleston, South Carolina, to Rebecca Mary Logan Bellinger Garvin, a homemaker and dressmaker, and George Washington Garvin, a carpenter. Fields finished the high school course at Claflin University in 1908, receiving her licentiate of instruction, and began teaching on John's Island. She also completed college-level courses at South Carolina State University. In 1914 she married Robert Fields, a brick mason. Between 1914 and 1924 the couple lived in North Carolina for a short time and then in New York. They returned to Charleston in 1924, and in 1926 Fields resumed her teaching, this time on James Island. She retired in 1943.

Sarah Louise Delany (1889–) was one of ten children born to Henry Beard Delany, an Episcopal bishop, and Nanny James Logan Delany, a homemaker and matron for Saint Augustine's School, where Henry was vice principal. Delany was reared on the Raleigh, North Carolina, campus and received her early education there. She earned a normal degree in 1910 and then became a Jeanes supervising teacher, serving rural communities in eastern North Carolina. After working several years in North Carolina and in New York as a factory operative, Delany enrolled at Pratt Institute in 1916, completing a two-year degree in 1918. She subsequently completed bachelor of science and master of education degrees at Columbia University Teachers College in 1920 and 1925. Delany retired from teaching high school domestic science in the New York public schools in 1960.

Sadie Peterson Delaney (1889–1959) was born in Rochester, New York, to Julia Francis Hawkins Johnson and James Johnson and graduated from public high school in Poughkeepsie, New York. Delaney graduated from the College of the City of New York in 1919 and subsequently earned a certificate in library science from the New York Public Library School. From 1920 until 1923 she worked at the 135th Street Branch of the New York Public Library. In 1924 she took a six-month leave of absence to help organize a library at the Tuskegee Veterans Hospital, and she did not return to New York. While at the Veterans Administration Hospital, Delaney earned an international reputation in the field of bibliotherapy. She was married twice, the second time in 1928 to Rudicel A. Delaney.

Florence Jacobs Edmonds (1890–1983) was born in Pittsfield, Massachusetts, the second of six children of Lydia Harrison Jacobs, a homemaker, and James Jacobs, a caterer. Edmonds was valedictorian of the Pittsfield High School class of 1908, and after graduation she worked as a receptionist in a doctor's office during the day while attending secretarial school at night. She attempted to enroll in the local hospital nurse training program after graduating but was told that they had never admitted black students and that she should go to New York, which she did. She graduated from the three-year program at Lincoln Hospital and Home Training School. Edmonds spent the next year studying hospital social service at Columbia University Teachers College on a scholarship. She then went to work for the Henry Street Settlement as a visiting nurse. Two years later (in 1922) she married William Bailey Edmonds, and they returned to Pittsfield, where William worked as a janitor and Edmonds became a homemaker and seamstress. They had four children, and after the youngest daughter entered high school in the 1940s, Edmonds sought and found work as a nurse in Pittsfield.

Mabel Doyle Keaton Staupers (1890–1989) was born in Barbados, British West Indies. Her family settled in New York in 1903. Her father was a brake inspector for the New York Central Railroad, and her mother was a homemaker. Staupers attended public schools in New York, and she graduated from Freedmen's Hospital School of Nursing in Washington, D.C., in 1917. From 1922 to 1934 Staupers served as executive secretary of the Harlem Committee of the New York Tuberculosis and Health Association. She was an early member of the National Association of Colored Graduate Nurses (NACGN)—she joined in 1916—and she became its first executive director in 1934, a position she held until 1946. She also served as the organization's last president from 1949 to 1951. She was married twice. In 1961 Staupers published a history of the NACGN titled *No Time for Prejudice* (published by Macmillan).

Layle Lane (1893–1972) was born in Georgia and reared in New England. She attended Hunter College and graduated from Howard University in 1916. She also earned a master's degree from Columbia University. Lane taught school in Harlem and the Bronx for more than thirty years. She was also an active unionist who was elected vice president of the American Federation of Teachers. She wrote a regular column for *American Teacher* and the New York *Age* and was a principal organizer of the 1941 March on Washington Movement. Between 1933 and 1947 Lane ran unsuccessfully for a district congressional seat, for an at-large congressional seat, for New York City comptroller, and for state senator of the Twenty-third District of New York, usually as the Socialist Party candidate. On retiring from teaching in the 1950s, she moved to Cuernavaca, Mexico.

Frances O. Grant (1895–1982) was one of two daughters of Fannie Bailey Grant, who worked as a proofreader until her marriage, and George F. Grant, a prominent dentist who invented the artificial palate for cleft palates and once served as president of the Harvard Odontological Society. Grant started school in the local public schools, but her father took her out because of what he perceived as the unprofessional conduct of Frances's teacher—she had participated in a protest march with members of the cigarmakers' union—and enrolled her in Bowdoin Grammar School. While in the sixth grade, Grant passed the entrance exam to the prestigious Girls' Latin School and enrolled there. She graduated at the head of her class and entered Radcliffe College in 1913, graduating in classics, magna cum laude, in 1917. She taught from 1917 until 1955 at Bordentown Industrial School in New Jersey. Then, after a short stint as a leave replacement in the New York Public Library system, Grant taught Latin from 1956 to 1965 at the Fieldstone School, a private academy in New York. She completed a master's degree in education in 1949 at New York University.

Mary Gibson Hundley (1897–1986) was born in Baltimore, Maryland, to Mary Matilda Syphax Gibson, a schoolteacher, and Malachi Gibson, an attorney. Hundley graduated from Dunbar High School in Washington, D.C., in 1914 and from Radcliffe College (cum laude) in 1918. She also completed a master's degree in French at Middlebury College (1927) and some graduate study at the Sorbonne in 1928. Hundley's first teaching position was in Maryland, and from 1930 until 1954 she taught at Dunbar. In 1955 she was transferred to Eastern High School to help desegregate the white school, but she left the position in 1959 because her "newcomer" status there did not allow her to teach French, the major area of her training. She taught at Howard University from 1959 until 1964. Hundley's first marriage to William M. Brewer ended in divorce in 1935. In 1938 she married Frederick F. Hundley, an art teacher in the public schools. Beginning in 1941, the Hundleys were the plaintiffs in a series of important lawsuits to strike down restrictive covenants.

Beulah Tyrrell Whitby (1897–1990) was born in Lynchburg, Virginia, and graduated from Oberlin College in 1920. She taught for the next two years in Nashville, Tennessee, where she met her husband, a Meharry Dental School graduate. They moved to Michigan in 1922, and Whitby spent the next forty years working there in various social work capacities. For the first two years she worked with the YWCA. From 1924 to 1931 she worked for the Detroit Police Department. In 1931 she joined the Department of Public Welfare, and though for the next twenty-five years or more she maintained a professional connection to the department, she also served with the Office of Civilian Defense during the war, was a member of the Commission of Community Relations during the mid-1940s, and taught in the School of

Social Work at Wayne State University and at Mercy College beginning in the 1940s. The Whitbys had two daughters.

Charlemae Hill Rollins (1897–1979) was born in Yazoo City, Mississippi, to Birdie Tucker Hill, a schoolteacher, and Allen G. Hill. Rollins grew up in Oklahoma and was a schoolteacher there during the middle 1920s. In the late 1920s, she, her husband, Joseph, and their son moved to Chicago, where she began work as a librarian. Rollins spent most of her career at the George Cleveland Hall Branch of the library, which opened in 1932. There she earned a national reputation as a children's librarian, a storyteller, and an editor and author of children's books. Rollins retired from the Chicago Public Library system in 1963.

Septima Poinsette Clark (1898–1987) was a South Carolina schoolteacher from 1916 until 1955. Her mother, Victoria Warren Anderson Poinsette, was a homemaker who sometimes took in laundry to supplement the family income. Clark's father, Peter Porcher Poinsette, was born in slavery and later worked as an unskilled laborer (sometimes a janitor). Clark had seven brothers and sisters. She graduated from Avery Institute in 1916 and began teaching in the Sea Islands after graduating. After the public schools of South Carolina opened to black teachers, she taught in Charleston and Columbia (beginning in the 1920s). Before then, however, Clark married Nerie David Clark in 1920 and moved with him to Dayton, Ohio, in 1922. He died in 1925, and Clark and their infant son went to North Carolina to live with her in-laws before moving back to South Carolina. After she lost her teaching position in South Carolina for being a member of the NAACP, she became a full-time workshop director for the Highlander Folk School. In 1961 Clark went to work for the Southern Christian Leadership Conference. She completed a bachelor's degree at Benedict College in 1942 and a master's degree at Hampton Institute in 1944.

Ethel Ray Williams Nance (1899–), born in Duluth, Minnesota, was one of four children of Inga Nordquist Ray and William Henry Ray. William worked as a riverboat porter and as a laborer in local hotels, and Inga worked as a hotel maid until she and William married. Nance attended public schools in Duluth and accepted her first job in 1918 with the Red Cross and Minnesota Fire Relief Commission. During the early 1920s she became the assistant head resident of the Phyllis Wheatley House in Minneapolis. In 1926 she accepted a position in the women's bureau of the Minneapolis Police Department. Nance married during the late 1920s and had two sons. She spent some time working in New York in the Urban League office, and during the mid-1930s she accepted a position as a stenographer in the state legislature in St. Paul. She also began to work in an unpaid position with the Minnesota Negro Council, an advocacy organization. She moved to San Francisco during the 1940s and graduated from college in 1978, years after the conclusion of her professional career.

Lucy M. Mitchell (1899–) was born in Daytona Beach, Florida. Mitchell's mother was a homemaker while she was married, and Mitchell's father owned an orange growing and shipping business. After her parents divorced, her mother moved with the two youngest children, including Mitchell, to Columbus, Ohio, where she worked in a factory, leaving the older children in Florida with her parents. Mitchell returned to Florida when it was time for her to begin her formal schooling, and she attended the Daytona Normal and Industrial Institute for Girls from kindergarten through high school, graduating in 1918. She went from there to Talladega College in Alabama, and, after graduating, she taught elementary school at the Daytona school for one year. Mitchell then joined her mother and brothers in Massachusetts and married her college sweetheart, who had by then completed a law degree at Harvard. They had two children. Mitchell completed a master's degree in education at Boston University in 1935 and became a prominent worker in early childhood education and social work in the Boston area.

Eunice Rivers Laurie (1899–1986) was a Macon County, Alabama, public health nurse for forty years. She was born in Early County (Jakin), Georgia, the oldest of three girls. Her father, Albert Rivers, was a farmer who sometimes worked in a local lumber mill, and her mother, Henrietta, died while Laurie was a child. Laurie attended private church schools for her primary and grammar schooling, and she enrolled at Tuskegee Institute in 1918, graduating from its nursing program in 1922. Laurie was a public health nurse during the early 1920s and later worked with the Bureau of Vital Statistics. In 1931 she went to work at John A. Andrew Hospital, and later that year she became the nurse assistant on the federal government's Tuskegee

Syphilis Project. Rivers officially retired from the Macon County Public Health Service in 1965, but she continued to work until 1975.

Mabel C. Northcross (1900–), one of four children, was born in Humboldt, Tennessee. Her mother was a homemaker who also took in washing and ironing, and her father was a bricklayer. Northcross attended elementary and secondary school in Humboldt, and in 1915 she enrolled at Meharry Medical College School of Nursing, Hubbard Hospital, graduating in 1919. She worked as a nurse and nurse supervisor at Homer G. Phillips Hospital in St. Louis, Missouri, from 1921 until 1970, and she completed a bachelor's degree in nursing education at New York University in 1946. Northcross also served as president of the National Association of Colored Graduate Nurses from 1930 to 1934.

Susan St. Clair Minor (ca. 1901–) was born in Louisville, Kentucky. Both of her parents were domestic workers. Minor graduated from Central High School in 1919 and Louisville Normal School in 1921, after which she began her teaching career in the elementary grades. She subsequently earned a bachelor's degree, and in 1946 she completed a master's degree at Indiana University. Minor married for the second time in 1940. She retired from teaching in 1970.

Constance Clementine Fisher (1902–79) was born in Birmingham, Alabama, the only child of Sallie A. McCarver Fisher and Isaac Fisher. Isaac was an educator who worked at Tuskegee Institute, at Fisk University as director of publications, and at Hampton Institute. Fisher finished high school at Tuskegee Institute and then enrolled at Fisk University, from which she received a bachelor's degree in sociology and physical education in 1924. She also earned a master's degree in social work from Western Reserve University in 1929. Her first professional position was as a camp counselor with the Phillis Wheatley Association in Cleveland, Ohio. She subsequently worked for the Cleveland Associated Charities (1924–25 and 1927–30). Fisher spent most of her professional career in Minnesota, where she became the supervisor of Totem Town, a boys' farm in St. Paul, and in Eugene, Oregon, where she worked primarily in maternal and infant care.

Ophelia Settle Egypt (1903–84) was born in Clarksville, Texas. Both of her parents, Sara Settle and Green Wilson Settle, were schoolteachers.

Her mother became a homemaker after marriage, and she died when Egypt was about five years old. After Egypt developed acute asthma, her father took her to Denver, Colorado, to live with his aunt. Egypt graduated from Howard University and earned a master's degree from the University of Pennsylvania. In 1928 she went to work as an instructor at Fisk University and as a field researcher under Charles Johnson. While working with Johnson, she began to interview former slaves she encountered, and ultimately she produced a book manuscript that was published in 1968. Egypt also published a juvenile book on James Weldon Johnson in 1973. She worked as a social worker in St. Louis, Missouri, and Louisiana before settling in Washington, D.C., where she earned a national reputation for her work with single mothers. She married Ivory Lester Egypt in 1940, and they had one son.

Geneva Estelle Massey Riddle Osborne (1903–81) was the youngest of seven children born into a south Texas family. She finished high school at age sixteen and then completed two years at Prairie View College, after which she taught for two years in a rural community near her home. Upon giving up her teaching position, Osborne went to St. Louis, Missouri, to live with her brother, a dentist. She subsequently (1920) enrolled in nursing school at City Hospital no. 2 (Homer G. Phillips) and graduated in 1923. With the assistance of a Rosenwald fellowship, she earned bachelor's and master's degrees from Columbia University Teachers College in 1930 and 1931. Osborne worked for the Rosenwald Fund in the 1930s; she directed the nursing program at Freedmen's Hospital during the late 1930s; and she worked as the nurse supervisor at City Hospital no. 2 during the early 1940s. She might, however, be best known as president (1934–39) of the National Association of Colored Graduate Nurses. Osborne was married twice and had no children.

Miriam Matthews (1905–) was born in Pensacola, Florida, the second of three children of Fannie Elijah Matthews, a homemaker, and Reuben Hearde Matthews, a painter. When Matthews was two years old, the family moved to Los Angeles, California, where her father, who was trained at Tuskegee, opened a painting business. Her mother was his business partner. Matthews graduated from public high school in 1922, studied for two years at the University of California, Southern Branch (Los Angeles), and transferred to Berkeley, where she finished her bachelor's degree in 1926. Matthews became a librarian in the Los Angeles system in 1927, and she worked her way up through the ranks, ultimately becoming director of the south-central region in 1949. She earned a master's degree in library science from the University of Chicago in 1945.

Lula Catherine Jordan McNeil (ca. 1905–) was from a family of eight children. Her father was a bolter in the Virginia shipyards, and her mother was a homemaker. McNeil was a member of the first graduating class (1923) of Huntington High School in Newport News. After graduation, she completed a two-year normal course in Petersburg and returned to Newport News to teach. After she quit teaching, McNeil went to work as a domestic worker during the day while taking secretarial courses at night. In 1931 she enrolled in Hampton Institute's nursing program, graduating in 1934 with the first class. She worked at Hampton Institute as a student health nurse until the end of the 1930s, when she went to Richmond to complete a public health nursing course at the Medical College of Virginia. After finishing the course in 1941, she returned to Southampton County, working first as a public health nurse and then as the infirmary nurse at Hampton. Needing only a few courses to complete a bachelor's degree, she resumed college coursework and finished the degree in 1944. She married in 1945 and worked as a public health nurse in Virginia until her retirement in 1967.

Sarah Webb Rice (1909–) was born in Clio, Alabama, to Elizabeth Janet Lewis Webb, a homemaker, a domestic worker, and sometimes a schoolteacher, and Willis James Webb, a farmer and a minister. Rice graduated from Eufala High School in 1925 and began teaching, first in a private school and then in public schools. She married in 1927, had a son in 1928, and divorced in 1929. Between 1929 and 1953 Rice intermittently taught school and did domestic work. She married Andrew A. Rice in 1953 and quit teaching.

Barbara Simmons Miller (1910–) was the only child of Vivian Truss Simmons, a domestic worker, and Andrew Warren Simmons, an oriental rug dealer, cleaner, and repairman. At age sixteen Miller was valedictorian of her class at Central High School in Louisville, Kentucky. Because her mother believed she was too young to leave home for additional schooling, Miller enrolled at Louisville Normal School, graduating two years later. She spent the next two years teaching sixth grade, then she went to the University of Michigan, from which she graduated in 1933 with a degree in music. She returned to Louisville, taught for two more years, and married Thomas Rowland Miller. Miller eventually returned to college, earning a degree in library science in 1951 and a master's degree in education in 1957. She worked in the public library system in Louisville from 1951 until she retired.

Henrietta Veronica Smith Chisholm (ca. 1910–) was the daughter of Marie Cole Smith and James Smith. She graduated from public high school in Pittsburgh, Pennsylvania, and attended Freedmen's Hospital School of Nursing, graduating in 1931. Chisholm earned a bachelor of science degree in nursing from Catholic University by going to school in the evenings and summers. She married Clarence J. Chisholm in 1937, and they had one daughter. Chisholm was a public health nurse for most of her career.

Lillian Holland Harvey (1912–94) was dean of the School of Nursing at Tuskegee Institute from 1948, when school administrators initiated a baccalaureate program there, until she retired in 1973. She earned her nursing diploma from Lincoln Hospital School of Nursing in New York and her bachelor's degree from Columbia University Teachers College. She also completed a master's degree and a doctorate in education. Harvey married Raymond Francis Harvey, a Baptist minister, during the 1940s. They had three children.

Thelma DeWitty (1912–) was born in Beaumont, Texas. Her father was an entrepreneur who owned a grocery store, a boardinghouse, and a baseball team. Her mother worked as a cook in the homes of wealthy white families. DeWitty graduated from high school in Beaumont as valedictorian (at the age of fourteen) and went directly to Wiley College, a private school. After graduating from Wiley, she taught in Texas for fourteen years until she decided to go to graduate school. She chose a major that was not offered at the only black graduate school in the state so that the state would have to pay her tuition out of state (because state law prohibited her being admitted to white schools). She chose to go to the University of Washington in Seattle. After finishing a master's degree, she resumed her teaching career in Seattle's public school system. She also became active in Democratic politics there and was a delegate to three national conventions. DeWitty was married and had one daughter.

Clara Stanton Jones (1913–) was born in St. Louis, Missouri, to Etta James Stanton, a schoolteacher, and Ralph Herbert Stanton, an insurance sales supervisor. Jones completed her freshman year of college at the University of Wisconsin–Milwaukee and then transferred to Spelman College, where she received a bachelor's degree in English and history. She worked in the library at Atlanta University until she went to the University of Michigan, earning a master's degree in library science in 1938. Over the next several years, Jones worked as a reference librarian at Dillard University in New Orleans and then at Southern University in Baton Rouge. In 1944 she and her husband, Albert Jones, a social worker, moved to Detroit, where she accepted a position in the Detroit Public Library system. Jones became the director of the system in 1970, a first for a woman and an African American. She and her husband had three children.

Fostine Riddick (ca. 1915–) was reared in Muncie, Indiana, where she attended public schools. She enrolled in John A. Andrew Hospital's nursing program, and after graduating, she went to work at the Norfolk Community Hospital as a nurse anesthetist and laboratory technician. She worked there for two years, giving up the position in the early 1940s when she married because her husband wanted her to be a homemaker. She finished her bachelor's degree at Tuskegee in 1956 and resumed her nursing career as a staff nurse at Norfolk Community Hospital in 1957. She completed a master's degree at New York University in the 1960s. Riddick's husband, Henry, worked for the Postal Service.

Mary Elizabeth Carnegie (1918–) was born in Baltimore, Maryland, and grew up in Washington, D.C., where she finished high school at age sixteen. Carnegie lied about her age on her application to Lincoln Hospital School of Nursing, saying she was eighteen, and was admitted to the course in 1934. After graduating from Lincoln, and passing the civil service examination, Carnegie worked as a staff nurse at the Tuskegee veterans' hospital and as a volunteer rural public health nurse until the early 1940s, then she went to West Virginia State College and completed a bachelor's degree in 1942. After working at Homer G. Phillips Hospital for three years, Carnegie became an instructor at the Medical College of Virginia in Richmond. From 1945 until 1953, she worked at Florida A & M College, where she helped to transform the hospital school into a collegiate program. She finished a master's degree in higher education administration at Syracuse University in 1952 and received a doctorate in public administration from New York University in 1972. From 1953 until 1970, she was assistant editor of the *American Journal of Nursing* and worked at *Nursing Outlook* (later absorbed into *Public Health Magazine*). In 1973 she became the editor of *Nursing Research*. In 1988 Carnegie published a study of black nurses titled *The Path We Tread* (published by J. B. Lippincott).

Joyce Cooper Arkhurst (1921–) was the daughter of Hazel James Cooper, who grew up in New Zealand, and Felix Bond Cooper, a dentist who attended Lincoln University for his undergraduate degree and the University of Michigan Dental School. Arkhurst had one brother who settled in Alaska after World War II. She attended public schools in Seattle, Washington, and graduated from the University of Washington with a degree in sociology. Arkhurst became a social worker in California after graduating but gave it up in 1949 to go to library school at Columbia University. She also taught at Fieldstone School before going to work in the New York Public Library system. She left the library upon marrying Frederick Arkhurst, a Ghanaian diplomat. They had one daughter, and around 1969 the family moved to Chicago, where Arkhurst accepted a position as a community relations person in the Chicago Public Library system.

Barbara Pickett (1926–), from Georgia, was one of two children born to Minola Lockett and Robert Lockett, both graduates of Haynes Institute (Lucy Craft Laney's private school that became the model school and feeder to Payne College, a private Methodist school). Robert was also a graduate of Lincoln University and Howard University Dental School, and Minola was a homemaker. Pickett attended Payne College in Augusta for two years and graduated from Spelman in 1945 with a degree in English. She then enrolled in Atlanta University's School of Library Service and received a master's degree in 1947. After moving to Louisville, Kentucky, to work in the Western Branch of the Free Public Library, Pickett met her future husband, Steward Pickett, an executive with the Boy Scouts of America. They had two sons. Pickett retired from the library in 1968.

Gloria Smith (ca. 1935–) was born in Chicago. Her father was a factory worker, and her mother was a homemaker who occasionally worked as a hairdresser in her home. Smith was the oldest child of seven who lived (several children born before her did not survive infancy). Smith attended Wayne State University's College of Nursing, graduating in the middle 1950s. She worked for a short time for the Detroit Visiting Nurses Association, and after marrying she moved to Oklahoma, where her husband was stationed in the army, and worked for the State Health Department. Smith became dean of the College of Nursing at the University of Oklahoma during the 1970s, and in 1983 she became the director of the Michigan Department of Public Health. Smith also earned two master's degrees and a doctorate.

Libraries and Archives

ARC-CC Avery Research Center for African American History and Culture, College of Charleston, Charleston, South Carolina

AMD-MHS Archives/Manuscript Division, Minnesota Historical Society, St. Paul, Minnesota

Amistad Research Center, Tulane University, New Orleans, Louisiana

DPL Detroit Public Library, Detroit, Michigan

FUL-SC Fisk University Library, Special Collections, Nashville, Tennessee

HULA Hampton University Archives, Collis P. Huntington Memorial Library, Hampton, Virginia

HU-MSRC Howard University, Moorland-Spingarn Research Center, Washington, D.C.

JML Johnson Memorial Library, Virginia State University, Petersburg, Virginia

KDLA Kentucky Department for Libraries and Archives, Frankfort, Kentucky

Labor Archives Walter P. Reuther Archives of Labor and Urban Affairs, Wayne State University, Detroit, Michigan

LC Library of Congress, Washington, D.C.

MEC-BNA Mary Elizabeth Carnegie Black Nurses' Archives, Hampton University, Hampton, Virginia

MHS Minnesota Historical Society

MMC-DNE Meharry Medical College, Department of Nursing Education, Nashville, Tennessee

NCCU-BLA North Carolina Central University, School of Library and Information Sciences, Black Librarians' Archives, Durham, North Carolina

RAC	Rockefeller Archives Center, Tarrytown, New York
RBHL	Richard B. Harrison Library, Raleigh, North Carolina
RSSL-SC	Robert Scott Small Library, Special Collections, College of Charleston, Charleston, South Carolina
Schomburg Center	Schomburg Center for Research in Black Culture, New York, New York
SL-RC	Schlesinger Library, Radcliffe College, Cambridge, Massachusetts
SLWPL	Stanford L. Warren Public Library, Durham, North Carolina
TUA	Tuskegee University Archives, Hollis Burke Frissell Library, Tuskegee, Alabama
UL	University of Louisville Archives and Record Center, Louisville, Kentucky
WB-LFPL	Western Branch, Louisville Free Public Library, Louisville, Kentucky
WL	Woodruff Library, Clark-Atlanta University, Atlanta, Georgia
WSA	Washington State Archives, Olympia, Washington

Collections Cited

Albertha J. Murray Papers, ARC-CC

Amelia Perry Pride Papers, HULA

ANA American Nurses' Association Records, Mugar Library, Boston University, Boston, Massachusetts

Angelina Grimké Papers, HU-MSRC

Anna DeCosta Banks Papers, HULA

Archibald Grimké Papers, HU-MSRC

Brown Fellowship Society Scrapbooks, RSSL-SC

BTW-LC Booker T. Washington Papers, Library of Congress

BTWP *The Booker T. Washington Papers,* ed. Louis Harlan and Raymond Smock, 13 vols. (Urbana: University of Illinois Press, 1976–81)

Charlemae Hill Rollins Papers, NCCU-BLA

Clara Stanton Jones Papers, NCCU-BLA

Constance Fisher Papers, FUL-SC

Constance Fisher Papers, TUA

Francis Grimké Papers, HU-MSRC

FUL-BOHP Fisk University Library, Black Oral History Program

GEB General Education Board Papers, RAC

Janie Porter Barrett Papers, HULA

LAC Lincoln Academy Collection, Amistad Research Center

Layle Lane Papers, Labor Archives

Layle Lane Papers, Schomburg Center

Lincoln Institute Records, KDLA

Mabel Keaton Staupers Papers, HU-MSRC

Mabel Keaton Staupers Papers, Schomburg Center

Mary Gibson Hundley Papers, SL-RC

MCT-LC Mary Church Terrell Papers, Library of Congress

MCTP Mary Church Terrell Papers, HU-MSRC

NUC-WL Neighborhood Union Collection, Woodruff Library, Clark-Atlanta University

OCAR Oberlin College Alumni Records, Oberlin, Ohio

OHC-UL Oral History Collection, University of Louisville

RC-BWOHP Radcliffe College, Schlesinger Library, Black Women Oral History Project

RFF Rosenwald Fund Foundation Papers, FUL-SC

RRM-SC Robert R. Moton Papers, Student Correspondence, TUA

NACGN Records, MEC-BNA

NACGN Records, Schomburg Center

Ophelia Settle Egypt Papers, HU-MSRC

Sadie Peterson Delaney Papers, Schomburg Center

Sadie Peterson Delaney Papers, TUA

Sarah Collins Fernandis Papers, HULA

Septima P. Clark Papers, ARC-CC

Septima P. Clark Papers, RSSL-SC

TNCS Tuskegee News Clipping Service

WSA-OAHP Washington State Archives, Oral/Aural History Project, Olympia, Washington

Oral Histories

ARC-CC
  Clark, Septima

FUL-BOHP
 Arkhurst, Joyce Cooper
 Boyd, Norma Elizabeth
 Egypt, Ophelia Settle
 Hutson, Jean Blackwell
 Jones, Clara Stanton
 Miller, Barbara Simmons
 Picket, Barbara

LABOR ARCHIVES
 Whitby, Beulah

MEC-BNA
 Carnegie, Mary Elizabeth
 Chisholm, Henrietta Veronica Smith
 McNeil, Lula Catherine Jordan
 Osborne, Estelle Massey Riddle
 Riddick, Fostine
 Staupers, Mabel

MHS
 Nance, Ethel Ray

MMC-DNE
 Harvey, Lillian H.
 Northcross, Mabel
 Smith, Gloria

RC-BWOHP INTERVIEWS, HU-MSRC
 Boyd, Norma
 Edmonds, Florence
 Grant, Frances O.
 Hester, Beulah Shepard
 Laurie, Eunice Rivers
 Matthews, Miriam
 Mitchell, Lucy M.
 Smith, Julia Hamilton

UL
 Minor, Susan St. Clair

WSA-OAHP
 DeWitty, Thelma

Periodicals Frequently Cited

(Note that the names of the institutions and the titles of their bulletins changed over time. Only one representative title is given below, but the appropriate titles are used in the notes.)

AM AMERICAN MISSIONARY

ATLANTA UNIVERSITY
   AUB *Atlanta University Bulletin*
   Catalog of the Officers and Students of Atlanta University

FISK UNIVERSITY
   Catalog of the Officers and Students of Fisk University
   Fisk University News
   FE *Fisk Expositor*
   FH *Fisk Herald*

HMM-BAPTIST HOME MISSION MONTHLY

HAMPTON INSTITUTE
   Catalog of the Hampton Normal and Industrial Institute
   HS *Hampton Script*
   Southern Workman

HARTSHORN MEMORIAL COLLEGE
   Annual Catalogue of the Officers and Students of Hartshorn Memorial College
   Union-Hartshorn Bulletin
   Union-Hartshorn Journal
   UJ *University Journal*

HOWARD UNIVERSITY
   Catalog of the Officers and Students of Howard University
   HUR *Howard University Record*

LINCOLN INSTITUTE
   LIW *Lincoln Institute Worker*

OBERLIN COLLEGE
   Catalogue of the Officers and Students of Oberlin College

RADCLIFFE COLLEGE
Society for the Collegiate Instruction of Women

SPELMAN COLLEGE
   Circular and Catalogue of Spelman Seminary for Women and Girls
   Catalog of Spelman College

CM Spelman Campus Mirror
SM Spelman Messenger

TUSKEGEE INSTITUTE
Annual Catalogue of the Tuskegee Normal and Industrial Institute
SL Southern Letter
TM Tuskegee Messenger
TS Tuskegee Student
Tuskegee Institute Bulletin

WABHMS WOMAN'S AMERICAN BAPTIST HOME MISSION SOCIETY, AN-NUAL REPORTS

WELLESLEY COLLEGE
Wellesley College Calendar
Boston Normal School of Gymnastics Annual Catalogue of Instructors, Students, and Graduates

Introduction

1. Zora Neale Hurston, *Their Eyes Were Watching God* (Urbana: University of Illinois Press, 1978), 31–32.

2. Elsa Barkley Brown writes about the African American cultural tradition that involves "be[ing] an individual in the context of the community" in "African-American Women's Quilting: A Framework for Conceptualizing and Teaching African American Women's History," *Signs* 14 (1989): 921–29. Quotation from 925. The phrase "socially responsible individualism" is used in Robert Bellah, Richard Madsen, William M. Sullivan, Ann Swidler, and Steven M. Tipton, *Habits of the Heart: Middle America Observed* (London: Hutchinson, 1975), 155. Although my study began as an exploration into the lives of black women workers and not as a contribution to the ongoing debate among "communitarianists" and "individualists," the debate is a lively one that has moved from either/or characterizations of American society and critiques of the same to studies that see neither individualism nor communitarianism as the complete picture but rather posit some blending of the two characteristics (or see one as a stage preceding the other). A detailed overview of the debate is provided in Robert Booth Fowler, *The Dance with Community: The Contemporary Debate in American Political Thought* (Lawrence: University of Kansas Press, 1991). A critique of older works is provided by Casey Nelson Blake, *Beloved Community: The Cultural Criticism of Randolph Bourne, Van Wick Brooks, Waldo Frank, and Lewis Mumford* (Chapel Hill: University of North Carolina Press, 1990). Selections from representative viewpoints are included in Shlomo Avineri and Avner De-Shalit, eds., *Communitarianism and Individualism* (Oxford: Oxford University Press, 1992), while original interpretive essays are presented in Donald L. Gelpi, ed., *Beyond Individualism: Toward a Retrieval of Moral Discourse in America* (Notre Dame, Ind.: University of Notre Dame Press, 1989). A volume that falls in the category of proposing an alternative to either/or positions is Jack Crittendon, *Beyond Individualism: Reconstituting the Liberal Self* (New York: Oxford University Press, 1992). Studies addressing the ramifications of these issues for feminists include Linda Kerber, "Women and Individualism in American History," *Massachusetts Review* 30 (1989): 589–609; Mary Ellen Ross, "Feminism and the Problem of Moral Character," *Journal of Feminist Studies in Religion* 5 (1989): 47–64; and Elizabeth Fox-Genovese, *Feminism with-*

out Illusion: A Critique of Individualism (Chapel Hill: University of North Carolina Press, 1990).

3. Indicating how nearly complete disfranchisement was, in 1868 96.7 percent of Mississippi's black voting-age population was registered to vote. By 1896 the percentage was down to 5.9. In Louisiana black voters constituted 50.5 percent of all voters shortly after the Civil War, but by 1896 they made up only 0.6 percent. Louisiana and Mississippi were two of the three states with a black population of at least 50 percent. All together, by the turn of the century African Americans who could vote and did were the exception rather than the rule. Statistics from Neil R. McMillen, *Dark Journey: Black Mississippians in the Age of Jim Crow* (Urbana: University of Illinois Press, 1990), 36; and Jack M. Bloom, *Class, Race, and the Civil Rights Movement* (Bloomington: Indiana University Press, 1987), 43.

4. See Robert L. Zangrando, *The NAACP Crusade against Lynching, 1909–1950* (Philadelphia: Temple University Press, 1980); E. M. Beck and Steward E. Tolnay, "The Gallows, the Mob, and the Vote: Lethal Sanctioning of Blacks in North Carolina and Georgia, 1882–1930," *Law and Society Review* 23 (1989): 317–31; Sarah A. Soule, "Populism and Black Lynching in Georgia, 1890–1900," *Social Forces* 71 (1992): 431–49; W. Fitzhugh Brundage, *Lynching in the New South: Georgia and Virginia, 1880–1930* (Urbana: University of Illinois Press, 1993). The first systematic studies of lynching were conducted by Ida B. Wells-Barnett. See her *On Lynchings: Southern Horrors, A Red Record, Mob Rule in New Orleans* (rpt. New York: Arno Press, 1969). Others of her publications are included in Mildred I. Thompson, *Ida B. Wells-Barnett: An Exploratory Study of an American Black Woman, 1893–1913,* vol. 15 of *Black Women in United States History,* ed. Darlene Clark Hine (Brooklyn: Carlson, 1990). Also see Ralph Ginzburg, *One Hundred Years of Lynching* (New York: Lancer Books, 1962).

5. See James D. Anderson, *The Education of Blacks in the South, 1860–1935* (Chapel Hill: University of North Carolina Press, 1988).

6. Harvard Sitkoff notes that even traditionally liberal journals, including *The Nation* and *Harper's Weekly,* joined in portraying African Americans as subhuman. See *A New Deal for Blacks: The Emergence of Civil Rights as a National Issue,* vol. 1, *The Depression Decade* (Oxford: Oxford University Press, 1978), 6–9. Many of these works are explored in I. A. Newby, *Jim Crow's Defense: Anti-Negro Thought in America, 1900–1930* (Baton Rouge: Louisiana State University Press, 1965); and George M. Fredrickson, *The Black Image in the White Mind: The Debate on Afro-American Character and Destiny, 1817–1914* (New York: Harper and Row, 1971). Samples of these writings may be found in I. A. Newby, *The Development of Segregationist Thought* (Homewood, Ill.: Dorsey Press, 1968). Causing extensive public debate among African Americans were Madison Grant, *The Passing of the Great Race, or The Racial Basis of European History* (New York: Charles Scribners' Sons, 1916); Thomas Dixon, *The Leopard's Spots: A Romance of the White Man's Burden, 1865–1900* (New York: Grosset and Dunlap, 1902); Charles Carrol, *The Negro a Beast, or In the Image*

of God . . . (St. Louis, Mo.: American Book and Bible House, 1900); and Lothrop Stoddard, *The Rising Tide of Color against White World Supremacy* (New York: Charles Scribner's Sons, 1920).

7. An appendix that summarizes their "biographies" in the order of their births follows the text.

8. Standard works on professionalism and professionalization include C. Wright Mills, *White Collar: The American Middle Classes* (New York: Oxford University Press, 1953); Phillip Elliott, *The Sociology of the Professions* (London: Macmillan, 1972); and Eliot Friedson, *Professional Powers* (Chicago: University of Chicago Press, 1986). Scholars who diverge from the tradition of studying the structure of occupational groups or the process of their becoming professions include Paul Atkinson, Margaret Reid, and Peter Sheldrake, "Medical Mystique," *Sociology of Work and Occupations* 4 (1977): 243–80, in which the authors raise questions about the idea of "expert knowledge" and provide compelling evidence of the importance of "indeterminate knowledge" in the profession of medicine; and Andrew Abbott, "The Order of Professionalization," *Work and Occupations* 18 (1991): 335–89, in which Abbott compares and contrasts the processes of professionalization that take place on local and state levels. Scholarly works that characterize professionalization and take up the debate over whether these (feminized) occupations represent professions, semiprofessions, quasi-professions, etc., include Amitai Etzioni, ed., *The Semiprofessions and Their Organizations: Teachers, Nurses, Social Workers* (New York: Free Press, 1969); Nina Toren, *Social Work: The Case of a Semiprofession* (Beverly Hills, Calif.: Sage, 1972); and Patrick B. Forsyth and Thomas J. Danisiewcz, "Toward a Theory of Professionalization," *Work and Occupations* 21 (1985): 59–76. General studies of the feminized professions include Susan M. Reverby, *Ordered to Care: The Dilemma of American Nursing, 1850–1945* (Cambridge: Cambridge University Press, 1987), and Daniel J. Walkowitz, "The Making of a Feminine Professional Identity: Social Workers in the 1920s," *American Historical Review* 95 (1990): 1051–75. Studies of professionalism usually focus on the ministry, law, and medicine and generally document a process of professionalization that parallels processes of modernization. Samuel Haber, however, turns that commonly accepted notion on its head in *The Quest for Authority and Honor in the American Professions, 1750–1900* (Chicago: University of Chicago Press, 1991) by working from the premise that the hallmark of professions is their premodern nature. Before Haber's study, revisionists (usually sociologists) had already moved from portraying professions as altruistic and service oriented and had started to emphasize their monopolistic and self-serving nature. See especially Julius A. Roth, "Professionalism: The Sociologist's Decoy," *Sociology of Work and Occupations* 1 (1974): 6–23; Jeffrey Berlant, *Professions and Monopoly* (Berkeley and Los Angeles: University of California Press, 1975); and Magali Sarfatti Larson, *The Rise of Professionalism: A Sociological Analysis* (Berkeley and Los Angeles: University of California Press, 1977), and idem, "The Production of Expertise and the Constitution of Expert Power," in *The Authority of Experts: Studies in History and*

Theory, ed. Thomas L. Haskell (Bloomington: Indiana University Press, 1984), 28–80.

9. One pioneering study of this type is W. E. B. Du Bois, *Efforts for Social Betterment among Negro Americans* (Atlanta: Atlanta University Press, 1909). More recent works include Cynthia Neverdon-Morton, *Afro-American Women of the South and the Advancement of the Race, 1895–1925* (Knoxville: University of Tennessee Press, 1989); Jacqueline Anne Rouse, *Lugenia Burns Hope: Black Southern Reformer* (Athens: University of Georgia Press, 1989); Anne Firor Scott, "Most Invisible of All: Black Women's Voluntary Associations," *Journal of Southern History* 56 (1990): 3–22; Darlene Clark Hine, " 'We Specialize in the Wholly Impossible': The Philanthropic Work of Black Women," in *Lady Bountiful Revisited: Women, Philanthropy, and Power*, ed. Kathleen D. McCarthy (New Brunswick, N.J.: Rutgers University Press, 1990), 70–93; Ralph E. Luker, *The Social Gospel in Black and White: American Racial Reform, 1885–1912* (Chapel Hill: University of North Carolina Press, 1991). The last is a study of the impact of American Christian institutions, leaders, and thought on racial reform during the Progressive Era, not exclusively a study of African Americans during this period. More focused on the African American community is Luker's "Missions, Institutional Churches, and Settlement Houses: The Black Experience, 1885–1910," *Journal of Negro History* 69 (1984): 101–13. A recent study that examines this reform work beyond the Progressive Era and also sees it as work for social change and eventually civil rights is Elisabeth Lasch-Quinn, *Black Neighbors: Race and the Limits of Reform in the American Settlement House Movement, 1890–1945* (Chapel Hill: University of North Carolina Press, 1993). Other studies, broader in scope, also provide some insight on the collective consciousness that encouraged women to work toward community development. See, for example, Paula Giddings, *When and Where I Enter . . . The Impact of Black Women on Race and Sex in America* (New York: William Morrow, 1984); and Jacqueline Jones, *Labor of Love, Labor of Sorrow: Black Women, Work, and the Family from Slavery to the Present* (New York: Basic Books, 1985). Taking an approach similar to the one I have taken, Michèle Foster examines the influence of family and community on the ways black female schoolteachers organized their personal and professional lives. See "Constancy, Connectedness, and Constraints in the Lives of African American Teachers," *National Women's Studies Association Journal* 5 (1991): 233–61.

10. Most notably, see philosopher Elizabeth V. Spelman's *Inessential Woman: Problems of Exclusion in Feminist Thought* (Boston: Beacon Press, 1988); law professor Patricia J. Williams's *The Alchemy of Race and Rights* (Cambridge: Harvard University Press, 1991); former New Zealand stateswoman Marilyn Waring's *If Women Counted: A New Feminist Economics* (San Francisco: Harper and Row, 1988); and historian Elsa Barkley Brown's " 'What Has Happened Here': The Politics of Difference in Women's History and Feminist Politics," *Feminist Studies* 18 (1992): 295–312.

11. I use the terms "internal" and "external" in the social-

psychological sense. Internal factors are those designed and controlled by the group, and external factors are larger societal conditions often imposed and always determined by others. Thus the legal segregation of schools was an external factor; the educational process instituted in black private schools was an internal one.

12. Such a position, which this book challenges, assumes that one can and does exist apart from society and that one's identity is completely self-determined. My position also provides a contrast to the traditional understanding of professionalization as moving away from or out of community, which Bellah and his coauthors describe. It is true that professional status set these women apart from the community in one sense, but the way professional training was obtained defined success not merely as an individual accomplishment but also as the creation of moral responsibility to a larger group. See Bellah et al., *Habits of the Heart*, 119–26, and their discussions of the social transition from "callings" to "professions" in chapters 2 and 3, "Culture and Character" and "Finding Oneself."

13. Quotation and idea of culture as persistent in David Hackett Fischer, *Albion's Seed: Four British Folkways in America* (New York: Oxford University Press, 1989), 895–97. Another observer similarly noted that "perhaps the greatest problem which any historian has to tackle is neither the cataclysm of revolution nor the decay of empire but the process by which ideas become social attitudes." Quoted in Warren I. Susman, *Culture as History: The Transformation of American Society in the Twentieth Century* (New York: Pantheon, 1984), 273.

14. Fisher, *Albion's Seed*. For related examples of the persistence of cultural traditions even as objective conditions changed, see Lawrence W. Levine, *Black Culture and Black Consciousness: Afro-American Folk Thought from Slavery to Freedom* (New York: Oxford University Press, 1977); Sterling Stuckey, *Slave Culture: Nationalist Theory and the Foundations of Black America* (New York: Oxford University Press, 1987); and Stephanie J. Shaw, "Black Club Women and the Creation of the National Association of Colored Women," *Journal of Women's History* 3 (1991): 10–25.

15. Mary Church Terrell was somewhat extraordinary in her educational preparation and class background. More generally, however, that these women's lives can be documented is what makes them extraordinary, not that they worked the way they did. For the most part, I am in agreement with Bernice Johnson Reagon, who describes her second-grade teacher, Mamie Daniels, as "an extraordinary teacher" in "My Black Mothers and Sisters; or On Beginning a Cultural Autobiography," *Feminist Studies* 8 (1982): 81–96. Daniels taught seven grades in one room and apparently was an outstanding teacher. But Reagon adds that Daniels was a "prototype," not a rarity.

For a discussion of the lack of archival material on black women's lives, see Deborah Gray White, "Mining the Forgotten: Manuscript Sources for Black Women's History," *Journal of American History* 74 (1987): 237–42. Historiographical discussions of black women's history include Darlene Clark Hine, "Lifting the Veil, Shattering the Silence: Black

Women's History in Slavery and Freedom," in *The State of Afro-American History: Past, Present, and Future*, ed. Darlene Clark Hine (Baton Rouge: Louisiana State University Press, 1986), 223–49; and Evelyn Brooks Higginbotham, "Beyond the Sound of Silence: Afro-American Women in History," *Gender and History* 1 (1989): 50–67.

16. Fortunately, this tradition is changing. Public records are more mixed now, and personal accounts of individual lives are more frank. For one example, Eunice Rivers Laurie's role in the Tuskegee syphilis project (discussed briefly in chapter 6) is now being studied more closely and was even a topic of discussion in a session at the Berkshire Conference on the History of Women in 1993. For another example, the narrative of Alabama schoolteacher Sarah Webb Rice provides a much more balanced self-portrait than most autobiographies yield. Rice speaks as frankly about her own elitism, selfishness, and sexuality as about her community work and her public image. See Sarah Webb Rice, *He Included Me: The Autobiography of Sarah Rice*, ed. Louise Westling (Athens: University of Georgia Press, 1989).

17. Recent scholarly explorations of history and memory, some of which caution historians about the sources we use, introduce several important points about the construction of memory and the use of historical documents. Benedict Anderson, in *Imagined Communities: Reflections on the Origin and Spread of Nationalism* (London: Verso, 1991), addresses, among other things, the newness of nationalism and how people come to imagine, accept, and speak of it as ancient. David W. Blight, in *Frederick Douglass' Civil War: Keeping Faith in Jubilee* (Baton Rouge: Louisiana State University Press, 1989), examines Douglass's particular memory of the Civil War and his efforts to keep that understanding—an understanding of the war as one for freedom and democracy—in the minds of Americans. Douglass believed that Americans' failure to remember the war in that way led to increased persecution of African Americans in the post-Reconstruction period. Thus Blight's study is also about the construction of memory. Presenting a variety of essays is David Thelen, ed., *Memory and American History* (Bloomington: Indiana University Press, 1990). The preface to this book is especially instructive for people who use oral history. In particular, Thelen discusses how memory is constructed and affected by "new understandings," "present needs," and other factors. And see Scott A. Sandage, "A Marble House Divided: The Lincoln Memorial, the Civil Rights Movement, and the Politics of Memory, 1939–1963," *Journal of American History* 80 (1993): 135–67. A useful study of oral narratives as history, biography, and literature is Gwendolyn Etter-Lewis, *My Soul Is My Own: Oral Narratives of African American Women in the Professions* (New York: Routledge, 1993).

18. "Gender" and "sex" are not used synonymously in this book. "Sex" refers here to the biological category of females; gender refers to the social content or meaning of womanhood (in this case) for black professional women.

19. Erlene Stetson, "Black Feminism in Indiana, 1893–1933," *Phylon: Atlanta University Review of Race and Culture* 44 (1983): 292, n. 1.

20. "Books, Black Beautiful to Her," Dallas *Morning News,* June 23, 1971, Clara Stanton Jones Papers, NCCU-BLA.

Chapter One

1. The literature on childhood and the socialization of children is vast. One classic study is Philippe Ariès, *Centuries of Childhood: A Social Study of Family Life* (New York: Vintage Books, 1962). Also see N. Ray Hiner and Joseph M. Hawes, eds., *Growing up in America: Children in Historical Perspective* (Urbana: University of Illinois Press, 1985). Focusing on black children and families are Walter R. Allen, "Family Roles, Occupational Statuses and Achievement Orientations among Black Women in the United States," *Signs: Journal of Women and Culture in Society* 14 (1979): 670–86; Janice Hall, "The Black Woman and Child Rearing," in *The Black Woman,* ed. La Frances Rodgers-Rose (Beverly Hills, Calif.: Sage, 1980), 79–87; Harriette Pipes McAdoo, ed., *Black Families* (Beverly Hills, Calif.: Sage, 1981), esp. 209–63; and Harriette Pipes McAdoo and John Lewis McAdoo, eds., *Black Children: Social, Educational, and Parental Environments* (Beverly Hills, Calif.: Sage, 1985).

2. The U.S. Bureau of the Census did not begin to report systematically on family income until after the Great Depression. Average wages and salaries can, however, suggest the importance of black women's incomes to the family economy. According to the U.S. Bureau of the Census, nonwhite males earned 41.4 percent of the income of white males in 1939. Nonwhite women earned only 22.1 percent of the income of white men. Therefore it is likely that married black couples did not receive an annual income equal to that of white men alone. In 1947 nonwhite males earned 54.3 percent of what white men earned, and nonwhite women's proportion had dropped to 18.3 percent. Marion Hayes, "A Century of Change: Negroes in the U.S. Economy, 1860–1960," *Monthly Labor Review* 85 (1962): 1364. Also see Claudia Goldin, "Female Labor Force Participation: The Origin of Black and White Differences, 1870–1880," *Journal of Economic History* 37 (1977): 87–108; and Elizabeth Higginbotham, "Employment for Professional Black Women in the Twentieth Century," in *Ingredients for Women's Employment Policy,* ed. Christine Bose and Glenna Spitzeg (Albany: State University of New York Press, 1987), 73–91.

3. National statistics bear out the parents' conclusions. The total proportion of black women working as agricultural and domestic laborers was 97 percent in 1890, 95.6 percent in 1900, 96.6 percent in 1910, 89.3 percent in 1920, 89.5 percent in 1930, and 77.5 percent in 1940. The 1940 census lists 59.5 percent of black women in "domestic service," 10.4 percent in "service work," and 3 percent in agriculture. I have added the first two figures for my total in domestic work because the "service work"

includes charwomen, waitresses, cooks, and other domestic service workers not in private homes. I have not included the percentages of women employed as unpaid workers in agriculture. Presumably some of these women worked on family-owned farms, which is *not* what their parents hoped to save them from. These statistics are taken or compiled from *Report on Population of the United States at the Eleventh Census: 1890*, vol. 1 (Washington, D.C.: Government Printing Office, 1897), 429–31; *Statistics of Women at Work: Based on Unpublished Information Derived from the Schedules of the Twelfth Census: 1900* (1907), 161; *Fourteenth Census of the United States Taken in the Year of 1920* (1923), 4:340; *Fifteenth Census of the United States: 1930* (1933), 5:74; *Sixteenth Census of the United States: 1940* (1943), 3:97. On black women as domestic workers see Elizabeth Ross Haynes, "Negroes in Domestic Service in the United States," *Journal of Negro History* 8 (1923): 384–442; C. G. Woodson, "The Negro Washerwoman, A Vanishing Figure," *Journal of Negro History* 15 (1930): 269–77; Debra Lynn Newman, "Black Women Workers in the Twentieth Century," *Sage: A Scholarly Journal on Black Women* 3 (1986): 10–15; Tera Hunter, "Domination and Resistance: The Politics of Wage Household Labor in New South Atlanta," *Labor History* 34 (1993): 205–20; and Elizabeth Clark-Lewis, *Living In, Living Out: African-American Domestics in Washington, D.C., 1910–1940* (Washington, D.C.: Smithsonian Institution Press, 1994). More generally on black women's work options, see Jacqueline Jones, *Labor of Love, Labor of Sorrow: Black Women, Work, and the Family from Slavery to the Present* (New York: Basic Books, 1985); and Sharon Harley, "Black Women in a Southern City: Washington, D.C., 1890–1920," in *Sex, Race, and the Role of Women in the South*, ed. Joanne P. Hawkes and Sheila L. Skemp (Jackson: University Press of Mississippi, 1983), 59–74.

4. Sociological studies that reach similar conclusions about later generations include Wilbur Bock, "Farmer's Daughter Effect: The Case of the Negro Female Professional," *Phylon* 30 (1969): 17–26; Cynthia Fuchs Epstein, "Positive Effects of the Multiple Negative: Explaining the Success of Black Professional Women," *American Journal of Sociology* 78 (1973): 912–35; Robert Staples, "The Myth of the Black Matriarchy," *Black Scholar* 2 (1970): 9–16; Diane K. Lewis, "The Black Family: Socialization and Sex Roles," *Phylon* 36 (1975): 221–37; and Bonnie Thornton Dill, "'The Means to Put My Children Through': Child-Rearing Goals and Strategies among Black Female Domestic Servants," in *The Black Woman*, ed. La Frances Rodgers-Rose (Beverly Hills: Sage, 1980), 107–23.

5. Poindexter began his term on the board in 1881. Poindexter quotation reprinted in Richard Clyde Minor, "James Preston Poindexter: Elder Statesman of Columbus," *Ohio State Archaeological and Historical Quarterly*, July 1947, 10. I am grateful to Adah Ward Clifton for bringing this passage to my attention. In Sarah Webb Rice, *He Included Me: The Autobiography of Sarah Rice*, ed. Louise Westling (Athens: University of Georgia Press, 1989), 76, 100, Rice describes black school trustees as "men who you would call if a problem came up, and they would back you up. They could go down to the courthouse and get you fired too, if they thought

you were unfit morally." Rice also noted: "In my day, what they deemed your character determined your job. If the school board disapproved of you, they would let you go in a minute. You didn't have anybody to defend you." In William R. Conners to the Julius Rosenwald Fund, July 17, 1933, b. 381, RFF, FUL-SC, Conners recommends nurse Juanita Vivian Gregory for a Rosenwald Fellowship, saying, in part, "Because of her splendid reputation, excellent training, high moral character and pleasing personality, we [the Negro Welfare Association of Cleveland, Ohio] recommended her for the position which she secured [as the first black public health nurse on the city staff]. The manner in which she deported herself on the job . . . [resulted in the hiring of] three additional colored nurses . . . on the staff of the City Health Department."

Much of the scholarship that focuses on the black upper classes assumes that such people ascended to important public positions in the black community merely because of their education, skills, and self-determination rather than because (or partly because) others allowed, and even chose, them to assume such roles. An illuminating exception to this generalization is Julie Winch's *Philadelphia's Black Elite: Activism, Accommodation, and the Struggle for Autonomy, 1787–1848* (Philadelphia: Temple University Press, 1988), which provides useful discussions on the relation between individual efforts to "lead" and the reactions of others to being led. Another insightful study of this dynamic is George Lipsitz, *A Life in the Struggle: Ivory Perry and the Culture of Opposition* (Philadelphia: Temple University Press, 1988).

6. Reminiscing on her childhood, Susan St. Clair Minor, a Louisville, Kentucky, schoolteacher, concluded that her parents' lessons on manners were designed to teach the children how to interact not only with one another but also with people beyond their family. She noted that her parents were actually presenting a "model for what's the best way to handle yourself in a larger group." See Susan St. Clair Minor, interview transcript, OHC-UL, 11. The resources that document these women's lives show that parents worked hard to encourage habits not always explicitly defined, but designed nevertheless to develop character. That is, they talked about character development without saying what it was. The behaviors and traditions that parents encouraged, however, can be characterized as I have done in the text. My attempt to translate their efforts into these words was enhanced tremendously by my reading of Clarke E. Cochran, *Character, Community, and Politics* (University: University of Alabama Press, 1982), 11–35 (quoted phrases from pp. 18, 27, 29, 31); and Warren I. Susman, *Culture as History: The Transformation of American Society in the Twentieth Century* (New York: Pantheon Books, 1984), 273–77. Isaac Fisher not only attempted to impress his daughter Constance with words, but he also acted on those lessons himself, setting an example. After defending Fayette McKenzie, Fisk's last white president, even though the students and powerful alumni (including W. E. B. Du Bois) wanted McKenzie out, Fisher wrote to Constance: "I counted the cost in advance—a cost in abuse, vilification, misrepresentation, and epi-

thets which will make my blood boil while I try to restrain myself. But, 'Jumbo,' I had to write it to feel that I am the gentleman I want so much to be." Fisher knew that his position might cost him his job, and he did in fact leave Fisk for a new job at Hampton soon after he wrote this letter. But he considered himself a man of character, and he took the stance he believed was the right one. This commitment and loyalty, even at the risk of personal loss, undoubtedly constituted a powerful demonstration of character. See Isaac Fisher to Constance Fisher, October 1, 1924, Constance Fisher Papers, FUL-SC.

7. Norma Elizabeth Boyd, interview by Clarencetta Jelks, FUL-BOHP; Norma Boyd, interview by A. Lillian Thompson, RC-BWOHP, HU-MSRC, ii. The RC-BWOHP transcripts have now been published. The page numbers in the published volumes do not correspond to the page numbers in the original transcripts. See Ruth Edmonds Hill, ed., *The Black Women Oral History Project*, 10 vols. (Westport, Conn.: Meckler, 1991).

8. Norma Boyd, interview transcript, RC-BWOHP, 1–2; Julia Hamilton Smith, interview by Cheryl Gilkes, RC-BWOHP, 16, 65; Beulah Hester, interview by Felicia Bowens Anderson, RC-BWOHP, 61; Frances O. Grant, interview by Maurine Rothschild, RC-BWOHP, 4; Septima Poinsette Clark with LeGette Blythe, *Echo in My Soul* (New York: E. P. Dutton, 1962), 19; and Sarah and A. Elizabeth Delany with Amy Hill Hearth, *Having Our Say: The Delany Sisters' First 100 Years* (New York: Kodansha International, 1993), 50, 129, 143. The Delany sisters learned that it was not enough to live "a clean life," people had to know they did. Like Boyd, the Delanys also learned that their appearance reflected on the family. For an excellent description of expectations regarding personal appearance, see Mamie Garvin Fields with Karen Fields, *Lemon Swamp and Other Places: A Carolina Memoir* (New York: Free Press, 1983), 86. In this instance Fields describes traveling by train: "We all used to dress for travel. . . . We had the idea that the way you looked when arriving reflected where you came from and how your people carried themselves."

9. See Isaac Fisher to Constance, June 21, 1923, b. 13, Constance Fisher Papers, Hollis Burke Frissell Library, TUA (emphasis deleted).

10. Archibald Grimké to Angelina Grimké, November 25, 1894, February 7, 1895, April 25, 1895, March 7, 1895, September 7, 1897, January 19, 1898, February 8, 1898, March 18, 1898, March 29, 1898, and March 31, 1898, b. 4, Angelina Grimké Papers, HU-MSRC. Archibald's letters to his daughter after he returned to the United States continued to reflect this interest in shaping good behavior. Also see Mary [?] to Portia Washington, September [?] 1889, r. 2, BTW-LC. In this letter Portia was instructed on behaving properly toward her aunt, who was helping to care for her after her mother's death. For further details on Grimké, see Dickson D. Bruce Jr., *Archibald Grimké: Portrait of a Black Independent* (Baton Rouge: Louisiana State University Press, 1993), 75–77.

11. Archibald Grimké to Angelina Grimké, October 29, 1895, No-

vember 4, 1897, January 4, 1898, and February 15, 1899, b. 4, Angelina Grimké Papers, HU-MSRC.

12. Archibald Grimké to Angelina Grimké, October 29, 1895, February 15, 1899, February 25, 1899, December 1, 1898, and October 6, 1897, b. 4, Angelina Grimké Papers, HU-MSCR. On June 6, 1899, he tells her to keep her laundry bill down. On February 4, 1900, in response to her request for money for shoes, he advises her to have old shoes repaired or to trade a pair she already has for another pair. Similar advice appears throughout this collection. Lessons in saving money are also discussed in Delany, *Having Our Say*, 5.

13. Miriam Matthews, interview by Eleanor Roberts, RC-BWOHP, 14.

14. Booker T. Washington to Portia Washington, June 9, 1904, *BTWP*, 7:526; Portia Washington to Booker T. Washington, June 27, 1906, *BTWP*, 9:36; Booker T. Washington to Kolonial Wirtschaftliches Komitee (telegram), February 27, 1905; Booker T. Washington to Portia Washington, March 28, 1906; and Booker T. Washington to Portia Washington, June 19, 1906, r. 2, BTW-LC; Ruth Ann Stewart, *Portia: The Life of Portia Washington Pittman, the Daughter of Booker T. Washington* (Garden City, N.Y.: Doubleday, 1977), 66–68. Note that when I began this research, I used the published papers of Booker T. Washington. Later, while researching the collection at the Library of Congress, I used microfilmed copies in some instances and the actual documents in others. Consequently later citations in this book will refer to box numbers rather than reel numbers or volume numbers.

15. Beulah Shepard Hester, interview transcript, RC-BWOHP, 18–20; Mabel Northcross, interview by Sam Cameron, MMC-DNE.

16. Catherine Watkins Duncan, a rural Georgia schoolteacher, noted about herself and her two sisters that "any money we made went to our father for the general going-to-Fisk fund for the family. . . . Meagre meals, we rationalized, were helping to make it possible for us to go to Fisk. Few clothes were likewise a part of the pattern." See fellowship application for Catherine Watkins Duncan, b. 409, RFF, FUL-SC.

17. It is not too much to assume that some white people, even children, learned that it was not important to respect black people. Certainly one can see this lesson being conveyed in lynchings that were planned, advertised in advance, and made into social events with men, women, and children gaily taking part. By the same token, neither is it difficult to believe that some children were taught to love the brutes (in a particular way) anyway, out of a sense of Christian duty. An interesting though brief relevant discussion may be found in Cochran, *Character, Community, and Politics*, 48, where Cochran describes love as "a constant disposition toward the good of others, perhaps even those who are not liked. The injunction to love one's enemies is the highest form of this type [of communion]. It is also the most difficult, since the good of my enemy seems somehow bound up with harm to myself." Because these parents badly wanted their children to achieve acceptance by (perhaps even communion

with) the larger society, Cochran's description might be a viable explanation for what sometimes seemed to be self-effacement in the presence of racism. To be sure, this posture became a pillar of the later civil rights movement. But the lessons some white children learned that led them to uncharitable attitudes toward black people were probably much less vicious than those conveyed by the lynch mob, though equally repugnant. For a convincing presentation of this less aggressive process see Melton A. McLaurin, *Separate Pasts: Growing up White in the Segregated South* (Athens: University of Georgia Press, 1987).

18. For examples of children's sometimes not being allowed to associate with others, and being taught to be respectful toward all, see Beulah Hester, interview transcript, RC-BWOHP, 41; Julia Hamilton Smith, interview transcript, RC-BWOHP, 25–26; Edmund L. Drago, *Initiative, Paternalism, and Race Relations: Charleston's Avery Normal Institute* (Athens: University of Georgia Press, 1990), 157; and Delany, *Having Our Say*, 45.

19. Archibald Grimké to Angelina Grimké, June 19, 1895, b. 4; and "Mama Day" to Angelina Grimké, August 3, 1898, b. 1, Angelina Grimké Papers, HU-MSRC. The letter from "Mama Day" indicates that Angelina had previously reported an improvement in her behavior. The relationship between Angelina and Mama Day is not clear, but in Archibald Grimké to Angelina Grimké, April 25, 1895, he instructed Angelina never to neglect their dear friend Mama Day. On October 29, 1895, he wrote that Mama Day was "the dear, dear friend who has indeed been a mother to you." Information on Angelina's attending Carleton Academy for the 1895–96 and 1896–97 school years was provided by Eric Hilleman, Carleton College Archives, Northfield, Minnesota.

20. Barbara Simmons Miller, interview, FUL-BOHP. An acknowledged exception to this obedience is Stewart, *Portia*, 64–72, in which Portia Washington establishes that after moving to Germany she lived her own life, especially in regard to socializing. She also admits that many of her actions would not have been approved by her father.

21. Julia Hamilton Smith, interview transcript, RC-BWOHP, 2.

22. Mary Church Terrell, *A Colored Woman in a White World* (Washington, D.C.: Randsell, 1940), 15–16.

23. In Sharon Harley, "For the Good of Family and Race: Gender, Work, and Domestic Roles in the Black Community, 1880–1930," *Signs* 15 (1990): 336–49, Harley contends that parents' stress on good behavior in their children was also a way for some families to acquire social status.

24. Archibald Grimké to Angelina Grimké, November 18, 1897; and Francis Grimké to Angelina Grimké, November 20, 1897, b. 5, Angelina Grimké Papers, HU-MSRC.

25. Booker T. Washington to Frank W. Hale, May 23, 1902, *BTWP*, 6:468. A similar characterization of Portia appeared in the Indianapolis *Freeman* just after she arrived to enroll at Wellesley College. See "An Article about Portia Marshall Washington," *BTWP*, 6:360.

26. For historical and theoretical discussions of the negative stereo-

types related to black women's sexuality, see Deborah Gray White, *Ar'n't I a Woman? Female Slaves in the Plantation South* (New York: W. W. Norton, 1985), esp. 28–61; Darlene Clark Hine, "Rape and the Inner Lives of African-American Women," *Signs* 14 (1989): 912–20; and Patricia Morton, *Disfigured Images: The Historical Assault on Afro-American Women* (New York: Praeger, 1991). Discussing both white racist views and black romantic views from historical and literary sources is Beverly Guy-Sheftall, *Daughters of Sorrow: Attitudes toward Black Women, 1880–1920*, vol. 11 of *Black Women in American History*, ed. Darlene Clark Hine (Brooklyn, N.Y.: Carlson, 1990), 37–90.

27. Archibald Grimké to Angelina Grimké, November 18, 1897, b. 4, Angelina Grimké Papers, HU-MSRC; Miriam Matthews, interview transcript, RC-BWOHP, 13–14; Fields, *Lemon Swamp*, 38. Part of the socialization of these girls was clearly age specific rather than sex specific. See for a comparison Lewis, "Black Family," esp. 233.

28. Hester's brothers worked during the summers as railroad porters. Lucy Mitchell occasionally sold perfume door-to-door during the summers, and therefore she could control which houses she approached and entered. Her brothers, however, spent the summers working at various resorts in New Hampshire. Sarah Delany's brothers worked as Pullman porters, but she and her sisters were not allowed to do domestic work. Instead they sought summer work in Northern factories after graduating from high school and in order to save money for college. Beulah Hester, interview transcript, RC-BWOHP, 18; Lucy Mitchell, interview transcript, RC-BWOHP, 16; Delany, *Having Our Say*, 76, 109–10.

29. Clark's autobiography used the word "tempt," but considering the configuration of power based on race, class, and sex in such work relationships, clearly many of these "tempted" women were forced. Clark was fortunate enough one summer to obtain a job working in a bakery. Clark, *Echo in My Soul*, 23, 28–29. For other observations on the dangers and indignities associated with domestic service work, see W. E. B. Du Bois, "The Servant in the House," in *Darkwater: Voices from within the Veil* (1920; rpt. New York: Schocken Books, 1969), 163–86; John Dollard, *Caste and Class in a Southern Town* (1927; rpt. New York: Doubleday Anchor Books, 1957), 145–56; "A Negro Nurse," "More Slavery in the South," *Independent* 72 (1912): 196–200; Gerda Lerner, ed., *Black Women in White America: A Documentary* (New York: Vintage Books, 1973), 155–59, 163–71; Angela Davis, *Women, Race, and Class* (New York: Random House, 1981), 90–98; and Bettina Aptheker, *Woman's Legacy: Essays in Race, Sex, and Class in America* (Amherst: University of Massachusetts, 1982), 111–28.

Shortly after the turn of the century, young black women who had achieved a certain level of education (usually into and beyond secondary school) had more options for summer employment as teachers in the newly developing rural school systems. Because white landowners wanted to keep a viable agricultural labor force, especially in the fall and spring, these schools, often open only in the summer, provided a perfect opportunity for the advanced women students who wanted to continue their education in the fall. While on these jobs, the young women usually lived in the homes of black community residents, an arrangement that also provided some protection of their reputations and their persons.

30. Adrienne Lash Jones, "Jane Edna Hunter: A Case Study of Black Leadership, 1910–1950" (Ph.D. diss., Case Western Reserve University, 1983), 61–62.

31. Lucy Mitchell, interview transcript, RC-BWOHP, 3. Mitchell reports that this relationship was a loving one, but also that her grandmother refused to move to the North with the unnamed white man. Minnesota social worker Ethel Ray Nance grew up near resort towns and recalled that many southerners worked in the hotels on Lake Minnetonka during the summers. See Ethel Ray Nance, interview by David Taylor, AMD-MHS, 6–7.

32. Stewart, *Portia*, 52; Miriam Matthews, interview transcript, RC-BWOHP, 13–14; Frances Grant, interview transcript, RC-BWOHP, 4–5; Beulah Hester, interview transcript, RC-BWOHP, 26. Also see Fields, *Lemon Swamp*, 145–46; Florence Edmonds, interview transcript, RC-BWOHP, 12; Ethel Ray Nance, interview transcript, AMD-MHS, 6–7; and Delany, *Having Our Say*, 43. Hester's mother did not want her to have a boyfriend until she finished school. Regarding Grant's comments, black men and women regularly attended summer school in New England because they worked the rest of the year, often as teachers or principals. For some, limited funds made even a ten-cent trolley ride a luxury. Grant's father might also have wanted to keep his daughters from becoming attracted to young men from less impressive family backgrounds than his own, however upwardly mobile those men appeared to be.

So fearful were parents of acts that might be construed as manifestations of sexuality that Ellen Tarry's sister, Ida May, was severely whipped after her parents learned that "for the fee of a quarter, she would stop in her tracks and do a shimmy-she-wobble that stopped the park traffic." After Ida May showed her knees at the same park one day, her mother had her moved from her school to the one Ellen attended. Ida May clearly had not enough shame, and someone had to keep an eye on her for the sake of her safety and reputation. Ellen Tarry, *The Third Door: The Autobiography of an American Negro Woman* (1955; rpt. Westport, Conn.: Negro Universities Press, 1971), 17. In a rare set of documents that reveals a little about sexuality among middle-class black people, Edward Walter Ricks (who later served as the principal of Lincoln Academy and a YMCA executive) confessed his weakness to his fiancée, Launard Cobbs, in a series of letters. On September 1, 1915, he wrote: "I would tell you [of] a deep feeling of my heart, but you might suspect me and say I had bad notions." In a subsequent letter (September 15, 1915), in which he proposed that they marry soon, he noted that "I realize that [marriage] to be the best for me as a young man struggling to be clean and pure, and with other interests which I need a wife [to] help me look after." See LAC, Amistad Research Center, Tulane University, New Orleans, Louisiana.

33. Beulah Hester, interview transcript, RC-BWOHP, 24; Rice, *He Included Me*, 65; Clark, *Echo in My Soul*, 63. Similar concerns about accepting gifts from boys are noted in Fields, *Lemon Swamp*, 68, 143.

34. Beulah Hester, interview transcript, RC-BWOHP, 60. Sarah Delany acknowledges that she learned nothing about sex when she was growing up. See Delany, *Having Our Say*, 57–58, 78.

35. Beulah Hester, interview transcript, RC-BWOHP, 63. Catharine Beecher and Harriet Beecher Stowe wrote in *The American Woman's Home:* "Monday, with some of the best housekeepers, is devoted to preparing for the labors of the week. . . . Tuesday is devoted to washing, and Wednesday to ironing. On Thursday, the ironing is finished off, the clothes are folded and put away, and all articles which need mending are . . . attended to. Friday is devoted to . . . housecleaning. On Saturday, . . . everything about the house [is] put in order for Sunday." See Catharine E. Beecher and Harriet Beecher Stowe, *The American Woman's Home* (New York, 1869), 226–27. Hester's mother attended Boydton Institute, and the Beecher/Stowe book could have been used there. But this was a common routine for "efficient" homemakers at the time. Another indication of how common the practice might have been is provided in the manuscript diaries of Nanie Wilson, 1933–34, 1936. Photocopy in my possession, provided by Ann Patton Malone of Northwestern State University, Nachitoches, Louisiana. The diaries confirm that Wilson, a Seguin, Texas, schoolteacher, always did her washing on Monday or Tuesday and her ironing on Tuesday or Wednesday.

36. Stewart, *Portia*, 37–42; "An Article about Portia Marshall Washington in the Indianapolis *Freeman*," BTWP, 6:361 and 2:235–36, n. 2. The article is not dated in the published Washington papers, but it suggests that she was attending Wellesley at the time of the interview (she attended in 1901). See "An Interview with Portia Marshall Washington in the *Birmingham Age-Herald*," 6:322–27. The article appeared in the Birmingham paper on December 1, 1901. And see T. Thomas Fortune to Booker T. Washington, November 3, 1902, 6: 571–72, in which Fortune is trying to ascertain why Portia left Wellesley. Several other documents erroneously imply that she was at Wellesley in 1904, 1905, or both.

37. Harley, "For the Good of Family and Race," 348–49.

38. Portia Washington to Booker T. Washington, November 19, 1893, and October 7, 1895, r. 2, BTW-LC.

39. [Theresa] Tessa Lee to Angelina Grimké, September 23, [?], b. 1, Angelina Grimké Papers, HU-MSRC. Archibald Grimké boarded with the Lees when he visited Massachusetts. (Original emphasis deleted.)

40. Archibald Grimké to Angelina Grimké [1895], and April 25, 1895, b. 4, Angelina Grimké Papers, HU-MSRC. See also Emma Tolles to

Angelina Grimké, May 7, 1900, b. 2, in which Tolles, Angelina's maternal aunt, discussed new dressmaking patterns and Angelina's sewing ability.

41. Beulah Hester, interview transcript, RC-BWOHP, 23. See also Miriam Matthews, interview transcript, RC-BWOHP, 17; and Mary Brinkerhoff, "Books, Blacks Beautiful to Her," Dallas *Morning News*, July 23, 1971, Clara Jones Papers, NCCU-BLA (also in vertical files, Biographical-Women, "Clara Jones," Labor Archives).

42. Quotation from Miriam Matthews, interview transcript, RC-BWOHP, 5. The Matthews family subsequently became good friends with the Armenian family. Miriam Matthews to Stephanie J. Shaw, May 20, 1986. See also Miriam Matthews, interview by Robin D. G. Kelley, October 11, 1985, tape 1, side 1, 7, Powell Library, University of California–Los Angeles. Permission to read and cite this transcript was granted by Mr. Dale Trelevan of the Powell Library and Ms. Miriam Matthews of Los Angeles.

43. The way "Bessie" Delany's mother handled serious confrontations with racism was probably common. Delany noted that her mother would sit silently "and look at me while I cried, and it comforted me. I knew that she understood, and that was the most soothing salve." Delany, *Having Our Say*, 74. A. Elizabeth Delany (Bessie) began her career as a schoolteacher but eventually became a dentist. An example of the notion that only those with superior conduct were superior people is found in Norma Boyd, interview transcript, RC-BWOHP, 2. Also see Rice, *He Included Me*, 14.

44. Charlotte Forten Grimké to Angelina Grimké, September 23, 1899, b. 5, Angelina Grimké Papers; Booker T. Washington to Portia Marshall Washington, November 15, 1906, *BTWP*, 9:127; Portia Washington to Booker T. Washington, June 29, 1906, *BTWP*, 9:37–38. Ethel Ray Nance's father regularly lectured his children about race relations as they grew up in Minnesota. In particular, he talked about lynching. Nance insisted, however, that he did not want them to hate people. "He seemed to want to make us aware." Nance, interview transcript, AMD-MHS, 4. Angelina's presence at the Boston Normal School is confirmed in the *Boston Normal School of Gymnastics Ninth Annual Catalogue of Instructors, Students, and Graduates, 1899–1900*, 9.

45. Their parents were preparing them for a successful public life, not race wars, but it is still important that many parents believed the more respectable (well behaved) children were, the less hostile white people would be. On race riots, see Joseph Boskin, *Urban Racial Violence in the Twentieth Century* (Beverly Hills, Calif.: Glencoe Press, 1976), 21–33; Edgar A. Schyler, "The Houston Race Riot, 1917," *Journal of Negro History* 29 (1944): 300–328; Elliot M. Rudwick, *Race Riot at East St. Louis, July 2, 1917* (Carbondale: Southern Illinois University Press, 1964); J. Paul Mitchell, ed., *Race Riots in Black and White* (Englewood Cliffs, N.J.: Prentice-Hall, 1970), 89–128; and Joel Williamson, *The Crucible of Race: Black-White Relations in the American South since Emancipation* (New York: Oxford University Press, 1984), 189–223.

46. Important older historical, sociological, and anthropological studies that document the tradition of sending girls to the best schools possible in the North and South, church schools in particular, include August Meier and David Lewis, "History of the Negro Upper Class in Atlanta, Georgia, 1890–1958," *Journal of Negro Education* 28 (1959): 130–35; Hortense Powdermaker, *After Freedom: A Cultural Study on the Deep South* (New York: Viking Press, 1930), 299–322; St. Clair Drake and Horace Cayton, *Black Metropolis; A Study of Negro Life in a Northern City* (New York: Harcourt, Brace, and World, 1945), 515–16, 664–67; John Dollard, *Caste and Class in a Southern Town* (1937; rpt. New York: Doubleday Anchor, 1957), 87, 189–93; and Clifton R. Jones, "Social Stratification in the Negro Population: A Study of Social Classes in South Boston, Virginia," *Journal of Negro Education* 15 (1946): 9.

47. Studies on public and private education for black children in the South include Henry Allen Bullock, *A History of Negro Education in the South* (New York: Praeger, 1967); and Louis Harlan, *Separate and Unequal: Public School Campaigns and Racism in the Southern Seaboard States, 1901–1915* (Chapel Hill: University of North Carolina Press, 1968). An exceptional recent study of some aspects of black education is James D. Anderson, *The Education of Blacks in the South, 1860–1935* (Chapel Hill: University of North Carolina Press, 1988). Anderson's detailed discussion of how cash-poor, recently freed men and women taxed themselves (beyond the already imposed local taxes) to provide adequate schooling for their children reflects the same concern for education that the parents in this book shared. Another important work that indirectly addresses the struggle of slaves to achieve literacy and schooling is Janet Duitsman Cornelius, *When I Can Read My Title Clear: Literacy, Slavery, and Religion in the Antebellum South* (Columbia: University of South Carolina Press, 1991).

48. James H. Jones, *Bad Blood: The Tuskegee Syphilis Experiment—a Tragedy in Race and Medicine* (New York: Basic Books, 1981), 109–10; Eunice Rivers Laurie, interview transcript, RC-BWOHP, 1–10. Laurie must have been enrolled in Tuskegee's "Homecrafts" section of the "Department of Women's Industries," which offered mattress making, basket and bread work, broom making, rug making, chair caning, and home decorating. See the *Tuskegee Institute Bulletin: Annual Catalog Edition, 1921–22*, 91. (The description of the nursing program is on p. 119.) Ethel Ray Nance grew up in Duluth, Minnesota, and attended integrated public schools. To make certain that she and her siblings, whose mother was white, were informed about African American history, her father subscribed to the *Guardian* and *Crisis* and maintained a large private library from which the children were required to read. Ethel Ray Nance, interview transcript, AMD-MHS, 4.

49. Beulah Hester, interview transcript, RC-BWOHP, 19; Stewart, *Portia*, 38–40; Archibald Grimké to Angelina Grimké, January 29, 1899, b. 4, Angelina Grimké Papers, HU-MSRC; Julia Hamilton Smith, interview transcript, RC-BWOHP, 12; Delany, *Having Our Say*, 79. For an early account of the history of the Minor Normal School that includes

transcriptions of letters and reminiscences of Minor, some of her early supporters, and students, see Ellen M. O'Connor, ed., *Myrtilla Minor: A Memoir* (1885; rpt. New York: Arno, 1969). A recent study of women's health and education that includes the Boston Normal School of Gymnastics is Martha H. Verbrugge, *Able-Bodied Womanhood: Personal Health and Social Change in Nineteenth-Century Boston* (New York: Oxford University Press, 1988). Angelina's attending the Boston Normal School is mentioned above (n. 44). Less well known is that Angelina also was an instructor there in 1902–3. See *Boston Normal School of Gymnastics Twelfth Annual Catalogue of Instructors, Students, and Graduates, 1902–03, 41.*

50. Miriam Matthews, interview transcript, RC-BWOHP, 2, 8, 81; Norma Boyd, interview transcript, RC-BWOHP, ii; Eula Wellman Dunlap, "Reminiscences" (manuscript), LAC, Amistead Research Center; Barbara Simmons Miller, interview, FUL-BOHP. Linda M. Perkins's article "The Impact of the 'Cult of True Womanhood' on the Education of Black Women," *Journal of Social Issues* 39 (1983): 17–28, indicates that it was common for black families to relocate for educational advantages in the antebellum period as well. She includes examples of families from Michigan and North Carolina who moved to Oberlin, Ohio, in the 1830s and 1860s, respectively, to enroll their daughters in school there. And see extensive discussions of antebellum patterns in Cornelius, *When I Can Read My Title Clear.*

51. Ethel Evangeline Martin Bolden, "Susan Dart Butler: Pioneer Librarian" (M.S. thesis, Atlanta University, 1959), 9; "Sketches of Graduates," *SM*, May 1901, 2.

52. Especially critical for these women, and other African Americans in the South, was the increase in the number of high schools. According to one government study, there were only 67 black public high schools in the South in 1916. (Other studies say 64.) A later study concludes that by 1930 there were 506 public and 112 private high schools. Harry S. Ashmore, however, puts the 1928 total (public and private) at 1,860. See Department of the Interior, Bureau of Education, *Negro Education: A Study of the Private and Higher Schools for Colored People in the United States*, vol. 2 (Washington, D.C.: Government Printing Office, 1917), 15; Ambrose Caliver, *Secondary Education for Negroes*, National Survey of Secondary Education Bulletin (Washington, D.C.: Government Printing Office, 1932), 25; and Harry S. Ashmore, *The Negro and the Schools* (Chapel Hill: University of North Carolina Press, 1954), 19, 26.

The appendix, composed of brief biographical sketches arranged in the order of the women's births, reveals the pattern in family economic background and in the schools the daughters attended. It also reveals some blurring of the line between the first and second generations. That is, some of the "oldest" women in the second generation resemble those in the first generation. The farther you move into the second generation, the more different it is from the first. More details on the education of most of these women may be found in Stephanie J. Shaw, "Black Women in White Collars: A Social History of Lower-Level Professional Black

Women Workers, 1870–1954" (Ph.D. diss., Ohio State University, 1986), 92–107. Women who lived on the West Coast before white flight from the cities occurred regularly attended integrated schools.

53. See Shaw, "Black Women in White Collars," 92–107. Further supporting this pattern, one of Mary Church Terrell's most intensive struggles in the 1920s was for the admission of Eva Ross, a young black girl, to some of the very same New England schools that the older subjects of this chapter attended. Several of the schools admitted Ross but revoked the admission when they discovered that she was "part colored." See Laura Terrell Jones to Mary Church Terrell, May 12, 1935, r. 2, MCT-LC; and Terrell, *A Colored Woman in a White World*, 287–94. This general pattern also reflects a national trend in which the earliest men and women (black and white) to work in these professions came from more affluent families that could take advantage of private schooling. As public schooling became more available nationwide, less affluent families could take advantage of it, and consequently the economic class backgrounds of those who eventually became teachers were often lower than in the previous generation of professionals. It is also possible that this pattern reflects bias in the sources: sources for the first-generation women include more manuscript material, which is generally more available for women of prominent backgrounds.

54. Details on the missions of some of these schools may be found in Helen Lefkowitz Horowitz, *Alma Mater: Design and Experience in the Women's Colleges from Their Nineteenth Century Beginnings to the 1930s* (New York: Alfred A. Knopf, 1984); James D. Anderson, "Training the Apostles of Liberal Culture: Black Higher Education, 1900–1936," in Anderson, *The Education of Blacks in the South*, 238–78; Maxine D. Jones and Joe M. Richardson, *Talladega College: The First Century* (Tuscaloosa: University of Alabama Press, 1990), esp. 1–142; Verbrugge, *Able-Bodied Womanhood;* John Barnard, *From Evangelicalism to Progressivism at Oberlin College, 1866–1917* (Columbus: Ohio State University Press, 1969); Joe M. Richardson, *A History of Fisk University, 1865–1946* (University: University of Alabama Press, 1980); Rayford W. Logan, *Howard University: The First Hundred Years, 1867–1967* (New York: New York University Press, 1969); and Joe M. Richardson, *Christian Reconstruction: The American Missionary Association and Southern Blacks, 1861–1890* (Athens: University of Georgia Press, 1986).

55. See Angelina W. Grimké, "A Biographical Sketch of Archibald H. Grimké," typescript, 11, b. 1, Archibald Grimké Papers; Archibald Grimké to Angelina Grimké, November 25, 1894, April 25, 1895, September 7, 1897, November 4, 1897, January 19, 1898, February 8, 1898, March 18, 1898, and January 4, 1899, b. 4, Angelina Grimké Papers, HU-MSRC. For similar evidence, see Clark, *Echo in My Soul*, 21; Jones, *Bad Blood*, 109; Eunice Laurie, interview transcript, RC-BWOHP, 2–4, 7; Beulah Hester, interview transcript, RC-BWOHP, 4–5, 19; and Ethel Ray Nance, interview transcript, AMD-MHS, 4, 9, 14.

56. Quotation from Isaac Fisher to Constance Fisher, n.d., b. 1,

Constance Fisher Papers, FUL-SC (emphasis deleted). On parents' efforts to secure certain types of work for their daughters, see Isaac Fisher to Constance Fisher, June 26, [?], b. 14, Constance Fisher Papers, TUA; G. P. M. Turner to Mary Church [Terrell], December 19, 1886, b. 4, MCT-LC; and Archibald Grimké to Angelina Grimké, March 23, 1901, b. 4, Angelina Grimké Papers, HU-MSRC.

The Turner letter indicated that Robert Church had shared his daughter's letters with Turner, who was associated with the Memphis *Daily Scimitar*. Turner consequently wrote to invite Mary to become an "occasional correspondent" to the paper. In the 1901 Grimké letter, Archibald Grimké reported that he was trying to arrange a teaching position for Angelina at what is now South Carolina State University, where his friend Tom Miller was president. And in the second Fisher letter, Isaac instructed Constance to copy, verbatim, the letter he was enclosing. The letter was to go to government officials organizing the National Youth Administration and addressed their need to employ an African American woman (Fisher) to help with the work. Isaac also provided Constance with the list of references she was to include.

57. Quotation from Archibald Grimké to Angelina Grimké, September 5, 1905, Angelina Grimké Papers, HU-MSRC (emphasis added). Also see June 24, 1905, October 6, 1905, October 8, 1905, October 13, 1905, and November 3, 1905, b. 4. For some time Grimké had been urging Angelina to pursue publishing her writings. See, for examples, June 12, 1899, June 22, 1899, July 8, 1899, and October 13, 1905. She did eventually become well known as a playwright, poet, and short-story writer.

58. Archibald Grimké to Angelina Grimké, November 3, 1905, b. 4, ibid.; Dickson D. Bruce Jr., in *Archibald Grimké: Portrait of a Black Independent,* 164, notes that Archibald eventually intervened directly by going to the school board.

59. On the way many African Americans historically viewed education as serving a collective rather than an individual function, see Anderson, *The Education of Blacks in the South;* Herbert G. Gutman, "Schools for Freedom: The Post-emancipation Origins of Afro-American Education," in *Power and Culture: Essays on the American Working Class,* ed. Ira Berlin (New York: Pantheon, 1987), 260–97. On similar antebellum patterns, see Perkins, "Impact of the 'Cult of True Womanhood' on the Education of Black Women." The work of Gwendolyn Etter-Lewis also suggests that such socialization was widespread and continued well into the twentieth century. See *My Soul Is My Own: Oral Narratives of African American Women in the Professions* (New York: Routledge, 1993).

60. Fannie Dell Jordan, "My Choice of a Calling," *SM,* March 1926, 3; Isaac Fisher to Constance Fisher, June 26, 193[?], Constance Fisher Papers, TUA; Brinkerhoff, "Books, Blacks Beautiful to Her"; Robert Kraus, "Black Library Chief Bears No Scars after Squabble," Detroit *Free Press,* February 18, 1970, vertical files—Biography, "Clara Jones," La-

bor Archives; Susan St. Clair Minor, interview transcript, OHC-UL, 10. Also see Delany, *Having Our Say*, 81, 107.

61. Willard Gatewood notes that the Washington branch of the NAACP "became the largest and one of the most active in the nation" under Grimké's leadership. Willard B. Gatewood, *Aristocrats of Color: The Black Elite, 1880–1920* (Bloomington: Indiana University Press, 1990), 315. Dickson J. Bruce Jr.'s more recent biography of Archibald Grimké provides great detail on his race work. Julia Smith's grandfather, a Massachusetts abolitionist, also served in the Massachusetts legislature (the General Court of the Commonwealth of Massachusetts) for two terms. Julia Hamilton Smith, interview transcript, RC-BWOHP, ii, 53. On the Duluth NAACP branch, see Ethel Ray Nance, interview transcript, AMD-MHS, 11–12.

62. Details on these types of activities among the families are provided in chapter 2.

63. Julia Smith, interview transcript, RC-BWOHP, 53, 71–72; Terrell, *A Colored Woman in a White World*, 9; Miriam Matthews, interview transcript, RC-BWOHP, 5. For contemporary newspaper accounts of Georgiana Smith's concerts, see Monroe A. Majors, *Noted Negro Women: Their Triumphs and Activities* (1893; rpt. Freeport, N.Y.: Books for Libraries Press, 1971), 123–24.

64. On the specific statements see Terrell, *A Colored Woman in a White World*, 1–2, 104; "Sketch of the Life of Mary Church Terrell," b. 1, 2, MCTP, HU-MSRC; Stewart, *Portia*, 8; Gerda Lerner, *The Grimké Sisters of South Carolina* (New York: Schocken Books, 1971), 359–61; Angelina Grimké, "A Biographical Sketch of Archibald H. Grimké," b. 1, Archibald Grimké Papers, HU-MSRC; and Brenda Stevenson, ed., *The Journals of Charlotte Forten Grimké* (New York: Oxford University Press, 1988). Details on Margaret Murray Washington's activities are available throughout Cynthia Neverdon-Morton, *Afro-American Women of the South and the Advancement of the Race, 1895–1925* (Knoxville: University of Tennessee Press, 1989), and in Elisabeth Lasch-Quinn, *Black Neighbors: Race and the Limits of Reform in the American Settlement House Movement, 1890–1945* (Chapel Hill: University of North Carolina Press, 1993).

65. Mabel Staupers, interview transcript, MEC-BNA, 2–3; Pauletta Bracey, "Charlemae Hill Rollins and Her Peers," *Public Libraries* 21 (1982): 104; Miriam Matthews, interview transcript, RC-BWOHP, 2–6; Joyce Cooper Arkhurst, interview, FUL-BOHP; "Charlemae Hill Rollins" (obituary), Chicago *Defender*, *Sun-Times*, and *Tribune*, February 7, 1979, Charlemae H. Rollins Papers, NCCU-BLA. The term "exodusters" is taken from Nell Painter, *Exodusters: Black Migration to Kansas after Reconstruction* (New York: Alfred A. Knopf, 1976).

66. Fields, *Lemon Swamp*, xv. *Lemon Swamp* is the memoir of Karen Fields's grandmother, Mamie Garvin Fields, a South Carolina schoolteacher. Suggesting that this type of socialization continued significantly beyond the 1930s, see Jim Zook, "For Stanford Provost, a New Pinnacle,"

Chronicle of Higher Education, September 29, 1993, A5. The subject of this article, Condoleezza Rice, former special assistant to the president of the United States and currently provost at Stanford University, notes, "My parents somehow convinced me that I could be President of the United States, even though I couldn't have a hamburger at Woolworth's."

Chapter Two

1. Beulah Shepard Hester, interview by Felicia Bowens Anderson, RC-BWOHP, 2.

2. Mamie Garvin Fields with Karen Fields, in *Lemon Swamp and Other Places; A Carolina Memoir* (New York: Free Press, 1983), 197, explained why her women's club built a home for girls by saying, "We all could see that we had a responsibility for those girls: they were the daughters of our community coming up."

The idea of community as process I owe to Elsa Barkley Brown, " 'Not alone to build this pile of bricks': Institution Building and Community in Richmond, Virginia," paper presented at the Age of Booker T. Washington Conference, University of Maryland, College Park, May 3, 1990. Aspects of my definition of community are also based on ideas discussed in Jessie Bernard, *American Community Behavior,* rev. ed. (New York: Holt, Rinehart and Winston, 1962); Clarke E. Cochran, *Character, Community and Politics* (University: University of Alabama Press, 1982), 36–59; Thomas Bender, *Community and Social Change in America* (New Brunswick, N.J.: Rutgers University Press, 1978), 7; and Robert Bellah, Richard Madsen, William M. Sullivan, Ann Swindler, and Steven M. Tipton, *Habits of the Heart: Middle America Observed* (London: Hutchinson, 1985). Also useful were Robert Booth Fowler, *The Dance with Community: The Contemporary Debate in American Political Thought* (Lawrence: University Press of Kansas, 1991); and Gerald Sorin, *The Nurturing Neighborhood: The Brownsville Boys Club and Jewish Community in Urban America, 1940–1990* (New York: New York University Press, 1990). Edward Magdol, in *A Right to the Land: Essays on the Freedmen's Community* (Westport, Conn.: Greenwood Press, 1977), 221, describes the postemancipation community of freed people eloquently: "Without a space of their own, without full free status, slaves created a community not so much of place but of feeling, thought, and action." And see Thomas F. Armstrong, "The Building of a Black Church: Community in Post Civil War Liberty County, Georgia," *Georgia Historical Quarterly* 66 (1982): 346–67. Armstrong explores an aspect of community building "where more than simple building construction is at work." He characterizes community building also as social interaction that reflects and yields interdependence and cooperation.

3. Although I have used the term slightly differently, the idea of communion is discussed in detail in Cochran, *Character, Community and Politics.*

4. Fields, *Lemon Swamp,* xiv.

5. John W. Davis, "Platform for Teachers in Colored Schools," *Bulletin* 12 (1931): 5, 24; Norma Elizabeth Boyd, interview by A. Lillian Thompson, RC-BWOHP, 8. Also see Registrar [of Tuskegee Institute] to Mr. and Mrs. L. P. Harper, May 8, 1920, b. 8, RRM-SC, TUA, which reads in part, "I am sure you can understand that we felt quite at home there with you, among classmates and friends, and yet I dare say that no one can fully appreciate how much it means for one who is traveling about when he can get into such a comfortable home as yours. . . . When you are in Tuskegee our homes are open to you." Mary Church Terrell regularly stayed in private homes rather than hotels when she traveled as a lecturer. She sent the addresses of some of these homes to her husband in Mary Church Terrell to Robert H. Terrell, October 27, 1912, r. 2, MCT-LC.

6. Isaac Fisher to Constance Fisher, October 1, 1936, b. 15, Constance Fisher Papers, TUA. The migration pattern with intermittent stops that Norma Boyd's family helped to facilitate has been well documented for African Americans moving toward cities or the North during the first half of the twentieth century. Peter Gottlieb, *Making Their Own Way: Southern Blacks' Migration to Pittsburgh, 1916–30* (Urbana: University of Illinois Press, 1987), 43–46, notes that this pattern was especially common among young single men.

7. On Charlotte Forten Grimké, see Brenda Stevenson, ed., *The Journals of Charlotte Forten Grimké* (New York: Oxford University Press, 1988), 3–55. Also see Ray Allen Billington, ed., *The Journal of Charlotte L. Forten: A Free Negro in the Slave Era* (New York: W. W. Norton, 1981), 7–41.

8. For a clear example of a father's views on women's/mothers' responsibilities to daughters, see Booker T. Washington to Portia M. Washington, November 17, 1904, *BTWP*, 8:137. In this letter he answered questions that Portia had addressed to him by saying: "Such matters as you write about . . . belong more properly to your mama." He did not "know about such matters" and moreover was too busy to take care of them.

Catherine Duncan, who taught school in New Mexico before becoming a rural Georgia teacher supervisor for the Rosenwald Fund, believed her early development was impeded by lack of contact with adult women. Duncan's mother died of tuberculosis when Duncan was six and her sisters were four and two. Their grandmother and two aunts volunteered to take one child each to rear, but her father refused the offer and chose to rear his daughters alone. As an adult, Duncan wrote that as much as she appreciated her father's efforts, she always "perceived many lacks in [her] development," which she could never articulate. She described the void as having to do with values transmitted through mothering. She chose to attend Fisk University because, she said, "I might get them made up during life there." And she recalled that at Fisk she did begin "to feel that I was making up some of the lacks I had felt. So many things which I would have learned from a mother, I learned from contacts with Fisk students and teachers." Catherine J. Watkins Duncan, "An Autobiography," typescript, 1–4, b. 409, RFF, FUL-SC.

9. Ruth Ann Stewart, *Portia: The Life of Portia Washington Pittman, the Daughter of Booker T. Washington* (Garden City, N.Y.: Doubleday, 1977), 17–23; Margaret James Murray to Booker T. Washington, November 1, 1891, *BTWP*, 3:177–78; Margaret Murray Washington to Booker T. Washington, July 17, 1892, r. 6, BTW-LC. In this last letter Margaret also made a pitch for continuing some of her public activities by saying, "In regard to my doing a part of my work, do not give an answer too quickly because we can talk it over when you come, and you will understand me better. And then if we cannot see our way clear, we can do something else, but I hope we both will feel the same about it. I had rather give up slowly than to give up all at once."

10. Sarah Stanley Grimké to Archibald Grimké, September 22, 1884, September 30, 1884, and January 11, 1885; quotation from April 25, 1887, b. 3, Archibald Grimké Papers, HU-MSRC (original emphasis).

11. Mary Church Terrell, *A Colored Woman in a White World* (Washington, D.C.: Randsell, 1940), 18–40. The Hunster household composition and the percentage of black population in Yellow Springs are determined from information in *Population Schedules of the Ninth Census of the U.S., 1870* Population Schedules, Ohio, Greene County, M-593, r. 1205. The Hunsters operated the only hotel in the town, and it served black and white patrons. On the black churches in Yellow Springs, see Austin McDowell Patterson, ed., *Green County, 1803–1908* (1908; rpt. Bowie, Md.: Heritage Books, 1990), 115.

12. Terrell, *A Colored Woman in a White World*, 39–45, 52–55; W. E. Bigglestone, "Oberlin College and the Negro Student, 1861–1940," *Journal of Negro History* 66 (1971): 199–209.

13. See Joseph Lee to Angelina Grimké, January 9, 1898, April 19, 1898, and October 9, 1897; and Tessa Lee to Angelina Grimké [June 10, 1908], b. 1; Archibald Grimké to Angelina Grimké, October 29, 1895, b. 3, and March 24, 1900, b. 4, Angelina Grimké Papers, HU-MSRC. On the disagreement with Mrs. Lee, see Archibald Grimké to Angelina Grimké, May 31, 1899, and June 6, 1899; and Angelina Grimké to Archibald Grimké, March 7, 1900.

14. Angelina Grimké to Archibald Grimké, July 13, 1911, b. 3, Archibald Grimké Papers, HU-MSRC; Dickson J. Bruce Jr., *Archibald Grimké: Portrait of a Black Independent* (Baton Rouge: Louisiana University Press, 1993), 179–81.

15. Bruce, *Archibald Grimké*, 43, 54; John Daniels, *In Freedom's Birthplace* (1914; rpt. New York: Arno Press, 1969), 95, 203.

16. Eunice Rivers Laurie, interview by A. Lillian Thompson, RC-BWOHP, 3. And see Juliette Dericott to Constance Fisher, October 1, 1923, b. 15, Constance Fisher Papers, TUA. In this letter Dericott tells Fisher that Annie Lee Hill, from Winston-Salem, North Carolina, is coming to Fisk, and she asks Fisher to make Hill "feel very much at home during her first days" there.

17. There are numerous examples of household restructuring that clearly related to economic needs. For example, after Jane Edna Hunter's father died in 1892, her mother sent two of her children to live with one aunt and two others to live with another aunt because she could not afford to take care of all of them. See Adrienne Lash Jones, "Jane Edna Hunter: A Case Study of Black Leadership, 1910–1956" (Ph.D. diss., Case Western Reserve University, 1983), 59–61. And there are other examples not so clearly related to economics. See Fields, *Lemon Swamp*, 1. One example that seems exclusively related to practical concerns comes from the oral history of Ophelia Settle Egypt, a Washington, D.C., social worker. When Egypt developed asthma as a child, her father took her to live with his aunt in Denver, Colorado. The rest of the children remained in Texas with their father, a widower. See Ophelia Settle Egypt interview, FUL-BOHP. And finally, families regularly joined other households temporarily, especially while they were relocating. See, for examples, Miriam Matthews, interview transcript, 3; and Eula Wellmon Dunlap, "Reminiscences," LAC, Amistad Research Center, Tulane University, New Orleans, Louisiana, [55].

18. Stewart, *Portia*, 29, 41–43, 66; Portia Washington to Booker T. Washington, June 27, 1906, *BTWP*, 9:36.

19. Stewart, *Portia*, 29–37, 41–44; On Washington's election to the Student Government Association, see Booker T. Washington to Portia Washington, February 24, 1904, r. 2, BTW-LC; on her friendships, see Portia Marshall Washington to Booker T. Washington, October 25, 1902, *BTWP*, 6:559–60. And see T. Thomas Fortune to Booker T. Washington, November 3, 1902, *BTWP*, 6:571–72; and Washington to Fortune, November 6, 1902, 6:577–78. Fortune enclosed a copy of a November 3, 1902, New York *Sun* article titled "Miss Washington's Failure," alleging that she left Wellesley because she failed her exams. The article also claimed that students at the school said her presence divided the campus into "northern" and "southern" factions. Southern white newspapers that supported Washington, including the *Montgomery Advertiser,* received the text of the *Sun* article but refused to run it. And Fortune was writing to Washington to inform him of the article penned, Fortune speculated, by "the Boston skunk" (Trotter) and to ask if Washington wanted to respond to the allegations in his (Fortune's) paper. See also "Leaving Booker T. Washington, Growing Opposition to Him among Those Who Were His Surest Friends, Assert He Does Not Live up to His Preaching, School He Advocates Not Good Enough for His Children—Educated with Whites," New York *World*, October 23, 1904, *BTWP*, 8:105–6.

20. See, for example, Portia Marshall Washington to Booker T. Washington, October 23, 1904; Portia M. Washington to Booker T. Washington, March 10, 1904; and Portia M. Washington to Booker T. Washington, n.d., r. 2, BTW-LC.

21. See Booker T. Washington to Julian LaRose Harris, October 16, 1902, *BTWP*, 6:549–50. In Booker T. Washington to Frank Hale, May 23, 1903, r. 2, BTW-LC, Washington inquired about his daughter's

chance for admission to the New England Conservatory of Music, and he added for obvious reasons, "May I beg of you that nothing be said about this correspondence where the newspapers can get hold of it, and if my daughter does enter the Conservatory, I wish as far as possible to guard against newspaper publicity."

22. "An Article about Portia Marshall Washington in the Indianapolis *Freeman*," BTWP, 6:360–63; "An Interview with Portia Marshall Washington in the Birmingham *Age-Herald*," November 23, 1901, 6:322–27; T. Thomas Fortune to Booker T. Washington, November 3, 1902, 6:571; "An Item in the New York *World*," October 23, 1904, 8:105. White administrators were equally conscious of what Portia's presence meant. Her father made a late application for her admission to Lasell Seminary for Young Women in Auburndale, Massachusetts, in 1901. He said he was willing to have her housed in an annex room, probably because her application was so late. The principal replied: "If your daughter were to become a pupil here, it would be, for her sake and for ours too, better that she should be in one of the best places in the house. . . . Do I make it clear what I mean? For instance, suppose the New York *Independent* or the *Outlook* were to (as they might easily) follow the child of so well-known parents, and to find that she had been given a room in the Annex, it might easily be construed as a slight, and this I would not think it was worth the year's attendance to permit." See C[harles C.] Bragdon to Mrs. Booker T. Washington, September 4, 1901, b. 522, BTW-LC; and Portia Marshall Washington to Booker T. Washington, September 4, 1901, *BTWP*, 6:200.

23. See Clara Stanton Jones, interview, FUL-BOHP.

24. Fields, *Lemon Swamp*, 31–32; Thelma DeWitty, interview by Esther H. Mumford, "The Supplies Are Here for the Teachers," WSA-OAHP, 26–27; Jean Blackwell Hutson, interview, FUL-BOHP.

25. Stewart, *Portia*, 52; Booker T. Washington to Portia Marshall Washington, March 12, 1904, *BTWP*, 7:466.

26. Portia first asked to go to Wellesley and to stay in a boarding-house she had previously visited. See Portia Washington to Booker T. Washington, March 10, 1904. She accepted her father's decision that she spend the time with the Moores on March 13, 1904, r. 2, BTW-LC.

27. See for examples Booker T. Washington to Portia M. Washington, June 19, 1906, and n.d., r. 2, BTW-LC; Booker T. Washington to Portia, July 19, 1906, *BTWP*, 9:44.

28. Julia Smith, interview by Cheryl Gilkes, RC-BWOHP, 57–58; Frances Grant, interview by Maurine Rothschild, RC-BWOHP, 7. When Sarah and Elizabeth Delany went to New York during the 1920s to work and go to college, the family with whom they boarded was not altogether hospitable. The Delany sisters had to take their meals in the kitchen rather than in the dining room with the family. Still, the Scotts took them in "as a favor to Mrs. Russell." Mrs. Russell was a former student of Sarah and Elizabeth's mother. See Sarah and A. Elizabeth Delany with Amy Hill Hearth, *Having Our Say: The Delany Sisters' First 100 Years* (New

York: Kodansha International, 1993), 100–1. For evidence of similar patterns in accommodations persisting into the women's adulthood and into the mid-twentieth century, Thelma Dewitty, her husband, and many other travelers and newcomers to Seattle roomed, for a time, in the spacious home of J. Arnell and David Hickey during the 1940s. Sadie Delaney opened her Tuskegee home to "friends of friends" in the 1950s. An intermediary who once arranged such accommodations wrote to her from his California home in the 1950s: "We had a letter from Lex and Katheryn Cox telling of the wonderful visit they had with you in your beautiful home. It seems that all our close friends there in Tuskegee found time to be nice to them, but they were right at home when they were with you." See Dewitty, interview transcript, WSA-OAHP, 26–27; "F. L." to Sadie P. Delaney, May 25, 1950, vol. 2, Sadie Peterson Delaney Papers, Schomburg Center. Volume numbers represent Delaney's organization of her papers in scrapbooks.

29. I have borrowed the expression "friends of friends" from Jeremy Bossevain, *Friends of Friends: Networks, Manipulations, and Coalitions* (New York: Oxford University Press, 1979), but in this instance I am attempting to describe a phenomenon different from "networks," a concept that cannot fully explain what these women experienced. For a discussion on "networks" in which some of these women operated, see Stephanie J. Shaw, "Black Women in White Collars: A Social History of Lower-Level Professional Black Women Workers, 1870–1954" (Ph.D. diss., Ohio State University, 1988), 389–448.

30. See Bellah et al., *Habits of the Heart*, 71–75. The authors write: "Whereas a community attempts to be an inclusive whole, celebrating the interdependence of public and private life and the different callings of all, lifestyle is fundamentally segmental and celebrates the narcissism of similarity. It usually explicitly involves a contrast with others who 'do not share one's lifestyle.' For this reason, we speak not of lifestyle communities, though they are often called such in contemporary usage, but of lifestyle enclaves" (72). If one accepts this definition, the best example of "lifestyle enclaves" among these women were the black resorts. They included Arundell, Maryland (Highland Beach on Chesapeake Bay), where Mary Church Terrell and Julia Smith's father owned summer homes, Sag Harbor on Long Island, New York, Opeqoun in West Virginia, and Oak Bluffs on Martha's Vineyard in Massachusetts. Many of the oldest women in this study vacationed at these resorts as children and adults; they or their parents sometimes owned property there. And some of the resorts, most notably Oak Bluffs, remain thriving gathering places—lifestyle enclaves—for well-to-do African Americans. A recent article suggests that these enclaves also function to socialize children for high achievement. See Jill Nelson, "An Island on An Island: Cherishing a Special Portrait of Martha's Vineyard," *New York Times*, August 23, 1993, 84. My thanks to Susan Hartmann for providing a copy of this article.

31. The best-known interpretation of the separation of the classes is E. Franklin Frazier, *Black Bourgeoisie: The Rise of a New Middle Class in*

the United States (New York: Free Press, 1957). A similar, though brief, account is provided in Langston Hughes, "Our Wonderful Society: Washington," *Opportunity*, August 1927, 226–27.

32. W. O. Brown, "The Nature of Race Consciousness," *Social Forces* 10 (1931): 90–97. Brown's conclusion is all the more interesting when one considers it in light of the provocative recent publications by southern historian Barbara Jeanne Fields and Southeast Asia specialist Benedict Anderson on the historical constructions of race and nationalism, respectively. See Fields, "Slavery, Race, and Ideology in the United States of America," *New Left Review* 181 (1990): 95–118; and Anderson, *Imagined Communities: Reflections on the Origin and Spread of Nationalism*, rev. ed. (London: Verso, 1991).

33. For a very explicit example of this type of encouragement in one woman's life, see Leila Gaston Rhodes, "A Critical Analysis of the Career Backgrounds of Selected Black Female Librarians" (Ph.D. diss., Florida State University, 1975), 63. In this instance Rhodes quotes librarian/educator Eliza A. Gleason (Fisk, 1930; Illinois, 1931; Columbia, 1936; Chicago, 1940) as saying: "I came from a more or less affluent background, though we were never allowed to think of ourselves as affluent. There was no lack of money in my youth. Neither was there any flaunting of it, and we were made aware of the fact that you had a responsibility to your fellowman." And see chapter 1, note 60. James Oliver Horton, in *Free People of Color: Inside the African American Community* (Washington, D.C.: Smithsonian Institution Press, 1993), also describes the processes of bridging social divisions.

34. "Mississippi Negroes Petition Legislature to Redress Wrongs," Baltimore *Herald*, March 30, 1920, r. 11, and "Negroes Petition General Assembly," *Columbia (S.C.) States*, January 22, 1919, r. 9, TNCS. On Mississippi voter registration statistics, see Paul Lewinson, *Race, Class, and Party: A History of Negro Suffrage and White Politics in the South* (London: Oxford University Press, 1932), 219. In 1900, when Mississippi's black population reached nearly one million (970,630), only 1,264 African Americans were registered to vote. And of course this was an entirely male voting population. See Buford Satcher, *Blacks in Mississippi Politics, 1865–1900* (Washington, D.C.: University Press of America, 1978), 209. Black residents of Newport News, Virginia, petitioned their city council in 1928 for the employment of black registered nurses to work with the more than 15,000 black residents of the city. See "Petition for Employment of Registered Nurses," *Journal and Guide*, November [?], [1928], r. 31, TNCS. Also note that both Septima Clark and Mamie Garvin Fields helped to collect signatures for the South Carolina petition. Clark even organized her students as canvassers.

35. See "The Bond Issue and the Negro," Atlanta *Independent*, December 26, 1914, and "A Campaign for Fair Play," New York *Age*, October 23, 1913, r. 2; "Criminal Discrimination," Atlanta *Independent*, n.d., r. 6; and "4000 Negro Children Are Barred from School by

Crowded Conditions," Atlanta *Constitution*, March 26, 1915, r. 4, TNCS; "Colored Women and School Improvement in Atlanta," *AUB*, ser. 2, October 11, 1912; "Social Betterment in Negro Communities," *AUB*, ser. 2, January 1913. Additional details about this campaign are available in Jacqueline A. Rouse, "Atlanta's African-American Women's Attack on Segregation, 1900–1920," in *Gender, Class, Race, and Reform in the Progressive Era*, ed. Noralee Frankel and Nancy S. Dye (Lexington: University Press of Kentucky, 1991), 10–23. Women in Atlanta, including members of the Neighborhood Union (discussed in chapter 6), formed the Women's Civic and Social Improvement Committee during the 1910s and went to the school board "as taxpayers" protesting double sessions, overcrowding, lack of recreational facilities, and so on. See L. B. Hope to "Gentlemen," August 19, 1913, b. 1, NUC-WL. Similar circumstances existed in Savannah between 1912 and the 1920s, and black community petition drives forced the local school board in 1915 to add classes in black schools. Unfortunately, the very year after classes were added, black Savannah schools also went to double sessions. See "Two Additional Grades Open at Cuyler St. School Monday," Savannah *Tribune*, [?] 1915, and "1,500 Negro Children Unable to Get Seats in Public Schools," Savannah *Tribune*, October 19, 1915, r. 4; "Can't Get Seats in Public Schools" (source not cited), October 4, 1913, r. 2; and "700 Unaccommodated Negro Children to Get Seats in Public Schools," Savannah *Tribune*, October 14, 1916, r. 5, TNCS. The problems were still evident in the 1920s. See "Wretched Conditions Found to Obtain in City Public Schools, Savannah *Tribune*, November 10, 1922, r. 15. Note that the Atlanta *Constitution*, which reported the number of black children closed out of school, is a white-owned paper. And the Savannah *Tribune* was Georgia's first black newspaper.

36. See "Incompetency and Cheap Politics Characterized the Management of Our Schools; Receivership the Remedy," Atlanta *Independent*, February 10, 1927, r. 28, TNCS. The article strongly accused the black community of doing nothing while conditions worsened. Further documentation of the school board's actions after the public pressure may be found in George W. Powell and Willis A. Sutton to Edwin R. Embree, July 18, 1928, b. 171, RFF, FUL-SC. See also Sutton to Embree, March 27, 1929; George R. Arthur to Sutton, September 29, 1928; Sutton to Arthur, October 15, 1928; Alfred K. Stern to Sutton, October 25, 1929; and H. Reid Hunter to Stern, November 13, 1929.

37. "Board Is Told of Poor Facilities in Race Schools," Atlanta *Daily World*, December 13, 1944, r. 87, TNCS. It is not clear exactly when this organization was formed. The article suggests that it was not a newly created group. It might, in fact, have been created during the late 1920s at the urging of the *Independent*.

38. James R. Grossman gives this number for the Chicago *Defender*'s circulation in *Land of Hope: Chicago, Black Southerners, and the Great Migration* (Chicago: University of Chicago Press, 1989), 79–80. According

to Roland E. Wolseley in *The Black Press, U.S.A.*, 2d ed. (Ames: Iowa State University Press, 1992), 54, the *Defender* reached a circulation of 230,000 in 1915. See also Henry Lewis Suggs, *The Black Press in the South, 1865–1979* (Westport, Conn.: Greenwood Press, 1983), and idem, *P. B. Young, Newspaperman: Race, Politics, and Journalism in the New South, 1910–1962* (Charlottesville: University Press of Virginia, 1988); Julius Thompson, *The Black Press in Mississippi, 1865–1985* (Gainesville: University Press of Florida, 1993); and Gayle K. Bernardi and Thomas W. Segady, "The Development of African-American Newspapers in the American West: A Sociohistorical Perspective," *Journal of Negro History* 75 (1990): 96–111. On the Associated Negro Press, see Lawrence D. Hogan, *A Black National News Service: The Associated Negro Press and Claude Barnett, 1919–1945* (Rutherford, N.J.: Fairleigh Dickinson University Press, 1984). Also see Frankie P. Hutton, "The Antebellum Black Press and the Quest for Inclusion: Ideals and Messages of Social Responsibility, Morality, Class, and Style" (Ph.D. diss., Rutgers University, 1990).

39. Frazier, *Black Bourgeoisie*, 146–61; quotation on 146.

40. Minnesota social worker Ethel Ray Nance helped publish a local magazine called *Timely Digest*, which also reprinted Associated Negro Press stories "to let [the black community in Minneapolis] know what was going on outside" the state. Ethel Ray Nance, interview transcript, AMD-MHS, 19.

41. "Reports from Tag Day Sales," Norfolk *Journal and Guide*, April 10, 1915, r. 4, TNCS. In this instance the amounts raised ranged from $20.24 in Big Stone Gap, Virginia, to $380.39 in Petersburg. And see "Negroes Raise School Fund; Draw Praise," Tampa *Tribune*, May 5, 1933, r. 43; "Ahoskie Negro High School Gets $974," Gatesville (N.C.) *Index*, November 2, 1938, r. 57; and "Mississippians Erect Schoolhouse with No County, State Aid," Kansas City (Mo.) *Call*, February 4, 1938, r. 57. For other examples of community work, see "Memphis Teachers Establish Record for Community Work," Pittsburgh *Courier*, January [?] 1941, r. 72; "Schools Built by Negroes," Milwaukee *Free Press*, September 10, 1914, r. 2; "Stanley Colored People in Drive to Aid Orphans," Albemarle, N.C. *News and Press*, November 15, 1940, r. 66; "Century Club Recital for Tuberculosis Fund," Wilmington *Journal*, n.d., r. 6; and "A Hospital for Negroes," Pittsburgh *Post*, May 27, 1918, r. 7. The *Journal and Guide, Call*, and *Journal* are black-owned papers. Several of the others cited here and below are not.

42. For examples related to paying nurses' salaries, see "Welcome Nurse Tuesday Night," Spartanburg (S.C.) [?], May 11, 1924, r. 21; and "Tuberculosis Nurse Giving Splendid Service," Dallas *Express*, June 23, 1923, r. 18, TNCS. In the former article, the local black Red Cross branch raised enough money to hire nurse Janice Jones for three months. They then established a subscription program in order to pay her salary permanently. The latter article describes the way Ruth Chambers, a tuberculosis nurse in the 1920s, came to be hired. The Dallas Tuberculosis Association paid half of her salary, "and the other half is being

paid by the . . . Excelsior Mutual Benefit Association, Dagie Mutual Benefit Association, Lone Star Mutual Benefit Association, Mississippi Life Insurance Company, Dr. R. T. Hamilton, Dr. C. L. Morgan, Golden Chain of the World." The Colored Women's Federation coordinated the entire effort. For an example of a library's being funded this way, see "Negro Branch Library," *Christian Science Monitor,* August 13, 1918, and "Race in Birmingham to Have Own [Library], Cleveland *Advocate,* August 10, 1918, r. 7.

See also "A New Colored Hospital," Norfolk *Journal and Guide,* October 24, 1914, r. 2; and Wilson A. Drake, "New Hospital Now Open," Norfolk *Journal and Guide,* January 16, 1915, r. 4, TNCS. In the latter instance, black people raised $10,000 to build the hospital, and the article solicited from "the friends of the hospital . . . linen, crockery, glassware, . . . towels, sheets, pillowcases, napkins, cups and saucers, water glasses, knives, forks, spoons, etc."

43. "Pleasant Grove Community," Tuskegee *Messenger,* October 31, 1913, and "St. Louisians Pledge Big Sum and Pay in $38,000 within a Week for Colored Orphan Home," Pittsburgh *American,* March 28, 1924, r. 20; "Teachers and Pupils Build $20,000 School from Salvaged Bricks," Pittsburgh *Courier,* January 29, 1927, r. 27; "Appoint New Negro Nurse," Winston-Salem *Sentinel,* February 26, 1937, r. 56; and "Reports from Tag Day Sales," Norfolk *Journal and Guide,* April 10, 1915, r. 4, TNCS. The paper identified as the Pittsburgh *American* in the Tuskegee clipping file was probably the Pittsburgh *Afro-American.*

An article printed in the Montgomery *Times* discussed the building of a two-room school in Notasulga, Alabama. The writer suggested that not all those who participated had building skills, but that "one [person] sawed, another drove nails, and others did work assigned." See "Negroes of Rural Districts of Alabama Building School-Houses," May 26, 1913, r. 2.

44. "Getting the Cash," Dublin (Ga.) *Courier,* September 14, 1931, r. 38, TNCS.

45. For a specific example of some organizers' demonstrating this principle, when J. H. Holloway, a Charleston minister, issued an invitation to select "friends of humanity" to attend a 1903 meeting to discuss a plan for supporting the elderly in the community who had spent their lives working for others and had failed to prepare for their own old age, he wrote, "I sincerely invite the friends who responded substantially [to an earlier call] and those who gave their moral support, and all friends who will and feel that they can contribute, at least, their presence to forward a worthy undertaking to meet me." See J. H. Holloway to the Friends of Humanity, April 28, 1903, Brown Fellowship Society Scrapbook, RSSL-SC. For a scholarly example of applying the theory of valuing different contributions equally, see Elsa Barkley Brown, "African-American Women's Quilting: A Framework for Conceptualizing and Teaching African-American Women's History," *Signs* 14 (1989): 912–20.

46. This process was repeated over and over during the civil rights movement. JoAnn Gibson Robinson, a member of the Montgomery, Alabama, Women's Political Council that started the Montgomery bus boycott, put it this way: "It was said the Ph.D.'s and the no d's got together and knew each other as brothers. . . . Each person bore his part of the burden." JoAnn Gibson Robinson, *The Montgomery Bus Boycott and the Women Who Started It* (Knoxville: University of Tennessee Press, 1987), 60.

47. "Teachers and Pupils Build $20,000 School from Salvaged Bricks" (cited above, n. 43). The construction of a black public hospital in Louisiana began when about three hundred black craftsmen (carpenters, masons, plasterers, and electricians) met in the longshoremen's hall in 1917 and pledged one or two days of labor each to the effort. Indicative of everyone's involvement in the process, one article noted that a Mrs. Poupart's twin daughters, Marcell and Yvone, had penny parties and raised $52.58. See "Negroes Aiding Nurses' Home," New Orleans, Louisiana, *Picayune*, April 29, 1918, r. 7; and [title not available], New Orleans *Times Picayune*, November 10, 1917, r. 6, TNCS. These newspaper titles are reported in TNCS. They might be incorrect. The New Orleans *Times* and the *Daily Picayune* might be the actual papers referred to.

48. Terrell, *A Colored Woman in a White World*, 7. Also see "Community, Class and Race in the Memphis Riot of 1866," *Journal of Social History* 18 (1984): 233–46; and Kevin R. Hardwick, " 'Your Old Father Abe Lincoln is Dead and Damned': Black Soldiers and the Memphis Race Riot of 1866," *Journal of Social History* 27 (1993): 109–28. Both of these articles note the involvement of Irish-Americans in the violence but also argue that white rioters represented a diverse group in terms of ethnic and class background.

49. Eunice Laurie, interview transcript, RC-BWOHP, 4–5; Lucy Mitchell, interview transcript, RC-BWOHP, 14. For a scholarly discussion of black "kinship clusters," which Lucy Mitchell's multiple-household extended family represents, see Shepard Krech III, "Black Family Organization in the Nineteenth Century: An Ethnological Perspective," *Journal of Interdisciplinary History* 12 (1982): 429–54.

50. In Mrs. Taylor to Portia Washington, October 7, 1895, BTW-LC, r. 2, Taylor advised Portia to expect a letter from W. H. Baldwin, owner of the railroad, about the attack. The details of the letter reminded Portia that "he [the conductor] struck me in the face—cutting my lip through and kicked me several times because I did not get up to let him turn my seat over so quickly as he thought I should." In order to reassure Portia, the writer added: "Mr. Baldwin has already discharged the conductor from the service of the Company, so he will not have the opportunity of fighting passengers any more." (Probably Mrs. Taylor wrote the letter for the assault victim.)

51. Terrell, *A Colored Woman in a White World*, 46–47.

52. James M. McPherson in *The Abolitionist Legacy: From Reconstruction to the NAACP* (Princeton: Princeton University Press, 1977). On Ober-

lin College specifically, see W. E. Bigglestone, "Oberlin College and the Negro Student, 1865–1940," *Journal of Negro History* 56 (1971): 199–209. In this article Bigglestone maintains that when Mary Church Terrell brought her daughters, Phyllis and Mary, to enroll in Oberlin in the fall of 1913 and decided to spend the winter there, the dean of students was worried about her possible reaction to the significant changes in the atmosphere of the school since she left almost thirty years earlier. By this time the school had quotas limiting black student enrollment, and black and white student contact was controlled through dorm assignments. The next year there would be four boardinghouses in Oberlin exclusively for black women. Terrell tried hard (unsuccessfully) to have both of her daughters housed in a dormitory (rather than one of the segregated boardinghouses). See especially Mary Church Terrell to Miss Fitch, October 1913, Mary Church Terrell File, OCAR.

53. Fields, *Lemon Swamp*, 43.

54. Lula Catherine Jordan McNeil, interview transcript, MEC-BNA, 6; Jones, "Jane Edna Hunter," 63–65. A black Louisville, Kentucky, teacher/missionary arranged for Susan St. Clair Minor to attend Hampton beginning in 1919 on condition that "sometime in [her] lifetime, . . . [she] would pay back the amount of money that had been invested in [her]." Minor declined the offer because she had already decided to go to Louisville Normal School, and her mother had bought her books. (Minor suggested this was a major investment by adding that they cost five dollars.) She also noted that the Hampton program was longer than the one at Louisville, and the incidental expenses—related to travel, for example—were beyond her parents' means. She also thought that she might have refused the offer simply because she was afraid of the post-graduation financial obligation. She explained, "we were very poor." Susan St. Clair Minor, interview transcript, OHC-UL, 3–5, 8.

55. On the community's generally claiming the success of an individual and on individuals' acknowledging a collective accomplishment, see "For the Adornment of Her Race Jennie Porter Wins an M.A. Degree and Now Strives to Be a Doctor of Philosophy," Pittsburgh *Courier*, June 20, 1925, r. 22, TNCS. The writer noted that Porter's success thus far represented "a decoration for her race" and that she was continuing her studies "so that what honors she gains may reflect to the good of her people." On her completion of the Ph.D., see "First Race Woman Receives PhD Degree from the Univ. of Cincinnati," *East Tennessee News*, July 5, 1928, r. 31.

56. Lucy Mitchell, interview transcript, RC-BWOHP, 10; "Miss Bethune's Daytona School a 'Civilizer,'" *New York Times*, n.d., and Harrison Rhodes to Editor of the New York *Tribune* ("Funds for Negro Education"), New York *Tribune*, February 9, 1916, r. 5; and "Friends of Dr. Mary Mcleod Bethune Give over $5000 to College on Her Birthday," New York *Age*, July 22, 1929, r. 61, TNCS.

57. Dunlap, "Reminiscences," LAC, [8, 30–31].

58. E. J. Josey and Ann Allen Shockley, eds., *Handbook of Black Li-*

brarianship (Littleton, Colo.: Libraries Unlimited, 1977), 32–33; Ethel Evangeline Martin, "Susan Dart Butler: Pioneer Librarian" (M.S. thesis, Atlanta University School of Library Service, 1959), 7–8. Ethel Ray Nance's father also opened his home to neighbors who wanted to read his books. But he did not allow them to remove the books from his home. See Ethel Ray Nance, interview transcript, AMD-MHS, 11–12. Records indicate that John Dart was not the only person in Charleston interested in such an undertaking. In S. H. Jenkins to Rev. J. H. Holloway, September 20, 1906, Brown Fellowship Society Scrapbook, RSSL-SC, Jenkins, acting manager of the Charleston *Messenger,* addressed a letter to friends "interested in the progress of the colored citizens of Charleston and . . . willing to assist and cooperate with other enterprising men of the race in organizing a free library for our boys and girls." And in the same collection, see G. S. Dickerman to J. H. Holloway, July 23, 1905, in which Dickerman (field agent and associate secretary of the Southern Education Board) responded to a letter from Holloway by providing information on starting a library. This was an effort to formalize John Dart's earlier efforts of the 1890s. Apparently they were not wholly successful, for the first permanent library was the one started by Susan Dart Butler and supported by black Charleston clubwomen during the 1920s. In this context of community, and especially in light of my claim that class and color might contribute to differences within the community but that manifestations of the meaning of the differences were equally, if not more, important, it is also useful to note that the Brown Fellowship Society, a group of mulattoes, educated men mostly of West Indies origin, supported the local black "public" school while also maintaining a private school for their own children. See Janet Duitsman Cornelius, *When I Can Read My Title Clear: Literacy, Slavery, and Religion in the Antebellum South* (Columbia: University of South Carolina Press, 1991), 81; and Robert L. Harris Jr., "Charleston's Free Afro-American Elite: The Brown Fellowship Society and The Humane Brotherhood," *South Carolina Historical Magazine* 82 (1981): 278–310.

59. Dunlap, "Reminiscences," LAC, [7, 76–77]; "Charlemae Hill Rollins," Chicago *Defender,* February 7, 1979, Charlemae Hill Rollins Papers, NCCU-BLA; Beulah Shepard Hester, interview transcript, RC-BWOHP, 2, 8–9; Delany, *Having Our Say,* 45–47.

60. Beulah Hester, interview transcript, RC-BWOHP, 18; Dunlap, "Reminiscences," LAC, [12–13]; Sarah Webb Rice, *He Included Me: The Autobiography of Sarah Rice,* ed. Louise Westling (Athens: University of Georgia Press, 1989), 4–5; Delany, *Having Our Say,* 51.

61. Although nineteenth-century defenders of racism used the expression "consciousness of kind" in "scholarly" justifications for white separatism, twentieth-century "liberal" sociologists used it to explain the community consciousness they saw among African Americans. See, for an example of the latter, Theodore Abel, "The Significance of the Concept of Consciousness of Kind," *Social Forces* 9 (1930): 1–10. On community consciousness, see note 2 above.

Chapter Three

1. Florence Lattimore, *A Palace of Delight (The Locust Street Settlement for Negroes at Hampton, Virginia)* (Hampton: Press of the Hampton Normal and Agricultural Institute, 1915), 4.

2. Tullia Kay Brown Hamilton, "The National Association of Colored Women, 1896–1920" (Ph.D. diss., Emory University, 1978), 140; Sadie Iola Daniels, *Women Builders* (Washington, D.C.: Associated Publishers, 1931), 54–55.

3. Lattimore, *Palace of Delight*, 4–7. Barrett's point is well taken. But even as a student, she should have anticipated working on Sundays after graduation too, for many day school teachers taught Sunday school and Sabbath school. Also, they regularly felt obliged to attend several church services on Sundays, depending on the affiliations of their students. One Atlanta University graduate went to Methodist Sunday school in the morning and Baptist church and Sunday school in the afternoon because of her role in the community and the denominational associations of her students. See Edgar H. Webster, "Our Students' Summer Work," *AUB*, October 1889, 3–4. Pauli Murray's Aunt Pauline (Pauline Fitzgerald Dame), a North Carolina schoolteacher, went to the church attended by most of her students in the evening and her own family church in the morning. See Pauli Murray, *Song in a Weary Throat: An American Pilgrimage* (New York: Harper and Row, 1985), 15.

4. In spite of its founder's connection to the American Missionary Association, the extent of Howard's support from missionary societies was a full-time matron for Minor Hall (the girls' dormitory) provided by the Women's Home Mission Association of Boston. See *Catalog of the Officers and Students of Howard University, 1881–82*, 23.

I have characterized Oberlin as an evangelical school because at the time most of my subjects attended (before and around the turn of the century), its mission was clearly evangelical. Oberlin did, however, begin to move toward a social gospel orientation by the end of the century and was more fully a progressive institution by the 1920s when Beulah Whitby enrolled. On Oberlin's modernization, see John Barnard, *From Evangelicalism to Progressivism at Oberlin College, 1866–1917* (Columbus: Ohio State University Press, 1969).

Spelman and Hartshorn were heavily supported by the Woman's American Baptist Home Mission Society. The American Missionary Association (AMA) supported Talladega and Fisk Universities and Hampton Institute. And though Atlanta and Howard Universities were independent, Howard's first president and many of its early trustees maintained close ties to the AMA. Howard University was founded by O. O. Howard, a well-known Congregationalist.

Also note that although Spelman was founded as the Atlanta Woman's Baptist Female Seminary in 1881, became Spelman Seminary in 1884, and changed its name to Spelman College in 1924 (the first college degree was conferred in 1901), I will be referring to it as Spelman College throughout this chapter. I will also use "Hampton Institute" and "Tuskegee Institute" rather than their original or current names.

5. James H. Fairchild, *Oberlin: The Colony and the College, 1833–1883* (1883; rpt. New York: Garland, 1984), 12–31, 50–75, 173–86; Rev. H. Lyman, "'Lane Seminary Rebels,'" in *The Oberlin Jubilee, 1833–1883*, ed. W. G. Ballantine (Oberlin, Ohio: E. J. Goodrich, 1883), 61–69. The first circulars announcing the school's program suggest that although the school was coeducational at its founding, there was some idea that the girls' school would eventually be separated. And see W. E. Bigglestone, "Oberlin College and the Negro Student, 1865–1940," *Journal of Negro History* 56 (1971): 199–209.

6. Evelyn Brooks Higginbotham, *Righteous Discontent: The Women's Movement in the Black Baptist Church, 1880–1920* (Cambridge: Harvard University Press, 1993), 28–29, 36.

7. Tefft's receiving her B.A. degree is recorded in the *Wellesley College Calendar, 1890–91,* 56. The calendar lists her, however, as Mary Field Taft.

8. *Catalog of Spelman College, 1929–30,* 14–20. Of seven new teachers who started working at Atlanta University in 1911, two were Wellesley graduates, one came from Oberlin, and one came from Mount Holyoke. See "The New Teachers," *AUB,* ser. 2, October 1911, 17–18.

9. More profoundly suggesting the importance of Oberlin College to black professional women's education during these years, Bettina Aptheker notes that of the (only) 114 black women attorneys and physicians who had graduated from nonblack colleges by 1910, 66 were from Oberlin. See "Quest for Dignity: Black Women in the Professions, 1865–1900," in *Woman's Legacy* (Amherst: University of Massachusetts Press, 1982), 92. Also see Ellen N. Lawson and Marlene Merrill, "Antebellum Black Coeds at Oberlin College," in *Black Women in United States History*, ed. Darlene Clark Hine (Brooklyn: Carlson, 1990), 15:827–35.

10. James M. McPherson, *The Abolitionist Legacy: From Reconstruction to the NAACP* (Princeton: Princeton University Press, 1975), 13–161 (quotations on pp. 13, 37); C. L. Woodworth, "The Duty of the North to the South, Especially to the Colored People," *AM,* January 1876, 11–16. On some of the missionary teachers, see Jacqueline Jones, *Soldiers of Light and Love: Northern Teachers and Georgia Blacks, 1865–1873* (Chapel Hill: University of North Carolina Press, 1980). Note that although McPherson refers to these teachers as neoabolitionists, they continued to call themselves abolitionists, even into the twentieth century. Therefore I have chosen to use that term.

11. Freed people had formed an education society and started a school several years before the AMA became involved in efforts to build Talladega College in 1867. In Virginia, the Reverend A. Binga Jr. encouraged the American Baptist Home Mission Society to start a school "where the young women of my race in this state may secure a higher education, without which our social condition cannot be permanently improved." They subsequently helped to found Hartshorn Memorial College. See A.

Binga Jr., "The Social Condition of the Freedman of the South," *HMM*, March [?] 1880, 41–42; Maxine D. Jones and Joe M. Richardson, *Talladega College: The First Century* (Tuscaloosa: University of Alabama Press, 1990), 1–3; James D. Anderson, "Ex-Slaves and the Rise of Universal Education in the South, 1860–1880," in *The Education of Blacks in the South, 1860–1935* (Chapel Hill: University of North Carolina Press, 1988), 4–32. All articles cited in this chapter from the *Home Mission Monthly* and some of the Woman's American Baptist Home Mission Society (WABHMS) annual reports were graciously provided by Elsa Barkley Brown.

12. Quotations from Malcolm MacVicar in "Report of Superintendent of Education," 231–32, copy provided by Elsa Barkley Brown. For a detailed example of the ABHMS's egalitarian views on the education of African Americans, also see T. J. Morgan, "What the American Baptist Home Mission Society Has Done for Negroes," *SM*, March 1901, 2–3, 7; and "Why Stress Higher Education," *AM*, April 1910, 24.

13. "Fisk University," *AM*, June 1900, 16; George E. Hall, "Report of the Committee on Southern Educational Work," *AM*, January 1902, 36–39; J. G. Merrill, "Fisk University after Thirty-nine Years," *AM*, June 1904, 165; Solitude, Jr. [pseud.], "The How," *FH*, March 1885, 2. Also see C. L. Woodworth, "The Duty of the North to the South"; and "Forty-first Annual Report of the Executive Committee: General Survey," *AM*, November 1887, 313–26.

14. Most of the teachers during the early years of the schools' histories (again, except at Tuskegee) were white. For example, during the 1894–95 school year, only one of Fisk's 31 faculty members was black. Talladega had one out of 30; Hartshorn, a much younger school, had 2 of 9; Spelman, 4 of 38; and Atlanta University, none of 16. By the 1914–15 school year there was some notable difference. At Fisk, there were 14 of 45; at Talladega, 10 of 41; at Hartshorn, 3 of 15; at Spelman, 3 of 51; and at Atlanta University, 4 of 33. Howard stands out for having 21 black faculty members out of 61 in 1894–95 and 73 of 106 in 1914–15. See McPherson, *Abolitionist Legacy*, 410–15.

15. "The Address of H. S. De Forest–Talladega," *AM*, December 1891, 452; Amory H. Bradford, "Our Most Imperative Missionary Enterprise," *AM*, February 1905, 34; David O. Mears, "The Centennial Problem: And Its Uncertain Factor," *AM*, December 1876, 287–89. Evelyn Brooks Higginbotham has recently noted the extent to which Baptist missionaries shared this viewpoint. She points out that some of the white Baptist missionaries saw their efforts to provide schools for black people as in the interest of "national security." See Higginbotham, *Righteous Discontent*, 26–27. Unfortunately, the missionaries also regularly equated material deprivation with personal depravity. For examples, see Bertha Robertson, "Work among the Freedmen," *AM*, January 1887, 19–22; and "Addresses by Field Workers," *AM*, December 1891, 451–72. As late as the 1920s, although no longer blaming these conditions on slavery, the missionaries were still making such claims. In "Racial Assets and Liabilities," a writer

in *AM*, March 1921, 668, said: "It would be false and easy optimism which would fail to take account of the millions, fully one-half of the entire race ten years of age or over, still in the density of ignorance, intellectual and moral, largely in the depth of superstition, thoughtless and degenerate." Also see Johnetta Cross Brazzell, "Education as a Tool of Socialization: Agnes Scott Institute and Spelman Seminary, 1881–1910" (Ph.D. diss., University of Michigan, 1991), 39–42.

16. "Presidential Election—Southern Massacres," *AM*, October 1876, 218–19; "Thirtieth Annual Meeting of the American Missionary Association," *AM*, December 1876, 270–81; "Addresses by Field Workers," 451–72.

17. McPherson, *Abolitionist Legacy*, 52–56.

18. George M. Fredrickson's work suggests that my labeling these and similar positions as racist might be too strong. Fredrickson, in *The Black Image in the White Mind: The Debate of Afro-American Character and Destiny, 1817–1914* (New York: Harper and Row, 1971), 101–2, characterizes the missionaries' position as "romantic racialism" rather than racism.

19. Most schools noted the importance of character in terms similar to that expressed in a Hartshorn statement: "This Department submits that both scholarship and good character must be required. Neither must be counted incidental. A good school cannot put the seal of a graduation upon scholarship when tainted and spoiled by unworthy and base character." See "Some Principles," *UJ*, January 1903, 12–13.

20. James Bond, [untitled, letter to the editor], *FH*, October 1899, 3–4; *Sixteenth Annual Report of the WABHMS, May 2–3, 1894*, 39–41. In an untitled article in *UJ*, February 1902, 13, the author writes, "No education is complete without the study of that supreme literature found in Holy Scripture. Faith as a faculty of the soul is not inferior to reason nor less important. Education which omits faith and religion is partial and sadly imperfect."

21. Quotation from H. G. Gross, "The Essential Factors of Race Education," *UJ*, January 1901, 5. The speeches to the students regularly invoked the image of Moses, the leader; Ezekiel, the prophet; Peter, the teacher; and Paul, the missionary. See "Commencement at Fisk University, Tennessee," *AM*, July 1900, 106–8; "Forty-first Annual Report of the Executive Committee," 313; "Thousands Gather at Forty Third Commencement," *TS*, June [?], 1924; "The Principal's Sunday Evening Talk: Taking an Inventory of One's Self," *TS*, January 20, 1917; and William Shaw, "Christian Endeavor: A Missionary Training School," *AM*, August 1902, 438–39.

22. Gross, "Essential Factors of Race Education."

23. The teachers' ideas were consistent with Scripture, which proclaimed, " 'He who finds his life will lose it, and he who loses his life for My sake will find it' " (Matt. 11:38). E. T. Ware's baccalaureate sermon, in which students were given this advice, was filled with such biblical allusions. In E. T. Ware, "Education as a Means to Freedom," *AUB*, ser. 2, July 1912, 6–10, Ware concluded: "Remember that the only proof of real

freedom is willingness to give up one's individual desires for the welfare of the larger whole." In Ware, "Your Young Men Shall See Visions," *AUB*, ser. 2, July 1914, 21, he notes that each person's freedom depends on the freedom of all others. Also see E. T. Ware, "The Need of People with Vision," *AUB*, ser. 2, July 1913, 8–9; and James Bond, [untitled, letter to the editor], *FH*. In "A Backward and Forward Look," *CM*, December 15, 1929, the writer insisted that "the success of society is measured, to a large extent, by group development, by what it can do as a group, by what individuals are willing to do for the welfare of the whole group—so is the Spelman community." And see L. B. Tefft, "Editorial," *UJ*, February 1905, 60–61; "The American Missionary Association," *FE*, February 1880, 2; T. J. Morgan, "The Education of the Negroes," *HMM*, October 1895, 370–72; and Rev. Lanson Steward, "The Need of All Young People," *SM*, March 1887, 2.

24. The quotation in the text is found in "Mr. Rosenwald Makes Us a Proposition," *LIW*, April 1917, 6. Lincoln Institute was founded in Kentucky in 1904 after several state-initiated anti-integration lawsuits forced the expulsion of black students and faculty from Berea College. For a brief history of the events leading to the founding of Lincoln, see "A Brief Historical Sketch of Lincoln Institute of Kentucky," *LIW*, April 1929, 4–11. All Lincoln Institute records, including copies of the *Lincoln Institute Worker*, are in the Lincoln Institute Records, KDLA. On Berea College, see P. D. Nelson, "An Experiment in Interracial Education at Berea College, 1858–1908," *Journal of Negro History* 59 (1974): 13–27; and McPherson, *Abolitionist Legacy*, 244–61. McPherson describes Berea as "the child of Oberlin" (p. 244). In "Essential Factors of Race Education," Gross claimed that "the great thinkers are also the great Seers and Doers and raise the ideals, mould the forms, and set the standards for the masses. Such a university as this [Virginia Union University, Hartshorn's 'brother' institution] is to do this work and raise up the thinkers, seers and doers who shall lead in every department of the higher life of the people. Every graduate who goes forth from these halls of learning should resolve to be, in his place and according to his powers, a true and unselfish leader among his people. Thus shall he make his education count in the divine work of race redemption." Hartshorn principal L. B. Tefft noted similarly, "The student is educated not for her own sake only, not for her own sake chiefly, but for the thousands who will feel her uplifting influence through the years to come." L. B. Tefft, *Sixteenth Annual Report of the WABHMS*, May 2–3, 1894, 40. A very useful study on the importance of schools to local leadership and community development is Faye Wellborn Robbins, "A World-Within-A-World: Black Nashville, 1880–1915" (Ph.D. diss., University of Arkansas, 1980). Some of the ideas discussed in this chapter are also presented in Adele Logan Alexander, *Ambiguous Lives: Free Women of Color in Rural Georgia, 1789–1879* (Fayetteville: University of Arkansas Press, 1991), 166–71, 180–81.

25. Rev. D. E. Satterfield, D.D., "The Education of Afro-American Girls," *AM*, July 1892, 239–42.

26. Jones's grandfather's remark, "You're going to get your education and its not yours, you're doing it for your people" (cited earlier), embodied a common sentiment.

27. Union Baptist Church to [R. R. Moton], September 8, 1918; and L. B. Norris to [Moton], n.d., b. 1, RRM-SC, TUA.

28. Chapter 2 discussed the community support of individual women's schooling and school building as a community venture, and letters in the Student Correspondence section of Robert R. Moton's papers at Tuskegee show that many girls and young women there were being supported in school by people from their communities. For one example, see Mrs. Lillian M. Smith to R. H. Moten [*sic*], January 20, 1920. This letter indicates that black women in Oakland, California, organized as the Fannie J. Coppin Club, paid the tuition of Tuskegee student Henrietta Martin. The point here, however, is that whether or not community people helped to pay for individual women's courses, the women were still community representatives.

29. J. R. Philpot to R. R. Moton, October 26, 1916; James Brown to [Moton], September 25, 1917; and P. H. Smith to [Moton], September 12, 1918, b. 1, RRM-SC, TUA.

30. *Twentieth Annual Circular and Catalogue of Spelman Seminary for Women and Girls, 1900–01,* 41. Also see *Eighteenth Annual Circular and Catalogue of Spelman Seminary for Women and Girls, 1899–1900,* 42.

31. *Second Annual Catalog of the Officers and Students of Hartshorn Memorial College, 1884–1885,* 9. Also on the need for and desirability of having educated African Americans lead their own people, see "The Education of the Negro," *HMM,* October 1898, 346–49.

32. *Catalogue of the Officers and Students of Fisk University, 1889–90,* 5; *Twenty-fourth Annual Catalogue of the Tuskegee Normal and Industrial Institute, 1904–05,* 12.

33. Quotation from "Mr. Rosenwald Makes Us a Proposition," 6. Baptist school supporters put it similarly: "When you have trained one student [in the trades] you have simply fitted one man to earn an ordinary living. When you have given a college education to a man with brains, you have sent forth an instrumentality that will affect hundreds or thousands." See "The Higher Education of the Negro," *HMM,* September 1896, 308. George Sale, superintendent of education for the Home Mission Society, noted in 1911 that "The Home Mission Society has stoutly maintained the position that industrial education is second in importance to the training of the few for higher service as leaders of thought and action of the Negro race." See George Sale, "A Missionary University," *SM,* October 1911, 1–2. Evelyn Brooks Higginbotham characterizes this tradition as the development of "the female talented tenth" in *Righteous Discontent,* 19–46. Also see H. L. Morehouse, "The Worth of Spelman Seminary to the World," *SM,* June 1896, 3, 5–6.

34. Horace Bumstead, "Girls Industrial Work," *AUB,* November 1885, 3. Spelman's 1892–93 catalog noted that "all boarders are required to learn the art of housekeeping in all its branches. The time of seven

teachers is devoted mainly to this department." See *Twelfth Annual Circular and Catalogue of Spelman Seminary, 1893,* 20.

35. *First Annual Catalogue of the Officers and Students of Hartshorn Memorial College, 1883–84,* 11; L. B. Tefft, "Ideas Dominant at Hartshorn College," *HMM,* August 1899, 315–16.

36. Morehouse, "The Worth of Spelman Seminary to the World."

37. Higginbotham, *Righteous Discontent,* 28–29. See explicit comparisons in *First Annual Catalogue of the Officers and Students of Hartshorn Memorial College, 1883–84,* 11; and Morehouse, "The Worth of Spelman Seminary to the World." The only real difference between the early college curricula at black and white women's schools was in the number of courses available. Not until the 1920s and 1930s did black schools offer a significant number of electives in their programs. Wellesley, on the other hand, offered courses in the romance languages beginning in the late 1880s, and students there had many more courses in art and art history than were available at Spelman and Hartshorn all the way up to the 1920s. See *Wellesley College Calendar, 1886–87,* 25–28. Radcliffe offered courses in Hebrew, Sanskrit, German, French, and Italian; twice as many mathematics courses as Spelman or Hartshorn; and electives in the fine arts as early as 1884. See *The Society for the Collegiate Instruction of Women, 1884–85,* 5–8.

38. *Eighteenth Annual Circular and Catalogue of Spelman Seminary for Women and Girls, 1899–1900,* 30–31; *Catalogue of the Officers and Students of Fisk University, 1894–1895,* 38–41; *Catalogue of the Officers and Students of Howard University, 1881–1882,* 17–18. Howard's program, however, was always more advanced than Spelman's. For example, Howard's curriculum included courses explicitly designated as political economy.

39. For example, by the 1890s Howard offered a classical course, a scientific course, and a literary course. And by 1920 Fisk had four bachelor's degree programs: classical, science, education, and home economics. See *Catalogue of the Officers and Students of Howard University, 1894–95,* 40–43; and Richardson, *History of Fisk University,* 73. Fisk University officials at one time rationalized the lag in adopting the elective system by saying that their students had not had enough schooling before arriving there, and that neither they nor their parents were capable of choosing appropriately among nonrequired courses. For that reason the curriculum was rigid, organized by the faculty, and designed somewhat narrowly to provide "a secure foundation for professional study." See Merrill, "Fisk University after Thirty-nine Years," 165. But the fact was that almost none of the black schools could afford to pay a staff large enough to offer elective courses until their second or third generation of students had enrolled. Staffing college courses at all was difficult at black schools because at first they also had to maintain and staff elementary, grammar, and secondary programs to feed their college programs.

40. Black students who finished college programs (as opposed to normal programs) at Talladega, Fisk, Atlanta, and Howard, in particular, frequently continued in graduate and professional work at Ivy League in-

stitutions and distinguished themselves by their scholarship. See Merrill, "Fisk University after Thirty-nine Years"; Jones and Richardson, *Talladega College*, 70; Richardson, *A History of Fisk University*, 161–75; Rayford W. Logan, *Howard University: The First Hundred Years, 1867–1967* (New York: New York University Press, 1969), 36–39, 93–99, 130–36; and Clarence Bacote, *The Story of Atlanta University: A Century of Service, 1865–1965* (Atlanta: Atlanta University Press, 1969).

41. Hampton, more established than Tuskegee (by twenty years) had a more sophisticated curriculum than Tuskegee had in place at the time. Hampton also included in the normal program rhetoric, English literature, chemistry, bookkeeping, and political economy. See *Catalog of the Tuskegee State Normal School at Tuskegee, Alabama, 1881–82*, 7–9; *Catalogue of the Hampton Normal and Agricultural Institute, 1881–82*, 24–25. On the common school movement, see Anderson, *Education of Blacks in the South*, 148–85.

42. *Twenty-first Annual Catalogue of the Tuskegee Normal and Industrial Institute, 1901–2*, 23–34.

43. For examples, see "Announcement of the Tuskegee Summer School for Teachers . . . June 29–August 7, 1903," b. 980, BTW-LC; and "Negro Summer School Opens at Tuskegee: Largest Enrollment for First Day in History of the Sessions," Montgomery *Advertiser*, June 25, 1913, r. 2; and "Tuskegee's Summer School," *Freeman*, June 22, 1918, r. 7, TNCS.

44. "The Young Women of the South," *FE*, February 1880, 1; "The Education of Girls," *FE*, February 1882, 2; Gertrude Hadnott, "The Mission of the Negro Woman," *FH*, March 1900, 6–7; "Fisk University: Facilities for the Education of Young Women," *FH*, March [April] 1886, 1; Morehouse, "The Worth of Spelman Seminary to the World"; Anna Cahill, "Training Colored Girls," *AM*, January 1883, 8–12; Nanie McPine, "An Ideal Woman," *FH*, March 1891, 4–5; W. J. Lucas, "A Call for Educated Negro Women," *UJ*, April 1906, 102–4; "Female Education," *AM*, January 1869, 9; A. H. Bradford, "What Some Women Are Doing," *AM*, January 1887, 4–6; "CVD," "The Opening," *Union-Hartshorn Journal*, November 1911, 18–20. See also "The Role of Women," *CM*, November 15, 1931; and "The Founders' Day Address," *CM*, April 15, 1928. The speaker for this Spelman program was Mary McLeod Bethune, and she too (and this late—1928) noted the race's dependence on the women.

45. Hall, "Report of the Committee on Southern Educational Work," 36–39. Also see Amory H. Bradford, "Our Most Imperative Missionary Enterprise," *AM*, February 1905, 33–35. In this article Bradford noted, "So long as the colored people are in the condition in which they now are[,] the heel of the white man will be upon their necks. When they prove their intellectual and spiritual equality with the white race, as I fully believe that they will in the not distant future, then even the whites in the South who honor character and manhood will accord to them the recognition that they deserve. . . . Education and character in the long run always command respect" (p. 35).

46. "Alumni Dinner," *FE*, June 1882, 8.

47. See, for example, "Hints to the Student," *FE*, February 1880, 5; "Sister Moore's Rules of Politeness," *SM*, January 1912; quotation from Carrie P. Walls, "Children's Exchange," *SM*, March 1888; Ruby L. Brown, "Pigeon Manners," *CM*, December 15, 1927; and "A Better School or an Etiquette Library," *CM*, October 15, 1929.

48. Spelman had the Eunomean Society, which "was organized for the purpose of teaching the pupils more about etiquette, how to appear and act well both in private and public life." At Hampton, the "etiquette group" not only taught fairly traditional lessons but also occasionally had surprise guests drop in on their meetings posing as some international dignitary (Lord Chesterfield, on one night), who also "taught" the students. See Susie E. Jones, "Societies of Spelman," *SM*, April 1906, 2–3; and "Etiquette Group Holds Successful Session," *HS*, February 9, 1935. Even later, the concern for refined manners influenced the development of a club at Spelman in 1934 called "Daughters of Refinement and Culture." The club existed until 1942 and was sponsored by Mrs. H. A. H. Reddick, Freshman Hall housemother. See Narvis Smith, "D.R.C.," *CM*, October 1947. "A Better School or an Etiquette Library," cited above, announced that members of the 1929 class organized their own etiquette "police." And see J. G. St. Clair Drake Jr., "Our Right to Culture," *HS*, November 24, 1928.

49. See Sarah H. Lay, "Politeness," *SM*, February 1887; "The Great Virtues," *Union-Hartshorn Journal*, November 1911, 16; M. I. Williams, "Manners," *SM*, May 1890, 3; and "Dr. Miller's Ten Commandments for Daughters," *SM*, January 1912, 8.

50. *Catalog of the Officers and Students of Fisk University, 1871–72*, 29; *Catalogue of the Officers and Students of Fisk University, 1881–82*, 25; *Tuskegee Institute Bulletin, Thirty-second Annual Catalogue, 1912–13*, 21–22; Jones and Richardson, *Talladega College*, 10–11, 56–58; *Catalogue of the Hampton Normal and Agricultural Institute, 1881–82*, 33; *1891–92*, 42; and *1895–96*, 53; Richardson, *A History of Fisk University*, 84–85; *Catalog of the Officers and Students of Howard University, 1869–70*, 26.

51. *Twelfth Annual Circular and Catalog of Spelman Seminary, 1892–93*, 26; *Catalog of the Officers and Students of Fisk University, 1871–72*, 28–29; *Thirty-second Annual Catalogue [of Tuskegee Institute], 1912–13*, 20–21; *Catalogue of the Hampton Normal and Agricultural Institute, 1881–82*, 33. The final quotation in the text is from [untitled], *Union-Hartshorn Journal*, November 1910, 21 (original emphasis).

52. V. W. Barnett to Captain Neely [*sic*], January 15, 1920, b. 8, RRM-SC; Richardson, *A History of Fisk University*, 87; [untitled], *UJ*, April 1902, 12–13. Probably also to impress the parents and the public, Spelman College administrators even noted in their official publications the percentage of their graduates whom they no longer recognized because of their unacceptable behavior. In *Twenty-eighth Annual Report of the WABHMS, 1906*, 77, the author noted that "only 5% [of the graduates] are unrecognized by us because their lives dishonor the school." Spelman officials announced from the beginning: "No students are wanted or re-

tained, who have not sufficient character to appreciate their advantages, and to listen to reasonable advice and admonition." And in its early years Hampton, while defending its coeducational course, would readily dismiss any student whose character might "spoil" other students. See *Twelfth Annual Circular and Catalog of Spelman Seminary for Women and Girls, 1892–93*, 26; and *Catalog of the Hampton Normal and Agricultural Institute, 1870–71*, 23.

53. R. R. Moton to Mrs. A. C. Buchanan, April 7, 1920; Norman Cruzat to Mr. Wilborn, April 7, 1920; Mrs. A. C. Buchanan to Moton, April 8, 1920; and Moton to Mr. Cornelius Buchanan, April 14, 1920, b. 8, and RRM-SC, TUA. On the suspension of a Fisk University student whose parents were friends of Isaac Fisher, see Isaac Fisher to Constance Fisher, February 3, 1937, b. 15, Constance Fisher Papers, TUA. The student was dropped "for cheating and general dishonesty and troublesomeness about boys." The friendship with a prominent staff member did not save her academic career.

54. R. R. Moton to Jeff Howell, January 26, 1920; and Moton to Anna L. Hall, February 3, 1920, b. 8, RRM-SC, TUA; "Making Love," *Union-Hartshorn Journal*, March 1912, 23–24.

55. See Mrs. J. H. Fobish to R. R. Moton, August 21, 1920, b. 8; and W. H. Drew to Moton, February 2, 1920, b. 7, RRM-SC, TUA; and Richardson, *A History of Fisk University*, 87. Probably parental pressure caused Orlena McDuffie to beg for readmission to Tuskegee after her suspension for breaking rules. The school council refused to reverse the decision. See Orlena McDuffie to Robert R. Moton, July 10, 1920; and Moton to McDuffie, July 27, 1920, b. 8, RRM-SC, TUA. Hartshorn officials encouraged the parents of their students to provide the school with a list of the persons with whom their daughters were allowed to correspond. See *Hartshorn Memorial College Catalogue, 1928–29*, 29.

56. *Catalogue of the Officers and Students of Howard University, 1892–93*, 51.

57. Jones and Richardson, *Talladega College*, 93.

58. Lucy Hale Tapley and Edith Villora Brill, "Annual Report to the Trustees of Spelman Seminary," *SM*, April 1920, 2, 3, 8; L. B. Tefft, "Hartshorn Memorial College," *HMM*, August 21, 1899, 58.

59. Quotation from *Sixteenth Annual Report of the WABHMS, May 2–3, 1894*, 39–40. In "About Hartshorn," *UJ*, May 1902, 15–16, the author noted that Hartshorn "is not a place to which girls may be sent for imprisonment to keep them from bad company or to break off unsuitable attachments. It is not a place for reforming those who lie and steal, or use vile and profane language. Such persons find no admission unless they are put upon the institution by false commendation." The essay continued, "If any student goes out from HARTSHORN to engage in the follies and the sin of unchristian society, to drink wine, to play cards, to dance, to 'live in pleasure,' she goes contrary to all the instruction and training which she has received, she misrepresents the institution. If she fails to be

a faithful and effective Christian worker and a blessing to her community, she fails of realizing the HARTSHORN IDEA."

60. *Thirty-first Annual Report of the WABHMS, May 5–6, 1909*, 106; "Some Good Pledges," *UJ*, February 1901, 13–14; *Twenty-seventh Annual Report of the WABHMS, 1905*, 74.

61. L. N., "Our Choice of Companions," *FH*, October 1888, 7, 12. Oberlin administrators never went into great detail about the company or behavior of their students. They simply wrote in one issue of the catalog that in spite of the wholesome community where the school was situated, "those who seek bad company will find it—or make it—anywhere, and the College does not offer itself as a reformatory for young people who are too wayward for home restraints." See *Catalogue of the Officers and Students of Oberlin College, 1881–82*, 75.

62. *Twentieth Annual Report of WABHMS, May 4–5, 1898*, 88–89.

63. [Untitled], *Union-Hartshorn Journal*, January 1908, 22.

64. Bertha Robertson, "Work among the Freedmen," *AM*, January 1887, 22; John Ogden, "Fisk University," *AM*, October 1869, 218–20; Anna M. Cahill, "Training Colored Girls," *AM*, January 1883, 8–12; [E. T.] Ware, "The Peculiar Service of Atlanta University," *AUB*, ser. 2, January 1912, 14. Hartshorn teacher Mary Tefft also expressed a preference for students from rural areas over those from cities, because she felt the rural students better "appreciate[d] their training" and were "more conscious" of their opportunities for schooling because of their presumed meager home environments. See *Twenty-ninth Annual Report of the WABHMS, 1907*, 73.

65. Chlora L. White to Mr. Bumstead, published in *AUB*, March 1896, 3.

66. Atlanta University rules noted that "during vacation, as well as during term time, students are held amenable to the authority of the school." See *Catalog of the Officers and Students of Atlanta University, 1894–95*, 26. At Hampton, acting contrary to the rules of the school "either on or off the grounds" could result in suspension or expulsion. See *Catalogue of the Hampton Normal and Agricultural Institute, 1895–96*, 53. Students at a Tennessee school boycotted meals and refused to participate in chapel programs after several coeds were disciplined for "dancing during their recent visit to a home in the city." See "Students Protest Rule of Faculty," *East Tennessee News*, January 14, 1932, r. 40, TNCS. And see Jones and Richards, *Talladega College*, 56; and *Catalog of the Officers and Students of Atlanta University, 1894–95*, 26.

67. One example that includes all these aspects is "Fisk University," *AM*, January 1900, 16–17. In this article the writer noted that "the student body honors scholarship, awakens ambitions, cultivates good manners, frowns upon untidyness of appearance, while by firmly sustained legislation the faculty forbids any display of extravagance in attire. Patches and darns are expected; soiled or neglected garments the school will not permit."

68. *Twenty-fourth Annual Catalogue of the Tuskegee Normal and Industrial Institute, 1904–05*, 18; *Thirty-second Annual Catalogue, 1912–1913*, 20.

69. *Hartshorn Memorial College Forty-second Annual Catalog, 1924–25*, 20; *Hartshorn Memorial College Catalogue, 1928–29*, 29.

70. See "Woman's Dress," *UJ*, December 1901, 14–15.

71. *Twelfth Annual Circular and Catalog of Spelman Seminary for Women and Girls, 1892–93*, 29–30; *Thirtieth Annual Circular of Spelman Seminary for Women and Girls, 1910–1911*, 14; *Catalog of Spelman College, 1929–30*, 55. Indicating the seriousness with which students accepted this advice (and its implications) related to dress, see "Our Dress," *SM*, March 1912, 3, 8; Rose Strickland, "The Old Fashioned Girl," *CM*, December 15, 1927; and Mary Louise Smith, "Sensible Clothes for College Girls," *CM*, November 15, 1930.

72. Fisk University codes, which eventually came to include quasi-uniforms, and codes at Atlanta University were very similar to those articulated at Spelman. See *Catalog of the Officers and Students of Atlanta University, 1907–8*, 23; *AUB*, ser. 2, April 1919, 27; *AUB*, April 1925, 27; *Catalogue of the Officers and Students of Fisk University, 1881–82*, 26; and *Catalogue of the Officers and Students of Fisk University, 1912–13*, 18–19. By the 1920s, the Fisk dress code for women students took up three full pages in the catalog. Howard University catalogs never noted a dress code.

73. Cheryl Townsend Gilkes notes in " 'Together and in Harness': Women's Traditions in the Sanctified Church," *Signs: Journal of Women in Culture and Society* 10 (1985): 685–86, that black women in the Sanctified Church adopted a dress code that helped to "restrain the most ardent racists" when the women traveled. Most of the women studied here who discussed preparations for travel noted that everyone always traveled in her best clothes, for the same reason.

74. In this manner Spelman College, Tuskegee Institute, Atlanta University officials, and others regularly wrote of "the 10,000" elementary school students reached each year by their graduates. And Howard University officials wrote during the school's second year of existence, "Every teacher trained is the nucleus of a school, more or less numerous; every school carries the lamp of civilization into the homes that make up a community; and every community thus blessed contributes largely to the general peace and welfare of the land." *Catalog of the Officers and Students of Howard University, 1868–69*, 37.

75. T. J. Morgan, "The Higher Education of Colored Women," *HMM*, May 1896, 162.

76. For an especially clear example, see Morehouse, "The Worth of Spelman Seminary to the World," 3, 5–6. This article by the field secretary of ABHMS praises the work being done at Spelman. In a most telling statement, Morehouse wrote that "Spelman is improving the civilization of the southern Negro." Morehouse was without doubt alluding to the work the students would do in black communities after they graduated, but he did not suggest that those students were not being "civilized" as well. In fact, because most of the article was about the education avail-

able at Spelman, one can only conclude that he was speaking of the students themselves. See also "What the American Baptist Home Mission Society Has Done for Negroes," *SM*, March 1901, 2–3, 7. In "The Principal's Sunday Evening Talk to the Students in the Chapel," *TS*, October 18, 1902, Washington described the difference between "persons of training and those without training": "We want you to be strong, progressive, independent individuals, who shall lead other people and control your surroundings, and not let your surroundings control you. It is young men and young women of this kind we want to see go out from Tuskegee every year. . . . Go out as leaders on the farm, leaders in the home, leaders in the school room, leaders in whatever direction your life may be thrown. Go out and show yourselves so strong, so progressive, that you will control your surroundings, and not let your surroundings control you." And see "The Principal's Sunday Evening Talk: 'Taking an Inventory of One's Self,' " *TS*, January 20, 1917; and Miss D. E. Emmerson, "Bureau of Woman's Work," *AM*, August 1887, 41. (In the last reference, the author discusses the differences in their girls "after they have learned to love the new way.")

77. Although, as Evelyn Brooks Higginbotham points out, the expression "the talented tenth," and the philosophy that developed around it, was first articulated by Henry Morehouse, an American Baptist Home Mission Society executive, after Du Bois popularized the idea it became an important philosophy among significant sections of the African American community. See Higginbotham, *Righteous Discontent*, 20–21, 25–26.

78. Gross, "The Essential Factors of Race Education," *UJ*, 7; "Editorial," *CM*, [May 15?], 1944; E. T. Ware, "The Servant and the Spirit of Service," *AUB*, ser. 2, July 1911, 17; "NMK," "Be What You Are," *SM*, December 1885, 3.

79. "Address of the Right Reverend Charles H. Brent," *HUR*, November 1910, 3–9 (quotation on 5, 7).

80. Samuel V. V. Holmes, "Education and Life," *AUB*, ser. 2, July 1912, 4; "Visitors on the Campus," *CM*, May–June 1928; "Editorial," *CM*, [May 15?] 1944. See also [untitled, on Booker T. Washington's visit and speech to the students], *SM*, November 1895, 5; and Ware, "Your Young Men Shall See Visions," *AUB*, ser. 2, July 1914, 15–22. Leaven, in the biblical parable and in the example of these women, was the small bit of yeast that caused the whole lump (mass of dough/people) to rise.

81. For example, see "Miss Vassar, a Student from Fisk University, Gave Her Experience as Student Teacher," *AM*, January 1891, 28–29.

82. Brazzell, "Education as a Tool of Socialization," 47; Richardson, *A History of Fisk University*, 3–4; Jones and Richardson, *Talladega College*, 1–2; Higginbotham, *Righteous Discontent*, 22–24.

83. See G. D. Pike, *The Jubilee Singers, and Their Campaign for Twenty Thousand Dollars* (Boston: Lee and Shepard, 1873); Joe M. Richardson, *A History of Fisk University*, 25–39; "Raising $1,000 among the Colored People," *SL*, January 1890, 2; and *Thirty-second Annual Report of the*

WABHMS, 1910, 123. One would not get a clear impression of the extensive student work by reading Max Bennett Thrasher, *Tuskegee: Its Story and Its Work* (1901; rpt. New York: Negro Universities Press, 1969). But the captions beneath the pictures betray the otherwise conspicuous silence on the topic. Students at Tuskegee also aided the teachers and the larger community in raising funds to endow scholarships. On one occasion the students were asked to give one cent a week for scholarships and to witness the power of self-help that their contributions allowed.

84. *Catalog of the Officers and Students of Fisk University, 1871–72*, 25; [untitled], *AUB*, ser. 2, April 1925, 22; *Twenty-fifth Annual Circular and Catalogue of Spelman Seminary for Women and Girls, 1905–6*, 10; *Forty-second Annual Catalog of the Officers and Students of Hartshorn Memorial College, 1924–25*, 20–21; *Catalog of the Hampton Normal and Industrial Institute, 1870–71*, 14–15; *1881–82*, 32; and *1891–92*, 37, 39–41; *Nineteenth Annual Report of the WABHMS, 1897*, 85–86.

85. "Uplifting of the Negro," *TS*, December 10, 1904.

86. Two new graduates wrote of their understanding of their (future) community responsibilities in Camilla Weems, "The Relations of the Rural School to Its Community," *SM*, May 1912, 2–3; and Isabelle B. Walden, "The Aims and Aspirations of the Senior Class," *Fisk University News*, May 1921, 23–24, b. 8, Constance Fisher Papers, TUA. Importantly, however, the schools' relationships with the local communities were both intensive and extensive, and students participated in many of these efforts. For examples of the distribution of food, clothes, and other supplies to surrounding communities, see [untitled], *TS*, November 26, 1904; "Friends Respond to Principal Moton's Christmas Appeal," *TM*, January 17, 1931; H. S. B. to Miss C[leaveland], December 28, 1892, reprinted in *Southern Workman* 22 (1893) 29; "Institute Woman's Club Takes Part in Relief," *TM*, January 17, 1931; Ella Tucker, "Our Christmas Mission," *AUB*, January 1892, 1–2; and "A Thanksgiving Story," *UJ*, January 1903, 15–16. Documenting how Hampton faculty prepared packages of clothing, books, and money and sent them, for redistribution, to their former students who had become teachers and social workers, see Janie Porter Barrett to [Myrtilla] Sherman, December 12, 1916, Janie Porter Barrett Papers, HULA; and Amelia Perry Pride to Miss Bellows, May 6, 1897, Amelia Perry Pride Papers, HULA. On developing libraries in communities surrounding the schools, see *AUB*, ser. 2, April 1919, 24; *Forty-second Annual Catalogue of the Tuskegee Normal and Industrial Institute, 1922–23*, 128; "A Community Worker," *SL*, July 1918; and Jones and Richardson, *Talladega College*, 118–19. On evening school programs for community adults, see [untitled], *TS*, December 10, 1904; and Richardson, *A History of Fisk University*, 124–28. And on developing community hospitals, see Jones and Richardson, *Talladega College*, 82; Darlene Clark Hine, *Black Women in White: Racial Conflict and Cooperation in the Nursing Profession, 1890–1950* (Bloomington: Indiana University Press, 1989), 8–9, 16; and *Tuskegee Institute Bulletin: Thirty-second Annual Catalogue, 1912–13*, 13. The Tuskegee Farmers and Laborers Conferences, the Hampton Negro Con-

ferences, and the Atlanta University Conferences, all held annually, also demonstrated the schools' interest in and connection to a larger community.

87. Tefft's remark is in *Thirteenth Annual Report of the WABHMS*, 24. On the work of Hampton see "Hampton Normal and Industrial Institute: Report of a Special Committee," *AM*, August 1869, 3. And for Channing Tobias's speech, see "The Commencement Address," *TM*, June 1932.

88. Quotation from Ligon A. Wilson, "A Challenge," *HS*, May 25, 1929. Also see "Thousands Gather at Forty-third Commencement," *TS*, June 1924; and "Excerpts from Mrs. Roosevelt's Anniversary Address," *HS*, April 30, 1938. Decades before the intense public debate over whether black students should pursue liberal or vocational educations, Hampton officials wrote that because their program was only for three years, "our students could never become advanced enough in that time to be more than superficially acquainted with Latin and Greek; their knowledge would rather tend to cultivate their conceit than to fit them for faithful educators of their race." The essay did, however, acknowledge the importance of classical study and in effect referred interested students to Howard University. See *Catalog of the Hampton Normal and Industrial Institute, 1870–71*, 22, and similar examples in "The Meaning and Mission of Education: Address of President Thirkeld," and "Address of the Honorable J. C. Napier at Fortieth Anniversary," *HUR*, November 1907, 10–16 and 4–8, respectively.

89. *Twenty-fifth Annual Report of the WABHMS*, May 6–7, 1903, 95; "Home News," *Union-Hartshorn Journal*, January 1908, 22–23. Also see "News Item," *UJ*, January 1901, 16; [untitled], *UJ*, February 1902, 12; C. C. Boone, "On the Congo," *UJ*, February 1902, 15–16; *Thirty-first Annual Report of the WABHMS, 1909*, 104–5; *Twenty-third Annual Report of the WABHMS, 1901*, 74; *Eighteenth Annual Report of the WABHMS, 1896*, 91; and [untitled], *TS*, November 26, 1904. On support for students in or from Africa, see Susie E. Jones, "Societies of Spelman," *SM*, April 1906, 2–3. Nora Gordon earned some acclaim as a missionary in the Congo. See M. I. Williams, "Mrs Nora A. Gordon," *SM*, December 1900, 5; *Nineteenth Annual Report of the WABHMS, 1897*, 89; *Twelfth Annual Circular and Catalog of Spelman Seminary for Women and Girls, 1892–93*, 24; and Sylvia Jacobs, " 'Say Africa When You Pray': The Activities of Early Black Baptist Women Missionaries among Liberian Women and Children," *Sage: A Scholarly Journal on Black Women* 3 (1986): 16–21.

90. *Hartshorn Memorial College Third Annual Catalogue, 1886–87*, 15, 17; *Hartshorn Memorial College Fifteenth Annual Catalogue, 1897–98*, 20–21; *Hartshorn Memorial College Thirty-fifth Annual Catalog, 1917–18*, 20; *Fourteenth Annual Report of the WABHMS*, May 4–5, 1892, 21; *Twenty-third Annual Report of the WABHMS*, May 1–2, 1901, 74–75; *Thirty-first Annual Report of the WABHMS, 1909*, 104–5; "Our College Societies," *UJ*, November 1902, 12–13; *Thirtieth Annual Report of the WABHMS, 1908*, 103–6.

91. *Eighteenth Annual Report of the WABHMS*, April 29–30, 1896, 91.

92. Higginbotham, *Righteous Discontent,* 45.

93. *The Forty-seventh Annual Catalogue: The Hampton Normal and Agricultural Institute, 1915,* 33.

94. By 1893 Spelman students supported seven Christian Endeavor Societies. See *Twelfth Annual Circular and Catalog of Spelman Seminary for Women and Girls, 1892–93,* 24. Also see H. S. De Forest, "Commencement at Talladega College," *AM,* August 1887, 227.

95. "A Thanksgiving Story," *UJ,* January 1903, 15–16; Ella Tucker, "Our Christmas Mission," *AUB,* January 1892, 1–2; M. Ernestine Anthony, "To Whom Shall Our Gifts Go," and Alma Long, "Christmas, the Season of Giving," *CM,* December 15, 1930.

96. *The Forty-fourth Annual Catalogue: The Hampton Normal and Agricultural Institute, 1912,* 78–79; *The Forty-seventh Annual Catalogue: Hampton Normal and Agricultural Institute, 1916,* 30.

97. Richardson, *A History of Fisk University,* 125–28. Also see Fisk University, Rural Life Committee, *The Fisk Rural Life Program: A Plan for the Development of Negro Leaders for the Rural South* (Nashville: Fisk University Press, 1945).

98. *Forty-second Annual Catalog of the Tuskegee Normal and Industrial Institute, 1922–23,* 128.

99. Ibid., 126–28; *Forty-first Annual Catalog of Tuskegee Normal and Industrial Institute, 1921–22,* 125–26; *Forty-eighth Annual Catalog of Tuskegee Institute, 1928–29,* 93. The Plantation Settlement (Elizabeth Russell Settlement), out of which the Mothers' Clubs operated, is discussed in Elisabeth Lasch-Quinn, *Black Neighbors: Race and the Limits of Reform in American Settlement House Movements, 1890–1945* (Chapel Hill: University of North Carolina Press, 1993), 81. Lasch-Quinn examines many of the southern settlements/schools started by African American women.

100. E. T. Ware, "The Peculiar Service of Atlanta University," *AUB,* ser. 2, January 1912, 13–14.

101. See "Atlanta University and Domestic Service," *AUB,* ser. 2, October 1913, 17–18; and *AUB,* ser. 2, April 1919, 14–15, 24. Also on the Gate City Free Kindergarten movement, see Cynthia Neverdon-Morton, "The Black Woman's Struggle for Equality in the South," in Sharon Harley and Rosalyn Terborg-Penn, eds., *The Afro-American Woman: Struggles and Images* (Port Washington, N.Y.: Kennikat, 1978), 47–48.

102. My view of the Hampton/Tuskegee model of education is not nearly as unflattering as that of James D. Anderson in *The Education of Blacks in the South.* Anderson sees these schools as socializing African Americans to subordinate roles in society. And he sees a conservative black leadership emerging from these schools "which did not foster the political and economic improvement of black workers and voters" (pp. 52–53). Finally, Anderson's work suggests that the educational program at the "missionary" schools was quite the opposite of that provided at Hampton/Tuskegee. I accept Elizabeth Jacoway's distinction between "industrial" and "vocational" education, quoted in Lasch-Quinn, *Black*

Neighbors, 79–80. Jacoway notes that "industrial" education was not education designed to prepare the students to work in industries. Rather, " 'industrial' education was a moral program" designed to provide basic skills and build character. Thus my book assumes that at both kinds of schools the programs were structured to effect the same kind of discipline.

103. "Summer Experiences of Our Students," *AUB,* November 1892, 5–6; "Our Summer Schools," *AUB,* April 1891, 4; "Miss Vassar, a Student from Fisk University Gave Her Experience as a Student Teacher," 28–29; "Our Girls," *FH,* March 1889, 10; "Summer Work of Students," *AUB,* June 1883, 4; "Infelicities in Georgia's School Law," *AUB,* January 1893; *Sixteenth Annual Report of the WABHMS, 1894,* 31–34; Jones and Richardson, *Talladega College,* 56–57.

104. Note also that some of these publications were intended to impress the general public with the good work the schools were doing and therefore generate donations. But that does not diminish the potential impact of the reports on the enrolled students; nor does it negate the writers' intention to impress them.

105. See "Personal," *FH,* October 1883, 3; November 1886, 8–9; and November 1887, 11, 14; and "Alumni Column," *FH,* March 1896, 8.

106. "Spelman Graduates, 1887–1891" [copy provided by Elsa Barkley Brown], 4–14.

107. "How I Spent Vacation" [letter from Bessie T. Roane], *SL,* October 1897, 3–4; (correspondence), *FH,* April 1885, 1; "Leading a Community" [letter from Mrs. J. A. Tyson, class of 1885], *SL,* September 1906, 1. Also see "Hartshorn Family News," *UJ,* December 1902, 15–16; Mrs. T. N. Chase, "Summer Work of Students," *Bulletin,* June 1883, 4; Edgar H. Webster, "Our Students' Summer Work," *AUB,* October 1889, 3–4; "Echoes for the Alumnae Meeting," and *UJ,* May 1901, 15; "The Negro Girl in the Rural District," *AUB,* November 1898, 4. The last concerns Mrs. Anna (Wade) Richardson, who graduated from Atlanta University in 1885 and in 1898 was a school principal in Marshallville, Georgia. The article reported that when Richardson arrived in Marshallville, "whisky dens" were on almost every corner, none of the children could read, and all their homes were disorderly. By her influence the town had been voted dry, almost all the children could read and write, many of her former students were now teachers, and many of the community people now owned their homes and had improved them. Also, all of Richardson's teachers professed to be Christians.

108. "Sketches of Graduates," *SM,* May 1901, 2.

109. "Improving School Surroundings" [letter from Parthenia Hickman, February 19, 1915], *SL,* March 1915; " 'Making Good' Her First Year" [letter from Rowena Adams, January 17, 1917], *SL,* June 1917; "A Community Worker" [letter from Irene Richburg, March 21, 1918], *SL,* July 1918; Ethel E. M'Ghee, "Why I Like My Job," *SM,* May 1926, 9; "A Tuskegee Institute Graduate Interests Her Pupils in Charitable Work," *SL,* September 1907. See also the anecdote about the call for a teacher that Fisk administrators received in the 1870s or 1880s in Richard-

son, *A History of Fisk University,* 54. The woman sent to Georgia "instantly became Sunday School superintendent, janitor, and moral leader of the community as well as instructor." Like some of the others whose stories are cited here, she also rented a building to house female students who lived too far from the school to commute.

110. *Thirtieth Annual Report of the WABHMS, 1908,* 81–83.

111. Mrs. A. K. Spence, "Interesting Thanksgiving Services at Fisk University—Causes of Gratitude—The Changes of the Last Few Years," *AM,* January 1876, 8; "Commencement at Talladega College, Alabama," *AM,* July 1900, 109. The lines quoted are from "Stronger Men" by Phillips Brooks. The poem graced the cover of *TS,* February 3, 1917.

112. The missionary teachers provided an important suggestion of the meaning of these young women's education. These teachers sometimes arrived at the southern locales before school buildings existed. Local whites usually ostracized and castigated them because they taught black people. And they had to work constantly to deflect charges that they were "foreigners" who intended to "make mischief between the races" in the South. They endured all manner of insults, and, on top of it all, they earned little and sometimes no pay. A few of them lost their lives (usually from illnesses and in one documented case, by lynching). See "Talladega College," *AM,* April 1904, 105; W. T. B. Williams, "The Yankee Schoolma'am in Negro Education," *AM,* November 1916, 409–12; [untitled], *AM,* November 1887, 313; Lillian M. VanCleef [report from Hartshorn College], *Tenth Annual Report of the WABHMS,* 24–25; "Women to the Rescue," *AUB,* January 1890; [untitled series of reports from northern papers], *AUB,* June 1890; Mary DuBose, "Two Noble Women," *CM,* April 15, 1928; Mrs. E. Kirkland, "The Atlanta University," *AUB,* June 1890, 7; "A Curiosity," *AUB,* February 1892, 4; and Septima Poinsette Clark with LeGette Blythe, *Echo in My Soul* (New York: E. P. Dutton, 1962), 25. Minnesota social worker Ethel Ray Nance's father, who left North Carolina before 1900, frequently told his children about the threats that white missionary teachers, particularly in North Carolina, endured and of black townspeople's organizing to protect them. See Ethel Ray Nance, interview transcript, AMD-MHS, 1–2. It should be emphasized, however, that black missionary teachers were also harassed, simply because they were black and because they taught black students.

113. On the general changes in college personnel see McPherson, *Abolitionist Legacy,* 262–95. On student protests, "Student Strikes," *Union-Hartshorn Bulletin,* November 1927, 8–9; Richardson, *A History of Fisk University,* 84–100; Anderson, *The Education of Blacks in the South,* 268–78; W. E. B. Du Bois, "The Hampton Strike," *Nation,* November 2, 1927, 471–72; and "School Disturbances" [on Howard University student strikes], Pittsburgh *Courier,* May 25, 1925; "Trouble Reported at Fisk University," Atlanta *Independent,* March 12, 1925; "Trouble Comes to Climax at Fisk; President Orders Students Jailed; and Officers Beat College Boys," Birmingham *Reporter,* February 7, 1925, r. 22, TNCS. Broader sup-

port for Fisk students is suggested by the fact that during their revolt, they continued to publish their student newspaper through the New York alumni office. Howard, Hampton, and Spelman students also launched major protests against the school administrations during the 1930s and 1940s. See "H.U. Women Strike; Dean Called Hitler," Baltimore *Afro-American*, May 31, 1941; and "Howard Students Seek More Privileges; Hold Mass 'Strike' Session," Washington, D.C., *Tribune*, April 26, 1941, r. 71; and "Spelman Strike Reported Settled," Atlanta *Daily World*, February 28, 1942, r. 77, TNCS.

114. The post–World War I riots, in which African Americans fought back, reflected a more assertive community. Subsequently the Garvey movement, the Harlem Renaissance, and the NAACP salary equalization and school integration campaigns of the 1940s established that a more organized and demanding African American community had emerged, as many scholars have described.

115. Not many coeds before the 1920s would have dared to write an article like the one Mabel Dockett penned in 1931 that "demanded" that college teach her "*how* to think" only, not "*what* to think." See Mabel Dockett, "A Student Looks at College," *CM*, April 15, 1931.

116. All the quotations in this paragraph are from "Editorial," *CM*, May [15?], 1947, 3. Showing again that the ultimate goal of the education did not necessarily change after the 1920s, this article, and a series of articles published in *CM* beginning in the 1920s, usually under the title "The Ivy Oration," suggests that the students at Spelman, at least, were very much aware of family, community, and school interests in preparing them for high individual achievement and racial advancement. The essays were usually written by the valedictorian, who used ivy as a metaphor for the graduate. The articles talked about "roots" and "foundations," which allowed the ivy to conquer all "obstacles" and ultimately to cover a building gloriously. For examples, see "The Growing Ivy," *CM*, May–June 1928; Irene C. Dobbs, "The Self-Activity of the Ivy," June [15?], 1929; Mary Reddick, "Ivy Oration," June 15, 1935; and Gloria Davis, "Ivy Oration," May [15?], 1948.

Chapter Four

1. Apparently some women were excused from the "double duty" of wage work and housework. Patricia A. Palmieri notes that white women who attended Wellesley College between the late nineteenth and early twentieth centuries were "destined daughters" or "designated daughters" whose promising futures excused them from domestic duties at home. See "Patterns of Achievement of Single Academic Women at Wellesley College, 1880–1920," *Frontiers* 2 (1980): 63–67.

2. Booker T. Washington to Portia Marshall Washington, January 9, 1906, *BTWP*, 8:490; Isaac Fisher to Constance Fisher, October 1, 1924, b. 1, Constance Fisher Papers, FUL-SC; Joseph Rollins to Charlemae Hill

Rollins, July 17, 1958, and November 26, 1962, Charlemae Hill Rollins Papers, NCCU-BLA; Thomas Church to Mary Church Terrell, November 15, 1915, r. 3, MCT-LC.

3. Amelia Perry Pride to H. B. Frissell, December 4, 1900, Amelia Perry Pride Papers, HULA.

4. Janie Porter Barrett to [Bessie] Cleaveland, March 16, 1893, Janie Porter Barrett Collection, HULA.

5. Ruth Schwartz Cowan, *More Work for Mother: The Ironies of Household Technology from the Open Hearth to the Microwave* (New York: Basic Books, 1983).

6. Florence Jacobs Edmonds, interview by Ruth Edmonds Hill, RC-BWOHP, 18–21, 26.

7. Ibid., 21, 31–32.

8. Beulah Shepard Hester, interview by Felicia Bowens, RC-BWOHP, 5–7.

9. Ibid., 4–5, 30–36. It was not uncommon for migrants to establish themselves in a house larger than they needed for the specific purpose of making a living and/or paying for it by taking in boarders. Whether the house was large enough or not, it was a way for women in particular to earn a living, and it was often the only affordable housing black newcomers to cities could find. See John Bodnar, Roger Simon, and Michael P. Weber, *Lives of Their Own: Blacks, Italians, and Poles in Pittsburgh, 1900–1960* (Urbana: University of Illinois Press, 1982), 102–8; James R. Grossman, *Land of Hope: Chicago, Black Southerners, and the Great Migration* (Chicago: University of Chicago Press, 1989), 132–33; and Richard W. Thomas, *Life for Us Is What We Make It: Building Black Community in Detroit, 1915–1945* (Bloomington: Indiana University Press, 1992), 92–93. See also Haydie Campbell to Mary Church Terrell, September 15, 1904, b. 2, MCT-LC. Campbell was a schoolteacher who took in boarders during the summers. She complained in this letter that the summer work had been such a great strain that by August she had had to take to her bed, with only a week left before having to resume her teaching duties. And see Tessa [Theresa Lee (Connelly)] to Angelina Grimké, ca. August 14, 1911, b. 38, Angelina Grimké Papers, HU-MSRC. Tessa reports that "Nellie Smith has bought a place at Cottage City and is taking boarders, charging nine dollars a week."

10. Ruth Ann Stewart, *Portia: The Life of Portia Washington Pittman, the Daughter of Booker T. Washington* (New York: Doubleday, 1977), 77–81. On chicken farming, see Booker T. Washington to Portia Pittman, February 26, 190[9?], r. 2, BTW-LC. On Portia's stress because of the illness of Booker Pittman, see Booker T. Washington to Mary Caroline Moore, May 17, 1909, *BTWP*, 10:106–7. On the full-time nurse from Freedmen's Hospital and the full-time wet nurse, see William Sidney Pittman to Booker T. Washington, May 24, 1909, 10:111–12, and 112, n. 3.

11. Stewart, *Portia*, 84–85; Portia Pittman to Booker T. Washington, November 3, 1910, *BTWP*, 10:437; Booker T. Washington to Portia Pittman, February 14, 1911, *BTWP*, 10:587–88.

12. Stewart, *Portia*, 85–92, 100–101. Stewart reports that Sidney hit Fannie, his and Portia's youngest child.

13. Mamie Garvin Fields with Karen Fields, *Lemon Swamp and Other Places: A Carolina Memoir* (New York: Free Press, 1983), 164–65; Stewart, *Portia*, 92–93, 97, 103–4, 106. All four women were normal school graduates. All except Pittman pursued additional schooling, discussed in chapter 5.

14. Mary Church Terrell, *A Colored Woman in a White World* (Washington, D.C.: Randsell, 1940), 46–47; Mary Church Terrell to Robert Terrell, August 18[?], 1900, and November 5, 1911, r. 2, MCT-LC. (All microfilmed correspondence between Mary and Robert is on reel 2.)

15. Mary Church Terrell to Robert Terrell, August 18[?], 1900, MCT-LC. See similarly extensive instructions after her children were older in Mary Church Terrell to Robert Terrell, July 24, 1915, and March 22, 1915.

16. In Mary Church Terrell to Robert Terrell, July 24, 1910, MCT-LC, she instructed him on storing her ball gown to prevent damage; she warned him not to put a sulfur candle in her room because it might harm some of her delicate clothes; she advised him on storing other clothes to prevent moth damage; and she asked him to mail numerous articles she had forgotten.

17. Robert Terrell to Mary Church Terrell, August 1, 1915, October 22, 1920, and September 25, 1913, MCT-LC.

18. In Robert Terrell to Mary Church Terrell, January 28, 1921, MCT-LC, Robert wrote, "It was too bad that you were not here to push the first button yesterday and witness the lighting of your house by electricity and thus gratify one of your life's ambitions. The performance had to take place in your absence, but it was a big success, nevertheless."

19. Mary Church Terrell to Robert Terrell, n.d. [ca. November 5, 1911], MCT-LC (original emphasis).

20. Mary Church Terrell to Robert Terrell, March 22, 1915, and October 27, 1912, MCT-LC.

21. Quotation from Mary Church Terrell to Robert H. Terrell, August 21, 1910. Also see July 24, 1910, and August 7, 1910, MCT-LC.

22. Mary Church Terrell to Robert Terrell, August 15, 1909, MCT-LC.

23. Robert Terrell to Mary Church Terrell, November 20, 1913, MCT-LC.

24. In Phyllis Terrell to Mary Church Terrell, March 21, 1930, Phyllis wrote that they needed a new fur neckpiece because their "brown fox as seen better days." In Mary Church Terrell to Phyllis Terrell, March 26, 1930, Mary informed her that the correct word was "has," not "as." Much later Terrell wrote to her then thirty-nine-year-old daughter describing her (Terrell's) stay in London and her lunch with Viscountess Snowden. Terrell reminded Phyllis to "be sure to pronounce the word 'Viscountess' as though it were spelled Vi *countess[;] the 'Vi'* rhyming with

'my.'" See Mary Church Terrell to Phyllis Terrell, July 13, 1937, r. 3, MCT-LC.

25. Two other women's public work routines kept them away from home much of the time. Estelle Massey Osborne and Mabel Keaton Staupers, administrators for the National Association of Colored Graduate Nurses, were regularly on the road. Unfortunately, however, the interviewers of both women focused on their public professional work, and even though there is a collection of Staupers's papers at Howard University, they all concern her professional life. Except for one letter in which a correspondent observed that Osborne's husband must have been glad when she returned home after working away so long, their private affairs and the interaction of their homelives and public lives cannot be documented. Both women, it seems, were divorced from their first husbands, however. A 1942 newspaper article on Osborne's resignation from Homer G. Phillips Hospital noted that she was returning to Akron, Ohio, "where her husband is a well-known physician." See "Nurse Head at St. Louis Hospital Resigns," St. Louis *Post*, October 17, 1942, r. 79, TNCS.

26. On Robert's not knowing precisely what Mary's work with the Harding campaign was, see Robert Terrell to Mary Church Terrell, October 6, 1920, MCT-LC. In this letter Robert writes, "Tell me about your work and what your plans are relative to it. Do you have to travel, or do you send others out on jaunts." Even when Mary was at home, Robert did not take for granted any domestic role for her. He once thanked her and the children "for leaving the apartment in such 'apple pie' condition." He added, "everything looks as smart and as neat as a pin." See Robert Terrell to Mary Church Terrell, July 24, 1915.

27. Lucy Mitchell, interview by Cheryl Gilkes, RC-BWOHP, 18, 21–23, 25–28, 38. For a similar example of women working where they could take their children with them, see Virginia Yans McLaughlin, "A Flexible Tradition: South Italian Immigrants Confront a New Work Experience," *Journal of Social History* 7 (1974): 429–55.

28. Clara Stanton Jones, interview, FUL-BOHP, FUL-SC; quotation from "The Emancipated Librarian," *McCall's*, April 1971, 41, Clara Jones Papers, NCCU-BLA. A related example of a cooperative spouse is in Eunice Rivers Laurie, interview by A. Lillian Thompson, RC-BWOHP, 21.

29. Fostine Riddick, interview transcript, MEC-BNA, 6–15, 19. It is hard to imagine how Riddick could work for so long without her husband finding out. It is possible, however, that she passed off some of these work days as private-duty assignments.

30. Ibid., 20–21.

31. Ibid., 22; Earl Lewis, *In Their Own Interests: Race, Class and Power in Twentieth Century Norfolk, Virginia* (Berkeley and Los Angeles: University of California Press, 1991), 81.

32. Septima Clark with LeGette Blythe, *Echo in My Soul* (New York: E. P. Dutton, 1962), 72–74. Clark's work routine is discussed in chapter 6.

33. Ibid., 84–86.

34. Quotations from Laura Terrell Jones to Mary Church Terrell, September 25, 1934, r. 3, MCT-LC. On Jones's separation and divorce, see Laura Terrell Jones to Robert and Mary Terrell, June 14, 1917.

35. Ruth Ann Stewart, *Portia*, 134, 140. Tuskegee officials offered Portia a permanent home in Alabama, but she refused it, preferring to remain in Washington, D.C.

36. Frances Grant does not describe her late adulthood as poverty stricken, but after Bordentown Institute closed in 1954, she went to New York to live with her sister and her sister's housemate while working at part-time and temporary jobs. After her sister died, she moved and eventually obtained a full-time teaching position in a New York private school. Grant seems to have been frantic after Bordentown closed. She was sixty years old, not yet eligible for full retirement (social security) benefits, and not an attractive employee because of her age. Frances Grant, interview by Maurine Rothschild, RC-BWOHP, 21, 25–28, 32–42.

37. Susan St. Clair Minor was one who delayed marriage until after the law changed in Kentucky (Louisville) to allow married women to keep their teaching positions. She married in 1940, two years after the legal change, when she was thirty-nine or forty years old. See Susan St. Clair Minor, interview transcript, OHC-UL, 48–49. It is entirely likely that many women, including Boyd, did not marry because marriage would have legally obligated them to give up their jobs.

38. Norma Boyd, interview transcript, RC-BWOHP, 25–26. Elizabeth Delany, a dentist, unlike the other women in this study, learned from her mother that she should choose between marriage and a career. She and her sister Sarah, who retired from teaching, are still single. See Sarah and A. Elizabeth Delany with Amy Hill Hearth, *Having Our Say: The Delany Sisters' First 100 Years* (New York: Kodansha International, 1993), 111. As noted in the introduction, few details are available on these women's private lives. It seems that those who did address their family lives did so to make a point about the adjustments they had to make in their public lives as a consequence of marriage. And the single women who talked about not marrying portrayed their decision in terms of wanting to have a career. Thus, it might also follow that married women who said nothing about this issue saw being married and having a career (if not a role as a public activist) as normal and not worthy of comment. This seems to be the case for Lillian Harvey, a Tuskegee nurse and educator, who relocated to Tuskegee precisely because she heard that there were single men there. She added that when she decided on the one she wanted, he did not stand a chance of getting away from her because she even prayed for him. There is no evidence that Harvey's marriage and having three children created any significant obstacles to her career. She eventually became dean of the nursing school. Lillian H. Harvey interview, MMC-DNE.

39. For example see Angelina Grimké to Francis Grimké, n.d., b. 8; and Angelina Grimké, [memo], n.d., Angelina Grimké Papers, HU-

MSRC; Anna DeCosta Banks to [Bessie] Sherman, December 7, 1905, Anna DeCosta Banks Papers, HULA.

40. Julia Hamilton Smith, interview by Cheryl Gilkes, RC-BWOHP, 27, 38, 41–42.

41. See various financial documents in boxes 7 and 8, Angelina Grimké Papers, HU-MSRC.

42. Dorothy Sterling, *Black Foremothers: Three Lives* (New York: Feminist Press, 1988), 133, 151; Beulah Hester, interview transcript, RC-BWOHP, 56; Miriam Matthews, interview by Eleanor Roberts, RC-BWOHP, 60; "Willie" to [Alberta Murray], May 11, 1934; and Hortense Fitzgerald, "Forty-eight Years in County Schools End for Veteran Teacher," Alberta Murray Papers, ARC-CC. (It is not clear whether the Murray letter above is from her niece, Wilhemina Johnston Wright, or her nephew, W. E. Johnston.)

43. See for example, W. E. B. Du Bois, *Efforts for Social Betterment among Negro Americans* (Atlanta: Atlanta University Press, 1909), 77–87; Howard N. Rabinowitz, *Race Relations in the Urban South, 1865–1890* (Urbana: University of Illinois Press, 1980), 135, 143–45; and Cynthia Neverdon-Morton, *Afro-American Women of the South and the Advancement of the Race, 1895–1925* (Knoxville: University of Tennessee Press, 1989), 143–45, 182–83.

44. Amelia Perry Pride to General [Armstrong], November 12, 1888; and Pride to [Myrtilla] Sherman, December 26, 1912, Amelia Perry Pride Papers, HULA. Pride's work roles are drawn from Amelia Perry Pride, undated "Hampton Survey."

45. Amelia Perry Pride to Miss Bellows, May 6, 1897; and Pride to [Bessie] Cleaveland, December 1892, ibid.

46. Amelia Perry Pride to Myrtilla Sherman, January 31, [?]; Pride to [Bessie] Cleaveland, December 1892; and Pride to Miss Bellows, n.d., ibid.

47. Amelia Perry Pride to Myrtilla Sherman, April 15, 1911, and February 13, 1918, ibid.

48. Amelia Perry Pride to General Armstrong, November 12, 1888, ibid.

Chapter Five

1. Among the first detailed discussions of contradictory status is Robert Park's "Human Migration and the Marginal Man," *American Journal of Sociology* 34 (1928): 881–93. Also see Everett Cherrington Hughes, "Dilemmas and Contradictions of Status," *American Journal of Sociology* 50 (1945): 353–59; and Cheryl Bernadette Leggon, "Black Female Professionals: Dilemmas and Contradictions of Status," in *The Black Woman*, ed. La Frances Rodgers-Rose (Beverly Hills, Calif.: Sage, 1980), 189–201.

2. E. Franklin Frazier, *The Negro in the United States*, rev. ed. (New York: Macmillan, 1957), 473; Mabel Staupers, "Story of the National Asso-

ciation of Colored Graduate Nurses," *American Journal of Nursing* 51 (1951), 222–23, b. 329, ANA. (Unless otherwise noted, all ANA records cited are from box 329.)

3. To reveal this pattern in education, the appendix, containing biographical sketches, is arranged in the order of the women's births.

4. See Thelma D. Perry, *History of the American Teachers Association* (Washington, D.C.: National Education Association, 1975); and Rolland Dewing, "The National Education Association and Desegregation," *Phylon: The Atlanta University Review of Race and Culture* 30 (1969): 109–24. According to Dewing, the NEA accepted black members into the national group during the 1940s, but efforts to merge the NEA and ATA did not begin until 1962. After passage of the 1964 Civil Rights Act, NEA officials gave state affiliates until 1966 to admit black members. In 1966 the six remaining segregated state organizations were given until 1969 to comply.

5. E. J. Josey, "The Black Caucus of the American Library Association," in *Handbook of Black Librarianship*, ed. E. J. Josey and Ann Allen Shockley (Littleton, Colo.: Libraries Unlimited, 1977), 66–77; "Segregation and ALA Membership," *Wilson Library Bulletin* 36 (1962): 558–62 ff., and 37 (1962): 12–14; John Axam, "The Black Caucus: A Meaningful Course of Action," in *What Black Librarians Are Saying*, ed. E. J. Josey (Metuchen, N.J.: Scarecrow Press, 1972), 208–17.

6. The National Conference of Social Work canceled its 1935 annual meeting, scheduled for Washington, D.C., because of extensive racial discrimination in public accommodations. See Walter G. Daniels, "Current Trends and Events of National Importance in Negro Education," *Journal of Negro Education* 5 (1936): 650. ("Current Trends" was a regular column.)

7. Quotation from Sadie P. Delaney to Clyde Cantrell, April 15, 1952, b. 1, Sadie Peterson Delaney Papers, TUA. The nurses' ultimate position on the issue, though worded slightly differently, was exactly the same in its meaning. They noted that "the time has come for the total mobilization of nursing services without limitations." See at n. 60 below.

8. Robert Bellah, Richard Madsen, William M. Sullivan, Ann Swidler, and Steven M. Tipton, *Habits of the Heart: Middle America Observed* (London: Hutchinson, 1985), 66, 69–71, 119–20, 287–88, 300.

9. Karen Buhler-Wilkerson, " 'Caring in Its Proper Place': Race and Benevolence in Charleston, S.C., 1813–1930," *Nursing Research,* January–February 1992, 15–16; Anna DeCosta Banks to [Bessie] Cleaveland, January 22, [1910]; Banks to [Myrtilla] Sherman, April 18, 1904; Banks to "Miss Davis," May 14, 1904; Banks to Sherman, April 13, 1912; and Banks to Sherman, January 25, 1922, Anna DeCosta Banks Papers, HULA. There is no evidence that Banks and her assistant, Viola Ford, were employed or paid directly by Metropolitan. Instead, there is every indication that Metropolitan paid the Ladies' Benevolent Society to see to the work, and it just became an additional caseload for Banks. See "The Ladies' Benevolent Society Annual Report for 1916." It should also be

noted that the Lucy Brown Club, a black women's club in the city, contributed to the creation of the Hospital and Training School. The members also recruited students, helped pay the head nurse's salary, and provided supplies for the hospital. See Darlene Clark Hine, *Black Women in White: Racial Conflict and Cooperation in the Nursing Profession, 1890–1950* (Bloomington: Indiana University Press, 1989), 20.

10. Anna Banks to [Hollis B.] Frissell, January 20, 1910; and Banks to [Myrtilla] Sherman, January 15, 1907, and April 13, 1912, Anna DeCosta Banks Papers, HULA.

11. Anna Banks to [Bessie] Cleveland [*sic*], January 5, 1899; and Banks to Sherman, January 9, 1916, Anna DeCosta Banks Papers, HULA. Banks's quotation is from I Cor. 3:6.

12. Quotation from Buhler-Wilkerson, " 'Caring in its Proper Place,' " 15. Also see "Nurse Training in Charleston," *Southern Workman*, June 1899, Anna DeCosta Banks Papers, HULA.

13. An excellent discussion of the characterizations of nurses is provided in Darlene Clark Hine, " 'They Shall Mount up with Wings as Eagles': Historical Images of Black Nurses, 1890–1950," in *Images of Nurses: Perspectives from History, Art and Literature*, ed. Anne Hudson Jones (Philadelphia: University of Pennsylvania Press, 1988), 177–96.

14. Louie D. Shivery, "The History of Organized Social Work among Negroes in Atlanta, 1890–1935" (M.A. thesis, Atlanta University, 1936), 43; Jacqueline Anne Rouse, *Lugenia Burns Hope: Black Southern Reformer* (Athens: University of Georgia Press, 1989), 65–66.

15. One example of the women's characterizing their work in this way is provided in Mary Church Terrell to Robert Terrell, August 18[?], 1900, r. 2, MCT-LC, in which, as noted above, she insisted she stayed on the lecture circuit not for the money, which was minimal, but for the good she could do. And in Norma Boyd, interview by A. Lillian Thompson, RC-BWOHP, 28, Boyd summarized her work ethic as a lifetime of service. "Satisfaction comes in service," she maintained, in "the number of people you have helped." Boyd was also a public lecturer, but in her view to have accepted pay for it, since she earned a living as a schoolteacher, would have demeaned its value. And finally, in Amelia Perry Pride to "Mrs. Langhorn," June 23, 1899, Amelia Perry Pride Papers, HULA, Pride concluded that she "would rather wear out working *among all classes of my race* than to *rust* out seeing so much to be done" (original emphasis). Pride was defending her name in this letter, and so some of the details might be exaggerations. It cannot be ignored, however, that she worked as a day school teacher, a night school teacher, a caretaker of an old-folks home, and a social worker, as well as in a variety of other areas.

16. In this first generation, five out of ten women were normal school graduates. Two earned college degrees; two held nursing diplomas; and one held no degree. In the second generation there were six normal school graduates: five of them subsequently earned college degrees and the other completed a nursing program. Five additional women were nursing school (not normal) graduates, and twelve entered

the professions straight out of college (with degrees). The education beyond high school for Rollins, who remained in the professions, is unknown. And Mamie Garvin Fields, a second-generation normal program
graduate, continued her education in a college program and "completed
(or was on the point of completing) all the degree requirements," but
"some murky explanations were apparently given about the nature of the
program at [South Carolina] State," and she did not receive her degree.
These details are provided in Karen E. Fields to Stephanie J. Shaw, January 20, 1995. Only one third-generation woman finished a normal course,
and she also earned higher degrees. Of the ten remaining women in this
generation, five went directly into college (one in a nursing program),
and five went from nursing schools to colleges.

   17. The movement to transform normal schools into colleges be-
gan around 1910, peaked during the 1920s, but lasted until the 1940s.
See Kathleen M. Heim, "Professional Education: Some Comparisons," in
As Much to Learn as to Teach: Essays in Honor of Lester Asheim, ed. Joel M.
Lee and Beth A. Hamilton (Hampden, Conn.: Linnet Books, 1979), 143–
47; and Merle L. Borrowman, "Education of Teachers—History," in *The
Encyclopedia of Education* (New York: Macmillan and Free Press, 1971),
74–77. Sociological studies on the organization of all four occupations un-
der study here are included in Amitai Etzioni, ed., *The Semi-professions and
Their Organization: Teachers, Nurses, Social Workers* (New York: Free Press,
1969).

   18. William J. Goode, "The Librarian: From Occupation to Profession," *Library Quarterly* 31 (1961): 306–20; Heim, "Professional Education," 155–57; Sarah K. Vann, *Training for Librarianship before 1923* (Chicago: American Library Association, 1961), 4–6, 10–18, 31–32, 64. Also
see Dee Garrison, "The Tender Technicians: The Feminization of Public
Librarianship, 1876–1905," in *Clio's Consciousness Raised: New Perspectives
on the History of Women*, ed. Mary Hartman and Lois W. Banner (New
York: Harper and Row, 1974), 158–78; and Wayne A. Wiegand, *The Politics of an Emerging Profession: The American Library Association, 1876–1917*
(New York: Greenwood, 1986). Although Butler and Horton became librarians after determining a community need, both of the second-
generation women who chose the profession sought library careers from
the beginning and entered library science programs in college. Miriam
Matthews studied library science at the University of California at Berkeley during the 1920s, and Clara Stanton Jones earned a master's degree
in library science from the University of Michigan in 1938.

   19. James Edward Hagat, *The Training of Social Workers*, quoted in
Heim, "Professional Education," 139–41; Leslie Leighninger, *Social Work:
Search for Identity* (New York: Greenwood, 1987), 27; Donald Brieland,
"History and Evolution of Social Work Practice," in *Encyclopedia of Social
Work*, 18th ed. (Silver Spring, Md.: National Association of Social Work-
ers, 1987), 739–83. Also see Roy Lubove, *The Professional Altruist: The
Emergence of Social Work as a Career, 1880–1930* (Cambridge: Harvard Uni-
versity Press, 1965) and revisionist interpretations of professionalization

including Nina Toren, *Social Work: The Case of a Semi-profession* (Beverly Hills, Calif.: Sage, 1972), and idem, "Semi-professionalism and Social Work: A Theoretical Perspective," in Etzioni, *Semi-professions and Their Organization*, 141–95. And see Andrea Tuttle Kornbluh, "James Hathaway Robinson and the Origins of Professional Social Work in the Black Community," in *Race and the City: Work, Community and Protest in Cincinnati, 1820–1970*, ed. Henry Louis Taylor Jr. (Urbana: University of Illinois Press, 1993), 209–31.

20. Susan M. Reverby, *Ordered to Care: The Dilemma of American Nursing, 1850–1945* (New York: Cambridge University Press, 1987), 3, 122–31; Barbara Melosh, *"The Physician's Hand": Work Culture and Conflict in American Nursing* (Philadelphia: Temple University Press, 1982), 40–47; Nancy Tomes, "The Silent Battle: Nurse Registration in New York State, 1903–1920," in *Nursing History: New Perspectives, New Possibilities*, ed. Ellen Condliffe Lagemann (New York: Teachers College Press, 1983), 107–32, esp. 111–14. Also see Vern L. Bullough and Bonnie Bullough, *The Emergence of Modern Nursing*, 2d ed. (Toronto: Macmillan, 1969), esp. 148–81.

21. Rice noted that this is precisely why she left teaching. Ethel Ray Nance left social work during the 1930s and took clerical positions. She went back to college in the 1970s, graduating when she was nearly eighty years old. Details of Nance's 1978 graduation were provided by Steven Eric Nielson of the Division of Archives/Manuscripts, Minnesota Historical Society, St. Paul, Minnesota.

22. Fostine Riddick, interview transcript, MEC-BNA, 6–10.

23. Louis R. Harlan, "South Carolina: Inequality as a Higher Law," in *Separate and Unequal: Public School Campaigns and Racism in the Southern Seaboard States, 1901–1915* (Chapel Hill: University of North Carolina Press, 1958), 170–209; statistics on pp. 208–9. Harlan notes that such inequality persisted at least through the 1928–29 school year, when South Carolina public school officials allocated $60.06 per white child and $7.89 per black child, on average. In the most extreme case, one county provided $124.29 per white child and $5.85 per black child. An extensive quantitative study of black education is Robert A. Margo, *Race and Schooling in the South, 1880–1950: An Economic History* (Chicago: University of Chicago Press, 1990).

24. The disparity was not unique to education. Forrester B. Washington, an early social work scholar, noted that before the 1920s, public agencies—mostly in the South but in the North too—employed "untrained Negro social workers whereas the same agency would not employ untrained white workers." See "The Need and Education of Negro Social Workers," *Journal of Negro Education* 4 (1935): esp. 82–83.

25. Septima Clark with LeGette Blythe, *Echo in My Soul* (New York: E. P. Dutton, 1962), 75, 83, 86. Susan St. Clair Minor, also a normal school graduate, received her diploma in 1921. Her interview does not note when she earned the bachelor's degree, but she completed a master's degree in 1946. See Susan St. Clair Minor, interview transcript, OHC-UL.

26. Evelyn Tomes, "Mabel Northcross: 'Old Miss,'" unpublished manuscript, 1–2; and Mabel Northcross, interview, MMC-DNE. Similarly, Veronica Smith Chisholm probably took fifteen years or more to complete her bachelor's degree. She married after finishing nursing school and subsequently gave birth to a daughter. Between her paid public work and her family domestic work, she took night and summer classes. During her interview, she neglected to say when she graduated. Instead, connecting her child-care responsibilities to her educational endeavors, she noted: "I finally finished [the bachelor's degree] when my daughter was old enough to go to graduation with me." Veronica Smith Chisholm, interview transcript, MEC-BNA, 7.

27. Mabel Northcross, interview, MMC-DNE. Also see Miriam Matthews, interview by Eleanor Roberts, RC-BWOHP, 26. Matthews took a six-month leave of absence without pay from her job in the Los Angeles County Public Library System to work and study in the New York Public Library System.

28. The southern public image of the black nurse as a devoted domestic servant rather than a professional is discussed in Hine, "'They Shall Mount up with Wings as Eagles'"; and Carter G. Woodson, *The Negro Professional Man and the Community* (1934; rpt. New York: Negro Universities Press, 1969), 147–48. Especially telling is Charles Dudley Warner, "Colored Schools South," *SM*, May 1887, 1. In commenting on the nursing program at Spelman, Warner notes that nursing was "for colored women, suited in every way to their natures and capacities. . . . The colored women are natural capital nurses—gentle, patient, dexterous."

29. Mabel Keaton Staupers, *No Time for Prejudice: A Story of the Integration of Negroes in Nursing in the United States* (New York: Macmillan, 1961), 12, 20; Mary Elizabeth Carnegie, *The Path We Tread: Blacks in Nursing, 1854–1984* (Philadelphia: J. B. Lippincott, 1986), 156–57; Hine, *Black Women in White*, 92–93.

30. Estelle Massey Osborne, interview transcript, MEC-BNA, 1; Carnegie, *The Path We Tread*, 39, 237; Hine, *Black Women in White*, 118.

31. Mary Elizabeth Carnegie, interview transcript, 7–16; and Mary Elizabeth Carnegie, Curriculum Vita, 1, MEC-BNA. When Carnegie later applied for Rockefeller Fund support for more training, General Education Board administrator Robert July did not believe that she would be an effective leader and concluded that he would support her fellowship application, unenthusiastically, if he had to. Carnegie eventually earned a Ph.D. in health services administration. See Robert W. July, notes from interview with Mary E. Carnegie, January 12, 1951, ser. 1, subser. 3, b. 548, GEB-RAC.

32. Beulah Hester, interview by Felicia Bowens, RC-BWOHP, 7.

33. Scholarship application of Latis Melba Caver, November 21, 1936, b. 381, RFF, FUL-SC.

34. The "oldest" woman is Fostine Riddick, who graduated from John A. Andrew Hospital during the 1930s and completed bachelor's and master's degrees during the 1950s and 1960s. The second "oldest"

woman is Mary Elizabeth Carnegie, who graduated from the Lincoln Hospital School of Nursing in 1937, then completed a bachelor's degree in 1942, a master's degree in 1952, and a doctorate in 1972. The "youngest" woman is Gloria Smith, who graduated from Wayne State University College of Nursing during the mid-1950s. She subsequently earned two master's degrees and a doctorate.

35. Miriam Matthews, interview transcript, RC-BWOHP, 62; Application of Ollie Jewell Sims, May 15, 1936, b. 381, RFF, FUL-SC; Mabel Staupers, interview transcript, MEC-BNA, 5; Norma Boyd, interview by A. Lillian Thompson, RC-BWOHP, 28.

36. Florence Edmonds, interview by Ruth Edmonds Hill, RC-BWOHP, 18; Julia Smith, interview by Cheryl Gilkes, RC-BWOHP, 10.

37. James T. Williams to "whom it may concern," July 27, 1954, vol. 5; M. Cleopatra Crutcher to Sadie P. Delaney, June 26, 1948; Jewell Gresham to Delaney, February 14, 1949; Dorothy Ferebee to Delaney, October 15, 1952; and NCNW to Delaney, November 15, 1952, vol. 3; Mabel Staupers to Delaney, n.d.; and Urban League to Delaney (telegram), March 9, 1950, vol. 2, Sadie Delaney Papers, Schomburg Center; "BTWA to Honor Three for Top Achievement," *Michigan Chronicle,* July 1, 1961; and "Honored for Service," *Michigan Chronicle,* December 1, 1956, vertical files, women—biographical, "Clara Jones," Labor Archives; Carnegie, *The Path We Tread,* 101, 240.

38. Clyde H. Cantrell, "Sadie P. Delaney: Bibliotherapist and Librarian," *Southeastern Librarian* 6 (1956): 108; T. P. Sevensma to Delaney, November 14, 1934; and S. L. Smith to Sadie Peterson [Delaney], April 21, 1927, vol. 1; John W. Lockett to Delaney, March 12, 1949, vol. 2; Joanne Dann to Delaney, August 9, 1950; and (Mrs.) N. M. G. Prange to Delaney, October 19, 1936, vol. 3; Harry C. Bauer to Delaney, June 9, 1954; and Ruth M. Tews to Delaney, February 16, 1955, vol. 5; and H. O. Teets to Delaney, February 21, 1957, vol. 6, Delaney Papers, Schomburg Center; Prange to Delaney, November 30, 1936; Virginia Lacy Jones to Delaney, March 25, 1947; and Felix Jager to Delaney, September 7, 1950, Delaney Papers, TUA. On the use of bibliotherapy in San Quentin, see Eric Cummins, *The Rise and Fall of California's Radical Prison Movement* (Stanford: Stanford University Press, 1994), esp. 21–32.

39. Perry, *History of the American Teachers Association,* 18–23; Ernest J. Middleton, "The Louisiana Education Association, 1901–1970," *Journal of Negro Education* 47 (1978): 373.

40. Harriet Hill, "The Division of Librarians of the Virginia State Teachers' Association," in Josey and Shockley, *Handbook of Black Librarianship,* 64.

41. Laura Lewis, "The Librarians' Section of the Georgia Teachers and Education Association," and Carrie C. Robinson, "The Alabama Association of School Librarians," in Josey and Shockley, *Handbook of Black Librarianship,* 52 and 49, respectively. Also see Mollie Huston Lee, "North Carolina Negro Library Association, 1934–1954," *Library Service Review* 2 (1955): 10–31.

42. Mabel Staupers, interview transcript, MEC-BNA, 9; Estelle Massey Riddle Osborne, interview transcript, MEC-BNA, 5; Florence Edmonds, interview transcript, RC-BWOHP, iii; Mary Elizabeth Carnegie, interview transcript, MEC-BNA, 19; Gloria Smith, interview, MMC-DNE.

43. Mary Elizabeth Carnegie, interview transcript, MEC-BNA, 17; Fostine Riddick, interview transcript, MEC-BNA, 12–14; Barbara Pickett, interview, FUL-BOHP; Barbara Simmons Miller to Stephanie J. Shaw, July 25, 1994, in the author's possession; Clark, *Echo in My Soul*, 77. In contrast, when Estelle Osborne was invited to ANA meetings at segregated hotels, she declined the invitations. Walter White, whose advice on the matter she sought, insisted (and Ruth Logan Roberts agreed) that no "self-respecting person" would submit "to the humiliation of using service entrance and elevators." White and Roberts thought that Osborne's role as an NACGN officer made it imperative that she not abide the discrimination. See Hine, *Black Women in White*, 130–31.

44. Hospital Division, ALA, to Sadie Peterson Delaney, July 3, 1947, Sadie Peterson Delaney Papers, vol. 1, Schomburg Center.

45. Mabel E. Willoughby to Sadie P. Delaney, November 20, 1951, Sadie Peterson Delaney Papers, TUA.

46. Sadie P. Delaney to Clyde Cantrell, April 15, 1952, Sadie Peterson Delaney Papers, TUA. Also see Cantrell to Delaney, April 10, 1952, and May 9, 1952; and "Minutes of the Meeting of the Bi-racial Committee [of the Alabama Library Association] January 18, 1952," vol. 5, Sadie Peterson Delaney Papers, Schomburg Center. The minutes were provided to Delaney by Cantrell, who supported integration. Also note that the "Bi-racial Committee" was apparently not biracial, but instead a committee designed to make a decision on integration.

47. Ethel Saunders to Sadie P. Delaney, April 7, 1954, vol. 5, Sadie Peterson Delaney Papers, Schomburg Center.

48. Ellinor G. Preston to Sadie Delaney, August 29, 1956, vol. 5, Sadie Peterson Delaney Papers, Schomburg Center. On controversies and protests concerning segregated accommodations at the 1936 ALA meeting (Richmond, Virginia), see Walter G. Daniels, "Current Trends and Events of National Importance in Negro Education," *Journal of Negro Education* 5 (1936): 648–50. On 1950s ALA meeting sites, see Ray N. Moore to David H. Clift, March 11, 1953, vertical files, "Negro Library Association," SLWPL.

49. Suggesting Delaney's plans to retire, see Joan Cloke to Sadie Peterson Delaney, July 21, 1951; and indicating that she did not retire, see R. A. Delaney to Sadie Peterson Delaney, January 7, 1954, vol. 4, Delaney Papers, Schomburg Center. In the latter document, her husband congratulated her for having completed thirty years of working in the hospital library. The letter did not indicate that she was, even then, retiring.

50. Estelle Massey Riddle to Susan Francis, October 19, 1937, b. 225, RFF, FUL-SC.

51. Mary Hickey to Estelle M. Riddle, March 28, 1938, NACGN records, Schomburg Center.

52. Mrs. Bedford [Estelle M.] Riddle to Mary Hickey, May 5, 1938, ibid.

53. "Minutes," Advisory Council of the NACGN, November 3, 1939 Meeting, ANA.

54. C. [Carrie] M. Sharpe to Mabel Staupers, September 2, 1939; Staupers to Sharpe, September 15, 1939, ANA.

55. Minutes, Advisory Council, November 3, 1939, ANA.

56. Minutes of the Joint Conference of the NOPHN, ANA, NLNE, Advisory Council of the NACGN, January 5, 1940, ANA.

57. Minutes of the Joint Conference [of the NLNE, NOPHN, ANA, NACGN], October 28, 1940; and Claribel Wheeler to Mabel Staupers, October 30, 1940, ANA. During World War I an influenza epidemic decimated the ranks of military nurses, who were already in short supply, causing the change in military policy. The entry of black nurses to World War I service represented no change of heart or permanent change in policy.

58. Julia C. Stimson to Staupers, November 26, 1941, ANA.

59. Mabel Staupers to Julia Stimson, January 12, 1942, NACGN records, Schomburg Center; Mary A. Hickey to Staupers, March 26, 1942, ANA.

60. Untitled typescript, April 12, 1945, NACGN records, MEC-BNA.

61. Mary I. Campbell to Mabel Staupers, January 11, 1946; and "Report of Conference of Representatives of the American Nurses' Association and National Association of Colored Graduate Nurses to discuss the question of ANA membership for Negro Nurses in states where they are not admitted to membership in the State Nurses' Association," January 1946, ANA.

62. "Biennial Nurses Convention," [September 1946, Atlantic City, New Jersey], NACGN records, Schomburg Center; Staupers, No Time for Prejudice, 132; "Statement from the American Nurses' Association to the National Association of Colored Graduate Nurses," August 1949, ANA.

63. Report of the National Association of Colored Graduate Nurses to the Board of Directors of the ANA, [ca. January 22, 1947], ANA.

64. Mabel Staupers, "The President's Message," National News Bulletin 4 (1950): 4. Also see Latis M. Campbell to Ella Best, May 12, 1948; and Ruth C. Balthrop to Katherine J. Densford, May 12, 1948, ANA. Also relevant is "Report of the National Association of Colored Graduate Nurses [to the American Nurses' Association]," November 8, 1947, ANA, in which Staupers quotes extensively from the new United States Civil Rights Commission's To Secure These Rights in her effort to convince the ANA of the urgency of ending segregation. Like the Commission report, Staupers's report clearly distinguished between desegregation and integration.

65. "Excerpts from the Verbatim Report of the Meeting of the

Advisory Council of the American Nurses' Association . . . ," January 24, 1947; and [Memo regarding conference with Alma Vessells and Margaret Jackson], March 14, 1947, ANA.

66. "Negro Nurses in the ANA," *American Journal of Nursing* 48 (1948): 750; "NACGN Member Named to Headquarters Staff of ANA as Assistant Executive Secretary," *National News Bulletin* 3 (1949): 1; "ANA Votes Individual Memberships, Elects Mrs. E. M. Osborne to Board," *National News Bulletin* 2 (1948): 1; Alida C. Dailey to Linnie Laird, November 22, 1948; and Statement from the ANA to NACGN, August 1949, ANA. Also see Staupers, *No Time for Prejudice*, 133, 136.

67. Report of the August 1949 Meeting of the NACGN, September 6, 1949, ANA.

68. NACGN goals are outlined in Staupers, *No Time for Prejudice*, 14–17; "The National Association of Colored Graduate Nurses," b. 225, RFF, FUL-SC; and Mabel Staupers to Pearl McIver, September 9, 1949, ANA.

69. See Agnes Ohlson to Mabel Staupers, October 2, 1950, and November 1, 1950; Minutes of the Board Meeting, National Association of Colored Graduate Nurses, January 25, 1951; and "Brotherhood Has to Be Lived," *American Journal of Nursing* 52 (1952): 163, ANA.

70. Alma Vessells John to Ella Best, March 6, 1951; Alma John and Mabel Staupers to NACGN members, March 12, 1951; Ella Best to Staupers, March 22, 1951; and [Mabel Staupers], "Why Should Club Groups Continue (if the National Association of Colored Graduate Nurses Will Vote to Terminate Its Program)," *National News Bulletin*, ANA. Also on the donation of NACGN records to the Schomburg Center, see "Library to Receive Gift from Nurses," (New York) *Amsterdam News*, November 7, 1953.

71. "Negro Nurses Will Disband Soon," *New York Times*, October 21, 1950, Mabel Staupers Papers, HU-MSRC; "Negro Nursing Unit Dissolves: Its Fight Won," New York *Tribune*, February 11, 1951; and "The Nurses Disband," (New York) *Amsterdam News*, February 10, 1951, NACGN Scrapbook, vol. 8, NACGN records, Schomburg Center. Quotation taken from untitled manuscript, January 1951, NACGN records, MEC-BNA. That manuscript reads very much like the text of Alma Vessells John to Joseph Herzberg (city editor of the New York *Tribune*), February 5, 1951, ANA.

72. Walter White, untitled typescript prepared for the Chicago *Defender*, ANA.

73. For reference to Osborne's being the first nurse in the District of Columbia with a master's degree, see Estelle M. Osborne, interview transcript, MEC-BNA, 7.

74. See related discussion in William Goode, "Encroachment, Charlatanism, and the Emerging Profession: Psychology, Sociology, and Medicine," *American Sociological Review* 25 (1960): 902–14; James G. Burrow, *Organized Medicine in the Progressive Era: The Move toward Monopoly* (Baltimore: Johns Hopkins University Press, 1977); Robert E. Kohler,

From Medical Chemistry to Biochemistry: The Making of a Biochemical Discipline (New York: Cambridge University Press, 1982); Eliot Friedson, *Profession of Medicine: A Study of the Sociology of Applied Knowledge* (New York: Dodd, Mead, 1970); Jeffrey Berlant, *Profession and Monopoly* (Berkeley and Los Angeles: University of California Press, 1975); and Peter Meiksons, "Professionalism and Conflict: The Case of the American Association of Engineers," *Journal of Social History* 19 (1986): 403–21. A general discussion of some of the literature on professionalism as it pertains to women may be found in Joan Jacobs Brumberg and Nancy Tomes, "Women in the Professions: A Research Agenda for American Historians," *Reviews in American History* 10 (1982): 275–96. Also see Introduction, note 8.

Chapter Six

1. Florence Lattimore, *A Palace of Delight (The Locust Street Settlement for Negroes at Hampton, Virginia)* (Hampton, Va.: Press of the Hampton Normal and Agricultural Institute, 1915), 19.

2. *Locust Street Social Settlement: Founded and Managed by Colored People* (Hampton, Va.: Press of the Hampton Normal and Agricultural Institute, 1912), 1–21; Lattimore, *A Palace of Delight;* Janie Porter Barrett to "Miss Tileson," December 4, 1885, Janie Porter Barrett Papers, HULA.

3. Janie Porter Barrett to [Hollis P.] Frissell, December 25, 1915, ibid. Also see Barrett to [Myrtilla] Sherman, December 25, 1915. The "home school" came to be called the Virginia Industrial School for Colored Girls. A contemporary discussion of the school may be found in William Anthony Aery, "Helping Wayward Girls: Virginia's Pioneer Work," *Southern Workman* 44 (1915): 598–604.

4. Alice Dunbar Nelson paid tribute to Barrett in Nelson's Pittsburgh *Courier* column in 1925 because Barrett did not "nurse her grief and sit down and bewail the hard future which had taken her mate from her when they were both young and avid of life." See Gloria T. Hull, ed., *Give Us Each Day: The Diary of Alice Dunbar Nelson* (New York: W. W. Norton, 1984), [147].

5. See Booker T. Washington to Ruth Anna Fisher, November 14, 1906, b. 564; Washington to D. C. Fisher [Ruth Anna Fisher's father], November 16, 1906; and D. C. Fisher to Washington, November 21, 1906, b. 321, BTW-LC. For details related to Fisher's subsequent career, her work with John Franklin Jameson for the Library of Congress, and her overseas work in major British libraries, museums, and archives, see Ruth Anna Fisher file, OCAR; Sylvia Lyons Render, "Afro-American Women: The Outstanding and the Obscure," *Quarterly Journal of the Library of Congress* 32 (1975): 315–19. A single woman accepting a position at Tuskegee could also completely lose her personal life because single women were expected to live in the dorms as unofficial "house mothers" and thus to be working practically all the time. They had to perform this

work in addition to their on-campus teaching, mothers' club work, and other extension work.

6. For a northern comparison to the Locust Street Settlement House, Mary Burnett Talbert made part of the "old Talbert home" in Buffalo into a girls' club soon after moving there with her new husband. She at first held weekly meetings "at which she talked to the young folk about dress, manners, and morals." During the summers, she also gave dances for the young people in the pavilion behind her house. See "Local Woman Benefactor of Negro People," *Illustrated Buffalo Express*, July 15, 1923, Mary Morris Burnett Talbert file, OCAR. Talbert was an 1886 graduate of Oberlin College.

7. Even though I am distinguishing "work" from "jobs," I am also purposely distinguishing "work" from "work culture," which some scholars describe as the difference between the work assignment and the process of getting the work done. Discussions of work culture, to this point, aim to explain workers' efforts to advance or privilege themselves, usually in opposition to management, in the workplace. "Work," as I am using it, includes aspects traditionally associated with work culture, but is more visibly concerned with advancing the larger community. Cheryl Townsend Gilkes, in " 'Holding Back the Ocean with a Broom': Black Women and Community Work," in *The Black Woman*, ed. La Frances Rodgers-Rose (Beverly Hills, Calif.: Sage, 1980), 217–31, similarly notes that "community work" became the occupation of the black professional women she studied regardless of their job titles.

8. Addie W. Hunton wrote that "Those who write most about the moral degradation of the Negro woman know little or nothing of that best element of our women who are quietly and unobtrusively working out the salvation of the race. Because the Negro women with whom they come in contact exhibit none of those higher qualities that are based upon virtue, it is assumed that these women are typical of all Negro women, and upon this assumption, an attempt is made to prove, to the shame of all, a wholesale immorality." See "Negro Womanhood Defended," *Voice of the Negro* 1 (1904): 280–81. In a 1900 article, Mary Church Terrell wrote that educated black women must come "into closer touch with the masses of our women, by whom, whether we will or not, the world will always judge the womanhood of the race." See "The Duty of the National Association of Colored Women to the Race," *AME Church Review* 6 (1900): 346–47. Later she wrote: "The literate do not interfere sufficiently with the illiterate, whose conduct and whose crimes bring shame to the race and disgrace to themselves, while the lot of all, the just as well as the unjust, is made increasingly hard thereby." See "The Mission of the Meddler," *Voice of the Negro* 2 (1905): 566–68. A most eloquent essay that lays responsibility for these social problems at the feet of the state rather than the community is Julia A. Hooks, "Duty of the Hour," in *Afro-American Encyclopaedia, or The Thoughts, Doings, and Sayings of the Race*, comp. James T. Haley (Nashville: Haley and Florida, 1896),

332–39. My thanks to Kenneth Goings for providing a copy of this document.

9. Sarah Collins Fernandis, "A Colored Settlement," *Southern Workman* 33 (1904): 346–50; Rosa Hunter Moore, "A Pioneer Settlement Worker," *Southern Workman* 52 (1923): 320–24; untitled, undated article, *Southern Workman*, Sarah Collins Fernandis Papers, HULA. And also see Ethel Ray Nance, interview by David Taylor, AMD-MHS, 15–16; Inabel Burns Lindsay, "The Contributions of Negroes to Welfare Services, 1865–1900," *Journal of Negro Education* 25 (1956): 15–24; W. E. B. Du Bois, *Some Efforts of American Negroes for Their Own Social Betterment* (Atlanta: Atlanta University Press, 1898); and Frances R. Bartholomew, "A Northern Settlement for Negroes," *Southern Workman* 35 (1906): 99–102. Darlene Clark Hine describes an exactly parallel example that takes place thirty years later and in the Middle West, when Ada Harris moved to Norwood, Indiana, a black community near Indianapolis that was supposed to be known for its crap games and prostitution rings. Harris later became the school principal, founded a boys' club, and raised money for a gym and clubhouse. See Hine, " 'We Specialize in the Wholly Impossible': The Philanthropic Work of Black Women," in *Lady Bountiful Revisited: Women, Philanthropy and Power*, ed. Kathleen D. McCarthy (New Brunswick, N.J.: Rutgers University Press, 1990), 72–73.

10. A study of black settlement work is Elisabeth Lasch-Quinn, *Black Neighbors: Race and the Limits of Reform in the American Settlement House Movement, 1890–1945* (Chapel Hill: University of North Carolina Press, 1993). Lasch-Quinn also sees black settlement work as a bridge between black residents and "the rest of the city," and as being aimed at individual and community development. And see Wilma Peebles-Wilkins, "Black Women and American Social Welfare: The Life of Fredericka Douglass Sprague Perry," *Affilia* 4 (1989): 33–44. A general comparison of black and white women's social welfare activism is Linda Gordon, "Black and White Visions of Welfare: Women's Welfare Activism, 1890–1945," *Journal of American History* 78 (1991): 559–90.

11. See "The Calhoun School," *Southern Workman* 45 (1916): 564; and Pitt Dillingham, "Black Belt Settlement Work," *Southern Workman* 31 (1902): 383–88, and 31 (1903): 437–44.

12. Constitution of the Neighborhood Union, 1908, article 2, b. 1, NUC-WL.

13. Ibid., articles 2–4; Neighborhood Union Application for Incorporation to the State of Georgia, County of Fulton, March 17, 1911; "An Open Letter from the Neighborhood Union to the Editor of the Atlanta *Constitution*," December 3, 1913; and "Annual Report of the Neighborhood Union, 1913–14," b. 1; and "The Neighborhood Union: A Survey," b. 2, NUC-WL. In a letter of recommendation written for Lugenia Hope, A. D. Williams wrote, "She has the happy faculty of being able to have all classes of women work together. Whenever we have wanted the women of our city to work as a unit, we have always secured Mrs. Hope

314

NOTES TO CHAPTER SIX

as a leader and we have never failed." See A. D. Williams to "whom it concerns," October 1, 1919, b. 2. Neighborhood Union work is also summarized in "Social Betterment in Negro Communities," *AUB*, ser. 2, January 1913, 13–20; and "Colored Women and School Improvement in Atlanta," *AUB*, ser. 2, October 1912, 24–31.

The work carried on in Washington, D.C., became decentralized in this way too. One contemporary wrote of the Cooperative Civil League, an offshoot of Fernandis's settlement work, that "starting with a membership of thirty-five it has spread among the women in all parts of the city until there are now separate groups in the different wards who work out their individual community problems and come together to report progress." See Moore, "A Pioneer Settlement Worker," 323.

14. Jacqueline Anne Rouse, "Lugenia D. Burns Hope: A Black Female Reformer in the South, 1871–1947" (Ph.D. diss., Emory University, 1983), 64–125. Rouse aptly titles this chapter on the Neighborhood Union "An Example of Community Building." The revised chapter in her book *Lugenia Burns Hope: Black Southern Reformer* (Athens: University of Georgia Press, 1989), 57–90, is retitled " 'Thy Neighbor as Thyself,' " the Union's motto. Also see Rouse, "The Legacy of Community Organizing: Lugenia Burns Hope and the Neighborhood Union," *Journal of Negro History* 69 (1984): 114–33.

15. Jane Addams, *Twenty Years at Hull House, with Autobiographical Notes* (New York: New American Library, 1910), 59–74; Roy Lubove, *The Professional Altruists: The Emergence of Social Work as a Profession* (Cambridge: Harvard University Press, 1965). Lubove's work, however, does not concern settlement house workers. Also see Allan Davis, *Spearheads of Reform: The Social Settlements and the Progressive Movement, 1890–1914* (New York: Oxford University Press, 1967); and Mina Carson, *Settlement Folk: Social Thought and the American Settlement Movement, 1885–1930* (Chicago: University of Chicago Press, 1990).

16. See Addie Watts Hunton, "The Southern Federation of Colored Women," *Voice of the Negro* 2 (1905): 850–54. In this article Hunton wrote: "It is generally admitted that the most womanly woman is she who, while making her hearthstone her throne, her children her jewels, can still have a warm heart and a ministering hand for the crying needs of humanity."

17. "A Tribute of Love and Appreciation to Lugenia Hope, Honoring Her on the Twenty-fifth Anniversary of the Founding of the Neighborhood Union," b. 3, NUC-WL. For very useful discussions on black professional women's developing careers as community resource persons, see Cheryl Townsend Gilkes, "Going up for the Oppressed: The Career Mobility of Black Women Community Workers," *Journal of Social Issues* 39 (1983): 115–39, and "Successful Rebellious Professionals: The Black Woman's Professional Identity and Community Commitment," *Psychology of Women Quarterly* 6 (1982): 289–311.

18. *The Stanford L. Warren Public Library* (Durham, N.C.: Trustee Board of Stanford L. Warren Public Library, 1947); and "Negro Library

Does Valuable Service Here," Durham *Sun*, November 25, 1923, Stanford L. Warren Records, SLWPL; Beverly Washington Jones, *Stanford L. Warren Branch Library, Seventy-seven Years of Public Service: A Phoenix in the Durham Community* (Durham, N.C.: Durham County Library, 1990), 3–21.

19. For one piece of evidence concerning the fiscal difficulties that Neighborhood Union women faced, see Angie Kendall to Lugenia Burns Hope, February 18, 1916, b. 1, NUC-WL. In this letter Kendall, who was Spelman Seminary's treasurer, was about to prepare her report to the college on the purchase of the Neighborhood Union House. She wrote: "I think I should give you all the notice I can so that if you can and wish to have that statement different from the way it stands just now, you may have a chance to consider it." She added, "Please do not take this as an unpleasant dun. I am in sympathy with your work and I know that you are doing the best you can, but I do not wish to embarrass you by my report to the trustees provided you see your way clear to put it in a little better shape before my report is due to be read." And on the fiscal difficulties that regularly plagued the National Association of Colored Graduate Nurses, see Stephanie J. Shaw, "Black Women in White Collars: A Social History of Lower-Level Professional Black Women Workers, 1870–1954" (Ph.D. diss., Ohio State University, 1986), 215–21.

In contrast, John Merrick owned extensive real estate in Durham. Loren Schweninger reports that by 1927 Merrick's holdings were appraised at over $135,000. See Loren Schweninger, *Black Property Owners in the South, 1790–1915* (Urbana: University of Illinois Press, 1990), 222. He was one of the founders of the North Carolina Mutual Life Insurance Company. For details on Merrick and Moore, see Walter B. Weare, *Black Business in the New South: A Social History of the North Carolina Mutual Life Insurance Company* (Urbana: University of Illinois Press, 1973).

20. Trezzvant W. Anderson, "Va. Girls' Reform School Is a Model Institution," Baltimore *Afro-American*, August 15, 1931; r. 38, TNCS; "Virginia State Federation of Colored Women's Clubs: Its Origin and Objectives" (typescript), Virginia Federation of Colored Women's Clubs Papers, JML-SC.

21. See Mrs. J. G. Horton to "Friend," [ca. April 15, 1908], Mrs. Daniel Gibbs Horton (Judith Ann Carter) file, OCAR, in which she wrote: "We, the 'Excelsior Club,' an organization of Negro women, earnestly request you and all friends of progress and a 'square deal' to aid us in raising ($5,000) five thousand dollars, with which to purchase and equip a building which . . . shall be known as 'Excelsior Library and Industrial Institute.'" As a founder and a member of the Oklahoma State Federation of Colored Women's Clubs, Horton also helped raise money to send orphaned black girls to college, and later she helped to create a training school for delinquent boys. See President of the Oklahoma State Federation of Negro Women's Clubs to [friends], January 27, 1915.

22. Anna DeCosta Banks to [Bessie] Cleveland [*sic*], January 5, 1899; Banks to [Hollis] Frissell, January 10, 1900; Banks to Cleaveland,

January 10, [1910?]; and Banks to [Myrtilla] Sherman, April 18, 1914, Anna DeCosta Banks Papers, HULA. Also see Anna DeCosta Banks, "Dixie Nurses in Charleston," *Southern Workman* 55 (1926): 180–83; and Karen Buhler-Wilkerson, " 'Caring in Its Proper Place': Race and Benevolence in Charleston, S.C. 1813–1930," *Nursing Research*, January–February 1992, 14–20, Anna DeCosta Banks Papers.

23. Ethel Evangeline Martin Bolden, "Susan Dart Butler—Pioneer Librarian" (M.S. thesis, Atlanta University School of Library Service, 1959), 14.

24. Bolden, "Susan Dart Butler," 13–19; E. J. Josey and Ann Allen Shockley, eds., *Handbook of Black Librarianship* (Littleton, Colo.: Libraries Unlimited, 1977), 32–33.

25. James D. Anderson, in *The Education of Blacks in the South, 1860–1935* (Chapel Hill: University of North Carolina Press, 1988), makes clear how common this practice was in regard to schools.

26. Rouse, *Lugenia Burns Hope*, 72–73; "The Virginia State Federation of Colored Women's Clubs: Its Origin and Objectives"; Bolden, "Susan Dart Butler," 18; Cynthia Neverdon-Morton, *African American Women of the South and the Advancement of the Race* (Knoxville: University Press of Kentucky, 1989), 116. In Delaware, the Federation of Colored Women's Clubs bought a farm and created an extensive program for black girls and women nine to twenty-one years old, who were, to that point, sent to state penitentiaries in Maryland and Pennsylvania. In one year, four out of five of the Delaware women and girls sent out of state died of tuberculosis, and so the effort to develop an institution in Delaware began at the clubwomen's 1919 state convention when Bessie Bowser put the first fifty cents on the table. In 1921, realizing "that the work they were doing properly belonged to the state and that the only way to ensure the continuance and usefulness of the school lay in its being a state institution . . . [they] . . . . deed[ed] the farm, house, and equipment to the state." Quotation from "Industrial School for Colored Girls Accomplishing Splendid Work," Wilmington *Star*, January 30, 1927, r. 28, TNCS. Also see "Success at Marshallton," February 6, 1927, r. 27; and "Industrial School for Colored Girls Made State Institution by Legislature," Wilmington *Advocate*, April 2, 1921, r. 13.

27. Many of the projects in community development discussed in chapter 2 became public institutions in this way. Also see S. L. Smith to Isaac Fisher, October 24, 1924, b. 15, Constance Fisher Papers, TUA. This letter concerned a Fisk graduate named Ella Grant, who "without any assurance that the board would build a school for her, organized the community and bought 5 acres of the best land in the community on the highway." The school board subsequently decided to build a school there. (The letter was later published in *Fisk University News*, November 1924.)

28. Public school expenditures from Henry Allen Bullock, *A History of Negro Education in the South from 1916 to the Present* (New York: Praeger, 1967), 180; Mamie Garvin Fields with Karen Fields, *Lemon*

Swamp and Other Places: A Carolina Memoir (New York: Free Press, 1983), 130; "Address Delivered before Women's New England Club," January 27, 1889, b. 541, BTW-LC.

29. Fields, *Lemon Swamp*, 130.

30. See Sharon Harley, "Beyond the Classroom: The Organizational Lives of Black Female Educators in the District of Columbia, 1890–1930," *Journal of Negro Education* 51 (1982): 254–65; and Lasch-Quinn, *Black Neighbors*, esp. 75–109.

31. "The Calhoun School," *Southern Workman* 45 (1916): 564; Pitt Dillingham, "Black Belt Settlement Work," *Southern Workman* 31 (1902): 383–88, and 31 (1903): 437–44; Camilla Weems, "The Relation of the Rural School to Its Community," *SM*, May 1912, 2–3.

32. "Teachers and Pupils Build $20,000 School from Salvaged Bricks," Pittsburgh *Courier*, January 29, 1927, r. 27, TNCS. And see chapter 2.

33. Spelman College taught women courses in "benchwork" that included drawing and execution, "use of and care of the Tri-square, ruler, rip saw, crosscut saw, plane, hammer, screwdriver, chisel, and auger." Officials noted that they had "a well-equipped bench work room," and that "emphasis is placed upon accuracy and technique." Spelman had for some time been teaching courses in agriculture, and by 1920 had an enlarged workroom to allow for a larger class in woodworking. See *Thirty-seventh Annual Circular and Catalogue of Spelman Seminary for Women and Girls, 1917–18*, 22; *Twenty-fifth Annual Circular and Catalogue of Spelman Seminary for Women and Girls, 1905–6*, 27. Hampton women students took a 100-hour woodworking course (boys took 200 hours) to open "the minds of the students in as many directions as possible and to give a varied and reasonable degree of skill in using different kinds of tools." See *Catalogue of the Hampton Normal and Agricultural Institute, 1895–96*, 28–29. And as soon as Fisk began to offer courses in woodworking for college preparatory students in 1888, women regularly joined the class and " 'measured as closely and sawed with as much deftness as their brothers.' " See Joe M. Richardson, *A History of Fisk University, 1865–1946* (University: University of Alabama Press, 1980), 60.

34. Ladson quotation from Edmond L. Drago, *Initiative, Paternalism, and Race Relations: Charleston's Avery Normal Institute* (Athens: University of Georgia Press, 1990), 153–54.

35. Bullock, *A History of Negro Education*, 180.

36. Anderson, *The Education of Blacks in the South*, esp. 148–85; and see chapter 2 above.

37. A participant at the 1904 Tuskegee conference reported that in his hometown of College Station, Alabama, black residents who organized a school taxed each family twenty-five cents a month "and by this means we got up enough to supplement the school term of three months to five months." See "Conference Report," February 17, 1904 (typescript), b. 980, BTW-LC. Also see Fields, *Lemon Swamp*, 99; Septima Poinsette Clark with LeGette Blythe, *Echo in My Soul* (New York: E. P. Dutton,

1962), 35–37; "Our Parent Teacher Association," and "School Teacher's Influence Felt throughout the School" (1959 typescripts), Albertha J. Murray Papers, ARC-CC; "Miss Vassar, a Student from Fisk University Gave Her Experience as a Teacher," *AM* 45 (1891): 28–29. The final document also reveals that in communities where white people opposed education for African Americans, the teachers had some difficulty finding housing because local black people feared white retaliation if it became known that they supported the teachers.

38. Lula Catherine Jordan McNeil worked as a waitress when school was not in session and before returning to school to study nursing. And Sarah Webb Rice did domestic work in private homes. See Lula Catherine Jordan McNeil, interview transcript, MEC-BNA, 6; and Sarah Webb Rice, *He Included Me: The Autobiography of Sarah Rice,* ed. Louise Westling (Athens: University of Georgia Press, 1989), 106–8, 119.

39. Mary Lee McCray to Margaret Murray Washington, July 20, 1900, b. 522, BTW-LC.

40. Fields, *Lemon Swamp,* 107, 114, 131, 206–8, 212–17, 219–20.

41. Fields, *Lemon Swamp,* 106–7, 114–25, 208; Clark, *Echo in My Soul,* 36–39; Rice, *He Included Me,* 76–80. Even in Memphis, Tennessee, the school board closed black schools on September 3 in 1922 to get around enforcing the new compulsory attendance laws. See "Rural Negro Schools in South Closed to Get More Cotton Laborers," *Negro World,* October 7, 1922, r. 15, TNCS. The sarcastic subtitle of the *World* article read: "Logic Is That Pupils Can Accomplish as Much by Dragging a Bag between Rows as Attending School, Causing a Labor Shortage." "Negro School Closed during Cotton Season," Memphis *Evening Appeal,* September 12, 1930, r. 36, TNCS, details Tennessee officials' opening black schools in July (after crops were laid by) in order to close them in September to start harvesting. "Wants Longer Term," *Afro-American Ledger,* April 24, 1915, r. 4, reported that the Maryland State Teachers Association had launched a campaign to have the black school term extended to at least seven and a half months. The white school term was already almost nine months long. And "Longer Term for Colored Schools," Charlotte *Daily Observer,* January 29, 1916, r. 5, reported that black schools operated four and a half months and consequently students had to sit in the same grade for several years. According to "Opposed to Long Term, They Dynamite School," Atlanta *Constitution,* June 30, 1914, r. 2, a black school was "destroyed by residents of the [Griffin, Georgia] district who are opposed to a school term longer than three months." And see S. H. Lee, "Unequal Chance—Suggested Remedy," *Bulletin* 9 (1928): 16–18.

42. Drago, *Initiative, Paternalism, and Race Relations,* 153–54.

43. Fields, *Lemon Swamp,* 218–19.

44. See "The Woman Who Has Helped Booker T. Washington Build Tuskegee," typescript, b. 586; and Mrs. Booker T. Washington, "Brief History of the Woman's Meeting Organized and Conducted in the Town of Tuskegee, Alabama," manuscript, b. 981, BTW-LC; Maenelle Dixon, Report on "Bullock County Negro Schools," October 1939, b. 407,

RFF, FUL-SC. Dixon's manuscript also reflected little sensitivity for rural students who needed or wanted to work to fulfill personal and family obligations. She criticized area teachers for "allowing" the students to leave school to do farm and household chores and to work in turpentine camps. My thanks to Kenneth M. Hamilton for copies of the Tuskegee documents.

45. Estelle Massey Riddle Osborne left her rural Texas teaching job out of frustration at her inability to change the people. In particular, she noted how early girls dropped out of school and how quickly they then became pregnant. Older women of the community, Osborne said, accepted it simply as "nature." See Estelle Massey Osborne, interview transcript, MEC-BNA, 19–21. And for comments specific to midwives' superstitions, see Lula Catherine Jordan McNeil, interview transcript, MEC-BNA, 21–25. Fields and Clark also comment throughout their autobiographies on the superstitions that were prevalent among the people with whom they worked.

46. For an extreme example, women of the Neighborhood Union drove several families out of their neighborhoods. One, a Pentecostal family, was forced out "on the grounds of disorderly conduct." See Rouse, *Lugenia Burns Hope*, 70. People with unacceptable lifestyles were also forced out of Mamie Garvin Fields's neighborhood. Fields noted that "Aunt Harriet would get the other neighbors together to 'run 'em out.'" See Fields, *Lemon Swamp*, 39–40.

47. Amelia Perry Pride to "Mrs. Langhorn," June 23, 1899; and Pride to [Myrtilla] Sherman, February 13, 1918, Amelia Perry Pride Papers, HULA. Alabama nurse Eunice Rivers Laurie also made certain between the 1930s and the 1950s that she visited the homes of black patients a number of times before she made any suggestions about their housekeeping. See Eunice Rivers Laurie, interview by A. Lillian Thompson, RC-BWOHP, 17; and Darlene Clark Hine, "'They Shall Mount up with Wings as Eagles': Historical Images of Black Nurses, 1890–1950," in *Images of Nurses: Perspectives from History, Art, and Literature*, ed. Anne Hudson Jones (Philadelphia: University of Philadelphia Press, 1988), 189.

48. Clark, *Echo in My Soul*, 39–54. Estelle Osborne performed similar social work duties when she taught school in rural Texas during the late 1920s. Osborne later went back to school for a nursing degree and became prominently associated with the National Association of Colored Graduate Nurses. Women teachers at Tuskegee began this form of socialization first by scheduling their mothers' meetings at the "cabin" of the woman they deemed "most promising." They presented her a gift of "a stout new broom" on the day of the first meeting. The Tuskegee women arrived early for that meeting, and Mrs. Washington suggested that they "all take a hand in cleaning the house a little before people should begin to come." See "The Woman Who Has Helped Booker T. Washington Build Tuskegee."

49. In "Colored Night School Has Governing Board," *Daily Her-*

ald, November 14, 1914, r. 2, TNCS, the reporter noted that "it will be news to the white people of the city to know that there is a Negro school superintendent and a colored board of trustees right here in Denison. It is true that they derive no power and acquire no pay from the city, but they have their titles just the same and actually operate and maintain a public school." On Chatham County Georgia, see [title unavailable], Savannah *Tribune*, June 26, 1920, r. 11. On "moonlight schools" in general, see "Kentucky's Moonlight Schools," Rochester (New York) *Democratic Chronicle*, May 6, 1915; and "A Moonlight School Record," Atlanta *Constitution*, December 16, 1915, r. 4; "The Moonlight Schools," Atlanta *Constitution*, April 13, 1917, r. 6; "School for Negro Adults Gets Aid," Montgomery *Advertiser*, June 15, 1931, r. 38; and "179 Negroes Learn to Read," La-Grange (Georgia) *News*, April 21, 1930, r. 36. In "Teachers of Texas Take Notice," Dallas *Express*, July 12, 1924, r. 20, TNCS, the writer noted that four thousand black Mississippi teachers each agreed to teach "one or more illiterate adults for one year without compensation." Also see Folia Butler, "Moonlight Schools," *CM*, December 15, 1927. For an example of community functioning both for the creation of the evening schools and in the teachers' work process, see Richard H. Thomas, "Learning to Read and Write in LA," Pittsburgh *Courier*, December 10, 1938, r. 57, TNCS. Some of the evening school teachers were accustomed to walking several miles to teach. In this instance a group of four women teachers in Louisiana resolved the problem by buying a car together and setting out for home each evening, "the first driving to her place, the second to hers, and so on." Also Catherine Watkins Duncan, in the 1930s, worked in Red Oak, Georgia, teaching children during the day and adults at night. Adult classes included Bible and newspaper reading, spelling, math, home hygiene, and home nursing. See Catherine Watkins Duncan, manuscript autobiography, 9, b. 409, RFF, FUL-SC.

50. See especially C. C. McDuffie to Board of Examiners, April 22, 1929; [Report of the College Committee], February 20, 1940; Mary Hundley to Harold A. Haynes, June 21, 1944; Hundley to Charles S. Lofton, June 23, 1948; LaVerna Murphy, "Dunbar Students Preparing for College Courses," Pittsburgh *Courier*, December 18, 1948; "Mrs Hundley Gives Sixth Annual Party Honoring Former Students," Pittsburgh *Courier*, January 31, 1953; and Board of Education, "A Tribute to Mrs. Mary Gibson Hundley," January 6, 1959, Mary Gibson Hundley Papers, SL-RC. Hundley also organized her female students into the Mary Jennings Club, whose members worked as volunteers in community schools, churches, and hospitals. See "The Coleman Jennings Club," typescript; Mary Jennings Club membership list with pledges; and Charles E. Burbridge to Hundley, April 14, 1954.

51. Norma Boyd, interview transcript, RC-BWOHP, 9.

52. Norma Elizabeth Boyd, interview by Clarencetta Jelks, FUL-BOHP, FUL-SC; Norma Boyd, interview transcript, RC-BWOHP, 15–18, 28. Susan St. Clair Minor organized her elementary school students simi-

larly in Louisville, Kentucky. She noted, "I took my bright children and made them what I might call mentors or helpers." Susan St. Clair Minor, interview transcript, OHC-UL, 21.

53. Norma Boyd, interview transcript, RC-BWOHP, 28.

54. Ibid., 16.

55. Ibid., 28. In this interview, Boyd says that she took students to hear Charlie Houston present bills before Congress. Probably Houston was instead testifying for or against a bill.

56. "The Valena C. Jones School Republic," *Bulletin* 10 (1930): 6, 23; "Valena C. Jones School," *Bulletin* 11 (1930): 23–24. The *Bulletin* was the organ of the National Association of Teachers in Colored Schools. See also Fields, *Lemon Swamp*, 52–55. Fields's aunt and teacher, Anna Izzard, had to provide her class with some of their history, civics, and social studies lessons surreptitiously while they were on "field trips." Izzard taught her students as they walked through "forbidden places," ostensibly to get to some other destination. For example, Fields recalled listening to Izzard's stories as the class walked through Charleston's segregated Battery Park at the edge of a prestigious white neighborhood. She noted that "although we couldn't stop in the Battery or use the park, we visited it anyhow. We got our history lesson. We got our 'sociology' lesson. And at the end we got our recreation" (quotation on p. 55).

57. Frances O. Grant, interview by Maurine Rothschild, RC-BWOHP, ii–iii.

58. Ibid., 18–21.

59. Undated Hampton Survey of Graduates, Amelia Perry Pride Papers, HULA.

60. "News from the Field," *Southern Workman* [31] (July 1902); undated Hampton Survey of Graduates; (untitled) *Southern Workman*, [47] (October 1898); "Pioneer Ends Busy Life" (source unknown); Pride to "Miss Bellows," n.d, and May 6, 1897; Perry [Pride] to [Bessie] Cleaveland, December 15, 1890, and December 1892; Pride to [Hollis] Frissell, June 4, 1898, and October 7, 1898; Pride to Miss Dais, March 5, 1904; and Pride to [Myrtilla] Sherman, December 6, 1918, February 13, 1918, and December 23, (1920), Amelia Perry Pride Papers, HULA.

61. Amelia Perry Pride to [Myrtilla] Sherman, January 11, 1902, ibid.

62. Lula Catherine Jordan McNeil, interview transcript, MEC-BNA, 9, 18–25.

63. Eunice Laurie, interview transcript, RC-BWOHP, 10–12, 17–18; James Jones, *Bad Blood: The Tuskegee Syphilis Experiment—a Tragedy of Race and Medicine* (New York: Free Press, 1981), 111, 168.

64. First quotation from Mary Elizabeth Carnegie, interview transcript, MEC-BNA, 7–8, 10. Subsequent quotations from Clara Hamilton to Robert W. July, February 16, 1951, ser. 1, subser. 3, b. 548, f. 5866, GEB-RAC.

65. Rossa Cooley, "A Tribute to Nurse King," *Southern Workman* 64 (1935): 70–71.

66. Adrienne Lash Jones, "Jane Edna Hunter: A Case Study of Black Leadership, 1910–1950" (Ph.D. diss., Case Western Reserve University, 1983), 92–96.

67. Jones, "Jane Edna Hunter," 95, 99–100; Mayme V. Holmes, "The Story of the Phillis Wheatley Association of Cleveland," *Southern Workman* 57 (1928): 399–402; Jane E. Hunter, "Phyllis [*sic*] Wheatley Association of Cleveland: An Institution Devoted to Better, Brighter Girls, Happier, Heartier Women," *Competitor* 1 (1920): 52–54. The 1923 Annual Report indicated that 1,188 women had resided there during the year and over 39,000 meals had been served in the Association cafeteria in an effort to help black individuals "cope with a metropolitan environment." Phillis Wheatley Association, "Annual Report for the Year 1923," b. 4, Constance Fisher Papers, TUA. Fisher's first professional position after graduating from Fisk was a summer job (June–September 1924) with the Phillis Wheatley Association Camp.

68. White southerners' fixation on their potential labor loss is discussed in detail in James R. Grossman, *Land of Hope: Chicago, Black Southerners, and the Great Migration* (Chicago: University of Chicago Press, 1989), 38–65.

69. Beulah Whitby, interview transcript, Labor Archives, 1–6.

70. Ibid., 6; "Biographical Form," Beulah Whitby file, OCAR. Ethel Ray Nance worked during the early 1920s as a social worker with the Phyllis Wheatley Social Settlement in Minneapolis. Soon thereafter, however, she accepted a position with the Women's Bureau of the Minneapolis Police Department. Although she did not seek the police department position, the administrator at the Phyllis Wheatley House "volunteered" her services when city officials decided to start a Women's Bureau. She was supposed to stay six months but stayed four years. See Ethel Ray Nance, interview transcript, AMD-MHS, 14–15, 18.

71. Beulah Whitby, interview transcript, Labor Archives, 2–19.

72. "Biographical Form," Beulah Whitby; "The Detroit Community Barometer: An Experiment in Gauging Community Tensions in Race Relations," paper prepared for presentation to the Michigan Sociological Society, November 1945; and "Oberlinian of the Month," *Oberlin Alumni Magazine*, February 1947, 1–3, Beulah Whitby file, OCAR.

73. Richard W. Thomas, *Life for Us Is What We Make It: Building Black Community in Detroit, 1915–1945* (Bloomington: Indiana University Press, 1992), 26.

74. Grossman, *Land of Hope*, 8.

75. Mark Naison, *Communists in Harlem during the Depression* (Urbana: University of Illinois Press, 1983), 31–56, 95–125.

76. Earl Lewis, *"In Their Own Interests": Race, Class and Power in Twentieth Century Norfolk, Virginia* (Berkeley and Los Angeles: University of California Press, 1991), 127.

77. Robin D. G. Kelley, *Hammer and Hoe: Alabama Communists during the Great Depression* (Chapel Hill: University of North Carolina Press, 1990).

78. On the Scottsboro case, see Naison, *Communists in Harlem,* 56–94; Dan T. Carter, *Scottsboro: A Tragedy of the American South,* rev. ed. (Baton Rouge: Louisiana State University Press, 1982).

79. See Estelle Massey Riddle Osborne, interview transcript, MEC-BNA, 36–39; and Estelle Massey Riddle to M. O. Bousfield, December 17, 1934, b. 225, RFF, FUL-SC. The violence that characterized the local white response to black workers' efforts to organize in Alabama is an important theme of Kelley's *Hammer and Hoe.* On philanthropic agency representatives' possibly designing Osborne's work to inhibit radicalism among southern rural African Americans, and clearly to discourage their migration to the cities, see also Leo M. Favrot, "Rural School Work," October 16, 1913, r. 2, TNCS, in which Favrot (of the General Education Board) framed their efforts in terms of working "to keep them better satisfied to live in the rural districts and to prevent so many from crowding into the cities."

80. Estelle Massey Riddle, "Education of the Negro Nurse," typescript, b. 225, RFF, FUL-SC.

81. Estelle Massey Osborne interview transcript, MEC-BNA, 33–34. Phillips worked hard at exposing the city's injustice, but he paid the ultimate cost for agitating: he was assassinated.

82. See "Nurse Head at St. Louis Hospital Resigns," October 17, 1942, r. 79, TNCS.

83. Katharine Faville to Mary Elizabeth Tennant, April 13, 1945, ser. 1, subser. 3, b. 549, f. 5877, GEB-RAC. Osborne also met with black nursing students who charged that they were regularly subjected to racial discrimination at Wayne State University. And Katharine Faville, the acting dean of the College of Nursing, later reported to Mary Elizabeth Tennant of the Rockefeller Foundation that Osborne "helped us to bring the matter out into the open in a way which otherwise might have been impossible." Faville noted that without Osborne's help, establishing black contacts in the city would have "been very time consuming and difficult" as well.

84. Clara Jones interview, FUL-BOHP, FUL-SC; "Mrs. Jones Named Lothrop Librarian," *Michigan Chronicle,* September 9, 1944; and "Honored for Service," *Michigan Chronicle,* December 1, 1956, vertical files—biography, "Clara Jones," Labor Archives.

85. Leon Wasker to Rosenwald Fund, February 4, 1947, Pauline Byrd Taylor Fellowship Application, b. 451, RFF, FUL-SC; Adelaide M. Enright, Warren Burger, and Mayor John McDonnough to Constance Fisher, June 8, 1944; and Fisher to Enright, June 12, 1944, b. 15, Constance Fisher Papers, TUA; Thelma DeWitty, interview by Esther Mumford, WSA-AOHP, 27–29; A. Pelzer Beckman to Albertha Murray, December 14, 1933, Albertha Murray Papers, ARC-CC. Although many of these women (Taylor, DeWitty, Murray, and Fisher among them) received no wages for such work, what is important here is that white administrators now called on them to perform these duties in an official, albeit unpaid, capacity. The women were still, however, performing

traditional amelioration work (in addition to their jobs) with the help of the larger black community. For example, Constance Fisher, a social worker, also collected food baskets from the black Cameo Social Club and doll clothes from individual citizens to distribute to her clients. See Fisher to George Brooks, January 3, 1938; and Fisher to Mrs. Josie Williams, December 15, 1931, b. 13, Constance Fisher Papers, TUA.

86. A referee for Taylor wrote that she "worked to serve as a link between [the black community] and the dominant part of our city and to influence their thinking along lines of integration rather than segregation." The referee also recognized the balancing act demanded of her and noted that as "one of the few educated Negroes in her community" there were "wide and varied demands which the community has made upon her energy and time. She is known by people from varying socioeconomic and religious groups. Her poise is demonstrated in the way that she has been able to maintain balance in spite of the many demands." See Clara Graybill [to RFF], January 27, 1947, Pauline Byrd Taylor Fellowship Application, b. 451, RFF, FUL-SC.

87. Suggesting the poor work options for most black women during the 1930s, see Julia Kirk Blackwelder, "Quiet Suffering: Atlanta Women in the 1930s," *Georgia Historical Quarterly* 61 (1977): 112–24, and idem, "Women in the Work Force: Atlanta, New Orleans, and San Antonio, 1930–1940," *Journal of Urban History* 4 (1978): 331–58; Lois Rita Helmbold, "Beyond the Family Economy: Black and White Working-Class Women during the Great Depression," *Feminist Studies* 13 (1987): 629–55.

88. Jones, *Bad Blood*, 168–69; Eunice Laurie, interview transcript, RC-BWOHP, ii, 12–18.

89. Jones, *Bad Blood*, 6–7, 111–16, 145–67.

90. See Lois Scharf, *To Work and to Wed: Female Employment, Feminism, and the Great Depression* (Westport, Conn.: Greenwood Press, 1980).

91. It is also possible that Terrell disappeared from the lecture circuit simply because Chautauquas and the like were folding and this kind of public lecturing began to disappear as a profession. It is equally possible that her husband's illness and death in 1925 influenced her to stop. On her work for McCormick and Hoover, see Mary Church Terrell to Thomas Church, September 28, 1929; Mary Church Terrell to Phyllis Terrell, January 20, 1930, February 11, 1930, and April 7, 1930; and Phyllis Terrell to Mary Church Terrell, October 31, 1932, and ca. November 11, 1932, r. 3, MCT-LC; Dorothy Sterling, *Black Foremothers: Three Lives* (Old Westbury, N.Y.: Feminist Press, 1979), 149; Ruth Hannah McCormick to Mary Church Terrell (copy), February 14, 1931, Mary Church Terrell file, OCAR.

92. Harvard Sitkoff, *A New Deal for Blacks: The Emergence of Civil Rights as a National Issue*, vol. 1, *The Depression Decade* (New York: Oxford University Press, 1978), 35–37; Mary Anderson, "The Plight of Negro Domestic Labor," *Journal of Negro Education* 5 (1936): 66–72; Ella Baker and Marvel Cooke, "The Bronx Slave Market," *Crisis* 42 (1935): 330–31, 340; Louise Mitchell, "Slave Markets Typify Exploitation of Domestics," *Daily*

Worker, May 5, 1940. Philip S. Foner reports the 1932 black unemployment rate in Detroit as 60 percent for men and 75 percent for women. See *Organized Labor and the Black Worker, 1619–1973* (New York: International, 1974), 190 (188–203 for a broader discussion); and Rita Lois Helmbold, "Downward Occupational Mobility during the Great Depression: Urban Black and White Working Class Women," *Labor History* 29 (1988): 135–72.

93. Sitkoff, *A New Deal for Blacks*, 47–57; Nancy L. Grant, *TVA and Black Americans: Planning for the Status Quo* (Philadelphia: Temple University Press, 1990).

94. Sitkoff, *A New Deal for Blacks*, 89–92; Ralph J. Bunche, *The Political Status of the Negro in the Age of FDR*, ed. Dewey Grantham (Chicago: University of Chicago Press, 1973), 572–606; C. Vann Woodward, *The Strange Career of Jim Crow*, 3d ed. (New York: Oxford University Press, 1974), 128–29. This new public power was best symbolized by the NAACP's successful campaign against the nomination of Judge John J. Parker for the Supreme Court. See Kenneth W. Goings, *"The NAACP Comes of Age": The Defeat of Judge John J. Parker* (Bloomington: Indiana University Press, 1990).

95. Fields, *Lemon Swamp*, 160, 234, 238–39; Minutes of the Neighborhood Union, July 19, 1935, b. 4, NUC-WL; Ethel Ray Nance, interview transcript, AMD-MHS, 18.

96. [NACGN], "The National Health Act of 1939: A Special News Bulletin," June 1939, NACGN Records, MEC-BNA.

97. D. Lachatenere and V. Hodge, Inventory to Layle Lane Papers; Lewis Waters to Layle Lane, n.d., and December 24, 1944; and Noridge S. Maglancy to Layle Lane, June 25, 1946; b. 1, Layle Lane Papers, Schomburg Center; Layle Lane, "The Negro and War Activities," speech delivered before the American Federation of Teachers, August 18, 1940 [or 1941], Layle Lane Papers, Labor Archives; S. Grace Bradley, "Atlanta Teachers Hear Miss Lane," *Daily World*, January 19, 1941, r. 72, TNCS.

98. See chapter 5.

99. Norma Boyd, interview transcript, RC-BWOHP, 16; Norma Elizabeth Boyd interview, FUL-BOHP. Boyd's interview does not indicate when she read this article. It was probably in the late 1930s, because the Alpha Kappa Alpha campaign began around 1938. Also, the Costigan-Wagner bill (S. 1978) was introduced in the Senate in 1934 and 1935. It failed both times. What became known as the NAACP antilynching bill (H.R. 1507) was introduced early in 1937. See Robert L. Zangrando, *The NAACP Crusade against Lynching, 1901–1950* (Philadelphia: Temple University Press, 1980). On women's earlier efforts for an antilynching bill, see Alfreda M. Duster, ed., *Crusade for Justice: The Autobiography of Ida B. Wells* (Chicago: University of Chicago Press, 1970); Mildred Thompson, *Ida B. Wells-Barnett: An Exploratory Study of an American Black Woman, 1893–1930*, vol. 15 of *Black Women in United States History*, ed. Darlene Clark Hine (Brooklyn, N.Y.: Carlson, 1990); and Rosalyn Terborg-Penn, "African-American Women's Networks in the Anti-lynching Crusade," in

Gender, Class, Race, and Reform in the Progressive Era, ed. Nora Lee Frankell and Nancy S. Dye (Lexington: University Press of Kentucky, 1991), 148–61.

100. Norma Elizabeth Boyd, interview, FUL-BOHP.

101. On Aline Black and the NAACP efforts to pursue her case, see Earl Lewis, *"In Their Own Interests,"* 155–65; and Mark V. Tushnett, *The NAACP's Legal Struggle against Segregated Education, 1925–1950* (Chapel Hill: University of North Carolina Press, 1987), 77–78. Tushnett's book, together with Richard Kluger, *Simple Justice: The History of Brown v. Board of Education and Black America's Struggle for Equality,* 2 vols. (New York: Alfred A. Knopf, 1975), details the history of the NAACP's work to integrate public education. And also see Genna Rae McNeil, *Groundwork: Charles Hamilton Houston and the Struggle for Civil Rights* (Philadelphia: University of Pennsylvania Press, 1983). At least one black newspaper launched the local campaign to gain equitable salaries for black teachers. See "Afro Will File Suit to Secure Equal Salaries," *Afro American,* April 9, 1920, r. 11, TNCS.

102. Clark, *Echo in My Soul,* 79–82.

103. The chronology of this suit is provided in Tushnett, *The NAACP's Legal Struggle.* Tushnett says of the first plaintiff in the suit, "he had to be replaced." Clark's autobiography says it was a woman in Charleston, who got married, and the suggestion is that upon her marriage she left the paid workforce and therefore could no longer be a plaintiff in the case. See Clark, *Echo in My Soul,* 81–82.

104. Tushnett, *The NAACP's Legal Struggle,* 92–93; Clark, *Echo in My Soul,* 83.

105. Clark, *Echo in My Soul,* 111–19. Clark regained her pension of $3,600 a year in 1976. In 1981 the state legislature awarded her back pay for the years 1956–64, amounting to $36,412. Clark was eighty-three years old. See Cynthia Stokes Brown, ed., *Ready from Within: Septima Clark and the Civil Rights Movement* (Navarro, Calif.: Wild Trees Press, 1986), 124. Specifically on Clark's work with Highlander (and later with the Southern Christian Leadership Conference), see Clark, *Echo in My Soul,* 119–231; John M. Glen, *Highlander: No Ordinary School, 1932–1962* (Lexington: University Press of Kentucky, 1988); and the Septima Clark Papers, RSSL-SC.

106. Clark, *Echo in My Soul,* 82, 100. Discussions of the idea of resistance as sometimes being subtle, covert, and nonoppositional include Stephanie J. Shaw, "Cussin,' and Fightin,' and Rarin': Female Slave Resistance in the Antebellum South," paper presented at the meeting of the Southern Historical Association, November 1989, Louisville, Kentucky; Tera W. Hunter, "Domination and Resistance: The Politics of Wage Household Labor in New South Atlanta," *Labor History* 34 (1993): 205–20; and Robin D. G. Kelley, " 'We are not what we seem': Rethinking Black Working Class Opposition in the Jim Crow South," *Journal of American History* 85 (1993): 75–112.

107. Clark, *Echo in My Soul,* 89–94. Clark's autobiography does

not say who was responsible for bringing Lampkin to Charleston. Presumably her point was that the mayor had something to do with it.

108. Pauletta Bracey, "Charlemae Hill Rollins and Her Peers," *Public Libraries* 21 (1982): 104–5; Charlemae Hill Rollins, "The Role of Books in Combating Prejudice," *Wilson Library Bulletin* 42 (1967): 176–77; Era Bell Thompson, "Crusader in Children's Books," *Negro Digest* 1 (1950): 30; Spencer Shaw, "Charlemae Hill Rollins, 1897–1979: In Tribute," paper presented at the Second Annual Charlemae Hill Rollins Colloquium, NCCU School of Library Science, April 2–3, 1982, 3, Charlemae Hill Rollins Papers, NCCU-BLA. The date for the initial publication of *We Build Together* is inconsistently reported in printed documents. Several say it was first published in 1938. The second edition of the guide, published in 1948, included two hundred entries. Also see Rollins, "Building a Better World through Books," *North Carolina Libraries* 3 (1944): 11–12, in vertical files, "Negroes—Library," RBHL.

109. A. P. Tillman to Charlemae Rollins, February 11, 1942; and Charlemae Rollins to Elizabeth Riley, February 14, 1958, Charlemae Hill Rollins Papers, NCCU-BLA.

110. Thompson, "Crusader in Children's Books," 31. In Florence Means to Charlemae Rollins, October 18, 1942, and June 7, 1943, Means wrote about her plans for the book and about canceling a trip to Tuskegee. In Frances Cavanah to Rollins, April 27, 1957, Cavanah said regarding "Little Hiram," "you undoubtedly saved me from doing something that I would have regretted afterwards. I am grateful that you were so frank." All the documents above are in Charlemae Rollins Papers, NCCU-BLA. And see Mary Terrell Tancil to Mary Church Terrell, January 24, [1953], r. 3, MCT-LC. "Little Hiram," published in the February 1953 issue of *Good Housekeeping*, has the name George Sumner Albee on its byline. A search in reliable reference works on pseudonyms did not turn up this name.

111. Augusta Baker, one of the nation's most prominent children's librarians and storytellers, began her career at the 135th Street Branch of the New York Public Library. After attempting to teach African American history to young patrons and finding too few resources that were not racist, she created a committee of library and community people to search for adequate materials. They established criteria for judging the books that considered illustrations, realism, language (time, place, and people accurate, rather than "author-created dialect"), and social worthiness. Baker also made the children's center at the 135th Street Branch into a "children's cultural club" of sorts, by having Countee Cullen and Langston Hughes come in and read poetry, and they in turn urged the children to write. Aaron Douglass came and discussed his murals with the children; Frederick O'Neal made presentations on black theater; and black foreign diplomats spoke and showed slides about their countries. Finally, in 1940 Frederick Melcher of the R. R. Bowker Company, which awarded the Newberry and Caldecott medals for children's

publications, took Baker to a meeting of children's publishers and told her to "speak her piece" on the lack of appropriate reading material about African Americans, which she did. See Augusta Baker, "My Years as a Children's Librarian," in *The Black Librarian in America*, ed. E. J. Josey (Metuchen, N.J.: Scarecrow Press, 1970), 117–23; and "Augusta Baker to Conduct Storytelling Workshop at Shaw Library," in vertical files, "Augusta Baker," RBHL.

112. Marjorie H. Allen to Rollins, August 23, 1944; Helen King, [title missing], Chicago *Courier*, February 27, 1971; Kathryn Christensen, "Charlemae and Her Long Affair with Books," Chicago *Daily News*, June 7, 1974; and "Charlemae Rollins—Librarian and Storyteller," *American Libraries* 5 (1974): 413, Charlemae Hill Rollins Papers, NCCU-BLA; Bracey, "Charlemae Hill Rollins and Her Peers," 105. Rollins published *Christmas Gif'*, on black family life and Christmas folklore, in 1963; *They Showed the Way: Forty American Negro Leaders* in 1964; *Famous Negro Poets* in 1965; *Famous Negro Entertainers on Stage, Screen, and Television* in 1967; and *Black Troubadour, Langston Hughes* in 1970. She also periodically expanded *We Build Together*, the bibliography she first compiled around 1938.

113. Letters indicating that Delaney asked authors to donate copies of their books to the library include Benjamin Brawley to Sadie Peterson, n.d.; Ellen Glasgow to Sadie Peterson-Delaney, November 10, 1932; Mary White Ovington to Sadie Peterson Delaney, February 18, 1935; and James W[eldon] Johnson to Sadie Peterson-Delaney, April 27, 1937, vol. 1, Sadie Peterson Delaney Papers, Schomburg Center.

114. Ray Nichols Moore, "Mollie Huston Lee: A Profile" (source unknown), 432–39, vertical files, "Mollie Lee"; and Mary Day Morecai, "Mrs. Mollie Lee and a Little Faith Built the Richard B. Harrison Library," (Raleigh) *News and Observer*, June 2, 1972; H. B. Branch to "whom it may concern," May 22, 1935; Temporary Library Finance Committee to Citizens Committee of Raleigh, May 14, 1935; Marjorie Beal to "whom it may concern," May 23, 1935; and Marjorie Beal to Mollie Huston, February [?] 1935, and June 20, 1935, vertical files, "Richard B. Harrison Branch," RBHL. Branch was then secretary of the Raleigh Chamber of Commerce, and Beal was secretary and director of the North Carolina Library Commission. Lee and the community committee had solicited their help in raising funds. Sufficient funds were not raised to purchase a "permanent" facility for the library until 1948. Lee had left a position as a librarian at Shaw University library during the depression and began to work at establishing a public library. It is possible that because of the financial crunch Shaw University released her, but there is no documentation to that effect available. Also note that her local sorority sisters (Delta Sigma Theta) helped raise money for the library.

115. For another example of the conversion to black branches, see Miriam Matthews, interview by Eleanor Roberts, RC-BWOHP, 42. Matthews discovered a letter in library files that explained her earlier placement at the Helen Hunt Jackson Branch of the library. The city as-

sistant librarian and the city librarian placed her there during the 1940s in an "experiment" with an all-black staff in a "mixed races" neighborhood.

116. See Barbara Miller, interview; Clara Jones, interview; and Jean Hutson, interview, FUL-BOHP; Miriam Matthews, interview transcript, RC-BWOHP, 62–69.

117. Mary Church Terrell, "Service Which Should Be Rendered the South," *Voice of the Negro* 2 (1905): 182–86 (punctuation slightly altered in last paragraph). Terrell was certainly not the first person to express these ideas in print. Anna Julia Cooper, for example, in *A Voice from the South* (Xenia, Ohio: Aldine, 1892), 210, wrote: "If the cultivated black man cannot endure the white man's barbarity—the cure, it seems to me, would be to cultivate the white man."

118. Many studies characterize much of this work as charity work. See, for example, Philip Jackson, "Black Charity in Progressive Era Chicago," *Social Service Review* 52 (1978): 400–417. A recent presentation of the same kind of work as community development is Andrea Tuttle Kornbluh, "James Hathaway Robinson and the Origins of Professional Social Work in the Black Community," in *Race and the City: Work, Community, and Protest in Cincinnati, 1820–1970,* ed. Henry Louis Taylor Jr. (Urbana: University of Illinois Press, 1992), 209–31.

119. Eunice Rivers Laurie, interview transcript, RC-BWOHP, 16.

120. Clara Jones, "The Black Librarian," in *The Black Librarian in the Southeast: Reminiscences, Activities, Challenges,* ed. Annette Phinazee (Durham: North Carolina Central University School of Library Science, 1980), 19; Vivian Hewitt, "Special Libraries, Librarians and the Continuing Education of Black People," in *What Black Librarians Are Saying,* ed. E. J. Josey (Metuchen, N.J.: Scarecrow Press, 1970), 268–69; Mary Church Terrell to Mary Tancil [Boudreaux], February 14, 1920, r. 3, MCT-LC. Also see Virginia Yates, "Community and Outreach Librarians: Challenge and Change," in Josey, *What Black Librarians Are Saying,* 241–48. Pauli Murray characterized her aunt's schoolteacher cohort as women who "combined the functions of instructor, social worker, truant officer, psychiatrist, counselor, adult education specialist, and community leader." See Murray, *Song in a Weary Throat,* 15. Although Terrell's entire autobiography demonstrates a lifetime of race work, in Terrell, *A Colored Woman in a White World,* 98–100, she talks about it explicitly as a mission to achieve racial equality. Also note that although Mary Church Terrell left teaching early in her career, her work history still parallels that of the other women studied here. When she began her career as a lecturer and writer, an important emphasis in her speeches and essays was black women's responsibility for building and developing the community. One of her speeches inspired Mamie Garvin Fields to join the City Federation of Colored Women's Clubs. Terrell said: "We have more to do than other women. Those of us fortunate enough to have education must share it with the less fortunate of our race. We must go into our communities and improve them." Fields noted that after the talk, "nobody wanted to wait till

morning to pick up our burden again." Terrell's most prominent public work in the 1920s and 1930s, however, was race work coordinated by her employers. Her job was to organize black women to vote the Republican ticket. And in the 1940s she began to concentrate on reform-oriented activism. In 1946 she challenged the whites-only policy of the American Association of University Women, eventually winning her lawsuit. In 1950 she helped organize the Coordinating Committee for the Enforcement of D.C. Anti-discrimination Laws. Between the ages of eighty-seven and ninety (during the early 1950s), with the aid of a cane Terrell walked picket lines in front of many Washington, D.C., department stores protesting their treatment of African Americans. She subsequently participated in a lawsuit against the owners of one restaurant for refusing to serve her. She was ninety years old when a 1953 Supreme Court ruling upheld the old statutes that prohibited Washington restaurant owners from denying service to any "respectable person." See Fields, *Lemon Swamp*, 189–91; Mary Church Terrell, "What Role Is the Educated Negro Woman to Play in the Uplifting of Her Race," in *Twentieth Century Negro Literature*, ed. D. W. Culp (Toronto: J. L. Nichols, 1902), 172–77; Janice Leone, "Integrating the American Association of University Women, 1946–1949," *Historian* 51 (1989); 423–45; Sterling, *Black Foremothers*, 153–55; and Gladys Shepperd, *Mary Church Terrell, Respectable Person* (Baltimore: Human Relations Press, 1959), 39–92.

Conclusion

1. Newer studies on the Civil Rights Movement have helped significantly to shift the discussion of leadership. See especially Aldon Morris, *The Origins of the Civil Rights Movement: Black Communities Organizing for Change* (New York: Free Press, 1984); Vicki L. Crawford, Jacqueline Anne Rouse, and Barbara Woods, eds., *Women in the Civil Rights Movement: Trailblazers and Torchbearers, 1941–1965* (Brooklyn, N.Y.: Carlson, 1990); Charles Payne, "Ella Baker and Models of Social Change," *Signs* 14 (1989): 885–99, and idem, *I've Got the Light of Freedom: The Organizing Tradition and the Mississippi Freedom Struggle* (Berkeley and Los Angeles: University of California Press, 1995); Septima Poinsette Clark, *Ready from Within: Septima Clark and the Civil Rights Movement*, ed. Cynthia Stokes Brown (Navarro, Calif.: Wild Trees Press, 1986); Jo Ann Gibson Robinson, *The Montgomery Bus Boycott and the Women Who Started It* (Knoxville: University of Tennessee Press, 1987); and Kay Mills, *This Little Light of Mine: The Life of Fannie Lou Hamer* (New York: Plume, 1993).

2. On the development of a black working class in a northern industrial city, see Joe William Trotter, Jr., *Black Milwaukee: The Making of an Industrial Proletariat, 1914–45* (Urbana: University of Illinois Press, 1985). On the black worker in the South, see Gerald David Jaynes, *Branches without Roots: Genesis of the Black Working Class in the American South, 1862–1882* (New York: Oxford University Press, 1986). For an em-

phasis on rural workers, see Robin D. G. Kelley, *Hammer and Hoe: Alabama Communists during the Great Depression* (Chapel Hill: University of North Carolina Press, 1990).

3. Robert H. Wiebe introduced the historical discussions of the development of "the new middle class" in *The Search for Order, 1877–1920* (New York: Hill and Wang, 1967). For examples of subsequent literature, historical and sociological, see Introduction, note 8.

4. A study of journal articles on the divergence of family and women's history is Louise Tilly, "Women's History and Family History: Fruitful Collaboration or Missed Connection?" *Journal of Family History* 12 (1987): 303–15. A very useful survey of family history, especially the relationship between the public and private spheres, is Katherine A. Lynch, "The Family and the History of Public Life," *Journal of Interdisciplinary History* 25 (1994): 665–84.

5. "Marie" to Constance Fisher, March 24, [?], Constance Fisher Papers, TUA.

6. Ibid. It is not clear why Mrs. Sears did not supervise Marie.

7. Ibid. Obviously it never occurred to Marie's inquisitor that because of the conditions encountered, work with "her people," though perhaps immensely gratifying, was hardly "happy."

8. Septima Poinsette Clark, interview transcript, ARC-CC, A. 6–7.

"abolitionist legacy," 62, 69–72
Addams, Jane, 170
African Methodist Episcopal
    Church, 183
Agricultural Adjustment Act, 198
agricultural work: circumventing,
    1; women in, 14, 251–52 n. 3
Alabama Library Association: ef-
    forts to integrate, 153–55
Alabama State Health Department
    of Vital Statistics, 195
Alpha Kappa Alpha, 201
American Association of Social
    Workers, 142
American Federation of Teachers,
    204
American Library Association,
    137, 141–42 , 151, 154; Hospi-
    tal Division of the Council of,
    153
American Missionary, 72
American Missionary Association,
    71, 72, 75, 77, 94
American Nurses' Association,
    151, 152; campaign to integrate,
    155–62
American Red Cross, 158, 193
American Teachers Association,
    137
antilynching bill: failure to pass, 2;
    campaign for, 200–201
Antioch College Academy, 33
Antioch College Model School, 47
Arkhurst, Joyce Cooper, 40, 236
Armstrong High School, 16, 37
Associated Negro Press, 57–58

Association of American Library
    Schools, 141
Atlanta Independent, 57
Atlanta University, 69, 140, 144,
    173; and community-oriented
    curriculum, 97–98; and Gate
    City Free Kindergarten Associa-
    tion, 97; and interclass coopera-
    tion, 91; and Oglethorp Practice
    School, 97–98; residency re-
    quirements, 87; and social re-
    sponsibility, 92; and student be-
    havior, 87; training for domestic
    work, 77–78
Austin, Rev. J. C., 92
Avery Institute, 49, 64, 144, 173,
    176

Baker, Augusta, 205, 328–29 n.
    111
Banks, Anna DeCosta, 138–39,
    172, 222
Banneker Junior High School, 182
Baptist Home Mission Monthly, 190
Baptist Home Mission Society, 71
Barnes Medical School, 193
Barnett, V. W., 83
Barrett, Harris, 139, 164
Barrett, Janie Porter, 68–69, 101,
    112, 139, 140, 142, 164–66,
    166, 170, 172,174, 221–22
behavior. See social behavior
Bell, Fressie, 75
Benedict College, 144–45
Bennett College, 115
Bethune-Cookman College, 63

Birth of a Nation, 29
Black, Aline, 201
Black Bourgeoisie, 58
Black Caucus of the American Library Association, 137, 151
Black Codes, 55
Black Muslims, 190
Bond, Rev. James, 73
Bontemps, Arna, 206
Booker T. Washington Business Association, 150
Bordentown Manual Training and Industrial School, 183–84
Boston Normal School of Gymnastics, 30, 32
Boston University, 124
Bowers, Leonora, 99
Boyd, Norma, 16–17, 33, 44, 130, 181–83, 200–201, 225
Bracker, Miss, 99
Bradford, Armory H., 72
Bradford, Consula, 76
Bradford Academy, 50–51, 118
Brent, Right Rev. Charles H., 91–92
Bridgeport, Connecticut, 49
Brooks, Gwendolyn, 206
Brown, Rev. Henry E., 70
Brown, Rev. James, 76
Brown, Rosalee, 177
Brown v Board of Education, 202
Brown, W. O., 55
Buchanan, Pricilla, 84
Bullock County, Georgia, 179
Butler, Nathaniel Lowe, 173
Butler, Susan Dart, 64, 140, 142, 172–73, 174, 206, 225

Cahill, Anna, 87
Calhoun School, 175
"callings," 136, 138–40
"Canaan," 191
Cantrell, Clyde, 153
Carleton Academy, 21, 33
Carnegie, Mary Elizabeth, 147–48, 152, 235–36
Carver, George Washington, 32

Cavanah, Frances, 205
Circle of King's Daughters, 95
chaperones, 25
character, 14,17, 20, 21, 23, 76, 90, 91, 207, 215, 252–53 n. 5; defined, 15–16, 73–74; families and development of, 15–17, 17–26, 255–56 nn. 16–17; schools and development of, 73–74, 75–90. *See also* respectability; social behavior; social responsibility
Charity Organization Society, 142
charity work, 8, 74, 169, 208
Charleston, South Carolina, 55–56, 138–39, 172–73, 195, 202–4, 275 n. 45
Charleston, West Virginia, 186
Charleston (S.C.) Normal and Industrial Institute, 64
Charlottesville, Virginia, 185
Chase, Mabel, 99–100
Chevalier Jackson Bronchoscopic Clinic, 145
Chicago: depression era unemployment, 197
Chicago Public Library, 204–6
child-rearing strategies, 1–2, 6, 7–8, 10, 13–16, 38–39, 215, 217
children's literature, 204–6
Chisholm, Veronica Smith, 234, 307 n. 26
Christian Endeavor Societies, 95
Church, Louisa Ayres, 39
Church, Robert, 38, 39, 65
Church, Thomas, 112
Citizen's Committee on Public Education, 57
City Hospital No. 2. *See* Homer G. Phillips Hospital
Clafflin University, 177
Clark, Septima, 25, 26, 49, 113, 118, 127–28, 129, 133, 143, 144–45, 147, 152, 177, 180, 202–4, 208, 217, 229

Clark County, Georgia, Board of Education, 175
class: consciousness, 54–55, 167, 168, 272 n. 33; divisions, 54–55; formation, 212–13; interclass cooperation, 58–60, 62–66; 169, 179–80, 211–12, 276 n. 46, 278 n. 58, 325 n. 86; minimizing difference, 55, 88, 91–92, 179–80; structure, 211–12. *See also* class privilege; community; community consciousness; race consciousness
class privilege: meaning of, 2, 55, 65, 91–92, 218. *See also* social responsibility
classical education, 79
Cleveland, Ohio: depression-era unemployment, 197
Cleveland County, North Carolina, 64
Cleveland (Ohio) Social Services Department: desegregation of, 214–15
clothing: proper, 18, 24; at school, 88–90; to minimize class difference, 58, 88, 90, 179
Cold War, 137
collective action: and community development, 56–60, 203–4; on Federal antilynching bill, 200–201; and funding public institutions, 58–59, 63–65, 172–75; in March on Washington Movement, 200; on National Health Act, 199–200; and petition campaigns, 55–56, 59; in salary equalization campaigns, 201–3
collective consciousness, 6, 15, 65–66. *See also* community; race consciousness; social responsibility
College Entrance Board Exams, 181
College of the City of New York, 153
Colored American Magazine, 53

Columbia College School of Library Economy, 141
Columbia University, 144, 145; School of Library Service, 206; School of Social Work, 142; Teacher's College, 147
Columbus, Ohio: Board of Education, 14
Commission on Community Relations, 190, 194
communion, 13, 41, 55, 60; defined, 42
Communist Party, 191–92
community, 7, 8; defined, 42, 271 n. 30; operating for travelers, 43–44, 52–54, 271 n. 28; as product and process, 42, 60, 266 n. 2; scholarship related to, 245–46 n. 2; and social justice, 6; threats to, 46, 50–52, 54–55, 91–92, 167, 178–79, 190, 192–93, 194–96
"community barometer," 190–91
community consciousness: development of, 2, 6, 7, 14, 15–16, 37–39, 42–44, 58–60, 76–77, 91–98, 99–101 (and see socializing institutions: family; community, schools); evidence of, 43–44, 47–49, 53–54, 55–60, 62–67, 75–76, 100–101, 149, 155, 156, 167–76, 180, 185, 186, 187, 193, 267 n. 5, 271 n. 28
"community day," 63–64
community (infrastructure) development, 8, 10, 58–64, 167–79, 208–10; mentioned, 69, 90, 164
Connelly, Theresa Lee, 28, 30, 48
"consciousness of kind," 65, 278 n. 61. *See also* community consciousness; race consciousness
Cooley, Rossa, 186
Cowan, Ruth Schwartz, 113
Cravath, Erastus Milo, 70
Crawford, Charlie Mae, 76
Cromwell, Otelia, 181

Croppers' and Farm Workers' Union, 193
cultural persistence, 6, 249 n. 13
Cunningham, Virginia, 205
Cushing Academy, 23, 32, 33

Dark Lillibel, 205
Dart, John L., 64
Dart Hall, 64, 173, 174
Davis, John W., 43
Daytona Normal and Industrial Institute for Colored Girls, 63
De Forest, H. S., 72
Delaney, Sadie Peterson, 150, 153–55, 206, 226
Delany, Henry Beard, 33
Delany, Sarah Louise, 33, 65, 225–26
Detroit: depression era unemployment, 197; and migration, 198; and race relations, 124–25, 189–91, 193–94
Dewey, Melvil, 141, 209
De Witty, Thelma, 194, 234
District of Columbia. *See* Washington, D.C.
Dixie Hospital, 138, 187
Dixon, Maenelle, 179
domestic arts and science, 32, 75. *See also* domestic work
domestic violence, 118, 299 n. 12
domestic work, 8, 208; and divorced women, 128–29, 133; efforts to circumvent, 1, 14, 24, 217; extended households and, 131–33; for wages, 68, 114, 116, 176; home training for, 26–29; husbands as performers of, 119–25, 147; husbands' insistence on, 117, 125–27, 133; impact of technology on, 112–13; married women and, 112, 113–27, 131–33; never married women and, 130–31, 133–34; school training for, 77–78, 116; status attached to, 27; widowed women and, 127–28, 133;

women as performers of, 112–16, 224, 126–27, 132–33, 219; women's responsibility for, 4, 111, 123, 125, 134
domestic workers: African American women as, 251–52 n. 2; employment of, 116–17, 119, 120, 127, 130; in hotels, 24–25
Dorchester Home, 185
double victory campaign, 198–99
Drew, W. H., 85
Dublin, Georgia, *Courier,* 58–59
Duluth, Minnesota, 38
Dunbar, Paul Laurence, 205
Dunbar High School (M Street School), 37, 181
Duncan Catherine Watkins, 109–10, 255 n. 16, 267–68 n. 8, 321 n. 49
Dunlap, Eula Wellman, 33, 63, 64, 65
Durham Colored Library Association, 172

Edmonds, Florence, 113–14, 119, 123, 147, 150, 152, 226–27
Edmonds, William Baily, 114
education. *See* schooling; socializing institutions
Edwards, Ann Elizabeth, 160
Egypt, Ophelia Settle, 231–32, 269 n.17
Emergency Welfare and Evacuation Services, 190
employment options: enhancing, 15
Excelsior Club, 172
"exodusters," 40
external forces, 5

Fair Employment Practices Commission, 200
family. *See* child-rearing strategies; socializing institutions: family
family economies, 14, 19–20, 27, 28, 34–35, 54, 67, 92, 114–18,

119, 127–29; black family income, 251 n. 2
family history: as institutional history, 213
family reorganizing. See household reorganization
Federal Emergency Relief Act, 198
Ferebee, Dorothy, 200–201
Fernandis, Sarah Collins, 140, 168
Fields, Karen, 43
Fields, Mamie Garvin, 24, 40, 62, 118, 143, 174, 176–77, 178, 199, 225
Fifteenth Amendment, mentioned on, 70
First Congregational Church, 76
Fisher, Constance C., 17, 36, 37, 111, 142, 214, 231
Fisher, Isaac 17, 37, 44, 134
Fisher, Ruth Anna, 165–66, 224
Fisk Expositor, 80
Fisk University: academic rigor, 70; community work programs, 96, 98; graduates' continuing education, 99–100; and leadership development, 35, 71, 77; and missionary support, 65; parents' correspondence to, 83; and social control, 87; student fundraising, 92; and women's responsibilities, 81
Fort Gaines, Georgia, 32
Framingham: Academy, 27, 28, 33: State Normal School, 50–51
fraternities, 57
Frazier, E. Franklin, 58
Freedmen's Hospital, 100, 152
"friendly visitors," 142
Frissell, Hollis, 164–65
Fuller, Hoyt, 206

Garveyism, 103, 189
Gate City Free Kindergarten Association, 97
gender: use of term, 250 n. 18; constructions of, 6, 29, 24 (see also womanhood, constructions of)
George Cleveland Hall Public Library, 204–5
German Colonial Society, 50
Girl Scouts, 186
Good Housekeeping, 205
Governor's Board of Discrimination (Seattle, Washington), 194
Grant, Frances, 25, 53, 184, 208, 227–28
Great Day in the Morning, 205
Great Depression, 188, 189, 191–92, 196, 197
Grimké, Angelina, 17–18, 21, 22, 23, 24, 28, 30–31, 32, 36–37, 39–40, 44–45, 46, 48, 49, 62, 131, 181, 222
Grimké, Archibald, 17, 18, 21, 23, 24, 28–29, 36, 38, 44–45, 46, 48, 49
Grimké, Charlotte Forten, 17, 21, 30–31, 39, 44–45
Grimké, Francis, 17, 23, 39
Grimké, Sarah Stanley, 46–47
Grossman, James R., 191
Guidry, Willie Mae, 85
Guthrie, Oklahoma, 172

Hadnott, Gertrude, 81
Hall, Florence, 84–85
Hall, Rev. George, 71
Hampton, Virginia, 98
Hampton Institute, 138, 145, 164, 168, 185; community work programs, 95–96, 98; and development of race consciousness, 69, 77, 165; and leadership development, 35, 71, 77; material conditions at, 68; student labor, 93
Harding, Warren G.: presidential campaign, 123, 196
Harlan, Louis, 144
Harlem: depression-era unemployment, 197
Harlem Renaissance, 103
Harley, Fred, 49

Harley, Gussie, 49
Harley, Sharon, 27
Hartshorn Memorial College, 19,
32, 69, 115, 118; academic program, 70, 79; and character development, 86–87; and community interests 94, 98; and
domestic training, 78; dress
codes, 88; Home Workers, 95;
Education and Missionary Society, 95; graduation ceremony,
41; and leadership development, 71, 76; and social control,
86; students' community work,
95; and Virginia Union Univer-
sity men, 85–86; White Shield
Society, 86
Hartshorn-Union Journal, 82
Harvard Law School, 124
Harvey, Lillian Holland, 301 n.
38, 234
Hester, Beulah, 19, 26, 29, 32, 41,
64, 65, 114–15, 118, 123,
131–32, 147, 148, 224
Hester, William, 115
Hewitt, Vivian, 209
Highlander Folk School, 203
Hill, Allen G., 64
Holmes, Rev. Samuel V. V., 92
Home Mission Monthly, 190
Home School for Girls, 164–65,
172, 174
Homer G. Phillips Hospital, 147,
193
Hoover, Herbert, 196
Hope, John, 171
Hope, Lugenia Burns, 139–40,
169–71, 222
Horton, Judith Ann Carter, 138,
140, 142, 172, 222
Hospital and Training School for
Nurses, 138, 172
hotel: black owned, 52; "Do Drop
Inns," 44; substitute, 43
household reorganization, 43–50,
52–53
Houston, Charles Hamilton, 183

Howard University, 16, 69, 100,
181; academic program, 70; and
instilling social responsibility,
91–92; and interclass (intrara-
cial) interests, 91–92; and leader-
ship development, 35; and sex
segregation, 85
Hughes, Langston, 206
Hull House, 170
Hundley, Mary Gibson, 181, 228
Hunster, Edward, 48
Hunster, Margarite, 48
Hunster, Sallie, 47–48
Hunter, Jane Edna, 25, 63, 140,
187–88, 223
Huntington High School, 62
Hurston, Zora Neale, 1, 217

Independent, 72
Indiana University, 145
Indianapolis *Freeman*, 27, 28
individualism, 6, 41; and professional status, 137, 213; and social responsibility, 5–6; and socialization, 2. *See also* socially
responsible individualism
industrial education: as distinct
from vocational education,
294–95 n. 102
internal control, 5
International Labor Defense, 192
Ironsides Echo, 184

Jackson, Judia, 175, 208
Jakin, Georgia, 31–32
Jane Addams Peace Book Award,
111–12
Jeanes teacher, 179
Jim Crow, 6, 153; Era, 13, 135,
137, 168; laws, 55; and social responsibility, 66; system, 2–3;
and travel, 43–44
jobs: as distinct from work, 66,
208–10
John A. Andrew Hospital, 144,
147, 195
Jones, Adrienne Lash, 63

Jones, Albert, 124–25
Jones, Clara Stanton, 10, 37–38, 52, 75, 103, 113, 124–25, 150, 194, 209, 235
Jones, Ida Burton, 100
Jones, Laura Terrell, 128–29
Jonesboro, Arkansas, 59, 175
Jordan, Fannie Dell, 37
journalists: anti–Booker T. Washington, 51–52; and developing community consciousness, 56–59, 65–66; pro–Booker T. Washington, 51
Jubilee Singers, 92
Junior High School Federation of Student Councils, 182

Kalamazoo, Michigan, 194
Kansas City Call, 58
Kelley, Robin D. G., 192
Kentucky Library Association, 152
King's Mountain, North Carolina, 32, 33, 63, 64
Kolonial Wirtschaftliches Komitee, 19
Krause, Martin, 19
Ku Klux Klan, 61

labor unions, 57
Ladies Benevolent Society, 138–39
Ladson, Genevieve Nell, 176, 177–78, 208
"land of hope," 191
Lane, Layle, 200, 204
Langston, Phyllis Terrell, 120–23
Larson, Nella, 184
Laurie, Eunice Rivers, 31–32, 49, 60, 152, 186, 195–96, 209, 230–31
leadership: and feminized professions, 218–19; and social change, 219; and "spokespersons," 211. See also socializing institutions
Lee, Christina, 48
Lee, Joseph, 48

Lee, Mollie Huston, 206, 329 n. 114
Lee, Theresa (Tessa). See Connelly, Theresa Lee
Lewis, Earl, 127, 192
liberty: and social justice, 6
librarianship, 153–55, 171–73, 174, 194, 204–6, 209
Librarianship, Board of Education for, 141–42
libraries, and community development, 171–74
"lifestyle enclave," 54, 271 n. 30
Lincoln Academy, 32, 33, 63–64
Lincoln Institute Worker, 74
Lincoln School for Nurses, 147
Lindenwood Beautiful Group, 125
Lion's Club, 150
literacy, 180, 204, 208
"Little Hiram," 205
Locust Street Settlement House, 139, 142, 164, 172
"Look Applauds," 150
Louisiana Education Association, 151
Louisville Free Public Colored Library, 33 171
Louisville Normal School, 38
Lowndes County, Alabama, 175
Lubove, Roy, 170
Lynchburg, Virginia, 184–85
lynching, 2, 31, 246 n. 4

M Street School. See Dunbar High School.
McBeth, Julia, 173
McBryan, Sallie Waugh, 100
McCormick, Ruth Hannah, campaign, 196
McCray, Mary Lee, 176
McDowell Millinery School, 173
McNeil, Lula Catherine Jordan, 62, 185–86, 233
Macon County, Alabama, 98, 195
McPherson, James M., 62, 70
MacVicar, Malcolm, 71
manners. See social behavior

March on Washington Movement, 200

"Marie": on desegregation of Cleveland Ohio Social Services Department, 214–15

Martha's Vineyard, 122

matinee dances, 25

Matthews, Miriam, 18, 24, 29–30, 33, 39, 132, 149, 232–33

Means, Florence, 205

Mears, Rev. David O., 72

Meharry Medical College, 19, 145

memory, scholarly literature on history and, 250 n. 17

Merrick, John, 171–72

Merrill, Rev. J. G., 71

Metropolitan Insurance Company, 138

Michigan Sate Committee for Intercultural Understanding, 194

Mickle, Miss R. A., 100

migration, 189, 191; impact for professional women, 118–19, 188, 198–99

Miller, Barbara Simmons, 33, 143, 152, 233–34

Milwaukee, Wisconsin, 52

Minnesota Negro Council, 199

Minor, Susan St. Clair, 38, 143, 231

Minor Normal School, 32

misbehavior, 21, 22, 26

missionary associations, and schools, 69, 70–75

Mitchell, Lucy M., 25, 61, 63, 113, 124, 125, 147, 230

Mitchell, Joseph, 124–25, 147

mobility, 44; economic, x; geographic, 40; political, ix–x; social, ix–x, 39–40

Montgomery, Alabama, 83

"Moonlight Schools," 180, 321 n. 49

Moore, Aaron McDuffie, 171–72

Moore, Fred, 53

Moore, Mary Caroline, 28, 50

morality. See social behavior

Morehouse, Henry L., 78–79

Morgan, Rev. T. J., 90

Moton, Robert R., 84, 139

Mt. Holyoke College, 70

Murray, Albertha, 132, 195

Murray, Margaret. See Washington, Margaret Murray

music lessons: taking, 19, 28, 32; giving, 115, 116, 117, 118

Naison, Mark, 191–92

Nance, Ethel Ray, 25, 38, 199, 229–30

National Association for the Advancement of Colored People, 38, 145, 150, 192, 201–2, 214

National Association of Colored Graduate Nurses, 137, 151, 152, 163, 193; advisory council, 156; campaign to integrate ANA, 155–162; and National Health Act, 199–200

National Association of Teachers in Colored Schools, 43, 137

National Council of Negro Women, 150

National Council of Teachers of English, 204

National Cyclopaedia of American Biography, 36

National Education Association, 141, 151

National Health Act, 199–200

National League of Nursing Education, 156, 157, 158, 162

National Nursing Council for War Service, 193–94

National Organization of Public Health Nurses, 156, 157

National Purity Congress, 121

National Recovery Act, 198

National Republican Committee, 196

National Teachers Examination, 202

National Urban League, 150

National Youth Administration, 147

Negro Organization Society, 58

Neighborhood Union, 56; creation of, 139–40; structure of, 169; work of, 168–71, 199; sale to federal government, 174

New Deal, 188

New England Conservatory of Music, 23

New York *Age*, 53, 200

New York City: depression-era unemployment, 197; and migration, 198

New York Public Library School, 153

New York School of Philanthropy, 142

New York School of Social Work, 142

New York State Library School, 141

New York Times, 200

Newport News, Virginia, 62

newspaper, black: circulation, 57

newspaper reporters. *See* journalists

"No Work, No Rent" parades, 192

Norfolk Community Hospital, 126

Norfolk *Journal and Guide*, 58

Norfolk (Virginia) Board of Education, 201

Normal graduates: and continuing education, 80; and limited opportunities, 112, 118–19

Normal school programs, 77; at Tuskegee, 79–80

North Carolina A & T State College, 144

Northcross, Mabel, 19, 143, 145, 231

nurses: image of, 139, 309 n. 28; military policy regarding, 159; and New York State Licensing Law, 143; obstacles to professional status, 146–47; and standardized training, 142–43

Nurse Board of Examiners, 143

"Nurse King," 186–87

nursing, 138–39, 146, 151–52, 155–62, 172, 185–88, 193–94, 195–96, 199–200, 209

Nursing Council of National Defense, 158

Oak Bluffs, Massachusetts, 122

Oberlin, Ohio, 61, 69–70

Oberlin College, 35, 48, 61, 69–70, 172, 189

Oberlin College Academy, 33, 48

Office of Civilian Defense, 190

Oglethorp Practice School, 97

Opequon, West Virginia, 122

orphanages, 43, 64–65, 132

Osborne, Geneva Estelle Massey Riddle, 147, 148, 152, 155–56, 160, 161, 192, 193, 194, 232

Paducah, Tennessee, 19

Palmer, Alice Freeman, 50

Parent Teacher Association, 199

perceptions, ix–x, 9; importance of, 216–17

petition campaigns, 55–56, 59, 272 n. 34

Philadelphia: depression-era unemployment, 197; migration, 198

Phillis Wheatley Association, 187–88

Philpot, J. R., 76

Pickett, Barbara, 152, 236

Pittman, Portia Washington, 19, 23, 25, 27, 31, 32, 39, 111, 113, 116–18, 129–30, 223

Pittman, William Sidney, 113, 116–18, 129

Plantation Settlement, 179

Poindexter, Reverend James Preston, quoted, 14–15

Poinsette, Mrs., 217

Pompeii, 36

Pride, Amelia Perry, 112, 132–133, 179–80, 184–85, 221

Princeton University, 181

Private sphere work, 8; as community work, 132–33, 168–69, 177–80; as non-waged work, 80–81, 111, 112–13, 114, 115, 116, 121–25, 127–28, 130–33; as waged work, 114, 115, 116, 117, 128, 217; encouragement beyond, 29, 31–33, 36–38, 78, 94, 111–12

professional credentials, 134; financial support for pursuing, 147–48; obstacles to gaining, 143–47

professional organizations: exclusion from, 151, 153–62; participation in, 150–62; campaigns to integrate, 152–62

professional status, 8, 134; anomalies related to, 213; community recognition of, 149–50; "callings" and, 136, 138–40; collective efforts to gain, 155–63; dualism regarding, 135, 136, 144, 146–47; education and, 80, 136, 140–43, 143–49; importance of, 134, 146; individual efforts to gain, 138–48, 153–55; obstacles to achieving, 136, 144–47; organization exclusion and, 153–62; organizational membership and, 136–37, 150–62; professionalization of training and, 80, 140–43; public recognition of, 150; the service ideal and, 138–41, 149

professionals: impact of migration on, 118–19; and opportunities, 112, 117; public image of, 139, 175, 307 n. 28; scholarship related to, 247–48 n. 8; use of the term, 3

Progressive Era, 4, 136; and changing educational standards, 136, 140–43; and social justice, 31

Promised Land School, 177

public health nursing, 185–87, 209

public image, 23, 78, 90; of rural school teachers, 175; of nurses, 139, 309 n. 8

Public sphere work: and assuming leadership roles, 164–66; and "callings," 136, 138–40; and collective efforts, 169–70, 171–76, 180, 187–88, 199–204; and constraints, 112–13, 117, 118–19, 173; and community support for preparation, 47–50, 62–63, 66–67; for community development, 116, 117, 125–26, 132, 164–80; and family encouragement of, 111–12; home training for, 1–2, 4–5, 7–8, 13–16, 23, 29–38, 149, 215–19; impact of private sphere conditions on, 111–34; impact of migration on, 118–19; impact of public policy on, 112; impact of public tradition on, 113–14; impact of social tradition on, 117, 125–26; in construction, 175–76, 185; in race relations, 188–97, 209; in race uplift, 167–68, 178–80, 207, 209; as race work, 164–88, 192; as reform work, 196–208, 209–10; in rural settings, 174–79, 180, 185–87, 192–93, 195–96; roles, 209; and school training for, 71–103; in urban settings, 168–70, 180–85, 187–88, 189, 193–94, 196. See also librarianship; nursing; social work; teachers

Pullman porter, 22

Purcell, Mae, 173

race consciousness, 55; development of, 37–38, 69, 74–77. See also community consciousness; "consciousness of kind"

Rachel Hartshorn Education and Missionary Society, 95

racial violence, 2, 31, 60–61, 189
Radcliffe College, 35, 70, 181, 184
Ray, William Henry, 38
Read, Florence Matilda, 70
recommendation, letters of, 76–77
Red Cross. *See* American Red
  Cross
"redemption," 72
reform movements, 69
reform work, 4, 153–63, 196–206,
  206–7, 209; and black migration, 198–99; and electoral shift,
  199; and Federal legislation,
  199–200; and Great Depression,
  197; and local policy, 199; and
  New Deal, 198; public shift to,
  196–97, 330–31 n. 120; and
  publishing industry, 204–6; and
  salary equalization, 201–3; and
  World War II, 198–99
respectability, 14–16, 20, 24, 26,
  27, 38, 40, 42. *See also* character;
  social behavior
Rice, Sarah Webb, 26, 65, 143, 233
Riddick, Henry, 125–27
Riddick, Fostine, 125–27, 144,
  147, 152, 235
Riffles for Wattie, 205
Rising Star Model School, 96–97
Rivers, Albert, 31–32
Rivers, Eunice. *See* Laurie, Eunice
  Rivers
Roane, Bessie T., 100
Roberts, Mary, 157
Robeson, Paul, 184
Rockefeller Foundation, 147, 194
role models, 14–15, 128, 211
Rollins, Charlemae Hill, 40, 64,
  111–12, 204–6, 229
Rollins, Joseph, 204
Roosevelt, Eleanor, 150
Rosenwald Fund, 147–48, 149,
  150, 192, 193
Rouse, Jacqueline, 140

Safford, Albert A., 70
St. Augustine's College, 33

St Louis, Missouri, 52
St. Paul (Minnesota) Council of
  Human Relations, 194
salary equalization campaigns,
  128, 129, 145, 201–3
San Quentin Prison, 150
Santo Domingo, 17
Satterfield, Rev. D. E., 74–75
Saunders, Doris, 206
Schomburg Center for Research
  in Black Culture, 161
school bond issue (Atlanta), 56
schooling: away from home,
  17–20, 31–32; and broad preparation, 175–76; and changing
  student attitudes, 102–3; and
  character development, 73–74;
  and community support, 47–50,
  55–60, 62–65, 101, 176; and
  community work, 92–99; and
  freedpeople, 73, 216–17; mission, 8, 69–77, 101–3, 104–5,
  188; and new professional standards, 140–43; and parental interest, 31–37, 68–69; patterns,
  33–35; and student organizations, 94–95. *See also* socializing
  institutions: school
schools: black graduate programs,
  136; black nursing programs,
  136; community funding of,
  58–59, 63–65, 173–74; development of, 69–71, 92–93; goals
  of, 69–77; government funding
  of, 2–3, 174, 161; overcrowding
  of, 56–57; suspension or expulsion from, 83, 84–85. *See also individual schools by name*
Scott, Alma, 157
"Scottsboro Boys," 192
Sea Islands (South Carolina), 174,
  176–77, 183
"Service Which Should Be Rendered the South," 207
sexual exploitation, 23–24, 25,
  257 n. 29
sexual restraint, 23, 258 n. 32

sexual stereotypes, 23; scholarly literature on, 256–57, n. 26
sexuality, 25–26
Shepard, Pattie Gilliam, 32, 41, 115
Sherman, Myrtilla, 185
Shipherd, John J., 70
Shivery, Louie, 139
Simmons College School of Social Work, 148
Sims, Ollie Jewell, 149
singlehood: defined, 129; and career options, 130; and economic security, 130–31, 133–34
singleness: and domesticity, 127–31
Sixth Avenue Baptist Church, 76
"slave markets," 197
slavery, 23, 55, 217–18
Sloan, Selena, 100
Smith, Gloria, 152, 236–37
Smith, Julia Hamilton, 21–22, 32, 39, 53, 131, 138, 150, 224
Smith College, 35
social behavior: rationale for learning certain, 14–15, 22, 23, 80–82, 89–90; teaching, 168–69, 178–80, 184; training in homes, 15–26, 30–31, 254 n. 8; training in schools, 82–87. See also character; respectability; socializing institutions: family; community; school
social change: agents of, 5, 170. See also social reform
social clubs, 57
Social Darwinists, 3
social justice, 6, 31
social reform, 167. See also reform work
social responsibility, 6, 38, 40, 42, 43, 47, 55, 60, 66, 74, 92; community fostering of, 41, 43–45, 47–50, 56–59, 62–64, 66–67; family examples of, 37–38, 63–65; individualism and, 2, 7, 213; press encouragement and, 56–

60; professionalization and, 249 n. 12; public work and, 109–10, 164–88, 192, 196–208, 209–10; school encouragement of, 69, 73–75, 91–92
Social Security Act, 198
social settlements, 168–71; and gender roles, 208–9. See also individual settlements by name
social work, 85, 139–40, 142, 164–65, 168–71, 174–82, 184–85, 187–91, 194, 203–4, 208–9
socialization, 1–2, 4, 6, 7, 8, 38, 149, 170, 207, 211, 213, 215–19; for domesticity, 26–29, 77–78; for leadership roles, 1–2, 7, 10, 14–16, 76–91, 215; for socially responsible adulthoods, 7, 37–38, 91–101, 141, 215
Socializing institutions, 4, 7
—family, 13–40; and character development, 15–16; and child-rearing strategies, 13; and concerns about sexuality, 23–26; and developing self-esteem, 29–31, 35–37; and developing social responsibility, 37–38; and formal schooling, 31–35; and lessons in domesticity, 26–29; and lessons on manners, 16–18, 20–24; and lessons in self-reliance, 17–20, 33; and lessons on social intercourse, 20–21; and role of family history, 39–40
—community, 41–67; defined, 42; development, 55–60, 63–65; failure to accommodate, 50–52; and interclass (intraracial) connections, 54–61; and parental involvement, 38, 42–43, 63–65; and racial violence, 60–61; and support for education, 62–65; as facilitated by black journalists, 56–58; in accommodating students, 44–50, 52–53; in facilitat-

ing travel, 43–44, 52–53
—school, 68–103; "abolitionist legacy" and, 70–75; academic programs, 78–80; and character development, 73–74; and Christian missionary influence, 69–75; and community expectations, 74–76; and developing social responsibility, 91–101; and dress codes, 88–90; and domestic arts training, 77–78; and interclass (intraracial) connections, 91–92; and leadership preparation, 76–91; and Oberlin College connections, 70; and overall mission, 67, 69–77, 101–3, 104–5; and post-1930s students, 102–3; and role models, 99–101; and sexual self-control, 83–86; and student recommendations, 75–76; and summer teaching, 98–99; and training in manners and morality, 80–88
Socially responsible individualism, 2, 5–7, 66, 75, 166, 218
South Carolina: Consent Decree, 202; teacher certification scheme, 202
South Carolina State College, 144
Southeastern Library Association, 154–55
Southern Illinois University, 145
Southern Letter, 100
Spelman College, 35, 52, 69, 103; academic program, 70, 71, 76, 79; domestic training, 78; dress code, 89; graduates' community work, 100–101; and interclass interests, 91–92; and Morehouse men, 85; student labor, 93, 98; and the White Shield Society, 86
Spelman Messenger, 82
Spingarn Medal, 150
"spokespersons," 211
Stanford L. Warren Public Library, 171–72

Staupers, Mabel Doyle Keaton, 40, 149, 150, 151, 157, 160, 161, 227
Stetson, Erlene, 10
Stewart, Philo Penfield, 69–70
Swartzell, Rheem, and Hensey Company, 131

"talented tenth," 91
Talladega College, 69, 124; academic program, 35, 70, 71, 77–78; coeducational activities, 85
Tampa, Florida, 58
Tancil, Mary Terrell, 121–22, 205
Taylor, Pauline Byrd, 194
teachers: and work, 144, 165, 175–85, 200–204, 208
Tefft, Mary, 70, 94
Temple University, 145
Tennessee Valley Authority, 198
Terrell, Mary Church, 8, 14, 22, 39, 47–48, 60, 61, 112, 119–24, 131, 138, 140, 181, 196, 205, 207, 209, 221
Terrell, Robert Heberton, 113, 120–23, 125
Thomas Y. Crowell (publishing house), 205
Thomasville, Georgia, 49
Thompson, Era Bell, 20
Tidewater Association of Colored Graduate Nurses, 152
Tobias, Channing, 94
Toomer, Jean, 206
Tuskegee, Alabama, 98
Tuskegee Alumni Club, 130
Tuskegee Institute, 50, 69, 70, 112, 116, 129, 164, 165, 186, 205; academic program, 79; applicant recommendations, 75–76; community work, 94, 96–98; domestic arts training, 27, 28, 32; dress code, 88; and extensive teacher roles, 165–66; graduates' community work, 100–101; and leadership development, 35; residency require-

Tuskegee Institute (*cont'd*)
ments, 87; and single female faculty, 128–29; student labor, 92–93; student suspensions, 84–85
Tuskegee Institute Moveable School, 97, 186
Tuskegee Institute Rural Extension Program, 97
Tuskegee Mothers' Clubs, 97
Tuskegee Syphilis Project, 195–96
Tyson, Mrs. J. A., 100

Union Baptist Church, 75
University Journal, 91
University of California—Berkeley, 18
University of Chicago, 145
University of Michigan, 145
University of Virginia Medical School, 185
University of Wisconsin—Milwaukee, 52

Valena C. Jones School, 183
Veterans Hospital (Tuskegee, Alabama), 153, 155, 186, 206
Veterans of Foreign Wars, 150
victimization, transcending, 5, 10, 13–14, 30–31, 38
Victorian ideals, 23, 25
Virginia Federation of Colored Women's Clubs, 172
Virginia Library Association, 154
Virginia Nurses' Association, 152
Virginia State Teachers' Association, 151
Virginia Tidewater, 186
Visiting Nursing Association, 152
Vocation. *See* "callings"
vocational education: financial support for, 71; and industrial education, 294 n. 102

voting: disfranchisement, 2, 246 n. 3; electoral shift, 198–99

Ward, William Hayes, 72
Waring, J. Waties, 202
Washington, Booker T., 19, 23, 25, 45, 50–51, 53, 111, 112, 164, 165
Washington, D.C., 16, 21–22, 33, 38, 181–83, 200
Washington, Margaret Murray, 45–46, 164, 176, 178
Washington, Olivia Davidson, 50
Washington, Portia. *See* Pittman, Portia Washington
Wayne State University College of Nursing, 152, 194
We Build Together, 204
Wellesley College, 27, 35, 50, 51, 70
West Side Human Relations Council (Detroit), 150
West Virginia State College, 43, 147
Western Reserve University, 36
Whitby, Beulah, 142, 150, 189–91, 194, 228–29
White, Chlora, 87
White Rock Baptist Church, 171
White, Walter, 161, 163
Williams, Frances, 157–58
Williams, Mrs. G. P., 100
Willoughby, Mabel E., 153
Wilson, Butler, 49
Wilson, Mary Evans, 49
womanhood: tradition of, 7; model of, 111–12, 170–71
—constructions of , 1–2, 4, 10, 13–16; in families, 13–40; in communities, 41–40; in schools, 68–103;
women's history: as movement history, 213
Woodward, Abbie Smarr, 100–101

work: as distinct from jobs, 166, 208–10
work culture, 313 n. 7
Working Girls' Home Association. *See* Phillis Wheatley Association
Works Progress Administration, 198, 199
World War I, 103, 157, 189

World War II, 137, 155, 198–99
Wright, Richard, 206

Yale University, 181
Yellow Springs, Ohio, 47
YMCA, 94, 199
YWCA, 17, 189, 191, 199, 203–4